MANAGING SPORT ORGANIZATIONS

Now in a fully revised and updated third edition, *Managing Sport Organizations* is still the most interesting, challenging, and student-focused introduction to sport management currently available. Bridging the gap between theory and practice, this book explores every key topic, issue, and concept in contemporary sport management, including:

- understanding management and its relationship to sport
- the new sport management environment
- decision making
- strategy
- organizational design
- leadership
- human resource management
- managing change
- facility management
- innovation.

This new edition contains expanded coverage of current topics such as corporate responsibility and ethics, social media, career pathways in sport management, and international sport. Each chapter includes a full range of useful features, such as case studies, management exercises, study questions, and definitions of key terms and concepts.

Managing Sport Organizations is the only book to fully introduce the core concepts and principles of management theory and to demonstrate their application in the contemporary sport industry. No other textbook combines the rigor of the business school with the creativity and dynamism of modern sport business. This is the perfect foundation text for any course in sports management, sports administration, or sports organization.

Daniel Covell is Professor in the Department of Sport Management, College of Business, Western New England University, USA.

Sharianne Walker is Professor and Chair, Department of Sport Management, Western New England University, USA.

Visit the companion website at: www.routledge.com/cw/covell

MANAGING SPORT ORGANIZATIONS

Responsibility for performance

Third edition

**DANIEL COVELL AND
SHARIANNE WALKER**

Routledge
Taylor & Francis Group

LONDON AND NEW YORK

First published 2002
by South-Western College Publishing

This edition published 2013
by Routledge
2 Park Square, Milton Park, Abingdon, Oxon OX14 4RN

Simultaneously published in the USA and Canada
by Routledge
711 Third Avenue, New York, NY 10017

Routledge is an imprint of the Taylor & Francis Group, an informa business

British Library Cataloguing in Publication Data
A catalogue record for this book is available from the British Library

Library of Congress Cataloging in Publication Data
Managing sport organizations : responsibility for performance / edited by
Daniel Covell and Sharianne Walker.
p. cm.
1. Sports administration. 2. Sports--Management. I. Covell, Daniel, 1963- II.
Walker, Sharianne.
GV713.M3618 2013
796.06'9--dc23
2012039683

ISBN: 978-0-415-62679-8 (hbk)
ISBN: 978-0-415-62677-4 (pbk)
ISBN: 978-0-203-55028-1 (ebk)

Typeset in Melior and Univers
by GreenGate Publishing Services, Tonbridge, Kent

Printed and bound in the United States of America by
Edwards Brothers Malloy on sustainably sourced paper

CONTENTS

7 DESIGNING THE ORGANIZATION AND THE SPORT AGENCY INDUSTRY 207

8 MOTIVATION AND LEADERSHIP AND INTERCOLLEGIATE ATHLETICS 246

ix

Contents

9 HUMAN RESOURCE MANAGEMENT AND THE TOUR SPORT INDUSTRY   299

10 MANAGING CHANGE AND THE PROFESSIONAL LEAGUE SPORT INDUSTRY   336

LIST OF ILLUSTRATIONS

FIGURES

TABLES

BOXES

xiv
List of illustrations

CHAPTER 1

THE SPORT MANAGEMENT CHALLENGE AND THE BRANDED AND LICENSED SPORT PRODUCT INDUSTRY

INTRODUCTION

So you want to work in sport? How's your brand?

Congratulations. You're reading this book because you've chosen to pursue a dream. You want to work in sport. Your parents or partner might be a bit wary of this. No problem. Have them consider the following: Nike, the leader in footwear and apparel sales, is estimated to be worth $15 billion, while industry runner-up Adidas is valued at $5 billion. In 2011, Nike's apparel sales reached $5.4 billion, with overall sales topping $18 billion (including $7.6 billion in North America, $3.8 billion in Western Europe, and $4.8 billion from China and emerging markets). Nike also owned 38 percent of the branded footwear market. Next time you are in class, or in the dining hall on campus, take a moment and look at the footwear people are wearing. Unless you are near the beach or the North Pole, your observations will probably support that 38 percent figure (Oznian, 2011). So is Nike not a global brand? Are they not generating significant revenues from sport products? Now, if you told someone you planned on majoring in chemical or industrial engineering, they might be clueless about the content of the major, but there would be little question about the viability of those industries. Nor, given the kind of economic value generated by the sport industries, should there be with sport.

If there are still doubters about the significance of the sport industries, however, try responding with a series of questions of your own. Ask your concerned party whether they own a hat or jersey from a favorite team, or how many athletes or teams they follow on Twitter. Or if they work out regularly or play in an organized recreational sport league. Or if a sport blog or website is the first (or only) sites they visit daily. Or how many hours are spent managing their fantasy teams. These examples are indicators of the significant breadth of interest of sport in our society, and that interest is a major component in all societies around the world. Every culture

1

has some kind of sport activities. The road to success in sport careers, however, is full of challenges. For example, if you were to ask what their dream job might be, more than a few sport management majors would probably answer general manager of the Cincinnati Reds, the Chicago Bulls, the New York Red Bulls, Bayern Munich, or whatever their favorite pro team is. With such a crowded field, does this mean that these students can never get that dream job? Absolutely not.

There are four ways someone like you can enter and succeed in the sport industries. The first is to buy your way in. You watch National Football League (NFL) games and you make better play calls than Tom Brady, Drew Brees, or Eli Manning, and you have a better handle on the annual draft than Mel Kiper, Jr. "I can do this better than these guys," you think, so you pony up the dough and buy a franchise. How much would you have to pay? It depends on the franchise, its facility, and its revenue streams. *Forbes* magazine estimates the value of the Major League Baseball's (MLB) New York Yankees, with its revenues from its subsidiary YES Network and other sources, to be $340 million. Soccer clubs Manchester United and Real Madrid are valued at $269 million and $264 million, respectively, and the NFL's Dallas Cowboys check in at $193 million. So you would need to start at, on average, probably $200 million, and then the other league owners would need to approve you to join their club before you drop the cash. Do you have a quarter billion dollars handy? No? Okay, no sweat, there are three ways left.

The second is to inherit a team from your family. In the NFL, for example, league rules require individuals rather than corporations to own teams, and many of these teams will be taken over by family members rather than sold to outsiders when transitions are required. Does anyone in your immediate family own an NFL team or any other professional league franchise? No? Okay, that's strike two, but in this game you still have two strikes left.

The third way to get into the game is to be an outstanding former player who moves from the playing field to the front office. There are athletic directors, general managers, coaches, and even some owners throughout sport who gained experience and connections from their on-field careers. How about you? Are you a blue-chip student–athlete on a National Collegiate Athletic Association (NCAA) Division I team looking to lead your squad to a national championship during the upcoming season? No? OK, are you a Division III standout? No? Not even the leading scorer on your intramural basketball team? Well, don't despair. You have one more shot – and it's a good one.

If you are reading this, you've already made a move toward the fourth step: education. In fact, more and more of the individuals who currently hold these positions have sport management academic backgrounds. But here's the lesson from these successful sport managers: to get a job in this highly competitive job market, you must have a strong knowledge, not only of sport and the specific sport industries, but also of

2

management and organizations in general. Knowing Albert Pujols' lifetime on-base percentage against left-handed pitchers with runners in scoring position from the seventh inning on in road games, or the all-time leader in National Hockey League Stanley Cup playoff plus/minus rating, can be of value in very limited industry positions, but in a career field where people will work for no pay as interns to get their foot in the door with an organization, it is not enough. Getting that dream job with the Winnipeg Jets or the Brooklyn Nets, with Gold's Gym or Planet Fitness, with Under Armour or New Balance, with the Ladies Professional Golf Association or the Professional Bullriders Association, requires more than being just a sport fan. Increasingly, success in a career in the sport industry requires an understanding of the best practices in organization and management as complete as the understanding of the sport itself. It means that you need to be in charge of creating your own brand – that is, you. You are the product you will be selling to sport organizations for internships and jobs. So what are your brand attributes? What are those characteristics that will make you stand out from all the others who want to work in your dream job? Think about it this way: what makes the Los Angeles Lakers a stronger brand than the Los Angeles Clippers? Arsenal stronger than West Ham United? The University of Notre Dame stronger than Purdue University? Adidas stronger than Puma? Each of these organizations possesses a collection of attributes that define how it is perceived by consumers, and a strong brand comes from positive associations, and is formed for sport organizations by a collection of elements that can include logos, players, traditions, facilities, rivalries, and ownership (Wood, 2000; Gladden, 2007). How many National Basketball Association (NBA) championships have the Clippers won? How does the Emirates Stadium compare to West Ham's Boleyn Ground? What's Purdue's fight song? How do you feel about the look of Adidas products versus Puma products?

So what is your personal brand? How will prospective employers view your attributes? This book will introduce you to the various sectors of the sport industry – branded and licensed products, Olympic and international sport, sport media, school and youth sport, health and fitness, facility management, sport agency, intercollegiate sport, professional leagues, and tour sport – as well as to the organizational and managerial concepts, practices, and skills required for a career in sport management. To achieve this realistic yet challenging goal, each chapter will contain two kinds of information:

1   Specific information about one of the major segments of the sport industry, including a segment profile and a discussion of some of the key developments and important issues confronting that segment, and
2   Consideration of one of the critical responsibilities – planning, organizing, quality, change, etc. – of managers in sport organizations.

This dual focus found in each chapter will enable you to enhance your understanding of both the various segments that make up the sport industry, and the challenges

and best practices of managing in sport organizations. This approach will be rein-
forced through an end-of-chapter managerial exercise with discussion questions
that explore the relevant important legal, marketing, and financial implications. All
this to help you define your personal brand and get that dream job in sport, whatever it may be. That's the goal of this book. Now let's get going.

Check the stats

Purpose
To provide apparel, footwear, and associated products for consumers.

Stakeholders
Apparel and footwear manufacturers, consumers, retailers, stockholders, organizational employees, sport organizations that enter into licensing agreements, third
party licensing coordinating companies, licensed product manufacturers, and government and legal trademark protection and enforcement personnel.

Size and scope
The following data outlines the scope of the branded and licensed product industries in 2011:

- Total year-to-date sales in the U.S. totaled $77.3 billion, up 4.2 percent from
  2010.
- Sporting goods equipment sales rose 2.5 percent, from $20.4 billion in 2010,
  to $20.9 billion. The largest categories of sporting goods are: firearms/hunting
  ($2.9 billion); golf ($2.5 billion); fishing ($2 billion); camping ($1.8 billion);
  optical goods ($1.3 billion).
- Wholesale sales of sport apparel were $31.4 billion, a 6.1 percent increase
  over 2010 ($29.6 billion). Branded activewear accounted for $14.4 billion of
  these sales.
- Sales in the athletic footwear category rose from $12.61 billion in 2010 to
  $13.18 billion, an increase of 4.5 percent. The top five athletic footwear cate-
  gories are: running/jogging ($3.89 billion); classics/originals ($1.88 billion);
  kids ($1.87 billion); basketball ($875 million); skate/surf ($831 million).
  Licensed merchandise sales rose slightly – 1.3 percent – to $7.385 billion
  ("SGMA's," 2012).
- Nike and Adidas each own about 15 percent of the annual sales in the $6 billion
  U.K. footwear and apparel market (Chamberlain, 2012).
- Under Armour is the fastest-growing sport apparel and footwear brand in
  the world. The estimated worth of the company is $1 billion, with revenues
  of $1.4 billion in 2011. Six percent of its revenue comes from abroad, com-
  pared with over 60 percent for Nike. Shoes make up 12 percent of revenue, just

4

one percent of the U.S. athletic footwear pie. Nike's share is over 42 percent, while Adidas' is 11 percent (Roberts, 2011).

■ EA Sports created 27 games that sold over a million units in 2010, with five titles (including *Madden NFL 10* and *FIFA 10*) which sold over four million copies (Oznian, 2011).

Governance

Most individual sport leagues, tours, and players' associations organize and operate their own licensing programs, as do some intercollegiate athletic departments. Others of this type of sport organizations employ third party companies to run their licensing programs for them.

Logos (also trademarks, word marks, and service marks) are the intellectual property of sport organizations. A trademark is defined under the Federal Trademark Act of 1946, commonly referred to as the Lanham Act, as "any word, name, symbol, or device or combination thereof adopted and used by a manufacturer or merchant to identify his goods and distinguish them from those manufactured or sold by others" (Berry and Wong, 1993, p. 620).

One of the world's most recognizable logos is the five-ringed, five-color design associated with the Olympic Games. The individual credited with promoting the revival of the modern Games, the French aristocrat Baron Pierre de Coubertin, also created this logo back in 1914, allegedly inspired by an advertisement for Dunlop Tires. Some recognize the five-rings as "a symbol for peace," while London graphic designer Sarah Hyndman, who operated an Olympic logo website in the months preceding the 2012 Summer Olympics, made this observation of the power of such a strong visual image: "A really strong brand or logo can have a greater lifespan ... the Olympic rings [are] a great logo because it can withstand being translated again and again" (Kennedy, 2012, p. 21). We will discuss the Olympics in detail in Chapter 2.

U.S. law defines trademark infringement as the reproduction, counterfeiting, copying, or imitation in commerce of a registered mark, and bars companies that do not pay for the right to use these trademarks from manufacturing products bearing those marks. Only the owner of a mark may apply for federal registration. The application must include a drawing of the mark, a written description of the mark, the identification of the goods and services for which the registration is sought, and basis for filing. Sport organizations "transferred the right of use" of their names, marks, and logos to other companies so that these companies may use them in producing products for sale ("Protecting," 2012, p. 1).

To be claimed as property, these names and logos must be registered with the U.S. Patent and Trademark Office (USPTO), an agency of the Department of Commerce. Trademark applications can cost as much as $375, and are reviewed by federal

5

trademark lawyers to ensure they comply with the law. Once this process is completed, these names and logos become trademarks of the organization. After creating affiliated marks and logos, sport organizations should conduct a trademark search to determine if a conflicting mark exists. To determine whether a conflict exists, the USPTO determines whether a likelihood of confusion exists (whether consumers would be likely to associate the good or services of one party with those of another as a result of the use of the marks) (Thomas, 2010; "Protecting," 2012).

To find a conflict with an existing mark, the marks need not be identical, just substantially similar. Certain specified Patent and Trademark Depository Libraries throughout the U.S. perform trademark searches for a small fee. The term of a federal trademark is ten years, with ten-year renewal terms. Between the fifth and sixth year after the date of initial registration, the registrant must file an affidavit setting forth certain information to keep the registration alive. If no affidavit is filed, the registration is canceled ("Protecting," 2012).

Sport organizations place a high value on protecting their images and marks because they established a strong sense of brand identity, loyalty, and commitment from their fans, which organizations work for decades to develop and to strengthen. Protected images and marks are an important source of revenue, which is generated directly through the fees and royalties paid for their use and indirectly by strengthening the loyalty of a paying fan base.

Inside look: China's Michael Jordan wants you (to buy his shoes)

Throughout the chapter we will discuss the power of brands for all sport organizations, as well as some of the iconic sport figures who have influenced the branded and licensed product industries. Most of the names are familiar to you and others across the globe. But what about Li-Ning? Doesn't ring a bell? Li-Ning is a male gymnast, described by writer Joe Nocera as "a Michael Jordanesque figure" in his native China, having won three gold medals in the 1984 Los Angeles Summer Olympic Games. Six years later, he used his image to found an eponymous athletic footwear company. In 2008, the company was generating $700 million a year in revenue. Nocera describes a visit to the company's headquarters this way:

> Almost everything about Li-Ning feels like your basic modern sneaker company: the airy, wide-open campus; the casually dressed young executives bustling about; the rows of basketball and tennis courts under construction; the huge posters of Chinese Olympians and other athletes who have endorsed Li-Ning shoes and clothing like the tennis player Ivan Ljubicic and, believe it or not, Shaquille O'Neal.
>
> (2008, p. B1)

The company even adopted a positioning statement (a.k.a. slogan) "Anything is possible," seeming like a corrected Chinese translation of Adidas' grammatically off-kilter "Impossible is nothing," and a logo that, according to Nocera, looks like Nike's swoosh "except with a checkmark stuck at the front of it." In addition, the Shaq figure stamped on his branded line of Li-Ning shoes (costing $120) looks "an awful lot like Nike's Air Jordan figure" (2008, p. B8). Such efforts to copy U.S.-branded products are not rare in China. Nike estimates that for every authentic pair of its shoes sold around the world, one counterfeit Nike item is sold. One Chinese counterfeit product salesman justifies the questionable practice this way: "The shoes are original, it's just the brands that are fake" (Schmidle, 2010, p. 44).

According to company Li-Ning COO, Guo Jianxin, by 2013 the company wants to achieve revenues of $2 billion, with 20 percent of that coming from international sales. "But to get there," said Nocera, "Li-Ning will have to become a brand like Nike or Adidas" (2008, p. B8). But what does that mean? Li-Ning may have positive scores on brand association factors from Chinese consumers, but what about from Americans? Or Brazilians, Germans, or South Africans? Nocera writes:

> It's easy when you live in the West to take brands – their power, their ability to conjure up feelings of status among consumers, the loyalty they can generate – completely for granted … But go to China, and you get a whole new appreciation for brands … What is the car of choice in China if you have some money? Surprisingly, an Audi. Why? Because Audi got [there] early and did the best job among foreign car manufacturers of persuading the Chinese that an Audi is a symbol that you've made it … There is a powerful sense among Chinese consumers that domestic brands are inferior – and a distinct lack of confidence among Chinese companies in the allure of their own brands.
>
> (2008, p. B8)

This issue of brand value has been a problem for Li-Ning, since their domestic market share has dropped to third against Nike and Adidas since the late 1990s, when each were first allowed to sell products in China. So if a Chinese company such as Li-Ning struggles to connect with domestic consumers as they compare it against established foreign brands, how will they compete against these brands in international markets? A branding consultant was hired to help the company with its branding challenges. Said the consultant: "I said to the Li-Ning executives, 'What does it mean to you when you wear a Li-Ning shoe?'" The consultant was trying to show them that branding wasn't just about copying Nike, but creating a distinct brand identity. Ultimately, said the consultant, Li-Ning personnel couldn't define their own brand (Nocera, 2008, p. B8).

So Li-Ning sought to redefine its brand in domestic markets in cities that Nike and Adidas haven't penetrated with shoes that have a patriotic Chinese focus. One new

7

shoe is named for Lei Feng, a famous Chinese soldier glorified by the Chinese government after his death in 1962 (Chang with Halliday, 2006; Nocera, 2008). But this won't be easy, since Nike has also set its sights on the Chinese market, investing billions in marketing there. Of these efforts, Nike CEO Mark Parker stated: "No matter how much you're investing [in China], it's not enough" (Horovitz, 2009, p. 2B).

As of late 2011, Li-Ning had experienced weak sales at its 900 domestic retail stores, and its stock price plunged, in part due to local competitors such as 361 Degrees. The company vowed to spend more on advertising and promotions to reverse the trend. The company has not given up on the U.S. market either. In 2012, the company created "Digital Li-Ning," based in Chicago, a joint venture with a $10 million investment that entailed the launch of an on-line retail site, www.Li-Ning.com, and development of a new apparel collection for the U.S. market. The company produced data that revealed there has been a significant shift in U.S. consumers' perception of Chinese brands over the past five years, indicating that 62 percent of Americans said they were more likely to purchase products from Chinese companies today than they were in 2007. Younger and more affluent consumers were most likely to regard Chinese brands favorably, and more than half of the survey respondents, according to Li-Ning, reported they believe the quality of Chinese brands will measure up to U.S.-branded goods in the next five years. Seeking a broader profile beyond the U.S., Li-Ning also provided apparel and footwear for Chinese Olympic diving, gymnastics, badminton, table tennis, and shooting teams for the 2012 London Summer Games. In 2008, the five teams collectively won 28 gold medals, compared with the 51 China won in total (Li, 2011; Liu, 2012; Tung, 2012).

So while Nike is still the world leader in footwear and apparel sales, there are hundreds of companies around the world looking to chip away at its base and move up the ladder. To understand more about this industry segment, let's continue to develop our own personal brand and learn more about how it evolved.

HISTORICAL PERSPECTIVES

Baseball historian Warren Goldstein (1989) noted that many early baseball teams, such as the Cincinnati Red Stockings, the first truly professional baseball team, got their names from their distinctive apparel, and that uniforms created a sense of apartness and defined who was a player and who was not. Davis (1992) commented that clothing styles are a transmitted code that can impart meanings of identity, gender, status, and sexuality. Licensed apparel communicates on each of these levels, and is based on the notion that fans will purchase goods to draw them closer to their beloved organizations and athletes. Writer Bill Simmons describes the early days of buying player-specific licensed products this way: "Fans bought them because they wanted to dress like players on the team. Not only were we supporting our guys, but the player we chose became an expression of sorts" (2004, p. 12).

While the American Needle Company (founded in 1918) was the first to sell licensed headwear, and was also an official supplier to many MLB teams beginning in the 1940s, many other sport organizations were slow to realize the financial potential of such connections. In 1947, University of Oregon Athletic Director Leo Harris and animator Walt Disney agreed to allow Oregon to use Disney's Donald Duck image for the university's mascot. While these were some early steps toward the development of licensable properties, the University of California, Los Angeles (UCLA) is generally credited with being the first school to enter into a licensing agreement in 1973 with a manufacturer when its school bookstore granted a license to a watch manufacturer. The NCAA formed its properties division to license championship merchandise in 1975, but it does not administer licensing programs for member schools. Significant revenue growth began in the late 1980s, when the University of Notre Dame, which began its licensing program in 1983, experienced growth of 375 percent from 1988 to 1989. Collegiate licensed product sales totaled $100 million in the early 1980s. In 1995, sales reached $2.5 billion. The peak for licensed sales for major college and pro licensed products was 1996, with sales of $13.8 billion. That figure had slipped to $11.8 billion by 2001 (Nichols, 1995; Plata, 1996; Hiestand, 2002; Belson, 2010).

The licensing programs in professional sport leagues are administered by a for-profit branch of the organization, generally referred to as a properties division. These divisions approve licensees, police trademark infringement, and distribute licensing revenues equally among league franchises. Properties divisions usually handle marketing and sponsorship efforts as well. The NFL was the first professional league to develop a properties component in 1963, under the leadership of then-commissioner Alvin "Pete" Rozelle. The first license was granted to Sport Specialties. David Warsaw, the founder of the company, had worked with Chicago Bears owner George Halas in the 1930s in selling Bears merchandise and later developed licensing agreements with the Los Angeles Dodgers and the then-Los Angeles Rams ("Sports merchandising," 1996). By the late 1970s, each NFL team's licensing share was believed to be nearly half a million dollars annually.

MLB followed with the creation of its properties division in 1966, although many teams who had strong local sales were reluctant to give up their licensing rights to the league. Indeed, some teams bristled at sharing their marks with licensees because of their perceptions that such actions would cheapen the product. George Weiss, general manager of the New York Yankees, recoiled at the notion of licensing agreements. "Do you think I want every kid in this city walking around with a Yankees cap?" said Weiss, evidently believing such wide-spread distribution would weaken the team's brand. NHL Enterprises began formal league-governed

9

licensing in 1969, and NBA Properties initiated activities in 1982 (Helyar, 1994, p. 70; Lipsey, 1996).

Players unions also administer licensing programs. The Major League Baseball Players Association (MLBPA) was the first to enter into such an agreement in the late 1960s when then-Executive Director Marvin Miller entered into a two-year, $120,000 pact with Coca-Cola to permit the beverage manufacturer to put players' likenesses on bottle caps. Such royalties helped fund the emerging union's organizing activities. Miller also negotiated a comprehensive agreement with trading card manufacturer Topps Company (see below) in 1968. Topps was permitted to continue manufacturing trading cards bearing player likenesses for double the player's previous yearly fees (from $125 to $250), and it paid the union eight percent on annual sales up to $4 million and ten percent on all subsequent sales. In the first year the contract earned the MLBPA $320,000 (Helyar, 1994).

As for branded products, in the 1920s a number of famous sport personalities began to endorse sporting goods products, including Notre Dame football coach Knute Rockne, and baseball standouts Honus Wagner and Napoleon Lajoie. Tennis greats Fred Perry and Jean Rene Lacoste helped launch the fashion-sportswear segment in the 1950s. German footwear and apparel manufacturer Adidas was the first to establish a strong international branded product presence. Founded in the 1920s by Adolph "Adi" Dassler (from whose name the company's is derived), as a family shoe business, the firm grew through the production of soccer cleats and track spikes. Dassler established his product in part by convincing U.S. track Olympian Jesse Owens to wear Dassler's spikes in the 1936 Berlin Summer Olympic Games. Adi's brother, Rudolf, would later go on to found Puma after a falling out between the two brothers. The two companies would compete for international market share for the remainder of the century, with Adidas ultimately prevailing, in part through its close partnership with FIFA (soccer's international governing body) (Smit, 2008).

In the 1980s and 1990s, the industry experienced the emergence of several industry giants, most notably Nike and Reebok. Nike, the brainchild of Phil Knight, began as an offshoot of Knight's original company, Blue Ribbon Sports. The "Nike" name came from one of Knight's colleagues in 1971. By 1980, Nike had pulled in $269 million and replaced Adidas as the U.S.' top sneaker. Although Nike temporarily lost its top ranking to Reebok in 1986, the advent of the "Air Jordan" and "Bo Knows" marketing campaigns in the late 1980s propelled Nike back to the top, and Nike was a $2 billion company by 1990 (Katz, 1993). Adidas countered Nike's ascendance in 2005 when it purchased Reebok for $3.8 billion, in part to gain control over Reebok's licensing agreements with the NFL and the NBA (Smit, 2008). Nike regained the NFL licensing business in 2012.

DEFINING ORGANIZATIONS AND MANAGEMENT IN SPORT

To begin to advance your personal brand as a future sport industry professional, we need to understand the concept of management and the concept of an organization. An organization is a group of people working together to achieve a common purpose. Organizations exist to achieve goals that individuals can't achieve on their own. Today, sport organizations exist to produce products or services that can't be produced by a single individual working alone. Sport organizations are far too complex, with far too many related products and services and necessary tasks.

As shown in Box 1.1, the traditional definition of management is the coordination of human, material, technological, and financial resources needed for an organization to achieve its goals. Management gathers the resources – the people, money, and equipment – required to make work and workers more productive. Management designs the tasks and organizes the work to be done. It ensures the skills and the coordination necessary for the kind of cooperative effort that is the essence of sport organizations. Finally, it provides the sense of direction and purpose that can unify diverse people in a productive enterprise.

BOX 1.1 ORGANIZATION AND MANAGEMENT DEFINED

Organization

■ Any group of people working together to achieve a common purpose or goals that could not be attained by individuals working separately.

Management

■ The coordination of human, material, technological, and financial resources needed for the organization to achieve its goals.
■ Responsibility for performance.

Throughout this text, we will use a more direct form of this larger definition of sport management: the responsibility for performance. Sport managers are always responsible for the organization's realization of its goals, even though the goals may vary depending on whether the organization runs bowling lanes, a professional league franchise, a youth ice hockey league, an international sport governing body such as the International Olympic Committee (see Chapter 2), or a retail sporting goods store such as The Sports Authority. In summary, sport organizations exist to perform tasks that can only be executed through cooperative effort, and sport management is the responsibility for the performance and success of these organizations.

11

Although earlier civilizations thought of sport as "play" in relation to the toil and labor of "work," many early sporting activities were undeniably also linked to aspects of organization and management. Consider the fact that Native Americans played an early form of the game lacrosse with hundreds of players from rival tribes on a side, on a field up to several miles long. This required organization and management. In addition, the popularity of horse racing in England in the eighteenth and nineteenth centuries led to the development of a system to organize formally betting and the running of races (Mandell, 1984; Vamplew, 1989; Gorn and Goldstein, 2004).

Although these efforts were not specifically called "management," the responsibility for organized performance has been part of human society essentially from the beginning. But it was only about two hundred years ago that the ideas that formed the basis for what we now call "management thinking" began to emerge. The following sections describe the evolution of management thinking and, more specifically, the intriguing range of answers that have been offered to what might be viewed as the key question of management: how do you improve the performance of organizations?

Understanding management and its relationship to sport

In the mid-twentieth century, Henri Fayol, a French engineer, provided a job description for managers. Fayol suggested that there are five functions that define the manager's job. His definitions were so clear and concise that they have evolved to define management for over a half-century. According to Fayol, management must perform the five key functions to ensure organizational success, as outlined in Box 1.2:

BOX 1.2 FUNCTIONS OF MANAGEMENT ACCORDING TO FAYOL (1949)

1 Planning the work that needs to be done.
2 Organizing the work and the workplace to ensure that the work is productive.
3 Commanding or leading and directing the workers.
4 Coordinating the efforts of everyone performing the work.
5 Controlling or monitoring to ensure performance is consistent with the plan.

We will discuss how these elements impact a wide range of sport managers throughout the book, but stop and think for a moment about how each of these five areas impacts a job in the branded and licensed product industry. In what

The sport management challenge and the branded and licensed sport product industry ways does the forecasting of events and the updating of organizational plans impact the director of product marketing for Under Armour? How does a manager at a retailer such as Dick's Sporting Goods set the organization in motion and deal with unproductive personnel? How does harmony and unity of purpose impact these organizations? How do they monitor worker activities and output? Fayol's response to the question of how to improve performance might be summarized as improve the management: train managers to plan, organize, command, coordinate, and control.

Later in the twentieth century, management researcher Henry Mintzberg (1980) offered a slightly different perspective on management. After carefully observing what executive managers actually do with their time, Mintzberg suggested that management might be defined more effectively in terms of the roles that managers perform, as listed in Box 1.3:

BOX 1.3 MINTZBERG'S TEN KEY MANAGERIAL ROLES

1 Figurehead – representing the organization at events and ceremonies.
2 Leader – exercising influence with people and events.
3 Liaison – interacting with other organizations.
4 Monitor – receiving information critical for performance.
5 Disseminator – sharing information within the organization.
6 Spokesperson – presenting information outside the organization.
7 Entrepreneur – initiating change to improve performance.
8 Disturbance handler – dealing with issues and crises inside and outside of the organization.
9 Resource allocator – determining where the organization's human and financial resources and technology will be used.
10 Negotiator – bargaining to arrive at agreements with groups and individuals both within and outside the organization.

Together, these two models provide an important understanding of the wide variety of functions and roles that managers are called to perform. However, even in the relatively short period of time since Mintzberg's research, our understanding of management in general, and sport management specifically, has shifted. Perhaps the most significant change is that managers are no longer the only ones engaged in the tasks, functions, and roles of management in sport organizations.

Management as shared responsibility

Over the past two decades, there has been a growing recognition that organizations are too complex to be managed by managers alone. Organizations have discovered that performance is often better when management is the responsibility not only of managers, but also of performance work teams as well.

Remember our understanding of sport management is true for management in every context throughout all of the sport industries. In the branded and licensed product segment, that means it is true for the companies that manufacture the products, to the organizations that provide the license for the products, down through the retail outlets that sell the product. All of these individuals and groups are engaged in sport management; each shares in the responsibility for the performance of their own organization. The shift in management by managers to self-managing work teams can be seen throughout all segments of the sport industry. Management is increasingly a responsibility shared among work team leaders, self-managing work groups, and all of the personnel involved with the performance of a sport organization. Increasingly, the definition of management must be expanded to include the growing dimension of shared responsibility for performance.

THE NEW SPORT MANAGEMENT ENVIRONMENT

The responsibility for performance involves combining and coordinating human, technological, and financial resources to achieve organizational goals. Organizations by their nature are complex and therefore difficult to manage. Still, as long as society, the economy, and technology remained somewhat stable or changed only slowly, management had time to make the adjustments necessary to maintain and improve performance.

Gradual change has been replaced by rapid change, however, and managers now face new challenges brought on by this changing environment. These challenges include intense competition and new performance standards that every organization must achieve. With so many sport product and service options now available to consumers, it is no longer enough for a sport organization simply to be managed well. To compete and succeed in today's environment, the challenge for every sport organization is to be *better*. Increasingly, competition is forcing organizations to increase the quality of the products and services they offer, to increase speed and flexibility in responding to customers, and to innovate to constantly provide new products and services. Achieving these new standards is the responsibility of the sport manager. Let's examine each of these factors within the framework of the branded and licensed product industry.

14

Quality

It is common sense that given the choice between two comparably priced sport experiences or products, the customer will almost always choose the one of higher quality. But quality can be defined in many ways. Consider the memorabilia and collectible segment of this industry, such as game-worn jerseys and unique artifacts connected in many cases to the historic elements of a sport or activity. Annual sales in this segment are estimated at $1 billion, and no U.S. sport relies on its connection with its history more than baseball. Indeed, the baseball trading card market (see above) essentially created the concept of collecting sport memorabilia, so much so that the Metropolitan Museum of Art in New York City, one of the foremost of such institutions in the U.S., has acknowledged the cultural significance of this activity by housing the Burdick Collection. The museum received donations over several decades of the baseball card and memorabilia holdings of Jefferson Burdick. Known as the father of card collectors, Burdick's collection exceeded 30,000 pieces and is in total presumed to be worth millions of dollars. However, one museum director described Burdick's life work this way: "He didn't collect cards because of their value but because of his interest in history." Ironically, Burdick had little interest in the actual game of baseball, and he said of his passion: "Card collecting is primarily an inherited love of pictures" (Branch, 2009b; Belson, 2012, p. 1).

So how does one determine whether a collectible is truly a quality item? As noted above, if baseball relies on its history and traditions more than any other sport in the U.S. to connect with current and potential consumers, then no other organization within the sport can use this tool more than MLB's New York Yankees. The franchise loudly and proudly touts its 27 World Series titles, and many of the game's iconic players and Hall of Fame inductees – Babe Ruth, Lou Gehrig, Mickey Mantle, Reggie Jackson – have worn the hallowed Yankee pinstripes. Most recently, after shortstop Derek Jeter notched his 3,000 hit – the first Yankee ever to reach that heralded benchmark – groundskeepers at Yankee Stadium dug up five gallons of dirt from the right-side batter's box, and officials authenticated the act so that the organization could sell tablespoons of the soil through its exclusive deal with Jeter and memorabilia company Steiner Sports. "That bucket of dirt will go a long way," said Steiner Chairman Brandon Steiner (Sandomir, 2011, p. B13). Indeed, as part of Steiner's "Dirt Collectibles" series, one can buy multiple Jeter dirt products, including a commemorative engraved bat with authentic field dirt for $219.99, or a framed 20″ × 32″ "Road to 3,000 hits" photo with game-used dirt for $349.99. Hardly dirt cheap. And this is several years after the organization started selling Yankees-brand grass seed, based on a special blend created in the 1960s for the Yankees Stadium playing surface (Branch, 2009a).

But what if you are a fan of the New York Mets or the Boston Red Sox, or of any of the other 27 MLB teams? Chances are you wouldn't take these items even if somebody paid you to take them (unless you thought you could resell them at a profit). Does that mean these items aren't high quality? Much of the memorabilia market is like free agency in pro league sports: if someone is willing to pay something, then that's what the product is worth. In addition, quality in this case can be highly subjective. If you like the Yankees and Jeter, then you are far more likely to purchase related items. If not, you're likely to pass. And it seems that many people think Jeter items – dirt and all – are quality. One MLB licensing official commented that in more than a dozen years working for the league, "other than the home run race in 1998, [the Jeter 3,000 hit product market] is the most significant business we've done ... for a player." A manager at Wincraft, an MLB licensee that makes banners, flags, and pennants, agreed. "Short of someone of Jeter's caliber retiring, you won't get an event bigger than this" (Sandomir, 2011, p. B13).

There are products that can top Jeter's in interest, however: those that are connected to the game's most famous slugger, George Herman "Babe" Ruth. A year after Jeter reached the 3,000 hit plateau, a 1920 road jersey worn by Ruth, "The Sultan of Swat," sold for $4.4 million, making it the most expensive sport artifact ever sold at auction (the previous record was $4.3 million paid for the original rules of basketball typed by the game's inventor, James Naismith). The garment came from Ruth's first year with the Yankees, after his contract was infamously sold to the club by the cash-strapped owner of the rival Red Sox. "This is the holy grail of sports memorabilia," said David Koehler of SCP Auctions, the auction house that sold the item. "It's the finest authenticated jersey we've ever sold." Another expert explained the sale this way: "The closer you get to the player, the more the value of the piece. The bat is worth so much. But the jersey he wore, well, they retire the jersey. Not the bat." And not the dirt. But Red Sox fans do not despair. "It would be great to find one of his Red Sox uniforms," said Koehler (Sandomir, 2012a, p. B13). And as for a similarly valuable item of Mets memorabilia? Well, keep waiting.

Achieving quality and continually raising the bar in terms of quality is now among the sport manager's most important responsibilities. While the beauty (and quality) of Jeter and Ruth items may well be in the eyes of beholder Yankee fans, the ways in which the items are presented and priced will certainly impact the likelihood of sale. And there can be no doubt that Ruth and Jeter were quality performers, and each had their own personalities – Ruth the carousing yet lovable home run king, Jeter the cool, suave ultra-professional – that helped bond them in their own way with fans. Recall that above David Koehler made a point in noting that the Ruth item was "authenticated." That is also a critical component to determining quality. No one would pay nearly $5 million for the item if they weren't sure Ruth had actually worn it. Later in this section we will discuss issues of authentication, for such items are important in terms of organizational integrity.

16

Innovation

No matter how successful a sport organization is, someone somewhere in the world is developing a product or service that is different or better. Innovation means providing different or better products and services or finding a better way to deliver them. The need for contemporary sport organizations to innovate has become essential. In the previous section and in Chapter 3 we discuss a number of innovations in the sport media sector that have been achieved through advances in technology. But whether through technology or rules changes in a sport, through enhanced fan participation or enhanced fan access to sport information, or even through product innovations such as Under Armour (see below), the pressure is on sport managers to compete through innovation. Actually, innovation has always been a part of sport. Consider rules changes like the forward pass in football, the designated hitter in baseball, and the three-point shot in basketball. When combined with continual improvements in equipment and related products, one sees the countless examples of entrepreneurial efforts throughout the history of sport management.

Now while many of you might have collected sport trading cards a few years back, the fact that this hobby began in the 1800s might make it seem both quaint and antiquated. The Topps Company began in 1890 as the American Leaf Tobacco Company, then switched to making chewing gum in the 1930s. In 1951, Topps started to use sport trading cards, specifically baseball cards, to sell bubble gum. Topps ruled the baseball card market until 1981, when a federal court antitrust decision broke their stranglehold, leading to an explosion of competition. By the late 1980s, new card companies like Upper Deck and the production of greater card varieties developed a speculative market, with consumers flooding the market with cash seeking to buy cards as investments. The market bubble grew until 1991, when sports cards sales topped $1.2 billion, then burst, settling to annual sales of $300 million by 2004, and to $200 million by 2008. Card shops closed at a rapid rate as well, from 5,000 in the early 1990s to 500 in 2009 ("Scorecard," 2003; Winn, 2009).

In response, card makers have struggled to regain market share with new products and sets, such as cards with pieces of bats or game-worn uniforms affixed to them. In 2003, four separate card companies released 87 separate sets of cards and, by 2005, brands such as Fleer, Pacific, and Sky Box had folded, and Topps had concluded that the trading card market was going to shrink 25 percent a year. According to one industry expert: "There was too much money going into competition and not enough into marketing, especially to younger kids." Topps now has the exclusive MLB trading card licensing rights (Duerson, 2007, p. 30; Winn, 2009; Chozick, 2012).

17

Author Josh Wilker wrote of his youthful devotion to collecting baseball cards growing up in rural Vermont in the mid-1970s in these terms when he recalled the experience of what it felt like to make a purchase, of

> the boundless possibilities in that slim moment when I levered my fingernail below the flap of an opened pack ... And in the tiny clicking sound of the flap disconnecting. And in the first strong whiff of gum. And in the first glimpse of some unidentifiable piece of a card, a swatch of grass in the photo on the front, a row of numbers on the back ... I looked for the first time directly at a brand-new card and felt the sunshine coming up from it as if from some better world, some wider moment suddenly so close I could hold it in my hand.
>
> (2010, pp. 8–9)

But what about kids today? Are they more like Josh Wilker, who bonded in part due to the strength of a very tactile connection with the purchase? Or are they more like Jefferson Burdick, who was more visually connected to the products? Or is it something else that can tap into kids' interests?

Since the sports trading card market today is only 30 percent kids, Topps is looking to the use of smartphone technology to continue to connect with more "techcentric" young consumers. As digital games such as Angry Birds vie for kids' attention, Topps recently released the iPhone and iPad app Topps Pennant, a data-based platform for the statistically infatuated, and Topps Bunt, an interactive game with properties similar to fantasy leagues. Topps hopes the new apps will be the beginning of an expansion into other digital and media offerings such as TV shows and movies. Topps CEO Michael Eisner, formerly of Disney, believes Topps' brand is strong enough to make the tech transition. "In the world of beverages, there's Coke, but it's very hard to find companies that have the emotional brand of Topps." Said a Topps product designer of the new offerings: "Our goal was to take that D.N.A. and reconstitute them to new platforms." The Pennant app (initially priced at $2.99, a little more than the price of a pack of cards) offers detailed interactive graphics on every player and every game played since 1952. Bunt (free) features rows of cards that rotate three-dimensionally to reveal biographical information, and allows users to build teams, trade players, and compete with other users as in fantasy leagues (Chozick, 2012, p. B4). Both apps require iOS 4.3 to download and operate.

The move is a good one, because, according to Evan Kaplan, VP of licensing and business development for the MLBPA, "certain businesses could go away for us, but baseball cards will always be essential" (Chozick, 2012, p. B4). So to keep something so essential for Topps, MLB, and its players, innovations like these must continue to emerge.

18

Speed and flexibility

As important as quality is, it is not the total answer. One executive put it this way: "Quality is your ticket into the stadium. You can't even come to the game unless you have a quality product and process in place ... But you have to compete on other dimensions today" (Byrne, 1992). In addition to quality, other dimensions such as speed and flexibility have become more and more important as a way to move ahead of the competition. Organizations that are too large to be flexible, or too rigid in terms of policies and procedures, are unable to take advantage of opportunities that emerge and disappear so quickly in all segments of the sport industry.

One sport that may boast the most invested fans is NASCAR, the National Association for Stock Car Auto Racing. Like other fans, NASCAR devotees not only wear the apparel of their favorite drivers (most have one favorite and several others they like, as well as a few they hate), but also purchase other types of collectibles unique to the sport. One such item is the die-cast stock-car replica, sales of which account for 14 percent of the $1 billion in NASCAR retail sales. The items typically cost $60, and are intricately designed and detailed based on the look of each driver's actual car, with some drivers having multiple models. The sport's most popular driver, Dale Earnhardt, Jr., has 18 versions available (Caldwell, 2010).

But sales of the die-cast products have fallen from a high of $250 million in 2002 to a third of that a decade later, while merchandise sales overall are down 20 percent. Some industry experts said this was a result of oversaturation in the market, the same issue that hit the sports trading card business in the late 1990s. As a result, NASCAR announced the formation of the NASCAR Team Licensing Trust to coordinate sales for many top racing teams. Previously, each team had negotiated its own separate deals. "The strong had always received the highest guarantees, and the weak just got the leftovers," said Ty Norris, VP and general manager for Michael Waltrip Racing. "For the first time, everybody has a voice in die-cast, toys and apparel." NASCAR also acted to establish connections with toy industry giant and model train manufacturer Lionel to make the die-cast cars. "We get to do what we know how to do," said Lionel's CEO, Jerry Calabrese. NASCAR has also worked to make its cars look more like the old-school models from the circuit's early days, when the cars raced were much closer in appearance to the actual cars sold in Chevrolet, Dodge, and Ford dealerships across the country. Of these various moves, Ty Norris of Waltrip commented: "We have to figure out a way to make die-cast collectible again" (Caldwell, 2010, p. Y5). Speed and flexibility on the part of teams, NASCAR, and manufacturers will contribute to the achievement of that end.

Sustainable growth

The concept of sustainable growth means that organizations neither seek to be as large as they can be nor to grow as quickly as they possibly can. Sustainable growth also means that organizations should only grow at a rate, and to a size, that can be maintained over the long term (Garfield, 1992). Certainly with so many sport organizations competing for the money and attention of potential consumers, every sport organization must commit itself to a goal of sustainable growth.

We have seen examples above from the licensed merchandise sales that experienced steep declines after the markets for sport trading cards and die-cast cars were oversaturated with products. Both MLB and NASCAR responded to reduce licensees so that the markets could stabilize. Today, sustainable growth has a larger meaning in terms of protecting natural resources and reducing the amount of waste created, and companies around the globe are using more recycled or biodegradable components in products. Prior to the 2010 FIFA World Cup (see Chapter 2), Nike used what is arguably the most popular sporting event in the world to announce that each team wearing Nike products during the competition (including the perennially strong sides from Brazil, the Netherlands, and Portugal, as well as the U.S. squad) would wear jerseys made almost entirely of plastic culled from landfills in Japan and Taiwan (Bhanoo, 2010).

Nike, an organization that has often been criticized for less-than-progressive policies toward its treatment of its factory workers (see below), began sustainability activities back in the early 1990s when it donated used materials to be incorporated into the production of running track surfaces. More recently, the company has created a long-term plan to "minimize or eliminate all substances known to be harmful to the health of biological or ecological systems." "Our customers expect this from us," said Lorrie Vogel, the head of Nike's team assigned to this task. "It's about changing the way our company does things in general." Company managers also note that these moves can make financial sense as well. "If this was not financially viable," said a VP at retail giant Walmart, "a company such as ours would not be doing it." The choice for other apparel manufacturers can be more difficult. Patagonia, the maker of outdoor and hiking apparel and products, is viewed by consumers as environmentally conscious – 75 percent of the clothes it sells are recyclable – but it has struggled to find non-toxic fabric dyes. "It's super-easy to find an environmentally friendly dye that will fade in three washes," a company spokesperson explained, "but a garment that lasts 20 years is much more friendly than one that lasts five months" (Bhanoo, 2010, p. B3).

Integrity

The final performance standard is of a different type than quality, speed, flexibility, and innovation and sustainable growth. It is, in a sense, the context for the others. Integrity serves a guiding principle by which all organizational decisions and actions are articulated and activated. Much like vision and goals (outlined in Chapter 4), mission (illustrated in Chapter 6), and codes of conduct (see Chapter 2), integrity serves to help sport managers to set the direction of their organizations, and to make decisions relative to what are appropriate operating procedures.

Every sport organization in each sport industry segment faces challenges that call into question its commitment to integrity in its operations. Recall that above in the discussion of quality we reference the issue of authenticity as a key component to determining the value of sport memorabilia. If someone is going to expect a bid of $4.4 million to purchase a jersey said to be worn by Babe Ruth, there better be a viable and legitimate way to prove it's really been worn by "the Bambino." The entire integrity of this particular segment of the branded and licensed product industry relies heavily on the authentication process. Around the year 2000, the Federal Bureau of Investigation reported widespread fraud in this industry, replete with forged signatures and fake items. MLB had to take the issue head on, so it now has at least one authenticator at every game, drawn from a pool of 120 active and retired law enforcement officials. At Yankee Stadium recently, when a home run dropped into Monument Park beyond the centerfield fence, a call came over the security walkie-talkie: "No one touch it until the authenticator gets there." Authenticator Cosmo Lubrano, a sergeant in the 23rd Precinct of the New York Police Department, retrieved the ball, stuck a hologram and a bar code sticker on it, and scanned the bar code with a hand-held unit to enter into a team database. Lubrano also witnesses autograph signings off-site, as well as the dividing of previously authenticated items, like the Jeter dirt described above (Branch, 2009b, B12).

The authentication process is "growing exponentially" according to an MLB official. At Citizen Bank Park, the home of MLB's Philadelphia Phillies, fans can visit a kiosk to buy authenticated game-used merchandise. A lineup card is $100, and broken bats can fetch up to $500. "As long as it is witnessed by an authenticator, there's no limit as to what can be authenticated," stated an MLB official. And years from now, says another MLB official, the league can verify that when the ball used for the first pitch at CitiField in New York is sold, "there won't be ten people coming out of the woodwork saying, 'No, this was the ball'" (Branch, 2009b, p. B15). Clearly the sport memorabilia segment must show that its products are what they say they are to maintain its integrity to customers.

The examination of the new sport management environment in the context of the branded and licensed product industry helps to underscore the importance of the increased emphasis on quality, innovation, speed and flexibility, sustainable growth,

21

The sport management challenge and the branded and licensed sport product industry and integrity. Ultimately, all sport managers will be judged by these standards, and successful sport organizations are already mindful of them and are actively pursuing them. The long-time viability of the branded and licensed product industry will depend on how well managers and decision makers recognize these factors and abide by them.

Before considering each dimension of the further challenges for sport managers in the various sport industries in greater detail, we'll first take a look at the development of management theories and thinking and how these apply to this industry. We'll trace the roots of these ideas and theories of how to improve the performance of organizations back more than a century, and present more contemporary management ideas that create the bridge between these earlier concepts and today's sport organizational climate. We have looked at the evolution of the branded and licensed product industry already. Consider this next step a similar look back, with the key issue here being relevance; specifically, how the history of management thought influences how sport organizations operate today.

APPLYING MANAGEMENT THEORIES TO THE BRANDED AND LICENSED PRODUCT INDUSTRY

Influential early ideas

J.B. Say and the concept of the "entrepreneur"

A fundamentally different response to the question of how to improve performance came in the early nineteenth century from the French economic philosopher J.B. Say. Essentially, Say suggested that improved performance is the result of better ideas. In fact, Say (1803/1964) created a term to describe people with ideas for better uses of existing technology; he called these people entrepreneurs.

The history of sport management is replete with technological and conceptual entrepreneurs. One of the earliest and best examples was Albert Spalding. Spalding was a standout professional baseball pitcher who in the late nineteenth century parlayed his baseball reputation and a loan of $800 to create a sporting goods manufacturing giant based on selling to the expanding American middle class. While also owner of the Chicago franchise of the National League, Spalding adopted technological advances to manufacture bats, baseballs, gloves, uniforms, golf clubs, bicycles, hunting goods, and football equipment. Many other manufacturers also focused on the production of sporting goods, but Spalding also understood that he had to create and foster the markets for these products as the newly affluent middle class sought to find uses for their leisure time. Spalding produced guides on how to play and to exercise, promoted grassroots sport competitions, and gained credibility with consumers by claiming official supplier status with baseball's National League (Levine, 1985).

22

This position of quality-by-association (a technique used today by every company that touts its status as the "official supplier" to any sport organization or by any company that uses a sport personality to endorse its products) allowed consumers to distinguish Spalding products from their many competitors. Spalding also created a profitable distribution system in which the company sold directly to retailers at a set price with the guarantee that retailers would sell at a price that Spalding set. This technique created stable markets for Spalding goods and eliminated price cutting at the retail level (Levine, 1985).

Many of the branded and licensed sport product organizations we have discussed thus far were founded and organized as makers of sport products. But many organizations in this industry, such as Lionel, the model train maker, have established association with sport only after being established as manufacturers of mainstream products. One such recent example is Vineyard Vines (VV), an apparel company self-described as "a preppy brand of clothing and accessories for men and women." VV's founders, brothers Shep and Ian Murray, started the business with a cash advance of $8,000 on their credit card in 1998 and began selling ties out of the back of their Jeep to local retailers on the Massachusetts resort island of Martha's Vineyard. Soon after they began sales via catalog. In 2002, the company dipped its toe in the sport product market, filling a custom tie order to Southern Methodist University. Three years later, VV conducted a "College Tour" road trip to campuses throughout the southeastern U.S. (where frat boys and sorority girls often sport the preppy look to social occasions and football games), and opened on Martha's Vineyard the first of its own retail shops. In 2008, VV became an official licensee of MLB, the NFL, and of dozens of colleges and universities, and with the National Hockey League (NHL) in 2011 ("Our story," 2012).

So how does one define what is "preppy"? In the seminal tongue-in-cheek treatise on the topic, *The official preppy handbook* (Birnbach, 1980), the persona is said to be based on having attended a prestigious private "prep" school (most likely in New England), ancestors who may have arrived in America on the Mayflower, an upper-class income, and possible residence in enclaves such as Fairfield County in Connecticut. Favored retailers include L.L. Bean and Brooks Brothers, and automobiles of choice include BMWs and Land Rovers. The preppy value system, instructs the *Handbook*, includes "nonchalance," "charm," "athleticism," and "drinking."

But, the book advises, preppy can also be an acquired mindset and ethos. "Stop thinking you're a lost cause simply because you've never been to either the Harvard–Yale (football) game or Martha's Vineyard. Even preppies had to learn at one point not to wear socks with loafers" (Birnbach, 1980, p. 11). To visualize the look, think of the character Sack Lodge (played by Bradley Cooper) from the movie "Wedding Crashers." That means madras, seersucker, blue blazers, and lots of pink and lime green. For both men and women sporting nicknames such as "Muffy," "Buffy," "Chip," "Skip," and "Trip." And loafers with no socks.

23

VV fully embraces this concept and expands on this notion to define its brand through its marketing and communication efforts, using its catalogs and website as a platform to share stories of how their customers and employees "live the dream and how they make Vineyard Vines a part of it." The dream lifestyle in this case is a mélange of sailing, deep-sea fishing, beach hijinx, golf, tennis, squash, and, of course, cocktail parties. VV has since expanded its product line to include all forms of casual and semi-formal clothing, operates 30 of its own retail stores in the U.S., and sells products through 600 other retail outlets (Connor, 2012).

The most recent move by VV to reach a sport market and expand sales is its partnership with the Kentucky Derby, America's most storied horse racing event. The Derby, its inaugural run in 1875, is the first leg of thoroughbred horse racing's "Triple Crown" and is held on the first Saturday of each May at Churchill Downs in Louisville, Kentucky. The 2012 event drew over 160,000 spectators, with an on-track wagering pool of $11.5 million, was the tenth most-watched U.S. sporting event of the year, and has an estimated brand value of $70 million (Oznian, 2011).

So what's the link between horse racing and VV? Utilizing a technique of Albert Spalding, VV became "the official style" of the Derby, based on the general connections between preps and the horse riding and racing culture. *The official preppy handbook* describes a phenomenon it calls "the Horse Phase," explaining it is "a standard condition of a girl Prep's adolescence" (Birnbach, 1980, p. 28), and there is a well-established alcohol-fueled party atmosphere associated with the Derby. While the infield at Churchill Downs might be closer to the scene found at the Indianapolis 500 or Talladega Superspeedway, the clubhouse and grandstand experience is somewhat more genteel. There, southern belles and grand dames are dressed in brightly colored frocks and sport all manner of hats, while the men wear garb closely aligned with the looks sold by VV, and all of the above imbibing in the region's famed libation, the mint julep. In 2012, VV issued a special catalog outlining its connection with the Derby, complete with young male and female models donning racing-themed apparel and accessories (with several clutching the famed juleps). VV also established a promotional presence at the event, giving away pink foam whale-shaped hats (based on the company logo) and putting signage on the tractor that groomed the dirt racing surface after each race on the day's card.

J.B. Say would point out that the entrepreneurial efforts outlined above improved performance by finding better uses for existing technologies and better ways to develop markets and to sell to customers. He would note that each example improved performance by finding better ways for using the resources we already have. So while Martha's Vineyard might be about a thousand miles away from Churchill Downs (and you can't get there via yacht or sailboat), VV understood that the event was a way to connect with customers who could identify with the look and vibe of their product line.

Robert Owen and the Soho Engineering Foundry

Management experiments like those of the entrepreneurs just discussed also occurred well before our time and often took different forms. Consider the efforts of Robert Owen, a Scottish cotton mill owner. Owen (1825) believed that improved working conditions for laborers would result in improvements in their performance. He shortened the workday from 13 to 10.5 hours, built better housing and a recreation center for his workers, provided a company store where necessities could be purchased at reasonable prices, and accessed schooling for workers' children. By all accounts, Owen's mills became highly profitable and had a significant impact on child labor laws.

Owen was able to improve performance by improving the way his workers were treated. Many manufacturers of branded and licensed sport products have much to learn from Owen. Industry giants Adidas, Nike, and Puma have been universally and repeatedly criticized for paying low wages and treating workers poorly. The most recent case involved evidence of managers in Bangladeshi sweatshops that supply the three companies verbally and physically abusing workers. At one supplier for Puma, two-thirds of workers claimed they had been beaten or slapped, and women working for Nike and Adidas reported sexual harassment incidents. Workers for all three companies also had to work illegally long hours for less than the established minimum wage (about $1.50 a day), with some working for as little as 12 cents an hour (Chamberlain, 2012).

All three companies dispute the claims or promise to address concerns. A Nike spokesperson told *The Guardian* newspaper of Great Britain that the company "takes working conditions in our factories very seriously. All Nike suppliers must adhere to our code of conduct ... we will get back to you as soon as someone ... has made an assessment" (Chamberlain, 2012, p. 1). Some of these issues are discussed in greater detail in Chapter 2, but the important point from Owen's perspective is that the way people are managed can make a significant difference in performance. To the question of how to improve performance, Robert Owen's answer was to make the workplace a community and treat people well.

These early answers to the question of management are interesting and important, but not until more recently were management and organizations actually studied and analyzed in a systematic way in an effort to understand which methods worked and which didn't to improve organizational performance.

More recent contributions

During the second half of the twentieth century, new answers to the question of how to improve organizational performance emerged. A number of the contributions to management thinking have endured and, taken together, they provide a sense of the range and diversity of the ideas within the management mainstream. The theories we will review are outlined below in Box 1.4:

BOX 1.4 RECENT CONTRIBUTIONS TO MANAGEMENT THINKING

Systems theory: recognizes the importance of factors and events occurring outside the organization and in the surrounding environment.

Stakeholder theory: suggests that an organization has relationships with many constituent groups, or "stakeholders," that affect and are affected by its decisions. Suggests that stakeholders are defined as those individuals that have a "stake" in the performance of an organization.

Contingency theory: adjust the management approach to match the requirements of the situation.

Learning organization: facilitate the lifelong learning and personal development of all employees while continuously transforming the organization to respond to changing demands and needs.

Systems theory

In 1928, biologist Ludwig von Bertalanffy introduced a theory of general systems suggesting that everything in nature is interrelated. According to von Bertalanffy (1951), every entity is part of a larger system. He pointed out that in nature nothing is totally independent and self-sufficient. Every living organism is part of a system and is affected by what happens both within and outside that system. Management thinker Herbert Simon (1965) extended systems thought to organizations by viewing them as systems that make decisions and process information.

THE IMPORTANCE OF LOOKING BEYOND THE ORGANIZATION

Traditionally, organizations were thought of as fairly closed systems. Organizations usually thought of themselves as mostly insulated or protected from whatever was happening outside their boundaries. Those in distinct organizations tended to think the events most critical to their success were those that occurred inside those boundaries.

Consider the case of New Balance (NB) and its 990 model running shoe. NB, based in Boston, is a privately held footwear and apparel company (which also owns the Dunham, PF Flyers, and Warrior brands). With global sales of $2 billion in 2011, NB is behind Nike and Adidas, and NB running shoes accounted for 6.4 percent

($400 million) of the $6.5 billion U.S. running shoe market (compared to $3.6 billion – 55 percent – for Nike) (Levere, 2012).

As some of the issues noted above illustrate, nearly all branded and licensed apparel and footwear (99.3 percent, in fact) is manufactured outside the U.S. NB's 990 shoe is a notable exception, assembled in factories in the towns of Norridgewock and Skowhegan in Maine, and Lawrence, Massachusetts. NB sought to capitalize on the 30th anniversary of the 990 in 2011 by promoting through a media campaign that cost nearly $1 million the fact that the shoes were made domestically by local workers more able to provide a quality product. One ad features an NB worker discussing "the people that have been here 20 or so years ... That's what they have done their whole life, is put good shoes in a box, to craft these shoes" (Levere, 2012, p. B2). This message of quality and concern for U.S. jobs and workers, the company believes, will provide a stark contrast to the products and practices of Adidas and Nike.

The major contribution of a systems perspective was the recognition that organizations are in fact open systems. That is, they receive input from their environment. They transform that input into output, and the output then re-enters the environment, resulting in feedback that affects subsequent input. The systems view forces organizations to recognize that what is happening outside its boundaries does matter. As we discussed earlier in the chapter, we are a society of organizations, and when one organization falters or fails, others are almost always threatened or damaged. Changes in the social, economic, political, and technological environments are also larger scale factors, as we see in Chapter 10 when we discuss professional league sports.

Today, successful sport organizations such as New Balance know they are open systems. They have learned that their environments are a key factor affecting their performance. The forms of their services and products are driven more by customer tastes and preferences than by their own. Their success in meeting customer demands is determined by many factors. Sport organizations must cultivate a work force capable of doing the necessary work. Each of these environmental factors must be recognized and responded to in managing the organization.

No organization can be concerned simply with what's happening within its four walls. All organizations must be concerned equally with customer relations, community relations, employee relations, supplier relations, and government relations. Von Bertalanffy and Simon were right: all organizations – from the smallest to the largest, and regardless of the sport industry segment – are part of a system, and anything happening within this system is happening to the sport organization as well.

Stakeholder theory

Above and throughout the text we cite the term "stakeholders" in describing the various groups associated with the management, organization, and operation in the various sport industries. But what exactly does this term mean? The concepts associated with stakeholder theory are aligned with the tenets of systems theory. Stakeholder theory suggests that an organization has relationships with many constituent groups, or "stakeholders," that affect and are affected by its decisions. Related theory also suggests that stakeholders are defined as those individuals that have a "stake" in the performance of an organization, that the interests of all legitimate stakeholders have intrinsic value, and that no set of interests is assumed to dominate the others (Freeman, 1984; Clarkson, 1995; Donaldson and Preston, 1995). Jones (1995) asserts that those organizations whose managers develop trusting and cooperative relationships with stakeholders will have a competitive advantage over other organizations. Theorists also suggest that all stakeholder interests must be attended to for the organization to be successful.

The concept of considering the various stakeholders connected to an organization is demonstrated through an examination of Under Armour (UA). As the football team's special teams captain (and a business major) at the University of Maryland in 1995, Kevin Plank, the founder and CEO of UA, saw teammates suffer from heat stress during practice and wondered whether their sweat-soaked t-shirts contributed to their maladies. In response Plank developed a performance undershirt that wicked moisture away from the skin. He initially financed the company with $20,000 of his own money, $40,000 spread on five credit cards, additional funds from family and friends, and a $250,000 loan from the Small Business Administration. But Plank couldn't convince large manufacturers to back him, so he took to selling directly to team equipment managers out of the trunk of his car (much like Phil Knight first did with Blue Ribbon Sports, as did Shep and Ian Murray of Vineyard Vines). In 1996, he booked $17,000 in sales, and made a deal with an Ohio apparel manufacturer (call in your orders by noon, said plant owner Sal Fasciana, and we'll make and ship the product by the end of the day). Plank established official supplier agreements with MLB, Major League Soccer (MLS), NHL, USA Baseball, and the U.S. Ski team, much like Spalding had with MLB over a century before. The company now makes shirts, shorts, pants, socks, hats, and underwear, and launched a women's gear line, along with "LooseGear" and "Performance Grey" products.

As noted above, Under Armour is the fastest-growing sport apparel and footwear brand in the world. The estimated worth of the company is $1 billion, with revenues of $1.4 billion in 2011, and owns three percent of the U.S. market. Even as competitors such as Nike, Adidas, Champion, and Russell Athletic have tried to match UA, Michael May of the Sporting Goods Manufacturers Association says: "Under Armour is the dominant brand in the high-tech sport apparel industry … people love Under Armour." Even as competitors try to buy him out, Plank refuses, stating: "As foreign as it would be for you to go running in regular shoes, I want it to be just as foreign for you not to work out in your Under Armour" (Graham, 2004, pp. 8, 9; Oznian, 2011).

In terms of brand strength, states writer Daniel Roberts, the interlocking UA company logo "is becoming as recognizable as the Nike swoosh," and in contrast to Nike's "deification" of individual athletes, "UA's brand identity was always about the team." UA has apparel and footwear agreements with several NCAA Division I athletic programs, including Maryland (a five-year deal signed in 2009 worth $17.5 million), Auburn University, and Boston College. In fact, some dubbed the 2011 BCS national championship game (eventual winner Auburn vs. the University of Oregon, the pet athletic department of Nike founder Phil Knight) as UA v. Nike (Roberts, 2011, p. 1).

In 2011, UA built further on this team-based approach and used the opening of the college football season and its relationship with the University of Maryland to introduce a brand-new UA "Maryland Pride" uniform, the first of 32 combinations the team would wear over the season. The new look (including player footwear) was based on the yellow–black–red–white design of the state flag, which in the opinion of one writer "made players look to some like chess pieces," while another suggested the design appeared like "a quilting bee enhanced by Jell-o shots." Some other reactions were more pointed. A headline on Deadspin.com read: "Maryland football players will dress in whatever clown suit Under Armour tells them to." However, Maryland students approved of the uniforms, as explained by the school's student newspaper. "People have taken a real sense of pride in what the football team wore … What a lot of people don't understand is that the people who grow up in Maryland have a huge sense of pride in our state flag." And the look resonated with Maryland recruits as well. One local prospect had this to say: "I like that [the uniforms] represented Maryland, the state flag, the state, everything." Team captains get to select the unie combinations for each week's game. A Maryland spokesperson justified the move, stating: "[UA is] trying to increase their visibility, and so are we" ("New uniforms," 2011, p. 7C; Roberts, 2011, p. 1; Tanier, 2011, p. A1).

But the uniform-as-fashion statement approach is neither new nor novel. Nike has been using Oregon teams as an incubator for new looks for several years (with nearly 400 different potential combinations for its football uniforms), and unveiled new looks for grid squads at the University of Georgia and Oklahoma State University the same weekend UA's Maryland duds were trotted out. Later in the year, Adidas did the same for both teams in the University of Michigan–Notre Dame game, choosing what one Adidas manager called "a retro-heritage look, which with these two programs makes all the sense in the world." "This company has got the world talking," UA's Plank defiantly declared to company workers soon after the Maryland Pride rollout (Tanier, 2011, p. B16).

29

So how is the Maryland–UA project a study in the terms of stakeholder theory? Through its uniform and apparel deal, UA is a partner with Maryland, and the two entities can work together for mutual success. The looks generate publicity and interest for both sides. The new looks are meant to capture state pride for students, players, and prospective recruits, who as a result may view the school as more in touch with its interests and perspectives. This last point sound far-fetched? In a 2010 poll of Division I college football players across the country, 53.7 percent ranked Oregon's uniforms the best. Said one Big Ten player ranked as a star by *ESPN Magazine*: "I don't even have to think about that one. I almost wanted to transfer there just for those uniforms." By the way, the University of Wyoming's brown and yellow uniforms were ranked worst, gaining 18.9 percent of the vote (Ain *et al.*, 2010, p. 80). By listening to all of those who have a stake in organizational success, Maryland might make it to No. 1 on the next uniform poll. And if it hasn't already done so, Wyoming is probably thinking about a complete redesign.

Contingency theory

The search for universal or general principles of management did not end with Fayol and Mintzberg. The emergence of systems theory, which highlighted the many environmental variables that influenced organizations, raised the question of whether it was still possible to develop universal management principles that would apply to all organizations and all situations. Social philosopher Mary Parker Follett developed the "law of the situation" in 1928. Follett suggested that leaders would be more successful if they would adjust their style of leadership to the needs of their followers and to the requirements of the situation (Metcalf and Urwick, 1941). For Follett there was no one best way. What was best would be determined by the situation. It was up to management to recognize what the situation required and to make the necessary adjustments.

Today, this approach is called the "contingency view," and it is reflected in nearly every dimension of management. In terms of planning, organizations now have contingency plans, options that ensure that a plan is in place for every situation likely to be encountered. In terms of organizing, the retail hat seller Lids recognizes that shipping the same products to all stores everywhere may be effective in terms of simplifying distribution, but management needs to listen to consumers and individual store managers and remain flexible to ensure that sales in stores in each market remain high. In terms of quality control, in some cases apparel manufacturer Under Armour may need to inspect every product; in other cases, where manufacturing or assembly is less precise, it may make more sense to test and to inspect only a statistically selected sample of the total output. The evidence is abundant: effective organizations adjust to the situation.

For a clearer understanding of the premises of the contingency view, consider the case of professional golfers and their selection of on-course apparel. For years, golf apparel was synonymous with bad taste (for another visual, think about the movie "Caddyshack" and the character Al Czervik, played so ably by comedian Rodney Dangerfield). Then, for years the looks on the PGA Tour were dismissed by many as staid and boring (think khakis and white polo shirts everywhere).

Recently, however, more PGA pros are wearing what *The official preppy handbook* coined "go-to-hell" pants. These are appropriate around prep country clubs, says the source, because "it is considered very spirited, very fun-loving to wear one off-beat, loud item … The favored color is lime green, but go-to-hell pants may come in other similarly shocking colors" (Birnbach, 1980, p. 193). This connection to both the traditional and the fun-loving has led designers such as Ralph Lauren to push the players wearing their product, such as Davis Love III and Webb Simpson, to wear bright pants colored pink (actually termed "Bubblicious" by the maker), paired with pastel striped shirts. Clothing companies often script the outfits for their golfers at major tournaments. "They tell me, 'Look, we sell more pink pants whenever you wear the pink pants,'" said Love. "Frankly, I'm not a fan of yellow or pink pants, but if they give them to me – and they do – I wear them. I figure they know better than me." Dustin Johnson, however, draws the line at wearing orange. Why? "I don't like orange," he explained. When Rickie Fowler (outfitted by Puma), who has made orange his signature color – a homage to his collegiate alma mater, Oklahoma State University – heard Johnson's remark, he said: "I've got to talk to him about that. Everybody needs some orange, man." A writer for *Golf Digest* magazine defends the approach this way: "People have to dress their personality … and there's nothing wrong with that." British golfer Ian Poulter, who once wore pants with the Union Jack British flag design (channeling the same theme used by Under Armour at Maryland), summed up his sartorial choices this way: "I wanted to liven up golf … What I always say is, 'Look good, feel good, play good'" (Macur, 2011, p. Y6; Pennington, 2012a, p. D7).

The challenge here for golfers is how comfortable they are in helping their apparel suppliers and pushing the fashion envelop with attention-grabbing looks. Contingency theorists would say that the solution to the problem depends on the situation, and no single answer exists for each individual golfer. When Davis Love III modeled the look Ralph Lauren proposed for his wife, the reaction was: "You've got to be kidding me." And the issue of fashion seems to be less controversial on the LPGA tour, as evidenced by a "The 18 best-dressed ladies on the tour" list recently posted on the website Bleacher Report (No. 1, by the way, was Paula Creamer, who, ironically, often features pink in her on-course attire). And writer Bill Pennington opined that "getting the right outfit on television for the final round of a women's major championship remains important to marketing." But it's not always colors and prints that are an issue. Creamer explained that women's designers only recently began putting functional pockets on their shorts, skirts, and pants for storage of items such as tees and ball markers. "Thank goodness they've learned that

31

you can hide the pockets and still be stylish," she said (Burke, 2011; Macur, 2011, p. Y6; Pennington, 2012a, p. D7).

Follett's contribution was an important one, but it is often difficult to understand what is required in situations as complex and chaotic as those that organizations in the widely varied sport industries face today. The challenge for management is clear: to improve performance, management must learn to adjust to the situation. What works for Ian Poulter and Ricky Fowler (and it seems to, as many fans were seen at the 2012 Open Championship at Royal Lytham & St Anne's in England decked out head-to-toe in orange. "I saw the all-orange ... I always notice the orange. Good to see it," said Fowler) may not make Phil Mickelson or Charl Schwartzel feel comfortable. And are golfers superstitious enough to copy the looks of a competitor who's playing especially well? Not David Toms, who has rejected pushes to wear more eye-catching looks. "I just kind of say, 'Nah, I don't really look good in that' ... They probably wish I was a little more flamboyant, but I'm old-fashioned" (Pennington, 2012a, p. D7; 2012b, p. Y7).

Learning organization

An extension of the continuous improvement approach to management is the concept of the learning organization (Senge, 1990). This approach integrates the principles and practices of continuous improvement with an emphasis on continuous employee learning and development. That is, a learning organization works to facilitate the lifelong learning and personal development of all of its employees while it transforms itself to respond to changing demands and needs. Facilitating lifelong learning involves constantly upgrading employee talent, skill, and knowledge.

In answer to the question of how to improve performance, advocates of the learning organization approach emphasize solving problems and changing to meet demands and needs by focusing on learning. This involves learning from organizational experience and history, learning from others (benchmarking and customer input and feedback), and ensuring that the newly acquired ideas and skills are transformed into superior organizational performance. We will investigate Senge's ideas further in Chapter 10.

One such case that can instruct on this issue is the recent legal dispute between the NFL and former licensee American Needle. In 2000, the NFL signed a ten-year, $250 million deal with Reebok to be its exclusive provider of licensed apparel, ending deals with other companies. But American Needle was then shut out of doing business with the league, and sued the NFL, arguing that based on Section 1 of the Sherman Act, the NFL and Reebok were conspiring to stifle competition and inflate prices. American Needle argued that immediately after the Reebok deal was signed, prices for NFL licensed products immediately rose. In 2008, a unanimous three-judge panel of the United States Court of Appeals for the

32

Seventh Circuit, in Chicago, ruled for the NFL on the ground that the league is a single entity (Belson, 2010; Belson and Schwarz, 2010).

As outlined above, professional league properties divisions have for decades negotiated such deals on behalf of all member franchises. These actions have been based on an exemption granted by the federal government to work as a single entity to negotiate broadcast deals. This "single entity" approach is the concept American Needle has sought to challenge in its suit, especially since its sales dropped 25 percent after the Reebok deal. Company President Robert Kronenberger (grandson of the company's founder who had convinced reluctant Chicago Cubs owner Philip Wrigley to let him sell Cubs caps at Wrigley Field on consignment) said of the suit:

> For me, it's a principled thing. We just want to be competitive. I understand that it's probably a business decision. It's just black and white and this is wrong ... It's not just headwear. It could be beyond that: television, concessions, food, beer. It's not just about me.
>   (Belson, 2010, p. B15; Belson and Schwarz, 2010, p. B15)

Kronenberger's comments are not merely the rhetoric of a jilted plaintiff. Industry experts believed that if the NFL were successful in defending its status in the case, and it is found exempt from Section 1 of the Sherman Act, it could extend its league-wide deals to stadium concessionaires, vendors, and parking operators, agreements that are currently managed by individual franchises. This could, potentially, drive up the cost of attending games. It could also mean that, according to legal experts, professional leagues could be empowered to unilaterally impose labor agreements when bargaining with players' unions. But other legal experts believed if the case were decided in favor of American Needle, all professional leagues could lose their single entity status exemption in negotiating labor agreements with players' unions and broadcast agreements. However, one legal scholar doesn't think an NFL win would mean a future with $200 licensed fleece sweatshirts, because "people would just go buy a baseball sweatshirt instead" (Belson and Schwarz, 2010, p. B15).

In January 2010, after the NFL won at the trial and appeals court level, the U.S. Supreme Court heard arguments from both sides of the case. The NFL had actually joined with American Needle in asking for the review, an action taken, according to one legal expert, "because they think they can win" (King, 2010, p. 9). Some experts felt that the NFL could count on four of the nine sitting justices – Chief Justice John Roberts, and Justices Samuel Aleto, Antonin Scalia, and Clarence Thomas – and would not get two others – Justices John Paul Stevens and Ruth Bader Ginsberg – leaving the league only needing to convert one of the remaining three justices (Stephen Breyer, Anthony Kennedy, and Sonia Sotomayor). Sotomayor, named to the high court in 2009 by President Barack Obama, has had the most direct contact with pro league sport issues, having issued an injunction as an appeals court judge against MLB owners in 1995, ending the player lockout that led to the cancellation of the 1994 World Series. She was also part of a three-judge appeals court panel that upheld the NFL's draft eligibility rule, which had been challenged by former Ohio State University running back Maurice Clarett. American Needle drew support from the existing players' unions and the NFL Coaches Association, while the NFL had support from the NCAA, the NBA, the NHL, and video game manufacturer Electronic Arts, which expressed concerns about the difficulty in negotiating agreements with each individual team, a move it felt would result in higher costs to consumers. Writer Bill King noted that a reversal in favor of American Needle would be in line with 30 years of lower court rulings which have found leagues to be joint ventures, even as most courts have upheld the single entity structure in those instances where it is seen to have benefitted consumers. An unsigned op-ed piece in the *New York Times* the day of the hearing sided with American Needle, stating, "the league is actually a cooperative effort of 32 separately owned, profit-making teams. They compete in everything from hiring to ticket sales. They should have to comply with Section 1" (Broughton, 2010; "Football," 2010, p. A26; Kaplan, 2010; King, 2010).

At the Supreme Court hearing, which lasted one hour and 11 minutes, eight justices chose to ask questions (this did not include Justice Thomas, who customarily remains silent). The justices sought to get each side to suggest, as in the words of Justice Kennedy: "A zone where we are sure a rule of reason inquiry ... would be inappropriate?" Neither side was willing to set parameters on how the court should act, and one observer remarked after the hearing:

> Both sides have to walk away from that argument not knowing what's going to come out of it because the questions were ... off the wall [and] unfocused ... There are simply no principle standards for deciding when sports leagues should be allowed to cooperate and when they should be allowed to compete.

Indeed, Justice Sotomayor said to NFL lead attorney Gregg Levy:

> I am very much swayed by your arguments, but I can very much see a counter argument that promoting t-shirts is only to make money. It doesn't really promote the game. It promotes the making of money. And once you fix prices for making money, that's a ... violation.
>
> (King and Kaplan, 2010, p. 28)

On May 23, 2010, the court unanimously found in favor of American Needle. "The league's decision to license independently owned trademarks collectively to a single vendor," Justice Stevens wrote for the court, deprived the marketplace "of actual or potential competition." "Although NFL teams have common interests such as promoting the NFL brand," Stevens continued,

34

they are still separate, profit-maximizing entities ... Each of the teams is a substantial, independently owned and independently managed business. The teams compete with one another, not only on the playing field, but to attract fans, for gate receipts and for contracts with managerial and playing personnel.

In addition, Stevens wrote that teams certainly compete in the market for intellectual property: "To a firm making hats, the [New Orleans] Saints and the [Indianapolis] Colts are two potentially competing suppliers of valuable trademarks" (Liptak and Belson, 2010, p. 1).

The ruling did not resolve the lawsuit. The court said American Needle's claims were not barred at the outset but must rather be analyzed under a standard that antitrust lawyers call the "rule of reason" to determine whether the league's licensing practices harmed competition. The case will be returned to the lower courts. Robert Kronenberger said of the decision: "This is to protect competition and consumers and right a wrong. We hope to prevail, but we'll see what happens" (Liptak and Belson, 2010, p. 1).

So what have these organizations learned from this case? The NFL's ten-year deal with Reebok expired and, in 2012, the league chose to work with Nike to produce its uniforms and on-field apparel for the next five years. The NFL is likely looking to capitalize on Nike's position as a market leader to help promote its brand; the same is also true for Nike, as the NFL is the most-popular professional sport league in the U.S. But the recent debut of the new NFL–Nike uniforms was met with a resounding yawn by experts and the media. Only the Seattle Seahawks look was significantly altered, but to many it looked a lot like the garb worn by the University of Oregon (in fact, one writer referred to the look as "the Oregon Seaducks"; Nike personnel described it as vaguely fluorescent and "rooted in the hues of the Seattle environment ... the deep blue of the ocean water, the greens of the evergreen trees, mosses, and ferns," which is probably quite similar to the environment in and around Eugene, Oregon). Nike personnel instead chose to focus more on the technical improvements of the new uniforms, including four-way stretch hydroponic materials on the sleeves, stretch twill numbers, and "aircraft-grade aluminum" in the belts. The new gear, Nike claims, will be five percent drier, eight percent lighter, and 22 percent cooler than its predecessors (McGrath, 2012; Tanier, 2012, p. B13).

And what do the players think? Pittsburgh Steelers QB Ben Roethlisberger told reporters at the introductory press conference that he loved it. "Super light and, uh, stylish? ... I don't know," said Roethlisberger, who also said the one clothing item he wanted most as a kid was a pair of Jordan brand shoes. But Tampa Bay Buccaneers running back LaGarrett Blount was less enthused with the look his team retained. "I have to talk with the [owners]. I think we need to be kind of trendy, because we are one of the younger teams" (McGrath, 2012, p. 42; Tanier, 2012, p. B16).

35

But Nike is also seeking to partner with the NFL so it can sell many other products such as coaches and player sideline apparel, as well as licensed apparel such as t-shirts and hats. And this is where the relationship might be limiting for the NFL. On a recent visit to the Niketown retail store in San Francisco, one could view a full range of new Nike licensed apparel. All of the individual team products were nearly similar in design, save for team logos and colors, making it seem like the products were Nike-first and connected with the NFL as an afterthought. In addition, the store was heavily promoting products of those players who had endorsement deals with Nike, as well as former NFL players with Nike connections, such as Bo Jackson. So it is reasonable to ask that for this deal, just exactly who is working for whom? The NFL has five years to learn whether the Nike deal makes sense for its purposes. We will learn more about the concept of learning organizations and adapting to change in Chapter 10.

These recent contributions to our understanding of management will certainly be followed by others. In the field of management it is clear that managers will continue to innovate and experiment with new approaches to make organizations more productive. The search will continue for more effective answers to the question of how to improve performance.

EPILOGUE: UA FOR HER

According to writer Elizabeth Olson, through its advertising and marketing campaign featuring "brawny athletes … in hard-charging situations, Under Armour became the brand of choice for young men in their teens and 20s." Now, says Olson, UA is looking at a new market segment: active young women. "Women's apparel some day will be larger than our men's apparel business," predicts Kevin Plank. Having first targeted male football players and other team sport athletes, UA is now aiming for the "team girl," described by UA's head of women's apparel as a female who is competitive and plays in high school or college. "The team girl is tough, intense, and passionate," said UA's Adrienne Lofton, "and she creates her own style." UA tried to reach this market about a decade ago, but failed, according to Steve Battista, the company's VP for brands, because they tried to take their men's styles and "shrink it and pink it," a hoary industry technique to make men's products suitable for women (Olson, 2010, p. B3).

The move makes sense for UA, as women's products are the only sector of the industry predicted to have steady growth over the next few years. But reaching this sector will not be easy for UA. "Guys buy clothes to look cool or feel cool," explained one market researcher. "Women buy for different reasons … And women demand that the brand does what it promises." Another researcher agreed, adding: "Women buy for fit and color. You can't just bowl them over with a logo."

36

But UA wants to keep its established brand strong while reaching out to women, and has taken the approach of showing both male and female athletes in recent advertisements. UA's Battista claims that their research showed that women "did not want to be treated separately. They said, 'We want to see ourselves up against men'... [They] don't see themselves as a female athlete but as an athlete" (Olson, 2010, p. B3). Whether UA is successful at reaching the female athlete segment will rest on how well company managers understand and apply many of the concepts outlined above.

SUMMARY

Organizations are groups of people working together to accomplish what they could not achieve separately, and management is responsible for the performance of an organization, and for the organization's achieving its goals. Sport organizations do not exist as separate units; they are interconnected. They are an integral part of a network of stakeholders, and whenever a sport organization fails to meet its performance goals, this entire network is threatened. For these reasons, management in sport organizations has never been more important. Management of sport organizations has become more challenging in the twenty-first century. The changing environment, the world that surrounds organizations, is marked by a new variety and intensity of domestic and international competition and the changing performance standards of quality, speed and flexibility, innovation, and sustainable growth.

Management is not a recent practice, and humans have been engaged in activities requiring management for millennia. From these contributions, the stream of management thinking finally gained impetus and momentum, and although these were not the only contributions of the period, they were certainly among the most important. At the time of the Industrial Revolution, a formal process of management thinking began to emerge. From the late 1700s to the early 1900s, J.B. Say, Robert Owen, and Albert Spalding all made contributions to our understanding of how to improve performance.

It was not until the twentieth century, however, that organizations were systematically studied to understand how performance might be improved. Systems theory considers the sport organization as part of a larger system. To improve performance, sport organizations must improve their relations with every element of the system in which it operates – with customers, employees, suppliers, the government, and society at large. Stakeholder theory suggests that an organization has relationships with many constituent groups, or "stakeholders," that affect and are affected by its decisions. Related theory also suggests that stakeholders are defined as those individuals that have a "stake" in the performance of an organization, that the

37

interests of all legitimate stakeholders have intrinsic value, and that no set of interests is assumed to dominate the others. Contingency theory is similar to the above approaches in that it provides a way of thinking about management rather than a specific management tool. Contingency theory recognizes that there is no "one best way" to manage. To improve performance, management must understand what the situation requires and then find a way to meet the needs of the situation, whether in the area of planning, organizing, or leading. Management must adjust to what the situation requires. Finally, the concept of a learning organization is one that recognizes that, to achieve continuous quality improvement, organizations must constantly upgrade employee talent, skill, and knowledge.

MANAGEMENT EXERCISE: LINSANITY™ (OR MAYBE LINDERELLA™)?

What's your all-time favorite sport movie? Is it "Rudy," "Hoosiers," "Miracle," maybe even "Bend it like Beckham," or "Blades of Glory"? Above we cited "Caddyshack," and the attire worn by comedian Rodney Dangerfield. This one might be on your list of faves (and is not to be confused with "Caddyshack II," which may be the worst movie, sport or otherwise, ever made anywhere by anyone). You might recall the scene where groundskeeper Carl Spackler (played by a slack-jawed Bill Murray) practices his golf swing as he decapitates flowers, imagining himself winning the Masters at Augusta National. This "Cinderella story," as Spackler calls it during his imaginary TV commentary of his charge at Augusta, is often the plot foundation for these films. Indeed, the boxing movie "Cinderella Man" made this connection quite plain. The "Cinderella story" line centers on the trials of an unheralded individual who rises from obscurity and, through perseverance, overcomes daunting odds and circumstances to achieve a lofty goal. In "Rudy," the hero was University of Notre Dame football wannabee Rudy Ruettiger. In "Cinderella Man," it was boxer James J. Braddock. In "Caddyshack," it was caddy Danny Noonan (and maybe the gopher, which eludes successfully Spackler's efforts to exterminate him, and rises from the dust of the explosive-ravaged and pockmarked Bushwood Country Club and dances triumphantly at the end of the film).

But many sport movies, including "Cinderella Man," "Hoosiers," "Miracle," and "Rudy," are based, however loosely, on actual individual and/or team achievements. And this is often what draws us to sport in the first place – the fact that the events that occur both in and outside competition allow individuals and teams to demonstrate in reality the fantastic and mythical exploits often associated with fairy tales and hokey Disney movies. And nowhere is this theme more in evidence than the recent example of Jeremy Lin.

You are probably familiar with the basics of the Lin, or may we call it, Linderella, story. Although his high school team won a state championship, Jeremy Shu-How

38

Lin – he is of Taiwanese–American descent – was a lightly recruited men's basketball hopeful from Palo Alto, California, who ended up matriculating at Harvard University, a middling program in the Ivy League, a conference that gains only one bid to the annual NCAA Division I men's basketball tournament. At Harvard, Lin, who sometimes played point guard, sometimes shooting guard, became a four-year starter and a unanimous all-league selection as a senior. While the program improved steadily during his time there, it won no league titles and did not qualify for any post-season play. Lin was a finalist for several individual national awards, and completed his career as the only player in the program's history to score 1,450 points and record 450 rebounds, 400 assists, and 200 steals (Pak, 2012).

Not surprisingly, Lin's name was not called by NBA Commissioner David Stern during the 2010 Draft, but Lin did manage to land a spot with the Dallas Mavericks during the NBA Summer League. He played well, and eventually caught on with the Golden State Warriors – near his home town, possibly a coincidence – but played sparingly, and spent some time in the NBA Developmental League. He spent the early part of the 2011–12 season with the Houston Rockets, but was cut on Christmas Eve, and was picked up by the New York Knicks as the team sought some bench depth after injuries to its starting backcourt. For a month, Lin played little, but that changed after a breakout 25-point performance versus the then-New Jersey Nets, then a 28-point effort against the Utah Jazz two days later. His ability as a slashing scorer and passer had emerged, but what was a nice little story became magnified due to the fact that he was Asian–American and playing in the world's preeminent media market. If Lin had remained in Houston, one wonders how big the hype would have ballooned. Calls to include Lin in the NBA All-Star Game came from various media sources, and in mid-season *USA Today*'s Christine Brennan called him "the most popular athlete in the world today" (2012, p. 3C). This wasn't so far-fetched, since the British Broadcasting Company's Radio World Service featured a story on him (Lin also made the cover of *People* magazine). An eager public learned that Lin was sleeping on his brother's couch in Manhattan because he had neither the time nor the money to get his own place. And the fact that he was becoming the league's first bona fide Asian star (with apologies to Yao Ming and Wang Zhizhi) gave the story another underdog twist, with some breathlessly calling his emergence "the most important event for Asian–Americans in sport history" (McGeehan, 2012, p. A19). Even Dan Covell, one of the co-authors of this textbook, who also works as the public address announcer for Harvard men's basketball games (and worked every one of Lin's home games during his career), was getting requests for media interviews. Linsanity/Linderella was born.

With the craze in full flower came opportunities for profit for branded and licensed product makers, but initially producers were caught off guard (no pun intended). After his first three starts (in which he scored a combined 76 points and handed out 25 assists), one couldn't buy a single item of Lin apparel, not even in the NBA's own

39

retail store a few blocks away from Madison Square Garden. The high demand and slow response led, not surprisingly, to the rapid emergence of a brisk counterfeit business in knock-off Lin merchandise in New York City, at the 2012 NBA All-Star Game in Orlando and in China and Taiwan. And as soon as authentic Lin items were available on the NBA's website, his became the top-selling jersey on the site, and sales at the Knicks' own on-line store increased 4,000 percent. In addition, an autographed Jeremy Lin rookie trading card from his 2011–12 season with Golden State sold on the on-line auction site eBay for $4,000 (after a bid of $21,580 was reneged upon by a buyer). Lin's whirlwind six months wrapped up when he was named the year's breakthrough athlete at the 2012 ESPY Awards in Los Angeles in July (McCarthy, 2012; Weinreich, 2012).

Even though Lin's season ended early due to a knee injury, in his 25 starts he averaged 18.2 points and 7.7 assists, and entered the off-season poised to turn his new-found notoriety into cash (his 2011–12 salary was just over $750,000) via free agency (which he did, opting to return to Houston for a three-year, $25 million deal). But while Lin and his agent Robert Montgomery handled the on-court dealings (for example, Lin has an endorsement deal with Nike), both were also looking at ways to control other potential revenue streams. The apparel distribution piece looked to have been settled (notorious Knicks fan and occasional film director Spike Lee seemed to have purchased a store's worth of Lin gear himself judging from his attire as he sat in his customary courtside seats at MSG). But this process had already begun way back in February, after a game against the Minnesota Timberwolves where Lin scored 20 with 8 assists, when he filed to register a trademark for "Linsanity" with the United States Patent and Trademark Office with the aid of an intellectual property group from a Washington, DC law firm. The action would give him legal protection against unauthorized and counterfeit use. Others had already filed for the term, including one to be used for an after-shave lotion, and others for dancer apparel, fire-retardant toddler pajamas, and chef's hats. "We've filed letters of protest against every other application that tries to play off Jeremy Lin's fame and personality," said Pamela Deese, Lin's trademark advisor. "There's a burden on a famous person to protect [one's] celebrity status." Experts believe Lin's claim will be supported by the USPTO. "Linsanity is a distinctive term with a distinctive meaning and is closely associated with Lin himself," said one (Sandomir, 2012b, p. Y7).

There is precedent for other similar trademarks. While head coach of the Los Angeles Lakers, current Miami Heat GM Pat Riley registered a trademark for the term "three-peat." NFL cornerback Darrelle Revis also sought to trademark the term "Revis Island" for use on apparel. "Basically anybody can market themselves," said Revis. "It don't matter if you're a high-profile player or not. You can find a way to market yourself and get your name out there" (Thomas, 2010).

So is this the correct approach for Lin? "There is extraordinary interest in Jeremy ever since he was injured and recuperated," said Deese. "We're approached multiple times a day from interests in Asia for endorsements and licensing. The Asian market holds incredible opportunities." In fact, when the Rockets – the former team of Yao – signed Lin, some experts believed the signing has much to do with trying to keep Chinese fans in the fold (Murphy, 2012, B14; Sandomir, 2012b, p. Y7). So while they're at it, Lin and his people should probably look at trademarking "Linderella" too.

QUESTIONS FOR YOU TO CONSIDER

1   Identify and explain the elements that comprise Jeremy Lin's brand, and what makes this brand of potential interest to companies seeking to align with him.
2   If you were a manager at a branded or licensed company looking to use Lin to endorse a product, explain how you would use each of the elements of the new management environment to get this product to market.
3   Is Lin of more value as an endorser to a large domestic company such as Nike, a smaller domestic company such as Under Armour or New Balance, or to an international company such as Li-Ning? Which should invest in signing Lin to an endorsement deal?
4   Identify and explain which of the influential early ideas and one of the more recent contributions of management theory would aid the company you identified in the previous question in maximizing its relationship with Lin.
5   Of the ten roles identified by Henry Mintzberg, identify and explain which five would be of most importance for a manager for Lin's marketing team to employ as they establish endorsement deals for him.

CHAPTER 2

GLOBALIZATION AND ETHICS AND INTERNATIONAL AND OLYMPIC SPORT INDUSTRY SEGMENTS

INTRODUCTION

This chapter deals with three issues that have gained priority as organizations move through the twenty-first century: the globalization of sport, social responsibility and ethics, and diversity. Each represents an important challenge to management. In this framework, globalization refers to the extension of sport – in all of its manifestations – to other parts of the world. In so doing, we must consider the ethical implications and social responsibilities arising out of this international engagement, including by its very nature the embrace of national, racial, gender, and cultural diversity. The chapter also introduces the international and Olympic sport sector and illustrates some of the specifics of this segment within the context of the managerial challenges listed above.

Check the stats

Purpose
To provide a mechanism for sport exchange, including competition, between participants of different countries.

Stakeholders
Athletes, coaches, trainers, referees, publicly elected officials, sport administrators, volunteers, sport organizations, media, corporate sponsors, and fans.

Size and scope
- At the 2012 Olympic Games in London, nearly 11,000 athletes from 204 countries qualified to participate in 302 events across 28 sports. Nearly four billion viewers worldwide tuned in to some of the television coverage over the 17 days

42

of competition from July 27 through August 12. The United States led the overall medal tally with 104 (46 gold), while host country Great Britain won 65 (29 gold) ("About us," 2012).

- At the 2010 Olympic Winter Games in Vancouver, 2,566 athletes from 82 nations participated in 86 events across 15 sport disciplines (governed by eight International Federations) ("VANOC Reports," 2010).
- Olympic marketing revenue reached $866 million for the period of 2005–2009, with broadcast revenues for the 2010 Winter Games and 2012 Summer Games totaling $3.5 billion ("IOC Olympic Marketing Fact File," 2012).
- Current members of The Olympic Partners (TOP), the IOC's corporate sponsorship group, include McDonald's, Coca-Cola, Panasonic, General Electric, Dow, Atos, Acer, Omega, Procter & Gamble, Visa, and Samsung. Each of the 11 partners pays upwards of $100 million in cash and value-in-kind for a four-year sponsorship (Mamudi, 2012).

Governance

INTERNATIONAL OLYMPIC COMMITTEE (IOC)

The IOC, headquartered in Lausanne, Switzerland, is the ultimate ruling body of the Olympic Games. The IOC decides where the games will be held and in which sport events will be held. There are currently 105 IOC members from 74 out of the 205 countries that have National Organizing Committees (NOCs). The IOC itself does not organize the competitions in the various sports; that is done by the NOCs in conjunction with the international sports federations (IFs) ("The organisation," 2012).

NATIONAL ORGANIZING COMMITEES (NOCS)

NOCs such as the United States Olympic Committee (USOC) serve "to recruit, supervise, and certify" Olympic hopefuls (Senn, 1999, p. 11). The IOC certifies one NOC per country, which is supposed to be independent of governments. Although the IOC states that the Olympics are open to the youth of the world, without NOC certification, no athlete can compete in the Olympics ("About the USOC," 2012).

INTERNATIONAL SPORTS FEDERATIONS (IFS)

The IFs (such as FIBA, the international governing body for basketball, ISAF, the international sailing federation, and FIL, the International Luge Federation) set the rules and hold the competitions at the Olympics, while the NOCs supply the athletes ("International Sport Federations," 2012).

NATIONAL GOVERNING BODIES (NGBS)

The USOC, like all NOCs, allows national governing bodies in each sport, such as USA Hockey, to focus on the preparation of athletes for Olympic competition (Senn, 1999).

43

OLYMPIC ORGANIZING COMMITTEES (OCOGs)

The OCOGs play a pivotal role in the successful management of each edition of the Olympic Games, as they are the responsible entity for ensuring the effective preparation of the physical environment and execution of the operational logistics for athletes, officials, media representatives, and spectators alike.

International sport: an overview

At its highest level, international sport competition is comprised of the best athletes and teams that a country has to offer, and in most instances are the products of significant investment of time and money. In other words, athletes train for many years to achieve their high level of performance and sport organizations provide substantial resources to develop and refine their talent pool in order to compete on the international stage.

In terms of global awareness and revenue generation, the two most prominent sporting events are the Olympic Games and the FIFA World Cup. Both are held just once every four years, where the quadrennial staging ensures that stakeholders, including fans, do not succumb to a sort of mega-sport fatigue and that these premier events remain the much anticipated celebration that they have become.

For the four-year period culminating in the 2010 World Cup in South Africa, FIFA (which is the French acronym for Fédération Internationale de Football Association, the worldwide governing body for what most Americans refer to as soccer) produced revenues of $4.189 billion ("Financial Report 2011," 2012), while the International Olympic Committee is expected to easily surpass $6 billion in revenue for the four-year period through the 2012 Olympic Games in London ("IOC Olympic Marketing Fact File," 2012). These vast sums of money are primarily generated from the sale of media rights paid by broadcasters to telecast these events, and corporate sponsors that pay handsome premiums for the privilege of being associated with these organizations and their events. Other sources of revenue include licensing agreements that permit a myriad of companies to link their product or service with the FIFA or Olympic "brand," as well as the sale of tickets to these marquee events.

The Olympics

Technically speaking, the term "Olympic Games" refers to the summer edition that was launched in 1896, while the "Olympic Winter Games" is the proper reference to the winter version that began in 1924. Starting in 1994, the IOC introduced a biennial schedule, whereby the summer and winter games alternate every two years. Thus, the Sochi Olympic Winter Games will be held in 2014, the Rio de Janeiro Olympic Games will be held in 2016, and the PyeongChang Olympic Winter Games will be held in 2018.

44

At the 1896 Olympic Games in Athens, there were only 245 athletes from 14 countries who competed in 43 events, and there were no female competitors (Wallechinsky and Loucky, 2012). Today, the Olympic Games have expanded to include upwards of 10,500 athletes from more than 200 countries and territories who compete in approximately 300 events across 28 sports. In 2008 in Beijing, women comprised 42 percent of athletes, and participation rates have continued to increase with each successive Olympic Games since 1960 ("IOC Fact Sheet," 2012). In contrast to the Summer Games, the Winter Games presents a program on a smaller scale for sports that are played on ice or snow, and features roughly 2,500 athletes from approximately 80 countries who compete in seven sports ("The organisation," 2012). The sport competition program for both editions is scheduled over a period of 17 days.

The FIFA World Cup

Although different versions of football (the global term for soccer) were played on the continents since ancient times, and games involving a kicking-and-rushing action with a ball were played across English schoolyards in the late 1700s, the rules of the game as we know it today evolved from a meeting in London that formed the Football Association (FA) in 1863 (Gifford, 2006).

The FIFA World Cup for men was established in 1930 and has been played continuously every four years except in 1942 and 1946 due to World War II. Currently, there are 209 national associations that are recognized by FIFA as being eligible to compete in the World Cup, which consists of a qualification phase and the month-long tournament known as the World Cup Finals. In the three years leading up to the World Cup Finals, national teams seek to qualify through a series of regional competitions to become one of the 32 teams to make it to the quadrennial tournament. At the World Cup Finals, teams first compete in a four-team pool called the group stage, with the two top teams advancing to the single-elimination knockout stage. The championship match of the FIFA World Cup is referred to as the World Cup Final.

Even though the FIFA World Cup involves a single sport (versus the multi-sport format of the Olympic Games), the World Cup Finals still require about a dozen venues and a period of a month to complete the two stages of the tournament. The Women's World Cup did not become a significant event until the 1970s. Competition formats are similar but includes fewer teams at the qualification and finals stages.

Inside look: I go to Rio

Most people are familiar with the Olympic Games because the media coverage is so pervasive that they can hardly avoid watching live or replayed television broadcasts of competitions, or other real-time accounts of the events. In fact, the IOC estimates that more than 4 billion people tune in to at least part of the 17-day global sport festival ("Faster," 2012). But watching your favorite athletes or sports on television and cheering them from afar is one thing; imagine for a moment that you are fortunate enough to find yourself in Rio de Janeiro in 2016, during the time of the Olympic Games.

After arriving at Galeão International Airport and exiting baggage claim, passport control, and customs, you find yourself a bit uneasy; first, because you do not speak Portuguese, the native language of Brazil, and also because of a lack of familiarity with the new and different environment. You are also overwhelmed by the smorgasbord of offerings that the Olympic Games present, which is unlike any sporting event that you have previously attended. You feel as though you are in a city that is hosting 28 sport world championships, practically simultaneously. You think, "Nobody in their right mind would ever contemplate staging the NBA Championships, MLB World Series, NHL Stanley Cup Finals, and NFL Super Bowl at the same place and at the same time," but this is a rough analogy of what the Olympic Games are about.

All of a sudden it hits you that you are at ground zero of the archetypal global village, because for the 17 days from the opening to closing ceremonies, there are citizens from every country of the world sharing the city's space with you. In fact, you have already heard people speaking a multitude of languages, many of which you could not begin to ascertain. At the same time, however, you are overcome with a feeling of pride that you are unique among your cohorts back home, and that for a moment at least, you are indeed a global citizen in probably the most internationally diverse place on the planet.

In addition to being inundated with television and print advertising prior to your arrival in Brazil by venerable Olympic sponsors McDonald's, Coca-Cola, Visa, and Samsung, among others, it has not escaped your notice that all of these companies appear to have a heightened presence in Rio with signage plastered on billboards and at commercial and other high-traffic locales. You realize that the city hosting the Olympic Games is transformed into a corporate bazaar, with Olympic sponsors and non-Olympic sponsors alike vying for valuable marketing platforms to expose their brand to prospective customers. You also notice that the dozen or so worldwide Olympic sponsors (the so-called "Olympic Partners") have exclusive access at official sites, but then you understand why when you learn that they have each paid in excess of $100 million for a four-year sponsorship.

As you attend your favorite sporting events at the Olympic Games, you are struck by the fact that despite the hyper-commercialization via corporate sponsorship and the plethora of licensed products that abound, there is absolutely no commercial advertising within the sport venues. Strangely, you feel as if the only safe

Globalization and ethics and international and Olympic sport industry segments zone from commercial bombardment is in the stadiums, fields, and arenas where the sporting competitions are held. You wonder why, of all places, that they do not permit commercial signage in and around the fields of play. In reflecting on this seeming anomaly, you finally conclude that it makes perfect sense. The IOC wants you to tune in to Olympic broadcasts, patronize its official sponsors and licensing partners, and buy tickets to your favorite events. But whether you watch your favorite sport, team, or athlete on TV or in person, the IOC wants you to have unfettered enjoyment of the viewing experience without distraction from corporate marketers. In fact, you see a bit of irony in the IOC exploiting commercialism to Olympian heights on the one hand while maintaining pristine, commercially Spartan-like venues on the other. But, hey, you think it's really neat to experience high-performance sport in a "clean" venue just this once, imagining that this is what it must have been like to watch the Ancients compete in Olympia.

In spite of the non-stop festive atmosphere of the Olympic Games, largely under-written by corporate sponsors, it dawns on you that this vast corporate presence is not just about being at party central, but rather, a considered strategy to extend their brand onto perhaps the greatest platform for global exposure. It is mind-boggling to keep track of the number of businesses that have assaulted your consciousness through signage, print advertising, and broadcast media, in addition to point-of-sale promotions, and you wonder if some of these companies actually do business in Brazil as you recall that, during the Torino Olympic Winter Games in 2006, American retailer Target plastered the public transport trains with its red bulls-eye logo, even though it does not have stores outside the United States. There is so much corporate clutter, it amazes you that the IOC and the Rio 2016 Organizing Committee even try to make a big deal of the fact that Coca-Cola, Nike, and Nissan are official sponsors, while Pepsi, Adidas, and Toyota are not. You also wonder if sponsor companies are getting their money's worth, since you believe that the average person in the street cannot clearly distinguish between Olympic sponsors and non-sponsors.

At the end of your stay in Brazil, you are no longer nervous and insecure as you learned a few words of Portuguese to engage in a simple exchange of pleasantries with the locals, and in just 17 days you have been transformed from an Olympic neophyte to a seasoned veteran observer of Olympic business practices and culture. What we will now consider is how sport organizations are impacted by globalization efforts, and how these efforts are influenced by the ethical principles of management.

47

THE GLOBALIZATION OF SPORT

The organization of the Olympic Movement and other key international sport organizations

Former IOC Vice President Dick Pound, a native of Canada, defined the Olympic Movement as "the aggregation of the IOC, international sports federations, national Olympic committees, athletes, officials, and organizers" (Pound, 2006, p. 12), which comprises the constituent parts of this global enterprise. In other words, this so-called Movement is made up of the people and organizations associated with and interested in the Olympic Games and the ideals that they espouse, with the goal of building a peaceful and better world through sport. Importantly, the IOC insists that individuals and entities comprising the Olympic Movement first be recognized by, and agree to abide by, the Olympic Charter.

The Olympic Charter serves as the International Olympic Committee's constitution and bylaws, and elaborates three main purposes as follows: (a) it sets forth and recalls the Fundamental Principles and essential values of Olympism; (b) it serves as statutes for the International Olympic Committee; and (c) constituents of the Olympic Movement, namely the International Olympic Committee, the International Federations, and the National Olympic Committees, in addition to the Organizing Committees for the Olympic Games, are all required to comply with the Olympic Charter ("IOC Olympic Charter," 2011).

The International Olympic Committee is the overseer of the Olympic Movement, including the Olympic Games and matters related thereto. As a non-governmental organization, it is neither an agency of any governmental entity nor a for-profit corporation. Since its inception in 1894, the IOC has been a self-perpetuating body on the order of a private club that elects its successor members in accordance with its own rules. Under reforms adopted in 1999, the total membership is limited to 115 and defined categories were established to ensure representation of the National Olympic Committees, International Federations, and athletes. The reforms also established that IOC members elected after 1999 must "retire" in the year that they attain the age of 70. Members elected prior to 1966 were eligible to serve for life, while those elected between 1966 and 1999 can serve until age 80 ("IOC Olympic Charter," 2011).

Note that there is no understanding that IOC members represent certain countries or geographic regions; in fact several countries have multiple members while the majority of countries have none. As of this writing, there are 105 members, with Switzerland, Italy, and Great Britain having five, four, and four members, respectively. Meanwhile, the top-two economic and sporting super powers – the United States and China – have three and two members, respectively. Curiously, the IOC maintains that its members are not a country's delegate to the IOC; rather it views them as the IOC's representatives in the countries where they reside. Of course, this

48

fiction is regularly tested each time a vote is taken that considers national interests, such as a country's bid to host an Olympic Games, and the perceived bloc support it receives from IOC members of the same region.

The IOC, which ordinarily meets once a year in a general assembly called a Session, is the final authority for all matters under its jurisdiction. A special session, referred to as an Extraordinary Session, can be called by the president upon the request of at least one third of the membership. The organization's business affairs are managed by a 15-member Executive Board, which includes the president, who is elected to an initial eight-year term and who may be re-elected for a subsequent four years; four vice presidents, who are elected to staggered four-year terms; and ten at-large members, who are also elected to four-year terms. Other than the president, Executive Board members may be re-elected for a subsequent four years, after which they may not be re-elected to the Executive Board until two years have elapsed ("IOC Olympic Charter," 2011). The Executive Board meets at least four times a year, but typically meets more frequently on call of the president.

All IOC members are volunteers in the sense that they are not employees and do not receive compensation for their services. They may, however, receive reimbursement of expenses and such other benefits that pertain to their office. For example, if the president elects to reside in Lausanne, Switzerland – the location of the IOC headquarters – as has been the tradition since 1980, then living expenses are provided accordingly.

While policy direction is set by the Executive Board and to the extent necessary ratified by the Session, the IOC's day-to-day operations are run by a professional staff of approximately 350 employees who come from over 30 countries and work at one of four office sites in Lausanne (Marchand, 2010). With the president essentially being the organization's CEO and indisputable leader of the worldwide Olympic Movement, the IOC's administrative work is led by a chief of staff who heads the president's executive office and a director general who oversees the functions of the organization's 15 departments, as outlined below in Box 2.1:

BOX 2.1 DEPARTMENTS OF THE INTERNATIONAL OLYMPIC COMMITTEE ("THE ORGANISATION," 2012)

- Human resources
- Planning/coordination
- Communication
- Marketing
- Technology
- Sports
- NOC relations
- Legal
- Olympic museum
- Information management
- Medical and scientific
- Finance and administration
- Olympic solidarity
- International cooperation
- Olympic Games

The IOC's work is aided by a number of commissions, which are appointed by the president and serve an advisory function to the Executive Board and the Session. Currently, there are 23 commissions, as listed below in Box 2.2:

BOX 2.2 INTERNATIONAL OLYMPIC COMMITTEE COMMISSIONS ("THE ORGANISATION," 2012)

- Athletes
- Audit
- Culture and Olympic Education
- Entourage
- Ethics
- Evaluation
- Finance
- International Relations
- Juridical
- Marketing
- Medical
- Nominations
- Olympic Coordination
- Olympic Philately, Numismatic, and Memorabilia
- Olympic Program
- Olympic Solidarity
- Press
- Radio and Television
- Sport and Environment
- Sport and Law
- Sport for All
- TV Rights and New Media
- Women and Sport

On an ongoing basis, among the most important decisions taken by the IOC's rank-and-file members at the Session are votes to (a) elect the IOC president, (b) determine the host cities for upcoming Olympic Games and Olympic Winter Games, and (c) include or exclude sports on the program of future Olympic Games or Olympic Winter Games.

In addition to the IOC, the other pillars of the Olympic Movement are the International Federations (IFs), National Olympic Committees (NOCs), and Organizing Committees for the Olympic Games (OCOGs) (see above). There are 35 International Federations, 28 of which govern sports on the program of the Olympic Games and seven that have the same responsibility for winter sports. The IFs are the worldwide governing bodies for their respective sport(s) and are responsible for promoting and developing their sport globally as well as organizing the competitions at the Olympic Games and Olympic Winter Games. Although most IFs correspond to a single sport, FINA (the IF for aquatic sports) has jurisdiction over swimming, diving, synchronized swimming, water polo, and open water swimming; and the International Skating Union (ISU) oversees both figure skating and speed skating. While there are well over a hundred international sports federations that govern every conceivable sport that is competed somewhere, the IOC has imposed a limit of 28 sports that can be competed at the Olympic Games due to manageability concerns (although there is no corresponding restriction at the Olympic Winter Games). The summer and winter IFs, some of which are referred to by their French name and acronym, are listed in Boxes 2.3 and 2.4:

50

BOX 2.3 SUMMER SPORT INTERNATIONAL FEDERATIONS ("THE ORGANISATION," 2012)

- Aquatics (swimming, diving, water polo, open water swimming): Fédération Internationale de Natation (FINA)
- Archery: International Archery Federation (FITA)
- Athletics (track and field): International Association of Athletics Federations (IAAF)
- Badminton: Badminton World Federation (BWF)
- Basketball: Fédération Internationale de Basketball (FIBA)
- Boxing: International Boxing Association (AIBA)
- Canoeing: International Canoe Federation (ICF)
- Cycling: Union Cycliste Internationale (UCI)
- Equestrian: Fédération Équestre Internationale (FEI)
- Fencing: Fédération Internationale d'Escrime (FIE)
- Football (soccer): Fédération Internationale de Football Assocation (FIFA)
- Golf: International Golf Federation (IGF)
- Gymnastics: Fédération Internationale de Gymnastique (FIG)
- Team handball: International Handball Federation (IHF)
- Field hockey: International Hockey Federation (FIH)
- Judo: International Judo Federation (IJF)
- Modern pentathlon: Union Internationale de Pentathlon Moderne (UIPM)
- Rowing: Fédération Internationale des Sociétés d'Aviron (FISA)
- Rugby: International Rugby Board (IRB)
- Sailing: International Sailing Federation (ISAF)
- Shooting: International Shooting Sport Federation (ISSF)
- Table tennis: International Table Tennis Federation (ITTF)
- Taekwondo: World Taekwondo Federation (WTF)
- Tennis: International Tennis Federation (ITF)
- Triathlon: International Triathlon Union (ITU)
- Volleyball: Fédération Internationale de Volleyball (FIVB)
- Weightlifting: International Weightlifting Federation (IWF)
- Wrestling: Fédération Internationale des Luttes Associées (FILA)

To exchange ideas and to discuss issues of common interest, the summer sport IFs have banded together to form an umbrella association called the Association of Summer Olympic International Federations (ASOIF). Similarly, the winter sport IFs established their own organization known as the Association of International Olympic Winter Sports Federations (AIOWF). Both ASOIF and AIOWF, in addition to the non-Olympic international sports federations that comprise the Association of IOC-Recognized International Sports Federations (ARISF), meet annually at an international sport convention known as SportAccord. Further, some sports (such as football) have regional sub-divisional organizations known as confederations that are based on geography. For example, the U.S. Soccer Federation is a member of FIFA, the International Federation for the sport of football, but it also belongs to CONCACAF, the hemispheric or continental confederation for football in North America, Central America, and the Caribbean. In addition to CONCACAF, the other five confederations are the Asian Football Confederation (AFC), the Confederation of African Football (CAF), Confederación Sudamericana de Fútbol (CONMEBOL), the Oceania Football Confederation (OFC), and the Union of European Football Associations (UEFA). In the sport of football, national teams qualify for certain international competitions, including the World Cup, through qualification matches against other national teams in their same confederation.

International Federations are membership organizations comprised of however many National Federations that it has duly recognized as members in good standing at any given time. Thus, National Federations have a corresponding responsibility to govern their sports at the country, or national, level. For example, the United States Soccer Federation is the National Federation for football and is one of 208 member associations of FIFA, which is the IF for football.

The National Olympic Committees are the organizations charged with developing, promoting, and protecting the Olympic Movement in their respective countries, but practically speaking, they assemble and prepare teams to represent their nation at the Olympic Games and Olympic Winter Games. The NOC for the United States is the U.S. Olympic Committee. Currently, there are 205 NOCs that represent countries that are independent states (member states of the United Nations) in addition to several territories that are possessions of independent states. For example, U.S. dependencies Guam, American Samoa, Puerto Rico, and the U.S. Virgin Islands each have their own autonomous NOC that is separate and apart from the United States Olympic Committee.

National Olympic Committees also play an integral role in the emergence of cities that host the Olympic Games and Olympic Winter Games because cities cannot attain this honor without first being nominated by its country's NOC. Then, if a city is designated by the IOC Executive Board as a "candidate city," the NOC must work to facilitate that city's bid to the entire IOC membership.

Analogous to the umbrella organizations formed by the IFs for purposes of facilitating communication and joint action in appropriate circumstances, the NOCs have a similar structure with membership in a global body called the Association of National Olympic Committees (ANOC), as well as in one of five continental associations as follows: the Pan American Sports Organization (PASO), the Association of National Olympic Committees of Africa (ANOCA), the European Olympic Committees (EOC), the Oceania National Olympic Committees (ONOC), and the Olympic Council of Asia (OCA) ("The organisation," 2012).

Three of the five continental associations organize their own hemispheric games on a quadrennial schedule that mimics the Olympic Games: Pan American Games (PASO), Asian Games (OCA), and All-Africa Games (ANOCA); and members of the Commonwealth countries, including territories and dependencies of the former British Empire, compete once every four years in the 71-country Commonwealth Games ("The role," 2012).

Sport organizations pursuing global markets

The IOC and FIFA are illustrative of sport organizations in the twenty-first century seeking to grow their product and build their brand by extending their presence into new, previously untapped markets. For example, in spite of concerns about infrastructure, security, and organizational capability, FIFA took the world's premier sporting event to the African continent for the first time in its 80-year history when it staged the 2010 World Cup Finals in South Africa. The IOC demonstrated a similar approach by awarding the 2008 Olympic Games to Beijing, the capital city of the world's most populous country and second-largest economy, granting China its first Olympic Games despite outcries against government abuses of human rights and civil liberties, and widespread apprehension about toxic air pollution and chronic traffic congestion. The IOC further tested its resolve to take its multi-sport festival to new lands by awarding the 2016 Olympic Games to Rio de Janeiro in Brazil, the first time ever in the South American continent.

It is intuitive that the IOC would be eager to stage its quadrennial celebration in China, which is projected to surpass the United States as the world-leading economy in the next decade, and Brazil, which ranks sixth among countries in gross domestic production. Even though as a non-governmental organization the IOC is essentially a not-for-profit organization, it reaps billions of dollars in revenue from rights fees, sponsorships, and licensing agreements; and its financial patrons – the corporations that foot the bill – are anxious to get a foothold in for what many of them are new and fertile territories.

In the case of FIFA and South Africa, the primary motivation might not have been commercial largesse, but rather, making a statement that football belongs to the world. With 17 of 18 editions of the World Cup having been played in either Europe or the Americas (with the 2002 World Cup having been co-hosted by Japan and Korea), it was important to FIFA that the sport played the world over be seen as being capable of being hosted elsewhere. In addition, FIFA surely recognized that with its 54 National Federations, the Confederation of African Football comprised more than a quarter of FIFA's membership. Perhaps surprisingly, the 2010 World Cup generated $3.7 billion in revenue, resulting in net income of $631 million for the 2007–2010 period, swelling FIFA's already substantial reserves to $1.28 billion ("FIFA has built," 2011).

Two sports recently dropped from the program of the Olympic Games – baseball and softball – have been working practically non-stop to regain their place in the quadrennial summer lineup. Baseball was added as a medal sport at the Barcelona Olympic Games in 1992, softball four years later in Atlanta. At the 2005 IOC Session in Singapore, however, both sports failed to survive retention votes in a sport-by-sport review of the Olympic sport program, and beginning in 2012 neither will be competed at the Olympic Games.

Thus, the International Baseball Federation (IBAF) and the International Softball Federation (ISF) have joined the ranks of the myriad sports that are lobbying the IOC to gain a spot on the sport program in a future edition of the Olympic Games. In petitioning the IOC, non-Olympic sports federations that are seeking inclusion in the Olympic Games work feverishly to raise the visibility and popularity of their sport across the globe, as well as facilitate the establishment of bona fide National Federations, to convince IOC members of their sports' broad sponsorship, following, and participation, and hence worthiness for the Olympic Games.

54

SOCIAL RESPONSIBILITY AND ETHICS

The question for us to consider now is what exactly does "socially responsible" mean? We can view the study of social responsibility and ethics from two perspectives. At the larger level is the obligation of organizations to be good corporate citizens, to provide society not only with goods and services, but also to contribute to the social well-being of the communities where they operate. At the more individual level is the ethical conduct of workers and managers in performing their daily tasks and planning for long-term growth. We will review both perspectives.

Socially responsible organizations

Through the 1950s, the relationship between business and the American public was usually positive. Consumers were eager to purchase products that had not been available during the Great Depression of the 1930s or during World War II, and businesses expanded rapidly to satisfy that demand. Business was viewed as the source of the jobs and the products that were at the heart of the American dream. A saying popular at the time was "What's good for General Motors is good for America." Large corporations made financial contributions for community projects, and most companies were strong supporters of the United Way and similar social service funds.

Beginning in the 1960s, however, the public began to view business differently. To meet the exploding consumer demand in the years following World War II, organizations increased production at such rapid rates that the results unfortunately included pollution of the air and water, environmental decay from the dumping of industrial waste, and effective and sometimes unsafe products and services. Frustration with the Vietnam War added to the public's discontent, as many people blamed big businesses with defense contracts, such as McDonnell Douglas and DuPont, for profiting from the prolongation of the war. An even stronger sense of resentment was directed toward Dow Chemical Company, maker of napalm, a chemical used by U.S. forces with tragic consequences for the landscape of Vietnam and its people. Additionally, there was the growing sense that business organizations were not offering equal employment opportunity to the minority members of society. In viewing this issue, one expert noted that suddenly issues such as consumerism, stockholderism, racial equalitarianism, antimilitarism, environmentalism, and feminism became forces to be reckoned with by corporate management (Jacoby, 1973).

The result of all of these factors was a significant increase in the public's demand that organizations of all types act in a more socially responsible way. Some areas of social responsibility, including protection of the environment, equal employment

55

opportunity, and safe working conditions, are now regulated by law and monitored by federal agencies. In the areas not covered by laws and regulations, however, the question of how much social responsibility business organizations should take on has generated a wide range of responses.

Two views of social responsibility

The most common approaches to social responsibility reflect either of two very different philosophies. These two views vary in their conception of the level and type of involvement management should undertake in terms of activities to benefit society.

The classical economic approach

The classical economic approach to social responsibility suggests that a business organization should limit its involvement to activities that improve its own economic performance. This approach maintains that the first and foremost responsibility of management is to earn profits for owners (stockholders). According to influential economist Milton Friedman (1970), a strong proponent of this view, there is a potential conflict of interest when society holds managers responsible to owners for meeting profit goals and at the same time holds them responsible to society to enhance social welfare. From this perspective, every dollar spent on social problems or donated to a charity is one less dollar distributed to the owners in the form of dividends and one less dollar available for the kind of investment that creates jobs. The classical economic approach further argues that requiring management to pursue socially responsible activities could be unethical, because the managers are spending money that belongs to other people (Friedman, 1970).

A final argument against managerial involvement in social responsibility programs is that businesses lack the expertise to determine which programs have the greatest needs. For example, should an organization donate to the United States Olympic Committee or a national governing body such as U.S. Track and Field, to support athletic activities for elite athletes, or should it, like many contemporary organizations in the U.S., found its community-based sport organization to provide such opportunities? Which would serve the needs of the community better? In summary, the classical economic approach to social responsibility insists that business organizations have the social responsibility only to do no harm to customers, employees, or the environment. In this view, managers do not have the right to invest stockholders' profits in activities focusing on social problems. Management's only responsibility is to follow the legal and ethical rules of society while making the business organization as profitable as possible.

56

The activist approach

The activist model of social responsibility argues that business does in fact have a responsibility to deal with social problems, because business is both part of the cause of the problems and part of society (Davis, 1975; Sturdivant and Vernon-Wortzel, 1990). Social responsibility activists argue that organizations do have the technical, financial, and managerial resources to help solve society's difficult problems. Growing evidence indicates that to some extent businesses agree with this view. For example, large and small companies all over the United States have entered partnerships with local schools; they provide training for teachers and administrators in key skill areas and donate surplus computers, furniture, and other equipment that the school might not otherwise be able to afford.

Another part of the activist argument is that business has a responsibility not just to owners and shareholders, but also to everyone who has a stake in the company's operations. These include employees, customers, suppliers, distributors, creditors, government, unions, special interest groups, and the general public. In the activist view, business – as a corporate citizen of a large community – has an obligation to respond to the needs of all these stakeholders while also pursuing a profit. In other words, business has an obligation to be responsible to all of the elements of the communities from which it profits. This argument gains strength considerably the more closely the success of the business is presented as linked to the health of the community that supplies it with workers and customers. Lastly, the activist argument holds that when business itself takes the initiative in addressing social problems, costly government intervention is less likely.

A difficult choice

In the classical economic approach, business is viewed exclusively as an economic entity whose nearly exclusive purpose is profit. The activist approach, in contrast, views business as a member of society, with broader social responsibilities. When an action is required by law or when investment in a socially responsible activity is profitable, there is no conflict between the two views, and both approaches would support the activity.

It is when the socially responsible activity is neither required by law nor profitable that the two approaches differ. The classical approach would argue against business becoming involved; the activist view would support involvement if the costs were not prohibitively high. The degree to which a business advances societal versus economic objectives depends to a great extent on factors such as the organization's size, the nature of competition in the industry, the type of problems involved, and the costs of pursuing an activity versus the consequences of not doing so. This example underscores the difficulties for some organizations, even those organized to perform social activism, to execute these duties fully and responsibly.

In the case of the IOC, we know that it is the organization responsible for staging the grandest of multi-sport spectacles at regularly scheduled intervals. But as the supreme authority for the Olympic Movement and overseer of the behemoth that is the Olympic Games, the IOC is not without responsibility in the realm of social obligations. Given the enormity of the carbon footprint produced by events of this magnitude and duration, in addition to the environmental impact on the city and region hosting the world in the years prior to, during, and after the Olympic Games, the IOC appears to have taken seriously its role as a model corporate citizen. In fact, in the Olympic Charter, Olympism is described as a "philosophy of life that seeks to create a way of life based on ... social responsibility and respect for universal fundamental ethical principles" ("IOC Olympic Charter," 2011).

The IOC's creation of commissions for Ethics, Sport, and the Environment, Women and Sport, Medicine, and Olympic Coordination, among others, ensures that it will keep a watchful eye on matters that affect competitive fairness, gender equity, and quality of life, as well as promote greater transparency in its business practices. The organization has also embraced Agenda 21, a United Nations initiative that envisions concrete actions to systematically address the human impacts on the environment. The IOC has taken the lead in encouraging its constituent members – the International Federations, National Olympic Committees, and Organizing Committees for the Olympic Games – to implement measures based on principles of sustainable development. In addition, the IOC has organized biennial World Conferences on Sport and the Environment, conducted regional seminars on related topics, and produced informational materials on sport, the environment, and sustainable development. To understand more fully the effects of an Olympic Games on a city, region, and nation, the IOC commissioned an Olympic Games Impact (OGI) Study that approximates an environmental impact statement. All cities that contemplate hosting an Olympic Games must participate in the OGI Study. As fiduciaries of what amounts to a public trust, the IOC appreciates that it has greater responsibility to bear, but it also understands that one of its most important legacies is to bequeath to the host cities and their citizens a heritage of undeniable improvement over conditions that preceded those cities' hosting of the Olympic Games.

Ethical conduct of individuals

There are other factors that are to be considered when reviewing social responsibility. Ethical sport organizations encourage and enable people at all levels to exercise ethical judgment. We expect sport organizations to conduct themselves in a way that is honest and fair in terms of how they treat their customers, employees, and society in general. To influence employee judgment and behavior properly, ethical practices must shape the organization's decision-making processes and be a part of the organization's culture. In sport organizations, the complexity of competing interests in sport makes moral and ethical dilemmas difficult to resolve. For the most part, athletic competition is a test of skill, strategy, and physical prowess. However, the industries and structures that have grown around sport have complicated the roles played by all sport organization personnel, from athletes, coaches, and managers, to officials, administrators, sponsors, and fans.

Sport is rife with examples of athletes who have resorted to bending or breaking the rules to gain a competitive advantage. At the 1988 Olympic Games in Seoul, Canadian sprinter Ben Johnson set the world afire with his then-world record time of 9.79 seconds in the final of the 100-meters event, only to be disqualified three days later for having tested positive for the banned substance stanozolol. Sadly, Johnson was neither the first nor last athlete to have been accused of taking performance-enhancing drugs, as hundreds more have been implicated or proven to be drug cheats at all levels of sport.

In 2003, federal agents raided the offices of BALCO (Bay Area Laboratory Cooperative) in Burlingame, California, and discovered containers with labels indicating that they were steroids and growth hormones, in addition to lists of customers that included NFL and MLB players, and Olympic athletes. The sordid ordeal was the basis for indictments and subsequent convictions of Olympic sprinter Marion Jones for lying to federal investigators, and San Francisco Giants slugger Barry Bonds for obstruction of justice for giving evasive testimony to a grand jury. More recently, retired MLB pitcher Roger Clemens was acquitted of charges that he lied to Congress when he denied ever taking performance-enhancing drugs (Wilber and Marimow, 2012), but it remains to be seen whether his otherwise stellar career will secure him a place in the Baseball Hall of Fame.

Lance Armstrong, seven-time winner of the Tour de France, has long been dogged by suspicion that he resorted to banned substances and/or methods in helping him capture cycling's premier event between 1999 and 2005. Although a federal investigation of Armstrong concluded in 2012 and did not result in any indictments, the United States Anti-Doping Agency (USADA), the entity responsible for enforcing the World Anti-Doping Code in the United States, recommended that same year that all of Armstrong's results from August 1, 1998 on be expunged, including his seven Tour de France titles, and that Armstrong be banned from cycling for life because of his doping actions. UCI, the IF for cycling, and the World Anti-Doping Agency supported the action (Dawes, 2012; Macur, 2012).

In December 1998, Swiss IOC member Marc Hodler announced to the media that several of his IOC colleagues had received improper payments and gifts in connection with Salt Lake City's bid to host the 2002 Olympic Winter Games. About a dozen IOC members were implicated in taking bribes or receiving some manner

59

of favor, presumably in exchange for their votes to give Salt Lake City the hosting victory it secured in 1995. In the weeks and months to follow, a frenzied atmosphere prevailed at IOC headquarters in Lausanne and at the Salt Lake Organizing Committee (SLOC) in an attempt to contain the crisis, which resulted in the resignation or firing of the top four SLOC officials (President and CEO Frank Joklik, Senior Vice President Dave Johnson, Bid CEO Tom Welch, and Bid Chief Administrative Officer Craig Peterson). In addition, six IOC members were expelled, three resigned, and several more were censured but permitted to retain their positions as IOC members (Mallon, 2000). Prior to the reform package adopted by the IOC in 1999 in direct response to the fallout from the corruption and bribery scandal, rules governing IOC members' visits to prospective host cities and the extent to which they could receive gifts were neither overly restrictive nor strictly enforced. Among the 50 recommendations made by the IOC Reform 2000 Commission and approved by the Session, rank-and-file IOC members are prohibited from visiting Olympic bid cities in an official capacity prior to the decision to award the hosting rights, and bid city officials are likewise prohibited from visiting IOC members ("IOC publishes," 1999). While there are certain exceptions for group presentations at meetings attended by IOC members where all bid cities are present, this rule is intended to minimize exposure and contact between bid city officials and IOC members for the purpose of lobbying. Another major development arising out of the Salt Lake City bid scandal was the creation of the IOC Ethics Commission in 1999, which includes a majority of outside members who are disassociated with the Olympic Movement.

During the ANOC General Assembly in Kuala Lumpur, Malaysia, in May 2002, United States Olympic Committee President Sandra Baldwin was basking in the limelight following a successful Olympic Winter Games in Salt Lake City that culminated in her election as a coveted member of the International Olympic Committee. As the first female president of the USOC, Baldwin's brief tenure was already tinged with optimism for her avowed intention to reach out to the international sport community, which was a departure from the USOC's isolationist past. Baldwin was a darling of assembled leaders of the National Olympic Committees and was respectfully courted by the male-dominated IOC and broader Olympic Movement. Then suddenly, in the midst of a blissful coming-out party for the newly elected IOC member from the United States, a story broke in the United States that Baldwin had for years fudged her résumé to reflect that she obtained her bachelor's degree from the University of Colorado, and her master's and Ph.D. degrees from Arizona State University. The story, written by a student reporter for the University of Colorado alumni magazine, revealed that Baldwin neither graduated from Colorado nor earned the graduate degrees. As the tempest swirled and grew into a firestorm Stateside, Baldwin abruptly departed Kuala Lumpur to assess the damage and contain the fall out. In media accounts, Baldwin admitted that she lied about her academic record, although she explained that she earned a bachelor's degree from Arizona State and completed course work for her Ph.D. A few days later, as the USOC Executive Committee was debating her fate, Baldwin notified CEO Lloyd Ward that she would resign her position immediately, thereby ending the sordid saga (Litsky, 2002).

More recently, the Hungarian President and longtime IOC member Pal Schmitt was forced to resign his largely ceremonial government post in March 2012 when it was revealed that Semmelweis University in Budapest stripped him of his doctoral degree after concluding that he plagiarized significant portions of his Ph.D. dissertation. The IOC has yet to act on his membership status pending review by its Ethics Commission (Karasz, 2012).

One way to simplify the decision-making process and to encourage ethical behavior in sport is to make the compliance requirements or standards of conduct of affected individuals or institutions clear. Codes of conduct or codes of ethics provide that clarification and outline the guidelines for employee or member behavior. Implementing such codes, however, is not always simple and straightforward for organizations to enforce, sometimes due to the close relationships between the individuals affected. This is why it is important, for example, that the majority of the IOC Ethics Commission be comprised of non-IOC members.

Rule 22 of the Olympic Charter sets forth the IOC's ethical framework and charges the Ethics Commission with promulgating ethical principles, including a Code of Ethics. In addition, the Ethics Commission investigates complaints related to such ethical principles and, if appropriate, recommends sanctions to the IOC Executive Board ("IOC Code of Ethics," 2009). The social responsibility and ethical behavior demands of contemporary society represent complex challenges for all organizations. For sport managers, the challenges can vary depending on the nature of the sport organization, but gaining an understanding of cultural differences in a multi-national setting is of critical importance. Increasingly, managers employed by organizations that function in a global environment rely heavily on the goodwill and positive associations held by colleagues and constituents alike, and as such must carry out business practices that meet their ethical expectations.

THE DIVERSITY CHALLENGE

A third emerging challenge for sport managers relates to diversity. The number of ethnic groups in workplaces around the world has increased dramatically in recent decades. In the United States, the work force is also becoming older as members of the huge "Baby Boom" generation move through their fifties and into their sixties. In addition, the Americans with Disabilities Act passed in 1990 sought to remove many of the barriers that formerly prevented individuals with physical disabilities from joining the work force. The net effect of all of these changes is that the

American work force is now and will continue to become increasingly diverse in terms of gender, race, age, and physical abilities.

While the coordination of human resources has never been easy, this growing diversity in the workplace represents a challenge as well as a special opportunity for management. The greater the differences that people bring with them to the workplace, the greater the management effort needed to blend these differences and to unify efforts in a single direction. Yet, as difficult as this challenge may be, many organizations feel this growing diversity also presents a special opportunity. The more the work force inside the organization mirrors the diversity of the customers outside, the more likely it is that the organization will satisfy the needs of those diverse customers.

Many sport organizations' administrative ranks, including the multitude of organizations that make up the Olympic Movement, are dominated by males, even those with a high percentage of female athletes. These organizations are rightfully criticized for their lack of commitment to organizational diversity by maintaining managerial staffs that do not reflect the composition of their prime constituency. In terms of the IOC's commitment to diversity, it created a Women and Sport Working Group in 1995 that was granted permanent status as the Women and Sport Commission in 2004. Chaired by U.S. IOC member Anita DeFrantz since its inception, the Women and Sport Commission develops programs to promote female participation in sport at all levels.

Although there we no female competitors at the inaugural Olympic Games in Athens in 1896, the number and percentage of female Olympic athletes have steadily increased, especially in recent decades. At the 2012 Olympic Games in London, female participation reached an all-time high of 45 percent, with every available event for women having at least one entrant (Whitley, 2012). In support of this, any new sport that hopes to be included on the program of the Olympic Games must include opportunities for female participation.

The first female member of the IOC, Flor Isava-Fonseca of Venezuela, was not elected until 1981. Some 30 years later, 20 out of 105 IOC members are women (19 percent), which is significant considering that the vast majority of electors are male never mind the vagaries of the elective process. On the important policy-making body, however, women comprise only 13 percent of the Executive Board (two out of 15 members), and do not hold any of the five officer-titled positions of president or vice president.

Guidelines for managing diversity

Given the lack of diversity in the sport industry (Ashe, 1992; Blum, 1993; Hums, 1996; Lapchick, 1996; Shropshire, 1996), steps must be taken to increase access to the industry. What follows are several guidelines for managing diversity (Rice, 1994).

Get the CEO's commitment
Addressing diversity issues is difficult to do well and is therefore easy to place on a back burner. When the head of the organization makes diversity a priority, everyone pays closer attention.

Set specific diversity goals
Set specific targets, such as 30 percent representation of females and minorities at all levels of the organization, especially management, by the year 2017. Measure managers' performance in terms of their contribution to these goals, and base compensation on their level of success.

Adopt a plan for addressing the concerns of white males
White males still constitute roughly half of the overall work force in the U.S. and hold 60 percent of all management positions. Individuals from this group may feel threatened when preference is given to women and minorities in the workplace, and they may view this practice as reverse discrimination. Organizations need to acknowledge and directly address their concerns. It needs to be made clear to every member of the organization why it is in everyone's best interest to participate in the development of a diverse work force.

Provide training in valuing diversity – carefully
It is important, but difficult, to provide training that allows others to experience what it is like to be a minority in our culture without also seeming to point a finger of blame at non-minority participants. People often feel threatened and uncomfortable when they are required to role-play difficult diversity situations. This is not the most effective emotional state for learning. One promising approach to diversity training is to present sport-themed films such as "A League of Their Own" and "Remember the Titans," and involve participants in discussions of what they experience and feel, and how this can be applied to improve their own organization's performance in the area of diversity. There are also numerous examples from sport organizations that underscore the value of organizational diversity, including the story of Jackie Robinson's breaking of the color barrier in Major League Baseball, Texas Western University's use of five African–American starters in winning their 1966 national championship game against the all-white squad from the University of Kentucky, and Billie-Jean King's victory over Bobby Riggs in the ballyhooed "Battle of the Sexes" tennis match in 1974.

63

Other guidelines for creating an organization where diversity is valued include celebrating differences among workers through special events, videos, and newsletters, as well as developing strategies to identify sources of diverse workers for the organization. Even with the most effective guidelines, however, creating a diverse force of skilled and talented workers and teaching them to work together in an atmosphere of genuine teamwork remains a major challenge.

Even though it is the most international of sports, soccer still faces challenges in some of these areas. At the 2012 Union of European Football Associations (UEFA) European Football Championship (i.e. Euro 2012), several groups of fans were accused of racial abuse and chants towards other fans and players. Croatian fans heaped abuse on Italy's Mario Balotelli, who is black, at a game in Poznan, Poland, making money noises and displaying right-wing nationalist flags during the match, a 1–1 tie. Piara Powar, the head of the anti-racism organization Football against Racism in Europe (FARE), a self-described "network of organizations from several European countries" dedicated to "fight racism and xenophobia in football across Europe," noted that "it was fairly consistent throughout the game. It was at its most intense as he was substituted and left the field." Croatian officials responded that those responsible were "not supporters, but hooligans who should be isolated from all sports events." During Euro 2008, UEFA, which is the continental confederation for football in Europe (see above), fined Croatia $20,000 for similar fan behavior in a match versus Turkey in Vienna, Austria. FIFA also fined Croatia $27,000 that same year due to racist abuse directed at England player Emile Heskey during a World Cup qualifying match in the Croatian capital city of Zagreb. Croats were not alone in this reprehensible behavior. Russians and Spanish fans were also alleged to have acted in this manner, as Czech Republic player Theodor Gebre Selassie told reporters he noticed racist chants directed at him during a match against Russia. It was also revealed that UEFA asked host city officials in Poland and Ukraine to provide more police to dissuade similar actions ("About FARE," 2012, p. 1; Conway, 2012; "Mario Balotelli," 2012, p. 1).

Given the complexities of an event like the UEFA European Championship, even the most internationally oriented sport organizations are challenged to eradicate racial and diversity problems. FARE's Powar noted that it was critical that UEFA take action with the evidence presented to them. "When it comes to tournament situations it's important to see proper sanctions taken so that the message can be given to the world" (Conway, 2012, p. 1). However, in the ever-more global sport industries, those sport organizations that embrace the key issues discussed in this chapter will ultimately be the most successful, in meeting the demands that come with global expansion.

EPILOGUE: RED, WHITE, AND BLUE – BUT MADE IN CHINA

For the IOC, International Federations, and all the other sport organizations that operate in the international community, as well as the hundreds of corporate interests that sponsor, market, broadcast, license, and otherwise trade on the Olympic Movement, all of their activities ultimately revolve around the globalization of sport. At least in part, all affiliated organizations are motivated by the generation of revenue, because they could not maintain their existence in perpetuity otherwise. However, this relatively direct mission can have complications for the issues of social responsibility and ethics, diversity, and their relationship to the globalization efforts of all sport organizations. If sport organizations look toward short-term financial success only, it could come at the expense of long-term organizational success in these other areas.

But how is this evolution toward globalization being felt in other ways in the United States? On the eve of the 2012 London Summer Games, members of the United States Congress expressed displeasure over the fact that the USOC had chosen to wear Chinese-manufactured apparel from designer Ralph Lauren (RL). In a rare moment of bi-partisanship, both Democrats and Republicans railed against the move due to the loss of jobs in the American textile industry. "I think the [USOC] should be ashamed of themselves," said Senate Majority Leader Harry Reid (D-Nevada). "I think they should be embarrassed. I think they should take all the uniforms, put them in a big pile and burn them and start all over again." House Speaker John Boehner (R-Ohio) agreed, stating plainly of the USOC: "You'd think they'd know better" ("China-made," 2012, p. 1).

U.S. Olympic and Paralympic athletes were slated to wear the Ralph Lauren clothes for the opening and closing ceremonies, and provided casual wear as well. Nike provided most of the competition apparel as well as medal-ceremony outfits. In defending the decision, spokesperson Patrick Sandusky called the uproar nonsense, and added: "Unlike most Olympic teams around the world, the U.S. Olympic Team is privately funded and we're grateful for the support of our sponsors. We're proud of our partnership with Ralph Lauren, an iconic American company ... which supports American athletes." Ralph Lauren, which has provided similar uniforms for past Olympiads, had no comment, while U.S. 800-meter runner Nick Symmonds tweeted: "Our Ralph Lauren outfits for the Olympic opening ceremonies were made in China. So, um, thanks China" ("China-made," 2012, p. 1).

We know from the last chapter that the overwhelming majority of footwear and apparel sold in the U.S. is manufactured overseas, which means that not only the Ralph Lauren garb but also the Nike apparel was not made in the U.S. The USOC also used Canadian clothier Roots for past Winter Games garb when no U.S. suppliers were interested in taking on the project. Could the USOC and Ralph Lauren have found a U.S. factory to assemble the uniforms? Sure. We

65

know from Chapter 1 that it is possible, since New Balance assembles some footwear in factories in Maine and Massachusetts. But even the components for those shoes – the leather and rubber pieces used in the construction – come from Asia. And what about the members of Congress who ranted against the USOC? Is everything they wear and buy made in the U.S.? Highly unlikely. But the fact remains that, in this case, the USOC has been perceived by some to have acted unethically in participating in the trends of globalization in sport. And if the USOC has acted unethically, then nearly every other American organization and consumer is equally culpable.

SUMMARY

Three issues have gained priority for sport organizations in the twenty-first century: social responsibility and ethics, diversity, and globalization. Each represents an important challenge to sport managers. Social responsibility is the concept that organizations, especially business organizations, have a responsibility for more than just economic performance; they have a responsibility to contribute to the social well-being of the communities where they operate. The classical economic view rejects this concept, saying that business organizations exist exclusively to generate profits for owners and stockholders. The activist perspective holds that all organizations have the obligation to involve themselves in solving problems in the communities from which they profit.

On an individual basis, sport managers need to be aware of the importance of ethics in the sport workplace. Incorporating codes of conduct or codes of ethics is one way to make the requirements and standards of behavior of a job or institution clear. Also demanding attention from management is the lack of diversity in the sport industry. Guidelines for managing diversity include getting the commitment of the chief executive officer (CEO), setting specific diversity goals, adopting a plan for addressing the concerns of white males, and providing training in valuing diversity. The goal is to create a diverse work force of skilled and talented workers and teach them to work together in an atmosphere of genuine teamwork.

Finally, there is competitive pressure for organizations to become involved in global markets. With intense competition in U.S. markets, business organizations must learn to succeed in markets around the world. There are a variety of options or degrees of global involvement, but regardless of the approach, success in global markets requires that management learn the culture, customize the product or service, recognize the risks involved in global environments, and be patient and persistent.

MANAGEMENT EXERCISE: THESE COLORS DON'T RUN – MERCENARY ATHLETES?

Christine Fay can remember watching the Olympics on television since she was eight years old, and although she was never inspired to become an Olympian herself, she was impressed by the athletes' feats of accomplishment and the fact that they came from all over the world. As she got older, Fay continued to follow the Olympics through the media and noticed that some athletes who were born in one country represented a different country at the Olympic Games. At first, she wondered how that was even possible, since she always understood the Olympics to be a competition of athletes and teams of the participating nations.

While in college, Fay studied immigration and demographics, and accepted as ordinary that people – including Olympic athletes – migrate from one country to another in the course of human events. She learned that people leave the country of their birth for a variety of reasons; oftentimes, it is to seek a better life elsewhere, whether escaping political repression or for rosier economic opportunities. Fay assumed that the migration pattern naturally flowed from poorer to richer countries or from despotic to democratic countries.

During the 2008 Olympic Games in Beijing, however, Fay was surprised when she heard that two Americans, Women's National Basketball Association All-Star Becky Hammon and former Bucknell University basketball player J.R. Holden, were playing for Russia as members of that country's Olympic Team. Now Fay was confused. She wondered how this was possible and, more importantly, why these Americans would even *want* to play for Russia. As she read the many stories written about these and other athletes who appeared to be "jumping ship" on their nationalities, she became intrigued by this phenomenon. In fact, Lopez Lomong, the flag bearer for the U.S. Olympic Team during the Parade of Nations at the Opening Ceremonies, was born in Sudan and lived in a Kenyan refugee camp for a decade before being relocated to the United States, where he excelled in track and field in high school and college. As Fay did more research on the topic, she found out that two Brazilian beach volleyball players who failed to make their country's Olympic Team made it to the Olympics anyway; but as members of the Georgian Olympic Team. She read a story about two New Zealand brothers who were trying to make it to the Beijing Olympics in their sport of triathlon; both made it, but one as a member of the New Zealand Olympic Team and the other as a member of the U.S. Olympic Team. Fay got the impression that there were dozens, if not hundreds, of these cases at every Olympics.

The more she thought about it, Fay became curious about the IOC's eligibility rule regarding nationality. As she understood it, an athlete had to be a citizen of the country that he or she represented at the Olympic Games. If this were true, how was it that athletes seemingly switched nationalities so easily? She also thought about the disturbing consequences of some countries aggressively recruiting – or poaching – other countries' top athletes in order to create a stronger national team to garner a bigger share of the medals, and especially gold medals. In consulting the Olympic Charter, Fay believes that Rule 41 governs these situations. The specific components of the rule are as follows:

1   Any competitor in the Olympic Games must be a national of the country of the NOC which is entering such competitor.
2   All matters relating to the determination of the country that a competitor may represent in the Olympic Games shall be resolved by the IOC Executive Board.

An additional bye-law to Rule 41 reads this way:

1   A competitor who is a national of two or more countries at the same time may represent either one of them, as he may elect. However, after having represented one country in the Olympic Games, in continental or regional games or in world or regional championships recognized by the relevant IF, he may not represent another country unless he meets the conditions set forth in paragraph 2 below that apply to persons who have changed their nationality or acquired a new nationality.
2   A competitor who has represented one country in the Olympic Games, in continental or regional games or in world or regional championships recognized by the relevant IF, and who has changed his nationality or acquired a new nationality, may participate in the Olympic Games to represent his new country provided that at least three years have passed since the competitor last represented his former country. This period may be reduced or even cancelled, with the agreement of the NOCs and IF concerned, by the IOC Executive Board, which takes into account the circumstances of each case.
3   If an associated State, province or overseas department, a country or colony acquires independence, if a country becomes incorporated within another country by reason of a change of border, if a country merges with another country, or if a new NOC is recognized by the IOC, a competitor may continue to represent the country to which he belongs or belonged. However, he may, if he prefers, elect to represent his country or be entered in the Olympic Games by his new NOC if one exists. This particular choice may be made only once.
4   Furthermore, in all cases in which a competitor would be eligible to participate in the Olympic Games, either by representing another country than his or by having the choice as to the country that such competitor intends to represent, the IOC Executive Board may take all decisions of a general or individual nature with regard to issues resulting from nationality, citizenship, domicile, or residence of any competitor, including the duration of any waiting period.

In reviewing the rules outlined above, aid Fay's efforts to understand the issue of nationality and eligibility for the Olympic Games in addressing the following questions:

1   In terms of the question of nationality, explain the basic requirement for an athlete to represent a country.
2   Explain how an athlete born in Kenya can represent Saudi Arabia at the Olympic Games.
3   If an athlete who represented Cuba at the last Olympic Games has since defected to the United States, explain whether she can represent the United States at the next Olympic Games.
4   Identify any safeguards that exist to minimize a country's concerted effort to recruit talented athletes from abroad to represent that country's Olympic Team.
5   Explain whether the nationality rule is fair and equitable – to athletes as well as to national teams – across all countries.

69

CHAPTER 3

INFORMATION TECHNOLOGY (IT) MANAGEMENT AND THE SPORT MEDIA

INTRODUCTION

Advances in information technology over the past decade represent perhaps the most dynamic set of opportunities and challenges in all of sport management. In this chapter, we explore the sport media, a segment of the sport industry that has significantly embraced innovation in information technology. The sport media is defined by its ability to produce and distribute sport information through a variety of platforms including live game television and radio broadcasts, live game blogs, pay per view, podcasting, satellite radio, print media, and a wide variety of social media outlets such as Facebook, Twitter, and YouTube. IT has significantly shaped the growth of sport media in the last decade in terms of content, speed of information delivery, international audience reach, information access, and information delivery. The sport media has become an increasingly powerful entity that shapes our games as well as how we perceive and how we interact with sport organizations.

In this chapter, we also take a broad look at IT from a management perspective. We consider how emerging information technology is applied in different functional areas of a sport business and how IT plays a critical role in enhancing individual and organizational performance. Then, we consider the challenges that must be met by sport managers if the full potential of IT is to be realized.

Check the stats

Purpose
To provide sport information to the general public through a wide variety of platforms and in varying formats including game stories and analysis, highlights,

feature articles, statistics, commentary, scores, and standings. To serve as a sport distribution channel through the production of game, contest, or event broadcasts.

Stakeholders

Fans, athletes, coaches, administrators, leagues, Commissioners' Offices, media personnel (writers, bloggers, reporters, broadcasters), alumni, sport governing bodies, licensees, corporate partners, and local, state, and federal government.

Size and scope

- The sport media consists of tens of thousands of sport media outlets including traditional sport media platforms such as magazines, newspapers, radio, and sport networks (national and regional). The sport media also includes social or electronic media-based platforms and outlets such as websites, blogs, sport affinity group chat rooms, Facebook, and Twitter.
- The sport broadcast media, which produces and delivers games, tournaments, or events to the consumer, includes not only the "on the air" talent (play by play, color analyst, on-field reporter, etc.), but also includes the "behind the scenes" staff that encompasses a wide array of broadcast specialists including camera crew, producers, sound technicians, editors, statisticians, and video technicians.

Governance

- Individual sport media outlets and their members operate under policies and guidelines established by its ownership; however, individual leagues and sport organizations establish rules pertaining to the media (e.g. when media members may enter the locker room or where cameras may be placed).
- Members of the sport media often belong to affiliate professional organizations such as the National Collegiate Baseball Writers of America (NCBWA), Pro Basketball Writers Association (PBWA), or College Sports Information Directors of America (CoSIDA).

Inside look: ESPN and navigating the multi-platform world

The development of ESPN in 1979 signaled the creation of the first all-sports national network in America. At a time when critics suggested that there wasn't enough sport content to drive a 24/7 sport network, ESPN quickly became the definitive source for information about the world of sports. With the advancement of cable technology, ESPN became available to more homes. Its popularity grew and traditional news programs began to scale back on national sport news coverage recognizing that many fans had instant access to the latest scores and game highlights through ESPN. In 1994, ABC purchased 85 percent of the network for

71

$202 million and, within seven years, the estimated value to its owner (ABC parent company Walt Disney) was $5 billion (Ostrowski, 1998).

Decades later, ESPN continues to be an influential leader in the sport media business. The network's sport news show, "SportsCenter," was the first uniquely positioned daily all-sport news broadcast. The program has not only become an icon of the American sport industry, but has affected the lifestyles of sport fans who have integrated SportsCenter viewing into their daily schedule. Many sport fans begin and end their day by watching SportsCenter. It is the show that fans and players alike watch and consider to be the gold standard in daily sport coverage. To make SportsCenter with a highlighted athletic performance is to achieve something special. There is little doubt that SportsCenter has become a central component of pop culture. Its catch phrases, anchor personalities, and even its advertising campaign, "This is SportsCenter," have captured the attention of viewers around the world.

To retain its position as a leader in sport media, ESPN/ABC Sports has continued to grow its business by developing related media properties including *ESPN Magazine*, ESPN radio, ESPN.com, and ESPN mobile. ESPN has moved into the restaurant and retail business with its ESPN Zones and ESPN merchandise. The company created its own annual award show (The ESPYs) to recognize and celebrate achievement in sport.

In 2005, ESPN had demonstrated success in the global marketplace by growing its international business operations. ESPN Star Sports, a joint venture of ESPN Inc. and News Corp., operated four networks in China: ESPN Asia, Star Sports Asia, ESPN Hong Kong, and Star Sports Hong Kong (Nethery, 2005). The Chinese version of *ESPN Magazine* boasted a 40,000 monthly circulation and ESPN properties had moved into the Chinese Internet and wireless mobile markets (Nethery, 2005). In 2009, *ESPN The Company* was published. The book chronicles the growth of the regional sports start up that grew into a media empire worth billions of dollars.

In part, ESPN has retained its first mover status in the sport media segment through innovation fueled by technologies such as WiFi, high definition television, satellite radio, broad band video, and social media. ESPN continues to aggressively adopt emerging technologies and to seek to enhance its global multi-platform strategy. There is broad recognition within the industry that the sport media marketplace is changing rapidly. The sport world is becoming increasingly global in nature. It is becoming more high tech in nature and fans' connection to the sport industry is becoming more complex. Fans no longer just sit at home and watch sports. They are constantly seeking new information about their favorite athletes and teams from a variety of sources. They want content on demand and through a variety of platforms.

ESPN executives have not only strengthened the ESPN brand through addressing these changes in the sport world, but they have also opened new markets and created new revenue opportunities for the company. For example, ESPN's ability to

72

deliver content globally through a variety of different platforms has been attractive to potential advertisers. As advertisers seek out new ways to reach specific target markets, ESPN is able to deliver multi-media delivery opportunities that link print, television, mobile, and Internet capabilities.

As ESPN continues to create its own platforms and explore emerging technologies including gaming, polling, podcasts, streaming video, fantasy sports, and video on demand, the challenge will be for the sport media giant to develop, acquire, and maintain quality delivery and content in an increasingly crowded sport media marketplace. Will technological delivery innovations enhance consumption as well as the fan's consumption experience? Can technology somehow detract from our games? High-tech delivery and social media platforms are very appealing to some fans. Others may be more skeptical of their value citing poor quality and meaningless content. Other criticisms of new technology might include long learning curves, equipment dependability, and associated high consumer cost of adopting such technologies. For some fans, this new technology feeds an obsession as they literally spend hours a day checking scores or highlights on a smart phone or following a favorite sport personality on Twitter. Is it possible that there is simply not enough time in the day to utilize the wide variety of available media platform delivery options? Is it possible that on-going engagement with social media is addictive?

The proliferation of media platforms and resultant need to develop compelling content for these platforms can be problematic. ESPN's hallmark had always been quality objective sport programming and reporting. Content such as sport quiz shows, made-for-television sport movies, reality shows, on-line polling, fantasy sport leagues, sport debate shows, and sport chat shows with ex-jocks and Hollywood celebrities have become part of the ESPN landscape. Do these programs enhance or detract from the ESPN brand?

Sport media companies adopt new technology in the belief that technological innovation adds to the quality of the content and allows the company to attract more viewers. Is high tech always better? For example, technology-based innovations such as instant on-screen fan polling, "catcher cams," "glowing pucks," cartoon characters, or extreme effects may have entertainment value but do they detract from legitimate sport content? Are sport organizations obsessed with showcasing new technologies to the detriment of content quality? Is technology-related entertainment value more important than the game itself?

One such technology that has been the subject of debate among sport fans is the use of wireless audio that allows viewers access to in-game comments by players, coaches, and officials. Personal microphones are used to capture "sounds of the game." While some fans may like to engage in this virtual eavesdropping, others may be uncomfortable with having such intimate access. Do these sound bites take away from the game itself? Is the content of legitimate value to the sportscast? Other technological advancements in graphics and animation have resulted in the integration of images promoting other shows along the bottom of the television screen during the live game telecast. While sport executives argue that these promotions are an important part of their network marketing efforts, many sport fans simply find them to be annoying.

For sport media executives and sport team/event managers alike the question is one of balance between legitimate sport reporting and entertainment value. When is an athlete's tweet educational and entertaining and at what point does it become the uncomfortable rant of a self-absorbed ego maniac? (Do we really need to know that the athlete ordered a berry smoothie at a fast food restaurant for breakfast or that he believes his biceps look really great in his new red shirt?)

While technology can enhance our relationships with sport organizations and sport media, it can also have the opposite effect. At what point does technology-based content become invasive? Members of the sport organizations and sport media are likely to continue to wrestle with this question of which technological advancements truly contribute to fans' enjoyment and which detract from it.

Media technology will continue to be a boon to the sport industry as media outlets and teams try to find new ways to use technology to reach more fans and generate new revenue. For sport media companies such as ESPN, the development of new technology-based platforms and quality content is an on-going challenge. Technological advancement will not only shape ESPN and the entire sport media, but will continue to support the development of a global sport marketplace and irrevocably shape how we consume and relate to sport for generations to come.

THE SPORT MEDIA INDUSTRY SEGMENT

The sport media segment is made up of tens of thousands of sport media-related organizations. These range from broadcast (television and radio) media outlets such as national broadcast network sport divisions (e.g. CBS Sports, HBO Sports, and NBC Sports) to national sport broadcast networks (e.g. ESPN) to affinity sport networks (e.g. MLB Network, NFL Network, or The Golf Channel) to regional sport networks (e.g. NESN, New England Sports Network). This industry segment also includes print media that encompass national sport publications such as *Sports Illustrated*, *ESPN Magazine*, and *The Sporting News* as well as sport sections of national, regional, and local newspapers. The sport media segment also includes the full spectrum of sport writers, authors, reporters, producers, anchors, broadcasters, bloggers, color and play-by-play announcers, celebrity analysts, and commentators. Allied technicians such as camera people, editors, and sound specialists are also included in this segment. Companies and individuals that provide support through equipment, services, or related platform design, technology development, and management can also be considered an integral part of the sport media segment. There is also a growing computer and wireless device (e.g. smart phone, iPad) media segment that includes professionals involved in developing and managing sport-related content, applications (apps), software, and services.

One of the most important things to consider when examining the sport media segment is that it is constantly changing and evolving. As technology advances and new devices and applications come to the market, consumers and organizations are always looking for the next best thing. The technology that is relevant today is likely to become obsolete very quickly. Sport managers realize the power of information in shaping public opinion, assessing customer interests and habits, branding and marketing the sport organization, and connecting with key stakeholders. Sport managers must appreciate the fact that today's sport organization stakeholders are increasingly sophisticated and tech savvy consumers who demand almost instantaneous and unfettered access to all kinds of sport information. Where sport managers historically relied upon traditional print and broadcast media to meet stakeholders' information requirements, organizations must now aggressively embrace new technology and social media platforms. Those organizations seeking to grow their business and become industry leaders must strategically utilize emerging technology to satisfy stakeholders' information demands.

Traditional sport media outlets have often been the first to adopt multiple social media platforms to enhance their own businesses. For example, it is not unusual for a sport media broadcast organization to feature live blogs, Facebook page, Twitter accounts, mobile applications, and on-screen interactive viewer texting to augment game telecasts. Individual athletes, coaches, and other sport figures including sport media members have also ventured into social media (e.g. Twitter) with the intent of connecting more directly with their fans while controlling their own message. Fans can now engage more actively and directly with sport organizations, athletes, and celebrities through social media platforms; however, it is not unusual for an individual athlete to manage such communications through a team of support staff. This approach is used for several reasons including assuring that communications are integrated with sponsorship promotional strategies, introducing a level of quality control of communications, maintaining consistency of branding, and assisting the athlete in on-going maintenance of the site or account given the multiple time commitments and competing priorities of the athlete.

Sport organization leaders as well as sport personalities are quickly coming to recognize the value of social media communication as a complement to existing traditional print and broadcast media and standard electronic platforms (e.g. websites). They actively seek ways to harness the speed and reach of the Internet for the purpose of expanding their markets, controlling their message, building relationships, enhancing promotional and sponsorship opportunities, and growing their

75

business. To not develop and execute a social media plan is to ignore one of today's most powerful business tools.

One of the benefits of social media and traditional Internet media such as organizational websites is that the individual or the sport organization determines what they want to say and when they want to say it. In effect, this approach may lessen the role of traditional reporters and may be viewed as cutting out the middleman. Some professional athletes have been less willing to talk to reporters or other media members in general and have said that they will make a statement on their own Twitter account or Facebook page.

This broadening of personal access to media platforms has added another layer to what has been the traditionally complex relationship of sport media, athletes, and sport organizations. Traditionally, the media's role in sport has been the same as it has been in general society. The media objectively reports the news to the public. They dig for the truth, analyze facts, and provide opinion or critical interpretation of what is happening in the world around us. In sport, the media provides game results and statistics, analyzes current events and issues in sport, and generally reports news about people involved in sport. The media plays an important role as sport industry watchdog, investigator, analyst, and critic. In some cases, such as investigations into the use of performance-enhancing drugs, the media has helped to bring important information to light and has encouraged public scrutiny of policy and behavior of athletes, teams, and organizations. One of the values of the press and media in general has been its outsider standing. Audiences are called upon to evaluate the source of the information they are receiving and to determine if they trust that the information is accurate and unbiased. For many stakeholders, information coming directly from an organization is often viewed as publicity rather than hard news. Surely, the message that is crafted and distributed by the individual or organization must be considered in context of that individual's or organization's agenda. Even when dealing with information being disseminated by the general media, audiences must evaluate how the information is spun or packaged and whether this represents unbiased reporting.

In the sport industry, the issue of biased reporting has become increasingly complicated as commercial partnerships with media organizations have grown. Do members of the media take on the role of cheerleader, supporter, or advocate for certain athletes or organizations? Is it likely that a member of the media would only report news that is favorable to the athlete or coach or organization? Are some sports reporters subjective rather than objective in their delivery of information? If so, does this approach diminish the credibility of the reporter? Why would a reporter allow some level of bias to creep into their work? For some members of the media, a less critical approach to reporting is a valuable strategy for building relationships with athletes or other sport personalities. It is hoped that these relationships will help the reporter gain access to information that might not be made available to someone who has taken a more critical approach in his or her reporting. The relationship between the reporter and sport personality may be viewed as symbiotic. The reporter or media member needs the athlete in order to do his or her job. Conversely, the athlete needs the media to enhance their exposure and build their relationship with the public. For the athlete, high levels of public recognition and appeal can translate into sponsorship deals and additional business opportunities both during and post career.

The advent of social media may shift this dynamic as more and more athletes are communicating with the public directly. Quite simply, the athlete and the sport organization now have direct and broader access to the public in a way that they never had before. Sport organizations and athletes will need to strike a balance between established media outlets and personally controlled media platforms in order to maximize the benefits of strategic communications.

For the foreseeable future, sport management professionals will need to continue to cultivate relationships with reporters and other members of the media. There is broad recognition of the role that the media plays in both public relations and marketing functions. It is important to note that, in the sport industry, there are other commercial interests at stake. For many sport organizations, the sport media provides a product distribution channel to constituents who consume the sport product through the media. This commercial relationship provides an important revenue stream to some sport organizations through the sales of broadcasting rights. In turn, the ability to broadcast popular sporting events provides important advertising revenue to the media outlet. For some sport organizations such as the National Collegiate Athletic Association (NCAA) and the National Football League (NFL), television rights fees are a significant source of revenue. In other cases, such as the Women's National Basketball Association (WNBA) and the National Hockey League (NHL), television rights fees provide lesser financial contribution.

In an attempt to maximize media revenues, teams, leagues, and/or events will create broadcast rights packages on the basis of a variety of dimensions including television, radio, local, national, language, and platform rights. Such rights fees are seen as a good investment by the media organization in that they can use this programming to attract advertisers. Sport broadcasts have delivered important and distinct target markets. Corporations around the world seeking to get their message to specific target customers have paid handsomely for advertising time on sport broadcasts. The NFL's Super Bowl, for example, has traditionally delivered large attractive audiences to advertisers and, in turn, commercial time during the Super Bowl has boasted some of the most expensive advertising rates in television with companies paying an average of $3.5 million per 30-second spot in 2012 ("Super Bowl ads," 2012).

Because sport programming has effectively delivered key demographic audiences and has attracted important ad revenue, competition among media organizations over sport broadcast rights has developed. It is not unusual for media outlets to engage in bidding wars to acquire premium sport programming such as the World Cup or the Olympic Games.

Both the media and sport organizations recognize that, in their partnership, they are playing a high-stakes game. It is in their mutual best interest to work together to promote the sport to increase audience share and related advertising revenue. It is this commercial partnership and financial interdependence that may also serve to compromise the media's ability to report on athletes and sport organizations objectively.

On the other hand, sports reporters recognize that compelling content is the key to generating audience. Some members of the media may adopt a confrontational or controversial approach to attract a large audience and are not concerned at all with how their coverage of the team may affect the commercial relationship. Their interest is in getting a good story that will attract viewers, grow numbers of friends, or generate followers.

Competition among sports reporters for stories is fierce. Given the sheer numbers of media members and media outlets, it is easy to see how members of the media constantly find themselves looking for a unique angle or new piece of information to create compelling content. As a result of this heated competition, sports reporters and media outlets seek to find ways to distinguish themselves in the marketplace. Some sports reporters have developed a particular niche as an expert analyst for a particular sport. This reputation may translate to book deals, paid-for appearances, or speaking engagements. Others have developed a particular persona or character that they have adopted and promoted to boost ratings, raise popularity, and generate business opportunities such as hosting a daily network sports show. This phenomenon of sport media member as celebrity has become more apparent in recent years as celebrity reporter-hosted sports talk shows and related media appearances are found in every market. Often these hosts boast hundreds of thousands of followers on Twitter and friends on Facebook.

The responsibility for managing these complex relationships with sport media members often rests with the sport organization's public relations director, marketing or communications specialist, or sport information director. Media relations staff in any sport organization are faced with the difficult challenge of maximizing positive coverage, protecting the interests of the sport organization, and cultivating a relationship with members of the media. In order to be effective, sport communications staff must be available, must be fair, and must maintain a high level of personal integrity and professional ethics. These people serve a critical function as liaison between the organization and the media. They always must remember the significant role the media plays in shaping public opinion and distributing the sport product to a wide variety of stakeholders. In recent years, the sport organization function has expanded to include updating of live stats, producing web-casts, designing and maintaining a high-quality relevant website, and managing strategic social media presence.

The line between the sport media and the sport organization has become increasingly blurred as sport organizations have ventured into in-house broadcasting. The New York Yankees, for example, own the YES network that broadcasts Yankee games. The NFL has developed the NFL network and produces NFL programming. Major League Baseball has its own MLB network. However, some critics suggest that media and sport organization shared ownership creates inherent conflicts of interest and allows for market exploitation through inflation of advertising rates and single interest control of game broadcasts.

Advancements in media information technology, specifically the development of broadband, high-definition television (HDTV), video streaming, digital recording, wireless technology, and social media have all resulted in an increasingly dynamic and fragmented sport media segment. There are more sport media products and services than ever before. One need only scan the digital cable on-screen guide, do an on-line search for sport media, or check the on-demand cable menu or satellite listings to get a clear sense of the explosion of sports on television. Not only is there a wealth of sport programming on television but on radio as well with the advent of satellite radio where dedicated sport channels are readily available. On the Internet, visit thousands of sports-related websites and retail sites, fan sites, chat rooms, blogs, Twitter feeds, Facebook pages, and fantasy leagues. Shop for sports-related apps for your mobile device, and you'll be surprised to see the number and breadth of options available. Check up-to-date scores or watch video highlight clips on your smart phone, your laptop, your notebook, your tablet, or your iPad. There are unlimited sport information media options for the dedicated sport fan.

Information technology has dramatically shaped not only how the sport media delivers sport information, but how the media manages and produces sport content. Broadcasts are supported by software packages that allow media crews to keep score efficiently, manipulate statistics, and provide fans with the most up-to-date information. Social media allows for instant polling, fan tweets that appear on screen, or a quick look at what is trending in sport discussion topics today. Other media-related technological innovations such as robotic cameras, on-line video streaming, interactive video boards, virtual signage, and instant replay are all examples of how technology has shaped the management and presentation of our games.

IMPROVED PERFORMANCE THROUGH INFORMATION TECHNOLOGY (IT)

Sport media organizations are certainly not alone in their integration of information technology in their operations. In fact, most sport organizations from all industry segments have embraced information technology advancements not only as they relate to communication functions but to all other areas of business operations.

Sport managers are learning to develop and adopt information technology that will help them provide better products and service to consumers and become more efficient in their operation. Once such example can be found in auto racing where technological advancements have provided crew chiefs with a wide variety of performance information before, during, and after the race. Such information is critical to decision making as teams rely on technology to provide important data that can help diagnose problems, forecast fuel efficiency, and track tire wear. In the sport facility industry, many stadiums and arenas now provide virtual view technology that allows fans to see the actual view from the seat location they have selected for on-line purchase. Managers throughout all of the segments of the sport industry recognize that information technology is a useful tool that presents both unique challenges and opportunities for the enhancement of the sport organization and its performance.

Information technology (IT)

IT refers to all of the resources – the processes, practices, and systems – an organization uses to gather, retain, and process the information it uses to pursue its mission. Most of us are familiar with the range of information technologies now in use in everyday life, everything from laptops and smart phones, to text messaging, e-mail, and video conferencing. All of these technologies, as well as an ever-expanding variety of information systems and software, have challenged managers to discover how IT can best be used to enhance performance and achievement of the organization's goals. To understand this challenge, it is helpful first to become familiar with some of the IT systems that are now part of our everyday lives as individuals.

Information systems

There are actually several levels of information systems available to organizations (see Box 3.1 below). The most basic is called a transaction-processing system (TPS). A TPS consists of a computer system designed to perform the most basic and recurring transactions of an organization. In a sport organization, a TPS would be used for credit card payments, for example, as well as the creation of invoices, facility

80

scheduling, tee-time reservations, on-line account management, retail sales, and payroll checks to employees. In general, a TPS is most useful for transactions that occur regularly and frequently, and in their basic format involve little or no change from transaction to transaction.

The next level of information system is called a management information system (MIS). An MIS is used to provide managers with information about the operation and performance of the organization. A sport media organization's MIS might be used to monitor the amount of maintenance or "down time" required for the various kinds of production equipment it uses, for example, or the percentage of advertising time sold for various upcoming programs or events. The MIS might also be used to track season ticket holder renewals, concessions inventory, or health club member attendance. This type of information allows managers to stay current in terms of how various elements of the organization are performing, and to recognize when problems occur. In the case of the health club manager, the club might require members to swipe a membership card with a bar code as they enter the club. This data would be stored in the MIS and a monthly systems report might then generate a list of frequency of attendance for all members. This information would then prove useful to the manager who might send a promotional flyer offering a reward to members who were attending frequently or the list might also trigger a phone call or letter to non-users inquiring about their absence and encouraging them not to let their membership lapse.

A more sophisticated form of MIS is called a decision support system (DSS). A DSS allows managers not only to monitor current performance in such areas as costs, sales, or revenues, but also to analyze trends over time in any of these areas, or the effects of changes in any of these areas on other areas of performance. A DSS also enables managers to monitor and factor in variables from the environment such as competitors' pricing or advertising expenditures, inflation, conditions in the national or regional economy, or any other external factor that might affect the organization's performance. A good example of a DSS' use is its application in player evaluation. In this system, managers collect a variety of statistics related to a particular player's performance over a period of time. This data is used to forecast future performance, establish relative value of the player to a particular team, and provide quantitative evaluation of a wide variety of performance metrics. Such information is used by sport organizations for the purpose of making decisions regarding player drafts, player trades, team development, and contract negotiations.

Using a DSS, managers can evaluate the impact of various options or alternatives before actually implementing them. For example, a sport facility can evaluate the impact of various levels of increases in the rate it charges for luxury boxes or suite rental, taking into account such factors as inflation, the prices its competitors charge, industry trends in premium seat sales and rental, the condition of the national economy, and so on.

81

In short, as a result of IT advances in TPS, MIS, and DSS, organizations now have the ability to dramatically streamline their day-to-day operations, to monitor virtually every performance area of the organization, and to significantly enhance the quality of analysis, problem solving, and decision making as the organization pursues its mission.

BOX 3.1 LEVELS OF INFORMATION SYSTEMS

Level I   TPS – transaction-processing system
              Designed to perform most basic and recurring transactions

Level II   MIS – management information system
              Provides managers with information about organizational operations and performance

Level III   DSS – decision support system
              Supports managerial decision making, identifies needs, monitors effects of environmental change

---

Organization-wide feedback on performance

One important change that has resulted from the use of IT in organizations is the availability of continuous feedback on performance, not just to managers, but also to individuals and teams at every level of the organization. It is no longer enough for the manager alone to know how things are going; for organizations to continuously improve, everyone must have access to information on performance. Through IT, this kind of organization-wide feedback on performance becomes possible.

Three examples of the integrated application of computer technologies utilized by sport organizations are the computerized maintenance management system (CMMS), enterprise resource planning (ERP), and the enterprise asset management (EAM) system. These systems are used by sport organizations ranging from professional sport facilities to sporting goods and equipment manufacturers. These systems consist of a series of relational database modules that communicate with one another. These modules may include equipment record management, work order management, preventive maintenance schedules, and inventory control modules. They may also include purchasing modules, personnel modules, report writing modules, and scheduling modules. While this technology provides the manager with continuous feedback on performance, it also allows the manager to identify strategies for enhancing organizational efficiencies and customer service. For sport managers, improved operations and service generated through streamlined management of these functions are highly desirable.

82

Sport organizations that use technology well are beginning to see the improvements in performance that are the result, at least in part, of the much wider range of feedback made possible by IT. In other words, the kind of organization-wide feedback made possible through IT allows not just managers, but also individual and team performers, to see what kind of progress they are making toward performance goals, and to more quickly identify performance problems.

It is also important to note that, in the sport industry, feedback made possible by technology is also being used not only in the front office, but on the playing field as well. Medical and training staff, coaches, and athletes have all effectively integrated technology into training regimens, injury diagnosis, and sport injury rehabilitation, as well as practice and game preparation. Video coupled with computer-based assessment and diagnosis is being used on a daily basis to improve golf swings and tennis strokes, develop individual speed and strength, determine opponents' playing tendencies, and analyze pitching and hitting performance. Virtually every sport has been able to utilize technology to improve individual and team performance.

Enhanced communication through IT

Where technology is available, children throughout the world aged ten years old and even younger are familiar with most of the recent IT-based advances in communication, particularly with social media and the latest tools for communication ranging from texting to tweeting to video chatting. (The authors fear that even as this book is published, it will be outdated by the latest technology to hit the marketplace.) What is less widely understood are the dramatic improvements that these technologies have made possible in terms of organization performance in the area of communication as well as in other functional areas of business.

To appreciate the scope of the improvements in these areas, it is helpful to consider what communication in organizations looked like prior to these advances. Even at the management level, if an individual or group identified a problem, or came up with an improvement idea, most often a memo had to be prepared, typed by a support staff member, and sent through the company's mail system to the appropriate parties. These parties would then respond through the same process of typed, mailed memo, most often independently, with little or no knowledge of the reaction of the others who'd received the initial memo. This process might continue back and forth for as long as it took to make a decision on the issue. Before voice mail, e-mail, texting, and teleconferencing, telephone messages could only be left for individuals with assistants to take the message, necessitating messages that were brief and less than complete.

In an effort to short circuit this extremely time-consuming process of memo and return memo and call and return call (telephone tag), a meeting might be called bringing together all of the parties required for discussion and decision. Of course the more parties required for this process, the more difficult it was to schedule a meeting, especially if some of the individuals involved were from outside of the area or from another company. The meeting form of communication does result in less time wasted in sending memos and calls back and forth and does provide an opportunity for interaction between participants. However, the logistics of scheduling meetings can often be cumbersome and, frequently, long periods of time pass before a mutually agreeable time can be found when all of the parties can come together at the same location. Today, teleconferencing and video conferencing provide a certain amount of flexibility that has enhanced the efficiency of group meetings. Texting has facilitated immediate communication. The breadth of information available through the Internet has facilitated world-wide access to important data and decision-making tools. We all can be connected every hour and every day of the year if we choose to be.

Changes in communication made possible through technology are affecting every aspect of organizational operations. For example, in the hiring process, we see how current IT advancements and changes in how we communicate have saved organizations time and money. Where sport businesses may have previously set up several in-person rounds of interviews or flown candidates to headquarters for an interview, phone interviews and video conferencing are now making the hiring process more efficient. Some employers now accept on-line applications for open positions and utilize software that screens résumés before human resources personnel begin the review of candidates. Employers also have more information about candidates available than ever before. On-line searches for public background information about candidates are common practice. In short, advances in IT have both accelerated and expanded communication processes throughout and beyond organizations, greatly enhancing their ability to respond rapidly and effectively both to problems and opportunities.

IT has also significantly affected the organization's ability to communicate with stakeholders. Web-based technologies such as blogs, live streaming, organizational websites, Twitter, and YouTube have allowed sport organizations to provide instantaneous information including game broadcasts, highlights, updates, game stories, game results, press releases, and statistics to both the media and other stakeholders including fans, sponsors, and parents of student-athletes. Sport facilities, youth leagues, and professional sport teams as well as other sport organizations are able to provide important immediate information such as schedule changes, announcements about up-coming events or promotions, and directions to sport facilities on-line. Some organizations encourage stakeholders to become more actively engaged with the organization by providing links for constituents to become friends of the organization's Facebook page, to follow the organization on Twitter, or view a highlight video on YouTube. This approach to communication can result in significant savings in publication design, printing, and mailing costs.

Many university athletic departments have been particularly successful in utilizing the web to communicate with key stakeholders including alumni, parents, donors, and prospective students who are located throughout the world. Parents, who may be located thousands of miles from the school, are now able to follow their student-athlete's team performance either through live game feeds or updates. Prospective students can research the school's athletic teams, coaches, and student-athlete services from the privacy of their own homes while alumni around the world can easily follow their alma mater's sport teams.

IT is also used to collect important feedback from stakeholders. Organizations may provide opportunities for on-line chats with sport stars or coaches, and may encourage fans to contact the organization for additional information or to provide comments on products, services, or policies that the organization is considering. The organization may set up on-line polls, prompt video or photo sharing, or solicit direct feedback or comments. Various media platforms provide tools for collecting contact information from users, counting numbers of visits, and even capturing user behavior patterns and preferences. All of this information can be utilized by the sport organization to better serve its constituents and market its products and services to them. For sport organizations, traditional web and social media technology creates an immediate direct link to a broad-based constituency.

It is also important to recognize the role that technology plays in facilitating commercial exchanges. Sport organization websites offer on-line purchase of goods such as tickets or merchandise as well as membership or registration services. For some sport organizations, the practice of doing business on-line has resulted in a better and more convenient service to customers while allowing the organization to cut back on personnel costs. For example, clerks who handled over-the-phone or walk-in business ticket sales might now become unnecessary as face-to-face customer traffic is lessened.

Use of on-line access goes far beyond purchasing products or services. Customers may use a sport organization's website to register for aerobics classes, youth soccer, summer camp, or tennis lessons. Golf courses offer on-line tee-time selection and access to the Golf Handicap and Information Network (GHIN) national on-line handicapping system where golfers can enter their scores and have their handicap calculated. Similarly, tennis clubs might provide an on-line court reservation service, computerized opponent selection, and tournament pairing service. At the ballpark or arena, fans might swipe a fan club card to receive discounts on stadium merchandise or concessions purchases. The Detroit Pistons of the NBA are giving season ticket holders team jackets with microchips embedded in the sleeves which will allow ticket holders to receive 20 percent off food and beverage and 30 percent off merchandise purchased at Piston home games ("Pistons giving," 2012).

Sport managers continue to experiment with mobile technology for sport concessions. One such example is Delaware North Company that runs concessions at Boston's TD Garden. The company is pilot testing BuyFi which allows fans to download the BuyFi app which is then used for food service orders and payment (Muret, 2012). Fans download the app and then enter a credit card and pin number that they wish to link to their BuyFi account. Fans may order from various menu options and then receive a text message when the order is ready for pick up. Other promotional incentives are made available through the app and users may pay a small fee for pick up or delivery. BuyFi may also offer discounts based on game events, e.g. points or goals scored, or may be connected to real-time inventory control systems which allow organizations to promote discounts on particular items.

Product and service innovations through IT

Yet another area of tremendous opportunity for organizations is the development of new products or services, or of new delivery mechanisms through the use of IT. Some professional football teams in the U.S. are now distributing laptop computers to players with preloaded electronic playbooks. These virtual playbooks not only replace traditional printed playbooks, but may include testing functions that allow the player to self-test learning and decision making in game scenarios (Newcomb, 2012). Sport medicine professionals are now using helmet and head cap technology to attempt to measure the intensity of hits or collisions and subsequent impact on the brain. Athletes are asked to take baseline computer-based concussion tests that attempt to establish a norm for brain function and reaction, and concussion training courses are now offered on-line.

Perhaps no IT-based change, however, has been more far-reaching than the changes that have come as a result of the development of the Internet. In every industry, the Internet has changed organizations dramatically. Transactions of every kind, from banking and stock market transactions, to account management, to catalog viewing and the purchase of everything from clothes to cars to music, are now web-based. To remain competitive, virtually every organization must at least make available to its customers the ability to "do business" with the organization over the Internet.

One of the great promises of emerging business information technology is its ability to be customized to the user. Individuals can create their own portfolio of media interests and sport organization information. One can choose the teams or individuals you wish to follow, or friend, like, or follow those people or organizations that are of direct interest to you. Organizations can create messages specifically designed for you based on your use and preferences. One can also download team wallpaper or ringtones, and you can receive advanced notification of broadcasts, or sales of products or services, that are important to you. One can also send a tweet directly to your favorite athlete, check game scores anytime night or day, send direct feedback to your sport organization, or blog with other fans as you watch a game. The choice is yours.

For students interested in a career in sport management, one of the best things you can do to prepare yourself for industry entry is to customize your own sport segment media portfolio. You should begin by identifying people who are respected industry analysts who comment on the business side of sports. Make daily visits to their Facebook page or website. Follow them on Twitter. Identify two or three sport industry segments, functional areas, or sport organizations of particular interest to you. What are the definitive websites, smart phone apps, experts on Twitter for the NFL? Sport facility management? Sport law? The English Premier League? Auto racing? Sport agency? Ice hockey? Utilize all of these information sources to keep up to date on the latest industry developments. When you know what's happening and what people are talking about in the sport segment you hope to work in one day, you have not only educated yourself, but you have given yourself an advantage over your competition.

THE MANAGEMENT CHALLENGES OF IT

The demonstrated benefits of recent advances in IT, both in terms of enhanced organizational performance and expanded and improved products and services for customers, are impressive. But there are significant challenges that must be met if organizations are to achieve the full dimension of these benefits. Among the most significant of these challenges are the need for quality information, the risk of information overload, ensuring continuous training to keep up with the continuing advances in IT, the challenge of maintaining security in terms of the organization's information systems, and the cost of IT development, training, and application.

The need to convert data into information

In all of the ways described above, advances in IT have significantly enhanced organizations' ability to use information. For IT to yield its full benefits, however, the information being processed must be *quality* information. Actually, there is a fairly common distinction drawn between information and data. Data consists of numbers or facts that represent some aspect or aspects of a situation. Nielsen ratings of a televised sports event, the prices competitors charge advertisers, and the number of "hits" on a sport organization's website are all examples of data, facts, or figures that in themselves have no meaning.

Information, on the other hand, consists of data that have meaning. A program's Nielsen rating, for example, when related to the ratings for other similar programs, or to the target rating established for that program, becomes information. By relating the data to other information, the data becomes information. In many ways, converting data to information is one of the critical tasks of the manager. IT can help ensure the availability of a continuous flow of essential data such as prices or ratings or website "hits," but it is the manager's job to apply knowledge and expertise based on education and experience to convert raw data into information that is useful for problem solving, decision making, and innovation. This means that one of the key challenges for organizations in optimizing the impact of IT is to ensure that there exists throughout the organization the knowledge and skills needed to convert data into useful information.

This is one of the reasons why higher levels of education are becoming required for more and more managerial jobs in sport. Higher levels of education translate into an increased ability to interpret, analyze, and understand data; in other words, to convert data into useful information. A major or degree in sport management has little value in itself; it is the knowledge of the sport industry gained through the major or degree program that is of value, because it is this knowledge that enables the sport manager to analyze and interpret data from the field, to convert that data into information that enhances decision making and problem solving. Business professionals often refer to this ability as having the skills to understand and utilize business intelligence.

Information and data-based decision making is supported through the practice of business analytics (BA). Business analytics may be best described as the process of carefully exploring and examining an organization's data through statistical analysis. BA may be successfully utilized to forecast and predict results, to find patterns or relationships, to determine causation, to test decisions, or to determine effects of manipulation of specific variables. This quantitative approach is being more widely embraced by business professionals who understand the value of data and how it might be better used to develop and evaluate both strategic and operational plans.

Ensuring information is on "TRAC"

Critical to the success of information and data-based decision making is ensuring that the information developed and used in organizations is quality information. Quality, in this case, generally means that information is timely, relevant, accurate, and complete, or as shown in Box 3.2, on "TRAC."

Timely

Even the best information, if it is not available at the time when it is needed for decision making or problem solving, is of little use to the manager. For example, inventory and sales statistics must be continuously updated and reported in order for them to retain their value to users. For the sport media and the sport communication function, timely information is essential. For example, sport organizations must pay particular attention to their websites and assure that site content is current. There is nothing worse than a website that has stories, scores, or promotional events that are days, months, or even years old.

Relevant

For information to be truly useful, it must relate to, and enhance understanding of, the issues and questions of direct concern to the organization. On the one hand this means not cluttering the organization's information systems with information that simply does not relate to the organization's needs, that is not used in the organization's decision making. On the other hand there is the challenge of ensuring that each decision maker in the organization has access to the kind of information needed for the particular decisions in which they are involved. For example, a national sport magazine manager would be particularly interested in collecting and maintaining a database of subscribers. The manager must determine what type of information would be important to collect and record about subscribers. What information would be useful to the organization? Does the manager want to know the age, gender, and income of the subscriber? Would it also be valuable to know what other magazines the subscriber reads, what products he or she uses, and what professional team the subscriber considers to be a favorite? Clearly, all of this information is considered in the magazine's marketing efforts and is, therefore, relevant to the organization.

Accurate

It almost goes without saying that for information to be of value to an organization, it must be accurate; that is, it must be a reliable and valid representation of what is really happening. In many ways, this is the most difficult challenge relating to information, especially in situations where the data are unclear. In these situations, the information being used is often the result of individual or group judgments about a situation, which are naturally subject to bias and interpretation. For example, members of the sport media are often faced with the challenge of reporting on games and events in the sport industry when few facts are known or may be unavailable. Consider the case where trade rumors surround a particular player. Locker room and press box speculation is rampant. A reporter may post a story to his or her blog or website. The story is little more than personal opinion, half-truths, and innuendo; yet, the reader has come to view the reporter as a legitimate news source and interprets the reporter's opinion as fact. In other cases, breaking news is reported via Twitter. Determining whether the poster is a fake or has hacked into someone else's account is necessary before the tweet should be reported or retweeted as fact. In all cases, the accuracy of such reports must be verified. In the rush to break or get something first in a very competitive media market, getting things RIGHT should not be sacrificed.

For the sport organization utilizing data to make managerial decisions, it is the manager's responsibility, as much as possible, to develop better data on the situation, either in the form of more reliable facts and figures, or by seeking the opinions of a wider group of people, preferably including "experts" with extensive experience with the situation under consideration. In other instances, it is critical to confirm information by two or three independent sources.

Complete

Finally, information must be sufficiently comprehensive to represent all of the important aspects of a situation. Incomplete information results in decision making that fails to take into account one or more important factors. This in turn jeopardizes the likelihood of the success or effectiveness of the decision or solution. For example, consider the case of the broadcast executive preparing to bid on a sport broadcast rights package. If he or she considered costs of production and advertising revenue forecasts, but did not consider information about competitors such as what they were likely to bid, how much they had bid in the past, and how much advertising rates were for a similar event in the past, he or she would be basing their bid on only part of the picture. The executive would also want to consider the state of the economy and industry trends as well. Sport managers must be cognizant of the fact that basing decisions on incomplete information often results in poor decisions.

BOX 3.2 THE "TRAC" MODEL OF QUALITY INFORMATION

Timely	Providing the most up-to-date information available
Relevant	Giving information that relates to and enhances understanding of key issues
Accurate	Ensuring that the information is a reliable and valid representation of what is happening
Complete	Providing information that is sufficiently comprehensive to represent all of the important aspects of the situation

---

Information that is on "TRAC" provides a solid foundation for an organization's decision-making and problem-solving processes. Shortcomings in any of these four areas results in decisions built on inadequate foundations, and the results are not likely to be positive.

Information overload and poor systems mismanagement

One of the downsides of the recent advances in IT is the risk of organizations and individuals being overwhelmed with so much information. The fact of the matter is that, on average, humans are somewhat limited in their ability to process anything more than a fairly moderate amount of information at any one time. The amount of information pouring in from a wide variety of sources has increasingly begun to threaten to exceed our capacity to organize and make sense of it all. The existence of so much information means risking either drowning as we immerse ourselves in this unending flow of information, or failing to recognize the most important information because it is buried in so much other information. Some critics also suggest that having so much data available causes over-reliance on quantitative inputs. There is valuable information and insights that the sport management professional gleans from years of experience and the development of personal instincts and opinions. Such qualitative assessment also brings value to the process. The best decision makers recognize that organizations can become stuck in analysis and in collecting and processing information. They know that the best decisions are made by considering information that is not only accurate and relevant, but represents a combination of information that is both qualitative and quantitative in nature.

The growth of technology in the workplace has also had an unintended consequence of presenting a challenge of employee time management. Engagement with media, particularly social media, becomes not only a time drain, but an addictive behavior. One of the challenges managers face is to develop practices and procedures that ensure, as much as possible, that everyone in the organization stays on task and limits media distraction. The manager also must be sure that information clutter is minimized, media use is targeted to work-related engagement, and that each employee has access to and receives only the information they need to perform their jobs well.

The continuous training challenge

It might be an obvious premise, but IT is only as good as the skills of the people who use it. This has always been the case between people and technology, but now there is a difference. In every age prior to the present, technology changed slowly. In fact, until the past two decades or so, the technical skills one learned at the beginning of a career most often were sufficient for an entire career. Whether in the factory or the office, it was fairly rare that a change in technology required significant additional training. With the advent of computer technology, this pattern has changed dramatically. Since the early 1990s, advances in IT have been continuous, requiring organizations to develop continuous training capabilities just to keep pace. In the past few years, technological development has accelerated even more quickly. In many cases, younger employees have a distinct advantage in this area as they most likely grew up in a technology-rich environment and are comfortable and familiar with its use and capacity.

Because of the explosion of technological advances, training is even more important than ever before. Traditionally, employee training has been viewed as "lost time," time when the employee is not working. Increasingly, this view is changing to recognize that training is an absolutely necessary investment to ensure that managers and employees have the skills needed to make maximum use of the capabilities of IT. Even with this changed mindset, however, arranging for continuous training in IT is difficult. As competition forces the requirement of greater efficiency on every organization, it becomes more and more of a challenge to find the time for training. But organizations are using innovative approaches to ensure that training occurs. One such approach uses IT to respond to this important IT challenge. In this approach training is available on-line, allowing employees to access training materials at whatever the best time for them might be, without ever leaving their desks. There may be disadvantages to this approach as well, including the problems associated with employees being required to find the time for training on their own. Additionally, some employees respond better to a face-to-face approach. To address this issue, some sport organizations are hosting on-site training sessions, while others are encouraging more professional development activities through conferences, seminars, or advanced degrees. But whatever questions specific approaches to training might raise, there is no doubt that if the full advantages of IT are to be realized, continuous training must become a reality.

The question of security

While the potential for improved performance through IT is significant, even when used appropriately, it is not without risks. An additional area of challenge for professionals is to effectively manage the access to information made possible by IT and required in the workplace.

The need for access and the threat of leaks

Increasingly, employees are sharing the responsibility with management for speeding up and improving the organization's performance. This shared responsibility increases their need for access to information on such factors as inventory levels, delivery schedules, costs, and levels of staff, as well as the performance of various units within the organization. Obviously, this greater access to information throughout the organization results in an increased possibility that important information might leak outside the organization to competitors, the media, and elsewhere. This is a reality, and organizations must learn to manage this reality and the risk it represents.

It is important to recognize, however, that some sports organizations routinely share information. For example, university athletic programs at public institutions have been sharing what some companies might consider secret information (e.g. budgets and salary information) with front-line employees and the general public for many years, with no evidence of resultant damage. It might also be argued that with the increasing availability of information through the Internet and other sources, what the organization is trying to protect may be already available through other sources. However, this is not to disregard the fact that in some segments of the sport industry information can be highly confidential and proprietary. For example, contract terms, grades of student-athletes, salary figures, or revenue information must be guarded in order to protect privacy or business interests of the organization and individuals. Sport managers must be aware of all legal requirements pertaining to information and information sharing. Personal information including credit card or bank account numbers, social security numbers, PIN numbers, and other access codes and passwords must all be well protected and stakeholders must be aware of information sharing and security standards and practices. In these cases, the sport organization is responsible for assuring the security of the information and must take every step possible to provide that the information is not hacked nor does it make its way to the media or to the very public domain of the Internet.

The possibility of sabotage

While internal leaks are of the utmost concern, another risk arising from the presence of IT in the workplace is the risk of an employee or outside user sabotaging the company's information system. A single angry employee armed only with a computer virus is now capable of doing irreparable harm to a company's databases and information systems. There is also the possibility of the one-person strike, where a single anonymous person, dissatisfied employee, or hacker team could interrupt the information system to call attention to a particular issue, attempt to gain concessions from management, or garner public attention. No laws, programs, and security arrangements can totally protect against this.

To guard against viruses or security breaks, employees can be trained in standard safety protocols. Organizations can be proactive and update computers with security and antivirus software. One of the best defenses against system breaches is employee education and customer service programs. In essence, it will have to be security technology itself combined with the vigilance of the organization, employee, and user that provides defense against IT sabotage.

Some sport organizations have recognized that either because of the size of the sport organization or lack of in-house professional expertise that they are unprepared to effectively manage information technology. As a result, tasks such as IT systems management, database management, software development, website design, social media coordination, and IT security maintenance may be outsourced to professionals or delivered through a collaborative partnership across leagues and organizations. A cottage industry of sports specialty IT companies and internal divisions has developed and they are serving a vital role in helping sport organizations integrate technology in their operations. It is important for students to recognize that expertise in technology management, business analytics, social media, and other web-based communications is highly valued by sport organizations. New employment opportunities in these areas are being advertised on a daily basis.

Cost considerations

One of the greatest challenges faced by managers seeking to develop and integrate information technology into the operation of the sport organization is the associated cost of IT. There is little doubt that research and development of new technologies is very expensive. Sport organizations must consider not only the upfront cost of securing the technology, but also training and maintenance costs must be considered as an on-going expense. The reality is that sport managers recognize that there are extensive technology start-up costs such as building infrastructure, purchasing hardware and software, personnel, and staff training.

For most sport organizations, it is no longer a question of **if** the sport organization should consider integrating advancements in information technology, but **how** the organization can successfully implement, realize, and sustain the competitive advantage that can be brought about through IT.

Negative consequences of IT growth in sport

While technological advancements in sport and sport media have revolutionized the management of sport organizations and greatly enhanced the fan experience, there are some negative consequences of the technology revolution in the sports business. One potentially damaging consequence of available technology in sport is related to on-line anonymity and chat rooms, comment boxes, blogs, and discussion forums. With the growth of these interactive communication options, a disturbing trend has emerged. Individuals may utilize these sites to make negative or vulgar remarks, issue competitive challenges, or taunt others or opposing teams. In the worst case scenario, demeaning, derogatory, or discriminatory remarks are posted. While some postings may be intended as good-natured trash talking, others rise to the level of cyber bullying and hate speech. For this reason, it is necessary for sport

94

organizations and media managers to be proactive in educating users about acceptable use and then, consequently, monitoring these postings for prohibited remarks or activity.

Another unintended negative consequence of the growth of on-line communication and social media is that individuals may post photos or comments without thinking through how their postings will be interpreted by their audience. For example, athletes may take photos of themselves or others and place them on a Facebook page or send them through Twitter. The nature of these photos may cause concern for the sport organization and could possibly do damage to the individual. For example, a photo of underage student-athletes drinking at a university team party while wearing their team sweatshirt can be a public relations nightmare. Photos or announcements of team beer pong tournaments, hazing activities, or sex parties and even photos of individuals flagrantly breaking team rules can have far-reaching negative consequences. Even when individuals believe that they have taken steps to block others from viewing postings, they have no way of ensuring that a permitted user won't repost or share with others in public forums. It is always best for the sport management professional to take a cautious approach when educating constituents and employees about Internet media use. A good general rule of thumb is that once something is posted or a message or text is sent, it is a good possibility that the image or words are there for anyone and everyone to see FOREVER.

Parents of prospective students, coaches, recruits, law enforcement officials, future employers, teachers, professors, and school administrators are increasingly present in cyberspace. While communication technology can be a valuable social and educational tool, users often overlook the broader audience that utilizes technology to gather information about the individual. Coaches, prospective intern supervisors, employers, and other decision makers are influenced by the results of a Google search, Facebook page, or Twitter account analysis.

While individuals and organizations may be diligent in paying attention to controlling their own on-line activity, it is virtually impossible to control all elements of on-line presence. For example, cell phone users or other digital camera users may take photos of student-athletes or other sport personalities and then use these images for their own purpose. In an extreme case, a photo might be used to blackmail or harm the reputation or relationships of the individual. Student-athletes or others not wishing these images to be posted or made available to parents, employers, coaches, recruiters, or other significant people in their lives may acquiesce to the blackmailer. Even in cases where blackmail is not threatened, damage can be done to the individual or the sport organization's reputation.

For some sport programs, the practice of athletes or officials posting or sharing personal photos on the Internet or through cell phones has become increasingly problematic. Even if the individual student-athlete is posting or sharing the photo him or herself, they may not realize the inflammatory nature of the image or who might have access to it. This is a practice that some professional athletes and sport organization officials have come to regret. Athletes who take personal or intimate photos intended for personal use often forget that, once the photo is sent, it is likely to be forwarded to others or posted on-line and, in some cases, even sold to the highest bidder. Sport managers must remember to communicate to their employees and other stakeholders that such communications may become evidence in legal cases, hiring decisions, disciplinary hearings, or other such proceedings and can have long-term and lasting negative effects on an individual or organization's reputation. Sport managers must be proactive in their knowledge of what is going on in cyberspace and must educate athletes and other personnel about the potential negative dangers and consequences of on-line personal communications.

Innovation and technology offer great promise for enhancing communication in the sport world and can contribute greatly to our understanding and enjoyment as fans and participants. Technology also has helped to rapidly advance the practice and profession of sport management; however, there is a dark side to the proliferation of technology that must be recognized as well.

EPILOGUE: TWEETING FOR DOLLARS

Do you know who Alex Morgan is? How about Skylar Diggins? Cappie Pondexter? Okiima Pickett? All are female athletes (Morgan is a forward on the U.S. women's national soccer team), and all use the social media site Twitter to communicate with fans, add sponsors, and promote games. At the conclusion of the 2011 Women's World Cup, Morgan had 100,000 followers on the social media site. "It made me a little nervous," said Morgan. "Some people even analyzed every little thing I said on Twitter. It took some getting used to." Morgan has been able to use the contacts established during the World Cup to stay connected to fans as well – and now she has four times as many followers (which exceeds the circulation of most major American newspapers). And according to writer Jane McManus, this expanded fan base "concretely translates into advertiser interest" in generating more revenue for the athlete (2012, p. 1).

Morgan's agent, Dan Levy of Wasserman Media Group (see Chapter 7), understands the importance of such a following. "Every single [prospective] sponsor, it's the first or second thing they look at," he said. "It's the difference between getting a deal and not getting a deal." But Levy also lauds the power of Twitter from the perspective of fans. "You used to have to rely on 'SportsCenter' or TV exposure. Now people can really handpick what they want to follow and care about" (McManus, 2012, p. 1).

96

And lesser-known female athletes can also benefit from use of the site. Okiima Pickett, a running back for the D.C. Divas of the Independent Women's Football League (see also Chapter 4), uses Twitter to promote her team and to let people know about upcoming games and events. "Women's sports don't have the money and the TV commercials that the men have," noted Pickett. "Our only mode right now of promoting the game is social networking and word of mouth." The site allowed Pickett to connect with basketball Hall of Famer Nancy Lieberman, who agreed to participate in a fundraiser for the team after Pickett contacted her. "I would never have had that connection without social media," Pickett said (McManus, 2012, p. 1).

As noted above, these athletes have chosen to utilize evolving social media technologies to gain a competitive advantage in the marketplace, and will need to remain committed to adopting technologies that will improve their performance. Professional sport managers will continue to assess and integrate rapidly evolving technology in an effort to gain a competitive advantage in the marketplace. The challenge is to use technology to advance quality, to adopt technology that will support the organization's mission, and to manage emerging technology in a way that adds value to the organization.

SUMMARY

In this chapter, we have examined the sport media segment which plays an integral role in connecting stakeholders to sport organizations. The sport media not only reports game outcomes, but also serves as a marketing distribution channel by which sport is delivered directly to consumers throughout the world. The sport media continues to reinvent itself through technologies and media platform development, which allows sport consumers to gain more immediate access to sport information and organizations.

The sport media has successfully utilized developing information technology (IT). IT refers to all of the resources – the processes, practices, and systems – an organization uses to gather, retain, and process the information it uses to pursue its mission. IT provides organizations with the ability to develop new products and services while improving management's ability to make effective and efficient decisions. Managers utilize several levels of information systems including transaction-processing systems (TPS), management information systems (MIS), and decision support systems (DSS). These systems help organizations dramatically streamline their day-to-day operations, monitor virtually every performance area of the organization, and significantly enhance the quality of analysis as it shapes strategies and operations to fulfill its mission. Increasingly sport organizations are relying on business analytics to inform their decision making and problem solving. Computer-based technologies, especially the Internet and social media, have greatly expanded

97

the capacity of individuals and of sport organizations. The sport media segment is leading the way in innovation and integration of technology in the sport industry.

Sport organizations have recognized the benefits and associated challenges of information technology. IT has helped to improve individual, organizational, and team performance through increasing efficiencies and facilitating improvements in operational standards, practices, and outcomes. In this chapter, the student was presented with several critical IT challenges including content quality, information overload, training, security, and cost considerations. Sport managers must also be cognizant of the deleterious effects of media and technology including the possible negative and harmful consequences of controversial postings as well as potentially problematic sharing of personal photos and comments.

There is little doubt that advances in information technology will continue to shape the management of sports organizations. As the sport media plays a leadership role in the sport industry in developing and integrating new technologies, it will continue to become an increasingly powerful entity that both shapes our games and also our understanding, participation, and perceptions of sport.

MANAGEMENT EXERCISE: PRO SPORTS COLLECTIBLES

Paul Hunter has recently purchased Pro Sports Collectibles, a local sport memorabilia and collectibles store that had been family owned for 40 years. Hunter, a long-time sport memorabilia collector, who was well known and respected in the sport memorabilia community, was excited about beginning his own business. He thought he had done his homework before purchasing Pro Sports Collectibles. He had created a business plan, secured the capital to support his investment, and had developed deals with several suppliers who would provide him with quality memorabilia and sport items. He was also a student of sport management, and was aware of the background and history of the memorabilia industry outlined in Chapter 1 of the course text.

One hour after Paul signed the papers, he walked into his new store and arranged to take Cy Thompson, the store's only full-time employee, to dinner that evening. What he learned during that dinner made him truly realize for the first time what he had undertaken. Paul carefully took notes as Cy began to talk about the operation of Pro Sports Collectibles. This is what he wrote.

Notes: Pro Sports Collectibles meeting

Only one full-time employee. Eight part-time college student workers. Schedule made up by owner and posted on the bulletin board on Saturdays. Sometimes part-time workers change hours. By the end of the week, the schedule is a mess with eraser marks, penciled in names. Sometimes no one shows to take a shift and the full-time employee or owner is stuck working the shift. Employees complain that hours are not distributed evenly and that pay checks are sometimes sent days late. The owner manually completes payroll every Wednesday morning.

Inventory arrives by truck on Tuesdays. Sometimes it is not unloaded until Saturday.

- Inventory system is maintained by hand on index cards.
- Shoplifting is a serious problem.
- Phone calls from out-of-state collectors take a great deal of time. Must search backroom or index cards to see if item is available.
- Most transactions take place with customers who live within 60 miles. No on-line transactions.
- Only cash and checks accepted for transactions.
- Marketing is limited to sporadic advertisement in the local newspaper.

When Paul got home that evening, he reviewed his notes and realized that he needed a plan to integrate technology into the management of Pro Sports Collectibles.

QUESTIONS FOR YOU TO CONSIDER

1   Based on Paul's notes, identify and explain the challenges facing Pro Sports Collectibles and how they might be addressed by the use of information technology.
2   Pro Sports Collectibles has failed to utilize Internet technology. Identify and explain what content would be important to include in a new Pro Sports Collectibles website.
3   Using IT, design a customer tracking system that specifies what types of customer information should be collected and how it will be used to enhance customer service.
4   Develop a social media plan to promote the store's opening under new ownership.
5   Identify and explain how Paul can utilize technology to begin to globalize his business.

CHAPTER 4

DEVELOPING GOALS AND SCHOOL AND YOUTH SPORTS

INTRODUCTION

Within the context of the school-based and youth sports industry segments, this chapter describes goal setting and how clearly stated goals can provide people and sport organizations with the focus, direction, and understanding needed for optimum performance. We define the task of developing effective goals in terms of several key criteria, review the numerous benefits from developing goals in this manner, and examine the challenges and difficulties that are part of the goal-setting process. The chapter also illustrates specifics elements of the school-based and youth sport industry segment, how goal-setting impacts this segment, and, once goals have been defined, how managers in this segment work to achieve them.

Check the stats

Purpose
To provide athletic participation opportunities to boys and girls of all ages up to and including enrollment in high school.

Stakeholders
Participant athletes, parents, coaches, related support personnel (trainers, officials), equipment suppliers, league administrators, school administrators, state association administrators, elected officials (local school boards, state and federal legislators).

Size and scope
More than 650,000 boys and girls ages 7 through 18 participated on more than 50,000 teams sanctioned by the American Youth Soccer Organization (AYSO) ("History of AYSO," 2011).

100

- Pop Warner Little Scholars, Inc. sponsors more than 5,000 teams in eight weight/age classifications for 240,000 football players, along with programs for 160,000 cheer and dance team members ages 5 through 16 ("About Pop Warner," 2012).
- Nearly four and a half million young men and over three million young women participated in high school athletics during the 2008–2009 school year ("2010–11 high school," 2011).
- More than 2 million coaches have been certified by the National Alliance for Youth Sports (NAYS); more than 65,000 families have gone through NAYS' parents' program; and more than 2,000 administrators have earned their certification credentials through NAYS' Academy for Youth Sports Administrators ("Frequently asked," 2010).

Governance

HIGH SCHOOL SPORTS – NATIONAL LEVEL

The National Federation of State High School Associations (NF), a non-profit organization headquartered in Indianapolis, Indiana, serves as the national coordinator for high school sports, as well as activities such as music, debate, theater, and student council. The NF encompasses all 50 individual state high school athletics and activity associations in the District of Columbia. NF represents over 11 million participants in more than 19,000 high schools, as well as coaches, officials, and judges through the individual state, provincial, and territorial organizations. In addition to compiling national records in sports and national sport participation rates, the NF coordinates official certification; issues playing rules for 17 boys' and girls' sports; prints eight million publications annually, including officials' manuals and case books, magazines, supplemental books, and teaching aids; holds national conferences and competitions; and acts as an advocate and lobbying agent for school-based youth sports. The NF also maintains a high school Hall of Fame ("Bob Gardner," 2010).

Three facets comprise the organizational structure of the NF. The legislative body, the National Council, is made up of one representative from each member state, provincial, or territorial association. Each council member has one vote, and the council meets to conduct business twice each year. The administrative responsibilities are handled by the 12-member board of directors, elected by the National Council from professional staffs of member associations. Eight board members are elected to represent one of eight geographic regions, with the remaining four chosen on an at-large basis. The board of directors approves the annual budget, appoints an executive director, and establishes committees for conducting association business. The NF has a paid administrative and professional staff of 50, including the current executive director, Bob Gardner, named to the post in 2010 ("Bob Gardner," 2010).

Other professional organizations and services offered by or affiliated with the NF include:

- The National Interscholastic Athletic Administrators Association (NIAAA), made up of 5,000 individuals responsible for the administration of high school athletics.
- The NF Coaches Association, comprised of 30,000 member high school coaches.
- The NF Officials Association, which includes 130,000 member officials who benefit from liability insurance and skills instruction.
- The NF Spirit Association, formed in 1988 to assist members and coaches of cheerleading, pompom, and spirit groups.

STATE HIGH SCHOOL ASSOCIATIONS

The NF model is typically replicated at the state level by state associations. State associations, which are also non-profit, have a direct role in organizing state championships and competitions in athletics and activities and are the final authority in determining athlete eligibility. The scope of activities, size of full-time administrative and support staff, and number of schools represented vary from state to state and are proportionally related to that state's population.

The legislative business of state associations is administered in much the same manner as the NF, with several general meetings each year attended by one voting representative from each member institution. While championships and competitions are administered by the associations, committees consisting of coaches and administrators perform most of the actual duties associated with the events, including determining criteria for selection of event participants, event management, and the general rules pertaining to regular season competition.

NATIONAL YOUTH LEAGUE ORGANIZATIONS

National youth league organizations focus administrative efforts on promoting participation in a particular sport among children. The activities and duties of these organizations are illustrated by examining one such association, Little League Baseball, the best-known youth athletic organization in the United States. Factory worker Carl Stotz founded Little League Baseball in 1939 as a three-team league in Williamsport, Pennsylvania. The organization, initially for boys ages 9 through 12 (girls were admitted in 1974), grew to 867 teams in 12 states over the next decade. By 1963, Little League boasted 30,000 teams in 6,000 leagues on four continents. In 2002, 2.8 million children ages 5 through 18 in 105 countries participated in t-ball, baseball, and softball at four age-group levels and for mentally and physically disabled children. Little League requires strict adherence to administrative guidelines, including standardized field size and use of uniforms; formalizes rosters composed via the draft system; and promotes its ability to provide adult supervision and safe play ("Little League chronology," 2010).

Little League governance structure is organized on four levels: local, district, region, and international. Each league program is organized within a community, which establishes its own boundaries (with total population not to exceed 20,000) from which it may register players. A board of directors guides each local league, and is responsible for the league's day-to-day operations. Ten to 20 teams in a given area usually comprise a district. The District Administrator organizes district tournaments. The District Administrator reports to the Regional Director, of which there are five in the U.S. and four internationally. All Little League operations are led by the President and CEO Stephen Keener, who reports to a Board of Directors comprised of eight District Administrators elected to rotating terms by their colleagues at the periodic International Congress. There are 110 full-time league employees and a million volunteers worldwide ("Structure of Little League," 2010).

Inside look: the patron saint of prep hockey

Sidney Crosby, Zach Parise, Jonathan Toews. What do they have in common? The first three picks by the respective captains for the NHL All-Star Game? The first three selections in your upcoming NHL fantasy league draft? Both options might be true, but these three share something else. All three attended Shattuck-St. Mary's School (SSM), a private, co-educational boarding and day preparatory school (Grades 6–12). The school is located in Faribault (pronounced "FAIR-eh-boe"), Minnesota (population: 22,000), about an hour's drive south of the Twin Cities of Minneapolis and St. Paul. SSM was founded in 1858 (initially the boys' school – Shattuck – was a military academy, while the girls' school – St. Mary's – was a separate entity) and is affiliated with the Episcopal Dioceses of Minnesota, and currently enrolls about 450 students.

On a recent visit to the campus, *ESPN Magazine* writer Gare Joyce drove through the school's entrance arch, took a look at the limestone neo-Gothic architecture design of the campus, repleat with a castle-like clock tower and a high-vaulted ceiling in its dining hall, and dubbed SSM "the Hogwarts of Hockey, where carbon-fiber sticks take the place of magic wands" (2008, p. 82). Just how magical? Crosby and Toews went straight from SSM to the NHL. A poll on the website "Bleacher Report" lists the Top 20 SSM alumni, all of whom are playing professionally – Crosby and Parise top the list, followed by Toews, Drew Stafford, Derek Stepan, Kyle Okposo, Emerson Etem, Ryan Malone, Patrick Eaves, and Brady Murray (Daniel, 2011). In all, the school boasts over 40 NHL draft picks ("Shattuck-St. Mary's," 2012). Also, seven former SSM players competed in the 2010 Vancouver Winter Olympics, including sisters Jocelyn and Monique Lamoureux, who earned silver medals for the United States women's team ("SSM alumni," 2010).

Although SSM is a high school, albeit private, its programmatic aspirations in hockey caused it to leave behind competition in the Minnesota State High School

League for affiliation with USA Hockey, the national governing body for the sport sanctioned by the United States Olympic Committee. SSM squads are registered as a "non-community-based team" and can represent Minnesota in the USA Nationals playoffs every year (Hunter, 2010). SSM's schedules include local prep schools such as Breck School (Minneapolis), regional prep opponents such as Culver Academy (Indiana), regional travel teams such as the Dallas Junior Stars, in-season tournaments in the U.S. and Canada, and national USA Hockey tournaments. Says one head NHL scout about the men's program: "You go see Shattuck whenever you get a chance, especially if they're challenged. There's something about their teams and their players that scouts love. They have this swagger, a confidence and their ability, and they earn it, every game and every shift" (Joyce, 2008, p. 82). The emergence of this program in the mid-1990s is hard to fathom when one considers that in the late 1980s the school had to run a cooperative hockey program with the local public high school, and only a half-dozen SSM kids were on the team.

Today, the school fields seven teams – five for boys, two for girls. The 2011–2012 Prep team – the most advanced level – boasted a roster of players from eleven U.S. states, one Canadian province, and Latvia. On its website, the school describes the benefits of its program: a seven-month schedule, with 50 to 75 games a year and tournament play throughout the U.S. and Canada; player on-ice access five to seven days a week, with one hour-15 minute practices; and proficient instruction from former NHL and NCAA Division I coaches ("Shattuck-St. Mary's," 2012). Compare this to local travel teams that might get ice time four days a week, more likely three, and certainly not on one of two rinks within walking distance from dorms, classrooms, and the dining hall.

Although undoubtedly a breeding ground for future college and NHL stars, alumni and other stakeholders laud the school's holistic educational approach. Crosby, who, in his one season at SSM before being selected first overall in the 2005 NHL Draft by the Pittsburgh Penguins, had 72 goals and 162 points in 57 games, described his year in Faribault this way:

> It was my first experience away from [home in] Nova Scotia, and I had to catch up academically. I struggled with it at first. But I loved the atmosphere … You get to know each other – everyone – a lot faster and a lot better. Leaving Shattuck [for the NHL] was the hardest decision I've had to make.

On the academic component, Toews stated flatly: "We never got a class off or any break," and one NHL GM (who was also a former NHL player) whose son attended SSM put it this way: "The school was a genuine concern for character development. All the right messages are sent. There are no corners cut, no elitism" (Joyce, 2008, pp. 82, 85).

Positive impressions aside, the development of the SSM hockey machine – some, like *ESPN Magazine*'s Joyce, refer to it as a factory – brings into question the proper goals of high school and youth sport programs, and the process of providing the

Developing goals and school and youth sports

clear sense of purpose for high school and youth league managers. For SSM, it is clear that one goal is for the school to attract promising hockey players to hone their on-ice skills. While there is anecdotal evidence to support the fact that SSM is providing a sound educational experience as well (and in the *ESPN Magazine* piece referenced above, a full-page photograph of three players on ice, with one – Etam – wearing skates and gloves but seated at a classroom desk with textbooks and notebooks spread out before him, surely met with the school's approval at promoting its academic image), it is not hard to imagine that if on-ice fortunes wane, or if other schools choose to adopt what we might call "the SSM Model" and start to compete to attract prospects from the finite pool of talent, the goal of college and NHL placement might supersede that of promoting academic rigor.

Chances are, you participated in either or both youth and school-based sports. Many of you had good experiences, and some of you probably didn't. What makes a team experience at this level either positive or negative? Did it come down to conflicts over winning and losing? Did the adults – your coaches, your parents, or others – seem to be more interested in winning than you were? Maybe. Research by Michigan State University's Institute for the Study of Youth Sports found that kids in youth sports play to have fun, be with their friends, and learn. A more recent study of youth football and basketball players in Connecticut verified these findings, and posits that no matter the age and sport, players cited having fun as the primary reason for participating. When viewing the results of the study, a local league official in the town of Darien commented that it was a "touch of reality" for adults. "It reminds us why kids play sports in the first place. It's not about winning a championship in the fourth grade," he said (Hyman, 2010, p. Y-9). Is this an issue for SSM? Whose needs are being addressed? Sure, a chance to play in the NHL might seem enticing, but not everyone is going to make it. Then what?

Historical perspectives and the challenge of vision

Management expert Peter Drucker has suggested that "it is the first responsibility of the manager ... to give others vision and the ability to perform" (1973, p. 3). Drucker defined vision as the clear, shared sense of direction that allows organizations to achieve a common purpose. He insisted that vision is the first contribution of management because a shared sense of direction makes possible the cooperation and commitment necessary for organizations to succeed. Only with a common vision can individuals and groups perform with a clear sense of the destination they are working toward and a clear sense of the direction of the organization. But in the context of youth and school sports, the question is: what direction is most important?

More recently, management thinkers James Collins and Jerry Porras (1998) described a well-conceived vision as having two parts: core ideology and envisioned future. Core ideology is defined as the enduring characteristics of an organization and includes core values and core purposes. Core values are those values an organization would keep even if it were penalized for retaining them, and core purposes are what defines an organization's reason for being. The envisioned future includes BHAGs, or "big, hairy, audacious goals," bold long-range goals that influence the direction of an organization for ten to 30 years, and a vivid description of what it will mean to achieve these BHAGs.

The recognition of the positive educatory and developmental aspects of athletic participation is not a recent phenomenon, and may be considered a kind of BHAG for school and youth sports. The history of youth athletic participation predates the signing of the U.S. Constitution and the formation of the United States. Native Americans played a game that French Jesuit priests called "lacrosse," because players used a stick that resembled a bishop's cross-shaped crosier. European settlers brought to the continent tennis, cricket, and several early versions of what would become baseball, and Africans brought to America as slaves threw the javelin, boxed, and wrestled. Despite all this, formally organized athletic participation, particularly those programs run under the auspices of secondary educational institutions, did not emerge until the mid-nineteenth century (Swanson and Spears, 1995).

Private schools in America rather than public ones were the first to provide athletic participation opportunities. The now-defunct Round Hill School in Northampton, Massachusetts, was the first institution known to have promoted the physical well-being of its students as part of its formal mission and curriculum. Many other early American private schools followed the model of elite English schools such as Eton, Harrow, and Rugby (characterized as "independent, non-local, predominantly boarding ... for the upper and upper-middle classes" (Ogilvie, 1957, pp. 8–10)), where athletic programs were more formalized, although managed by students, with campus-based club teams focused on intramural-type play forming the early modes of competition.

The foundations of athletics in private secondary schools in America is examined in detail in Axel Bundgaard's *Muscle and manliness: The rise of sport in American boarding schools* (2005), in which the author researches the motivating factors behind the eventual establishment of interscholastic athletic programs at Eastern private schools. Many such schools were founded in the late nineteenth century in large part due to growing dissatisfaction with the developing public school system (McLachlan, 1970). These schools, much like colleges and universities in the same region such as Harvard, Princeton, and Yale, would influence colleges and universities across the country, would be equally influential to other private secondary schools, as well as public schools, in forming and promoting a rationale for athletic programs. In the early years of these schools, students at some institutions were encouraged to pursue unstructured play. Bundgaard cites that character development (meaning moral education) through sport participation was the overarching goal to be gained by students, with physical fitness also seen as an important benefit.

Eventually, formalized sports such as football and baseball would soon be viewed as effective settings for teaching physical and moral development.

Initially, athletic programs at American private schools, like at their English counterparts and much like those at American colleges and universities, were organized by students. As a result, students were responsible for rule making and game management, and securing playing sites and outside opponents. Most early school leaders merely permitted such activities, while some actively promoted them. In 1859, the Gunnery School in Washington, Connecticut, was the first to feature games against outside competition in athletic programs actively encouraged and promoted by school founder Frederick Gunn. Students who attended the school at the time noted that students were required to play baseball. In 1878, St. Paul's School in Concord, New Hampshire, hired the first full-time faculty member specifically to coach team sports. St. Paul's is also credited with being the site of the first organized ice hockey game in the U.S. in 1883 (coincidentally, St. Paul's was founded by George Shattuck, a graduate of the Round Hill School who was also an early benefactor for Shattuck-St. Mary's). In 1895, Phillips Exeter Academy, also in New Hampshire, appointed the first permanent faculty member as Director of Athletics, indicating the intentions of schools to institutionalize all athletic programs within their education purviews (Hardy, 1997; Bundgaard, 2005; "SSM history," 2013).

Bundgaard examines in detail the factors that led to the eventual ubiquity of interscholastic programs at these types of schools, and concludes that these schools "aimed to produce young men who could take their place and serve with distinction in society" (2005, p. 31). Bundgaard also raises some compelling questions never addressed by school leaders of the time, such as whether these positive outcomes can be learned during practice as well as games, in intramural settings as well as those varsity contests against outside rivals, whether participation was compulsory or voluntary, or in one sport more so than another. But a telling perspective is offered by Alfred Stearns, head of Phillips Academy in Andover, Massachusetts, when he wrote in *The Atlantic Monthly*: "Were athletics, especially football, taken out of the life of our schools we should search long, and probably in vain, for a suitable substitute" (Bundgaard, 2005, p. 193).

The development of youth and school sports in America during the twentieth century provides an excellent example of the power of vision and what is possible when people share a committed sense of direction. But the challenge over this period was how to determine this direction, and in whose interests. During the early 1900s, educators aligned with the Progressive Movement, including John Dewey, G. Stanley Hall, and William James, first articulated the vision of athletics as a tool to prepare young people for the rigors of modern life in American society. Several years later, in the period during and immediately following World War I (1914–1918), the nation began to recognize the health benefits of athletics for male youths and adults alike. In particular, school sports for

107

males were promoted as a source of physical training for the armed forces without directly encouraging militarism and a means to encourage the cooperation and discipline valued by an increasingly ethnically diverse and industrialized society. During the period, when only one-in-three children entered high school and only one-in-nine completed it, educators began to recognize interscholastic athletic programs as an important way to keep students in school and to boost graduation rates. These became part of the envisioned future for those organizations promoting youth sports.

With this recognition, the vision of youth sports as a potentially valuable learning experience took root and began to grow. By 1931, 36 states had passed laws pertaining to physical education in high schools, and 47 states had athletic associations that monitored and controlled boys' high school athletics, and conducted state championships in baseball, basketball, football, and track and field (O'Hanlon, 1982). Not surprisingly, this period was also marked by dramatic growth for youth sports outside the high school arena. As a result of the Great Depression and the difficult conditions for youth at that time, a number of private and parochial sports organizations emerged to promote youth participation in sports. These included American Legion Junior Baseball (1925), Pop Warner youth football (1929), the Catholic Youth Organization (basketball, boxing, and softball) in 1930, the Amateur Softball Association (1933), and Little League Baseball (1939). Today, nearly four million young men and over three million young women participate in high school athletics, and as many as 70 million children are involved in youth sport programs annually ("2010–11 high school," 2011). These numbers are clear testimony to the success of the articulation of the vision of youth sports and school athletics as valuable learning experiences.

As with the pioneers of youth and school sports, the first responsibility of sport managers in every segment of the sport industries is to provide a clear sense of vision, to provide the direction that will ensure effective organizational performance, and to enable every member of the organization to contribute meaningfully to the organization's success. According to Peter Drucker, the most effective way to achieve a shared understanding of the organization's vision is through well-defined goals. The challenge in school and youth sports continues to be how to define program goals. This means it is management's first responsibility to develop a system of goals that provides a sense of direction so clear that it guides the organization on its course.

DEVELOPING EFFECTIVE GOALS

Consider the following two statements that might be made by a school regarding its athletic offerings:

108

- To provide high-quality athletic opportunities for youth participants.
- To provide a sport program for each season of the year at both the interscholastic and intramural levels within three years.

The first statement is not a goal; the second is. What is the difference? A goal is a commitment to a specific outcome within a specific time frame. The first statement describes a general direction of having high-quality athletic opportunity for youth participants, but it is not as specific as it might be in terms of exactly what the desired outcome is and when it is to be achieved. The second statement is much more specific in terms of both desired outcome and time frame. It commits to organizing a different sport activity on a year-round basis at different levels of competition (interscholastic and intramural) within three years. This type of specificity is a fundamental requirement for developing goals. Box 4.1 adapts an acronym suggested by Hersey and Blanchard (1981) as a way to remember the essential characteristics of effective goals. For goals to improve performance, they must be "S.M.A.R.T."

BOX 4.1 S.M.A.R.T. GOAL ACRONYM

- Specific enough for focus and feedback
- Meaningful enough to motivate
- Accepted by the participants
- Realistic yet challenging
- Time-framed

Specific enough for focus and feedback

Specificity contributes to improved performance in two ways. First, goals that specify a targeted outcome provide a clear focus for everyone in the organization. For example, a program that provides opportunities at different levels of competition must include intramural sports as well as interscholastic sports (if we are talking about a high school athletic program). The more general statement of providing "high-quality athletic programs" can be interpreted in many different ways, with some people perhaps focusing on intramurals as a way to ensure maximum participation and others focusing on making the interscholastic teams as competitive as possible. The more specific statement makes it clear that the focus includes both intramural and interscholastic sports. The more specific goals are, the more likely that everyone in the organization will have the same understanding, rather than his or her own individual interpretation, of the target. And when the destination is clear to everyone, it ensures both better decisions about how to get there and better cooperation along the way.

109

Table 4.1 Goal-setting formula for a school athletic department

	Specific outcome	Time frame
Goal 1	To decrease the number of athletic injuries by 20%	By the end of the school year
Goal 2	To recruit ten girls for the school soccer team	By 2014
Goal 3	To recruit ten new participants for the girls' soccer program	By 2015
Goal 4	To add a new sport program for the fall season	By the end of the school year

A goal-setting formula can assist managers and employees in developing goals that satisfy the specific and time-framed criteria. The first component is an action statement that includes a specific outcome that should be expressed in numbers, whenever possible (as the first three goals demonstrate). When the outcome cannot be expressed using numbers, then satisfactory completion of an activity is the next best way to ensure the desired outcome is specific (as in the fourth goal statement). Commitment to an outcome specific enough to provide focus and feedback, however, is not the only requirement for a goal to be effective.

Second, goals that are specific make it possible to track progress toward the goal. This information about progress toward a goal is called feedback. When there has been steady or significant progress toward the goal, feedback can be a source of positive reinforcement, increasing motivation to continue toward the goal. For example, with the general goal statement of "quality athletic opportunities for youth participants," it would be difficult to know how much progress the addition of any particular program actually represents.

Conversely, where progress has been less positive, feedback can serve as a warning, indicating that either greater effort or a different approach is needed if the goal is going to be achieved. Table 4.1 shows a formula for expressing goals in the most specific terms possible.

Meaningful enough to motivate

Earlier, we noted that significant progress toward the vision of athletics as a part of the curriculum throughout public schools gained momentum when educators realized that interscholastic sport programs are an effective way to keep students in school and to increase graduation rates. With this realization, the goal of establishing athletic programs in the schools became meaningful to educators. Because they viewed this goal as consistent with their own goal of educating students, they became motivated to accept this goal and to join the effort to achieve it.

110

When the people involved view a goal as a means for satisfying their own needs and for achieving their own goals, we say the goal is meaningful for them. When the goal is meaningful enough to motivate, performance improves. More recently, educators recognized the importance of making goals meaningful by linking performance in the classroom to eligibility to play high school sports. The "no pass/no play" policies that have become common in recent years are an effort to make the goal of acceptable classroom performance more meaningful to student-athletes. With "no pass/no play," educators attempt to make the goal of passing grades in all courses more meaningful by making this goal a requirement for participation in interscholastic sports, a goal they know is already meaningful to student-athletes.

However, some schools, programs, and coaches have seen the need to take other specific measures to assure that their players recognize and understand the importance of the link between athletic participation and education. Consider the cases of the football program at Calvin Coolidge Senior High School in Washington, DC, and the boys' basketball program at Medora (Indiana) High School.

At Coolidge, the head football coach is Natalie Randolph, a science teacher at the school. Randolph was a track student-athlete at the University of Virginia and also played six seasons with the D.C. Divas of the Independent Women's Football League (see Chapter 3). Randolph is one of the very few women in the U.S. to serve as head coach for a high-school football program, and was hired to the post over 15 male applicants (two of whom were former NFL players), because, as noted by *New York Times* writer Juliet Macur, "she emphasized one thing [they] did not: helping the players in the classroom." Still, the players were skeptical. Said one junior fullback/linebacker:

> When we heard that Ms. Randolph was the new coach, a lot of us thought it was a joke. I was like, "Ms. Randolph? The science teacher here? No way." She doesn't look like a stereotypical coach who's big, masculine and who yells [Randolph is 5′ 5″, 130 pounds, and is described as a tough but quiet leader]. But she knew what she was talking about.

(2010, p. D6)

At Medora, the head boys' basketball coach is Marty Young, whose name was rather significant as when named head coach at age 23 in 2009 he was the youngest head coach in the state. Indiana is often portrayed as the spiritual fount for boys' high school basketball, given the mythic trappings put forth in the film "Hoosiers" (a fictionalized account of a small-town team's path to the state title, based loosely on the actual 1954 Milan High School championship), and the fact that for many years the state's high school association operated an open boys post-season tournament, meaning that schools of all sizes were pitted against each other based on solely geographic proximity without consideration

111

of institutional enrollment. While Medora (population 500), located 65 miles west of Milan and midway between Indianapolis and Louisville, Kentucky, does have one championship banner – from 1949 – it is now the fifth-smallest school in the state (with a senior class of 16) and hasn't had a winning team in decades. One town resident, the mother of one of the team's players, described post-game parties at a local pizza restaurant (which has since closed). "It used to be such a big deal," she recounted. "Basketball is what you lived for." The town is dying because local factories and feed mills have closed. "There ain't much to do in this small town," surmised Wes Ray, a member of the team (Branch, 2009, p. B10).

For goals to improve performance, the goals must not only reflect the goals of the organization, but also must meet the needs of the individuals and groups involved in attaining the goals. In the case of Coolidge High, the year before Randolph was hired the team had a record of 6–4, but the academic performance of the players was not acceptable, according to school administrators. Only 36 percent of all Coolidge students met reading competency standards, and 43 met the math standard. In addition, school attendance is a problem, as are disciplinary issues and teen pregnancy. As a result, football players are required to attend after-school study halls where they complete homework, receiving tutoring, or prepare for upcoming standardized tests such as the SAT. Randolph requires each player to have his teachers fill out a weekly behavior and progress report. Players who fail to submit these reports miss practice and game playing time (Macur, 2010).

At Medora, players are subject to the problems endemic to poor, rural areas, which challenges their ability to attend school and participate in basketball. "You've got kids who struggle with clothes or coats or shoes," said Medora assistant coach and AD Dennis Pace, "yet their parents always have cigarettes or beer or satellite TVs." School principle Brad McCammon (who has a picture of basketball great Larry Bird, a celebrated small-town Indiana product, on the wall in his office – "it shows a kid can do anything if you have that desire," said McCammon of the picture) noted that two-thirds of the school's students qualify for subsidized lunches and ten percent of the students had drug problems. Of the impact these factors had on his teammates, one Medora player said: "I don't think they're used to people expecting something out of them" (Branch, 2009, p. B10). So the athletic programs at both Coolidge and Medora became meaningful to educators since these programs are recognized as an important means of support for their own goals of educating all students. Educators hope that the goal of participating in interscholastic sports will be meaningful enough to motivate students to put in the effort required to stay engaged in school.

Accepted by the participants

It has been assumed that for goals to improve performance, a sport organization had to allow its employees and stakeholders to participate in goal setting. This kind of participative goal setting was viewed as a problem by managers who felt there wasn't enough time available to get these groups involved, and that by involving these groups management would be giving up control of the process. Research, however, has revealed that goal setting does not have to be participative to be effective. Having a goal that is accepted by stakeholders is more important than whether or not they participate in the setting of it. The acceptance of the goal, not the degree of participation, is the key to whether the goal will result in improved performance. Stakeholders are willing to pursue goals set for them by others as long as they find them acceptable.

The question is, therefore, when are goals likely to be accepted? The answer is much like the question of a goal's meaning: a goal is likely to be accepted when achieving them also allows stakeholders to achieve their own goals. In the case of Coolidge football and submitting the weekly academic reports, when Randolph asked one player for his, he rolled his eyes and stormed out of the room. Others brought in good reports; others received poor marks for disrupting class, failure to submit assignments, or forgetting to bring to class simple items such as a pen. At Medora, head coach Young works his players hard in practice, and also jumps into drills to demonstrate proper technique. Most work hard and are eager to improve, but one player became overly aggressive and shouted at Young. The coach kicked the player out of practice, and the player took off his jersey and threw it to the ground as he left. After practice, several other players stayed late for extra work, then asked Young if he had any extra food in his office. Young tossed them his keys and they lit out down the hall on the hunt (Branch, 2009; Macur, 2010).

The goals in question in these cases would be accepted by administrators as they emphasized preparedness for academics and for life beyond athletics; for student-athletes, it presents a clear guideline on why academic work and the appropriate habits and behavior are important and what levels they must achieve to be eligible to compete. For parents and community members, the goal will be accepted because it shows that the school has made educating students the top priority.

Realistic yet challenging

There is another consideration, however, that affects the extent to which a goal will be accepted by stakeholders. Academic and behavioral standard rules reflect the efforts of educators to define a goal for student-athletes that is realistic. These standards represent for some students a definite increase in performance, but to a level that is realistic in terms of attainment. Some critics of such policies suggest that students might be capable of higher performance than coaches are setting, or that performance outside of team activities should have no bearing on how playing time is meted out. However, classic research in this area of management shows that difficult goals result in greater improvements in performance than goals that are perceived as easy to attain (Stedry and Kay, 1964). People work harder to achieve challenging goals and are inspired to rise to a challenge, as long as that challenge is meaningful and realistic. There has been concern that some students would view the standards set in these areas as unattainable and unrealistic. Indeed, goals that are viewed as too challenging can actually result in diminished effort and lower performance because the group or individual may simply withdraw effort and not perform even to previous levels. Performance increases as goal difficulty increases. The higher the goal, the higher the performance, but only up to a point. Beyond a certain point that varies depending on the task to be performed and the people performing it, as goal difficulty continues to increase, performance actually declines. The concern is that these students may actually work less hard at meeting these goals, thinking, "I'll never achieve the goal, so why even try?"

The key is to define goals in such a way that they are challenging, but not too challenging, and for school officials and coaches to define goals that are both challenging enough to improve performance and realistic enough for the group or individual to feel the goal is attainable. "Some of them will curse and hem and haw and try to make you cry, but what they really want is structure," noted Coach Randolph. "They want to be told what to do. Otherwise they'll do nothing" (Macur, 2010, p. D6). At Medora, Coach Young worked his connections to get a promising senior tryouts with several college coaches, but when the time came, the player was a no-show. The player now works at a local logging mill. "It's a struggle when they're given a chance and they don't take it," said Young, who was also thinking about his long-term viability as coach at Medora. But Young's college coach felt Young understood the importance of his role at Medora: "He recognizes that there is more to it than how many games he wins" (Branch, 2009, p. B10). This final example shows that coaches and officials can also struggle with the elements of realistic yet challenging goals.

Time-framed

The final criterion of an effective goal is that it must have a time component – more specifically, a deadline. Deadlines are one of the most powerful and effective means available to sport managers for ensuring performance. Even goals that are specific, meaningful, accepted, and realistic yet challenging, if they are without a time frame these goals are at risk of never being met. In the case of academic performance at Coolidge, the issue in terms of time is at what point is performance assessed. Since the reports are weekly, players and coaches can act on timely data and make decisions about practice and game playing time each week. If the reports were collected less frequently, let's say every two weeks or every month, some students might let their performance slide if they knew that their reports weren't due for another several weeks. More regular deadlines prove to be more effective in enabling students to meet the goal of academic and behavioral performance.

At Coolidge, most players see the impact of the system. One player who received an inquiry letter from Yale University (and who later matriculated at Morehouse College in Atlanta) said: "What I like most about Coach Randolph is that she's more focused on getting us in to school." It also seems that team performance has also benefitted. In 2010, the team went 4–6 and qualified for the city playoffs. In 2011, the Coolidge Colts went 8–2 and went on to play in the Turkey Bowl, the city football championship, losing to rival Dunbar, 33–21, while the team GPA rose to 3.0. And Randolph benefitted from the goals set as well, signing a deal to serve as a spokesperson for Crons, a Pittsburgh-based uniform and apparel manufacturer. CEO and founder Pat Cavanaugh explained the arrangement: "We were drawn to her because of her commitment to teach life lessons and help kids get into college … She's in a challenging situation and she's got a great opportunity to make a real impact" (Smith, 2010, p. 9).

While showing a slight improvement, the Medora Hornets boys' hoop team continued to struggle. In 2011–2012, the team went 3–18 (2–6 in conference), with wins over Lighthouse Christian Academy, Martinsville Tabernacle, and Washington Catholic. "I have friends who say, 'Why do this? They keep losing,'" said one player. "I say I grew up playing basketball … I'm going to finish it out" (Branch, 2009, p. B10; Macur, 2010, p. D6; Hruby, 2011). In summary, just having goals is not necessarily sufficient to improve performance. For goals to be effective, they must be specific enough for focus and feedback, meaningful enough to be accepted, and also realistic, challenging, and time-framed.

WHY GOALS IMPROVE PERFORMANCE

A reasonable question at this point is why S.M.A.R.T. goals do lead to consistently higher levels of motivation and performance. There are several reasons, as shown in Box 4.2.

BOX 4.2 THE BENEFITS OF S.M.A.R.T. GOALS

- Blueprint for performance
- A basis for feedback
- Focuses attention on the right agenda
- A basis for cooperation and teamwork
- Criteria for decisions

Let's consider the issue of religion in the management of school and youth sport. As we learned above, private institutions were the leaders in creating and maintaining school-based athletic programs, and many (including SSM) were founded with affiliations to religious organizations. Today, schools affiliated with the Catholic Church and those connected to evangelical Christian churches produce some of the most successful athletic teams and programs in the country. Quite possibly you attended such a parochial school, and are familiar with an institutional educational philosophy that advocated adherence to a set of clearly stated religious principles.

But public schools, those organized, operated, and funded by local municipalities with additional funding from state and federal sources, are barred from any such endorsement of or connection with private religious organizations. However, public schools are usually comprised of students from a specific prescribed geographic area, which are often inhabited by a fairly homogenous population in terms of demographic profile (race, ethnicity, income, religious affiliation).

Such is the case with Fordson High School, a public secondary school (grades 9 through 12) located in Dearborn, Michigan. More than 90 percent of the approximately 2,400 students at Fordson are Muslim. Dearborn is a city of 98,000, where a third of the population is of Arabic descent, while Michigan is home to one of the largest concentration of Muslims in the U.S. (Longman, 2011b). So it is not surprising that public school policies are influenced by the religious practices of its students. In 2011, pre-season football practices coincided with Ramadan, the Islamic holy month of fasting, during which adherents refrain from drinking and eating during daylight hours, so Fordson High moved its double-sessions to late at night, from 11 p.m. to 4 a.m. This allowed players to eat a light meal and drink liquids at sunset and practice in the cooler nighttime hours. "Honestly, it's more of a safety issue than a religious issue," commented head coach Fouad Zaban, who also played at the school, a state football power. "If kids were going to fast, and the majority are, it was much safer not to be outside in the daylight in 90-degree weather for hours each day." A third of the players at nearby Dearborn High School also fast during Ramadan, so practices there are held between 6 and 11 p.m. (Longman, 2011b, p. B13).

Although this approach to practice as described by Coach Zaban makes sense on the basis of player health and safety, some at Fordson are still wary of the publicity the move generates, since the city, according to *New York Times* writer Jere Longman, has sometimes been "a flashpoint for anti-Muslim sentiment since the terrorist attacks of September 11, 2001" (Longman, 2011b, p. B17). Some misinformed politicians across the country erroneously state that the city was being run under Shariah Islamic law. Fordson principle Youssef Mosallam responded this way: "Dearborn is no different from any little big city in the United States. Kids have the same dreams and ambitions as any other kids. They want an education, and a lot of them want to play football" (Longman, 2011b, p. B17). The Fordson

Tractors (the nickname a nod to the region's automobile assembly heritage) finished the 2011 season with a record of 5–4 and failed to qualify for post-season play.

But in other regions of the country, stakeholder, school, and athletic management groups are less willing to accommodate or to accept into their associations schools that demonstrate such organizational differences based on religious affiliation. Recently, the 220-member Texas Association of Private and Parochial Schools (TAPPS) had to deal with two issues relating to membership and institutional goals and objectives. TAPPS is a state association founded in the 1970s to coordinate athletic competitions among private Christian schools. In some states, private and public schools compete in combined state associations, while in other states and regions separate associations govern athletic management and competitions. In 2012, TAPPS had scheduled a state semi-final Class 2A boys' basketball playoff game on a Friday evening between Robert M. Beren Academy, a Modern Orthodox Jewish K-12 school located in Houston, and the Covenant School, a K-12 Christian school located in Dallas. Since the game time conflicted with observance of the Jewish Sabbath, or Shabbat (during which adherents must rest and refrain from labor from sundown Fridays to sundown Saturdays as a homage to God who, according to Biblical accounts, rested for a day after six days of labor completing Creation), Beren officials appealed to TAPPS to change the start time. TAPPS refused, citing the rules set in its organizational bylaws. Lawyers for several Beren players filed a complaint and an application for a temporary restraining order against TAPPS in U.S. District Court. The complaint stated that the players were "being put to the choice of violating their own religious beliefs ... or forfeiting the opportunity to participate in the state basketball championship tournament," and that TAPPS discriminated against the players by refusing to reschedule the game (Pilon, 2012, p. B10).

Another recent governance issue for TAPPS involved the membership application of Iman Academy SW, an Islamic school of 500 students located in Houston. Iman sought membership to TAPPS in 2010, but was denied admission to the organization after the school received a questionnaire that contained, in the words of school principle Cindy Steffens, "loaded and provocative" questions, including the following: "It is our understanding that the Koran tells you not to mix with (and even eliminate) the infidels. Christians and Jews fall into that category. Why then are you interested in joining an organization whose membership is in disagreement with your beliefs?" Steffens said the school only sought the chance to compete against other private schools, and nearly considered withdrawing the application (as two other Islamic schools had previously). Steffens also reported that one TAPPS board member told her: "I know not all Muslims are terrorists, but all terrorists are Muslims." "We don't want to change your children," responded Steffens. "Our children are not different. They are Americans. We want to be inclusive and to play ball and compete." A spokesman for Texas state

Senator Rodney Ellis (D-Houston) said the senator considered potential legislation that would help prevent situations like what happened with the Jewish and Islamic schools. Ibrahim Hooper of the Council on American–Islamic Relations, a Chicago-based non-profit group focused on civil rights and discrimination issues involving Muslims, called for the association to change its policies, asking: "Is there no law from discriminating based on faith?" Hooper said his group will revisit possible legal action (Mulvaney, 2012, p. 1).

So it is important to consider how goals can be used to address the issues of inclusiveness and membership needs for an organization such as TAPPS, which according to its bylaws cites that the purposes of the athletic program for the participant schools are

> to assist, advise, and aid the private and parochial schools in organizing and conducting interschool athletics; to devise and prepare eligibility rules that will equalize and stimulate wholesome competition between schools of similar size, and reinforce the curriculum; to regulate competition so that students, schools, and their fans can secure the greatest educational, social, recreational, and aesthetic benefits from the contests; and to reinforce the concept to all participant schools that athletics is an integral part of the educational program.
>
> ("Section 130," 2011, p. 1)

We've already discussed some of the powerful effects of S.M.A.R.T. goals. They provide the kind of focus that channels a sport organization's energies and efforts, and they make possible the kind of feedback needs for motivation and performance adjustments. There are other significant contributions that goals can make as well to help an organization such as TAPPS.

Blueprint for performance

A blueprint ensures that everything a builder does is consistent with the design or plan. Goals serve the same purpose for sport organizations. At every level of an organization's membership, including individual schools and their related stakeholder groups, the goal to eliminate organizationally sanctioned discrimination provides the critical means for ensuring performance stays on course. Rather than just reacting to future problems such as these, a clearly defined goal to eliminate discriminatory practices will allow TAPPS to respond in ways that are consistent with its stated mission. Without such a goal in place, TAPPS' officials would just continue to "put out fires," respond to potential lawsuits, and lose sight of that organizational mission.

Basis for feedback

We know that specific goals make it possible to track progress made toward goal achievement. This information is called feedback, and is critical for improving performance. Feedback comes from a comparison of where you are at any given point in time and where you want to be. Feedback in a performance situation is essential for at least two reasons. First, feedback can be an important source of motivation. It can either reinforce performance where progress is positive or spur greater effort where it is not. If TAPPS monitors its bylaws and actions and discriminatory practices are still occurring, then it will know that greater effort is needed to combat the problem.

Second, knowing how much progress has been made allows sport organizations to make the adjustments and corrections necessary to move closer to the goal. Feedback alerts sport organizations not only where they stand relative to a goal, but also can help clarify what adjustments or corrections are necessary to achieve the goal. If TAPPS discerns that discriminatory practice is no longer occurring in the scheduling of post-season tournament games, but persists in its review of potential applicant schools, then managers know how they must adjust their educatory efforts.

A goal that is not specific makes collecting feedback on progress all but impossible, and if a sport organization doesn't know where it stands in terms of progress, managers and stakeholders cannot determine what adjustments and corrections are necessary to move closer to achieving the goal.

Focus attention on the right agenda

Each stakeholder brings his or her own needs to the activities within a school or youth sport organization. For some, it's the need to compete; for others, it's the need to bond with others; for still others it's a sense of self-worth related to security and achievement. The existence of a strongly shared set of clearly defined organizational goals helps to ensure that everyone's primary focus is on achieving these goals rather than on satisfying their own individual needs. Some managers and stakeholders involved with TAPPS may have been interested primarily in winning games, and were willing to overlook or ignore the signs that discriminatory practices were occurring. It is natural to want to set a goal to win in such a setting, but clear organizational goals focusing on addressing these concerns would ensure that all stakeholders understood the negative repercussions of such practices, and that the individual goal of winning championships would not interfere with the organizational goals TAPPS espouses.

Basis for cooperation and teamwork

Just as individuals have their own priorities, so too do the different departments within a sport organization. A well-defined set of overall goals helps ensure that activities and efforts throughout the sport organization do not conflict. Specific performance goals can also have the effect of leveling the members of a sport organization, of eliminating some of the problems that can occur between stakeholders. In 2010, when Iman Academy first applied for membership, TAPPS surveyed its membership on the question of accepting the Islamic school, asking members "whether it was in the best interest" of the association to admit Iman, and whether any schools would leave should Iman be allowed to join. Some members were uncomfortable with the tone of the inquiry. The head of school at TAPPS-member Keystone School, a non-denominational K-12 school in San Antonio, declined to participate, and told TAPPS of his concern with the tone of the survey. But 83 schools did respond (roughly 38 percent), with 63 reporting that TAPPS should not admit Iman, with ten schools stating they would leave if Iman were admitted (Pilon, 2012).

Successful sport organizations concentrate on how each individual can best contribute to reaching the goal. In the case of TAPPS and the data collected from their membership survey, member schools and board members can make the case that eliminating discriminatory practices will not conflict with the goal of competition and winning valued by players, coaches, and other stakeholder groups, but, based on the elimination of the negative results of discrimination (such as litigation), can actually reinforce these other stated goals.

Criteria for decisions

As we will examine in Chapter 5, the first step in the decision-making process is to define the goal or goals of the decision. One of the greatest benefits of clear goals is that they then become the standard for evaluating decision options. Without clearly defined goals, decisions become arbitrary and potentially inconsistent. Without a strongly shared sense of exactly what the organization is attempting to accomplish, decision makers are more likely to base their decisions on the demands of a particular situation or stakeholder group rather than the stated goals of the organization. After the Beren and Iman cases, a well-defined goal to address discriminatory practices will ensure that all decisions reflect the long-term direction of TAPPS rather than the immediate perceived needs and beliefs of the decision makers and stakeholders.

TAPPS' initial refusal to reschedule the Beren–Covenant game garnered national scrutiny, including criticism of TAPPS by Houston mayor Annise Parker and former Houston Rockets and New York Knicks coach Stan Van Gundy. Rabbi Rick Jacobs of the Union for Reform Judaism, a New York-based organization that offers programs, information, and networking opportunities to nearly 900 member congregations across North America, wrote to TAPPS, noting that "asking the Beren Academy team to choose between observing their faith and participating in a game which they have rightfully qualified for sends the message that TAPPS values the religious convictions of Beren Academy less than other member schools" ("URJ encourages," 2012, p. 1). The day before the scheduled game, TAPPS' director Edd Burleson admitted he had received "hundreds of emails" referring to the issue, and announced that due to "legal concerns" the start time would be moved to 2 p.m., and that the final tip-off would be slated for 8 p.m. Saturday. "In this particular case [TAPPS] felt that it was in our best interest not to fight and delay the tournament," said Burleson (Pilon, 2012, p. B9).

Beren officials publicly thanked TAPPS "for ultimately making the right decision," and the team won the semi-final game over Covenant, 58–46. In the Class 2A state final versus Abilene Christian School, Beren closed a 12-point deficit to two in the final minute, but ultimately lost 46–42. Said one Beren player: "I'm happy we got the chance and that I was able to stay true to myself and my beliefs. I'm happy TAPPS gave us the chance. It was a tough loss, but Abilene Christian was a heck of a team" (Jennings, 2012, p. 1; Pilon, 2012, p. B10).

In the case of Iman Academy, Keystone School considered leaving TAPPS over the issue, but head of school Brian Yaeger said it would remain a member "for the time being. We feel it is important to try and effect change in the situation through positive action within TAPPS." Iman Academy maintains its athletics programs by arranging games with local schools, with some of its students opting to play in local city-based leagues. "We're trying to be inclusive," said head of school Steffens (Pilon, 2012, p. B10).

PROBLEMS WITH GOALS

While a system of goals can certainly benefit organizational performance, some problems associated with goal-based management can emerge. One recent example of this phenomenon is in relation to a recent action taken by Pop Warner Little Scholars, Inc., a non-profit organization headquartered in Langhorne, Pennsylvania, that coordinates youth football, cheerleading, and dance programs for male and female participants in 42 states and several countries around the world. As noted above, national youth league organizations such as Pop Warner (the organization is named for the famed early twentieth-century college football coach who led programs at Stanford University and the Carlisle Indian Industrial Training School – alma mater of football and Olympic great Jim Thorpe) focus administrative efforts on promoting participation in a particular sport among children. As noted above, Pop Warner serves approximately 425,000 children aged five through 16 years old

(240,000 of whom play football), and is the self-described largest youth football, cheer, and dance program in the world ("About Pop Warner," 2012).

Recent national concerns about the prevalence and debilitating impact of head injuries has impacted the sport of football at all levels (so much so that the video game *Madden NFL 12* was programmed so that any virtual player sustaining a concussion would not be able to continue in a game). Combined with recent research at the high school level showing that more than half of all sport concussions occur in football, Pop Warner acted to dictate to member programs that contact be limited during practices beginning in the 2012 season. The move was not without precedent – the year before the Ivy League, an NCAA Division I Football Championship Subdivision conference acted to limit the number of full-pad/contact practices for similar reasons (Conaboy, 2011; "Ivy League," 2011; Schwarz, 2011).

Pop Warner posted on its website that "no full speed head-on blocking or tackling drills in which the players line up more than 3 yards apart" would be permitted, although "having two linemen in stances immediately across the line of scrimmage from each other and having full-speed drills where the players approach each other at an angle, but not straight ahead in to each other" was permissible. "However, there should be no intentional head-to-head contact!" the site warned. In addition, the site decreed that "the amount of contact at each practice will be reduced to a maximum of 1/3 of practice time [either 40 minutes total of each practice or 1/3 of total weekly practice time]," although the definition provided was not clearly explained ("Pop Warner," 2012, p. 1).

"The science shows that this should be done," said Dr. Julian Bailes, chairman of the Pop Warner medical advisory board and co-director of the NorthShore Neurological Institute in Illinois. "We think right off the bat that with this change we can eliminate 60-plus percent of the brain impacts or concussions." "This is absolutely a step in the right direction," said Chris Nowinski, a former football player at Harvard University (and WWE professional wrestler) and the executive director of the Sports Legacy Institute, affiliated with the Boston University School of Medicine, which seeks to advance the study, treatment, and prevention of brain trauma in athletes. "Limiting contact during practice is the single easiest way to reduce the risk of concussions and sub-concussive injuries" (O'Connor, 2012, p. 1).

Four major hurdles must be cleared to achieve the improved performance that goals can bring. In reviewing the issue of seeking to curtail head injuries in youth football, we can see how each of the problems has the potential to hinder the development of an effective goal-based management system. The potential problems with defining goals in sport organizations are summarized in Box 4.3:

- **Measurability**: in some areas performance results are difficult to quantify or measure.
- **Stress**: goals that are too demanding can result in stress and performance problems over the long term.
- **Too narrow a focus**: some goals are so concentrated in their focus that they could cause unwanted results.
- **Too many goals**: when sport organizations head in too many different directions, performance loses focus.

Measurability

In the case of head injuries in youth football, *New York Times* writer Anahad O'Connor wrote that "research has shown that the damage from concussions can be cumulative, and that the brains of younger athletes may be particularly susceptible" (2012, p. 1). We discussed earlier the importance of goals being specific enough for focus and feedback and emphasized the importance of defining goals in such a way that it becomes possible to measure progress toward the goal. However, for some types of performance, it can be extremely difficult to define goals that are specific enough to be measurable. In 2010, in response to pressures from outside the organization, Pop Warner instituted a rule two years ago that only "medical experts," not coaches or parents, could make return-to-play decisions for concussed athletes. Pop Warner acted to initiate the limited contact rules in response to a study of second-grade football players published in February 2012 – which used data from sensors installed in helmets – that showed that the average player sustained more than 100 head impacts over a period of ten practices and five games. "Though most of those hits were moderate," wrote O'Connor of the *New York Times*, "some exceeded a force equivalent to a big hit in college football" (2012, p. 1).

In response to both pressure and research data, Pop Warner is now mandating that only "medical experts" be available to make decisions on whether players can return to play. Otherwise, coaches and others throughout the organization will interpret how to perform their duties based on their own understanding of what constitutes a head injury. This can result in inconsistency and sometimes conflict throughout a youth football organization. Dr. Matt Grady, a pediatric sport medicine specialist at the Children's Hospital of Philadelphia, said the new rules, while a good start, did not go far enough, and that the emphasis in football for players who have not yet reached high school should be on developing skill and technique, not learning how to tackle. But Jon Butler, the executive director of Pop Warner, said that while the organization's officials wanted to reduce head-to-head collisions, they stopped short of more drastic measures "because there has to be some full-speed contact in practice so players are prepared for it when they get into a game" (O'Connor, 2012, p. 1). Otherwise, the likelihood of additional injuries becomes magnified.

So the issue of measurability in terms of head injury prevention comes back to individual coaches, who must now not only manage the traditional elements of conditioning, skills mastery, and game strategy, but must also limit the amount of measurable "contact" that can be incorporated into each team activity. Mark Mueller, a Pop Warner coach in Hoffman Estates, a suburb of Chicago, said the rules would affect coaches more than players, forcing them to re-evaluate some of their time-honored drills, such as "bull in the ring," where teammates encircle an individual player and repeatedly rush him one at a time. The drill is intended to teach young players how to recognize where a block is coming from. "But most of the time the kids in these drills are just getting knocked around like a pinball," said Mueller.

> None of us are doctors, so when you're having the medical advisory board of Pop Warner saying these are some things you have to think about in the long term, most coaches are going to think about whether these things are good and safe.
>
> (O'Connor, 2012, p. 1)

But just how good and safe becomes an issue of measurability.

Stress

Earlier in the chapter we emphasized the importance of defining goals so they are realistic but sufficiently challenging to raise motivation and performance. We also cautioned that unrealistic, overly challenging goals can actually discourage those involved, possibly resulting in a decrease in motivation and performance. Another problem with goals that are too challenging, however, is the problem of stress. Some goals are so challenging that they place a high level of pressure on groups and individuals to perform. Over time, these kinds of very demanding goals can result in fatigue and burnout rather than improved performance. They can also cause individuals or groups under pressure to make compromises or cut corners to reach these goals. Sport managers working with youth have a special responsibility not to encourage goals that cause performance-sapping stress.

Stress also impacts those who manage these youth programs, often burdening them with duties and responsibilities for which they are not qualified to handle. Dr. Bailes reported that Pop Warner was open to additional safety measures, like banning linemen from getting set in a three-point stance, because it results in head-to-head collisions (O'Connor, 2012; Rohan, 2012). Such a move would alter considerably how a coach might teach certain game techniques (and could contribute to other types of injuries), further adding to his or her teaching workload and adding to the level of stress each might feel in terms of creating both a safe learning environment and a successful team. To avoid such potential added stress, Bailes (whose son plays football) said the league would wait until the 2012 season was over, and then review how the new rules influenced players and coaches. "I think when you make a change like this, you want to study it," he said. "And we'll ask: 'Will this be enough? Do we need to work further to take the head out of the game?'" (O'Connor, 2012, p. 1).

Too narrow a focus

An effective goal statement provides direction and focus. But when this focus is too limited, it could cause unwanted results. A goal with too narrow a focus might actually hinder Pop Warner coaches from adequately teaching the skills necessary for playing football. For example, Grady of Children's Hospital went so far as to suggest that

> playing tackle football at 10 years old doesn't translate to being a pro athlete. I think the ability to catch and run and throw translates to being a pro athlete. Players should develop these skills, and then we can add in the collisions later.
>
> (O'Connor, 2012, p. 1)

What is problematic about this statement is that it makes two false assumptions: first, that football can be taught in a realistic manner without physical contact; and second, that the goal of Pop Warner programs is to develop professional athletes. If the goal is to make Pop Warner 100 percent safe without the risk of any physical injury, the organization will fail to meet this charge and cease to exist as a football organization. Injuries will occur in all school and youth sport organizations. The key in managing injuries is a realistic approach toward prevention and treatment.

Too many goals

There are potential conflicts in managing school and youth sports effectively. Researchers have commented that organizational effectiveness is difficult to understand because it is inherently paradoxical. To be effective, an organization must possess attributes that are called competing values, such as control and flexibility, and internal and external focus (Quinn and Rohrbaugh, 1983). Jon Butler, the executive director of Pop Warner, said that research would continue to drive the organization's rules changes as it tries to limit concussions. Dr. Bailes added this perspective:

> The NFL's bore the brunt of this ... but how do we know that it's not the adolescent exposure? How do we know it's not the youth exposure? How do we know it's not the college exposure? Hopefully, this will be looked back upon as a common-sense approach.

Stefan Duma, the head of the biomedical engineering department at Virginia Polytechnic University, oversaw the research published recently that prompted Pop Warner to issue its rules changes. Of any future actions, Duma stated that

> there has to be scientific data that makes that decision. It can't be a group of people telling stories of how they used to play football. You've got to actually quantify what drills are causing what level head impact, and target those, and minimize those.

(Rohan, 2012, p. 1)

Situations like this remind us that sport managers must craft a vision that reflects a shared sense of direction to achieve the cooperation and commitment necessary for his or her athletic program to be successful. These examples of problems with goals in school and youth sports provide a clear message: achieving organizational performance requires the development of a comprehensive network of effective and appropriate goals to focus and energize the efforts of the sport organization. We have emphasized that goals must be specific enough to provide focus, but the challenge for sport managers is to develop goal statements that do not limit the focus to the point where unwanted outcomes result.

GUIDELINES FOR CREATING A GOAL-BASED ORGANIZATION

Let's consider how stakeholders and athletic administrators are addressing the growing challenge of how to incorporate the growing number of home-schooled participants into school-based sport programs. This may have been an issue on teams at schools in your hometown, or maybe you or a friend were a home-schooled student who sought the opportunity to play on a school-based team. NFL "quarterback" Tim Tebow sought such an opportunity growing up in a suburb of Jacksonville, Florida, and some believe Tebow's fame has fueled the focus on the issue. "People joke," says Matthew Gillespie, assistant executive director of the Tennessee Secondary School Athletic Association, "but everybody thinks they have a Tim Tebow in the backyard waiting to be found. Who's to say?" (Longman, 2012, p. B12). Twenty-five states now allow the rising number of home-schooled students to play sports at public schools with varying restrictions, according to the

Virginia-based Home School Legal Defense Association (HSLDA), a self-described "non-profit advocacy organization established to defend and advance the constitutional right of parents to direct the education of their children and to protect family freedoms". That same year, three other states (Alabama, Mississippi, Tennessee) also deliberated on whether to provide wider access to athletics for home-schoolers ("About HSLDA," 2011, p. 1). In 2012, senators in the Virginia legislature opted to kill a proposed measure (known as the "Tebow Bill") that had passed the state's Republican-controlled House of Delegates earlier that year. Patrick Foss, a top teenage soccer player from Virginia, wanted to try out as a kicker on the football team at Freedom High School in South Riding, his local public high school, but since he is home-schooled he was ineligible. "My parents pay the same exact taxes as my next-door neighbor who plays varsity sports," he said. "I just want to be part of the community. You shouldn't have to pick between athletics and academics" (Longman, 2012, p. A1). Virginia state officials say that nearly 32,000 children are home-schooled in the state, but the HSLDA claims there are twice that number (Kumar, 2012a).

Whether the issue for home-schooled students and their desire to compete is based on real concerns over academic standards, and the actual taxes paid by the Foss family, are both subject to debate, there is undoubtedly concern and interest relating to this issue. The potential of goals to improve performance is clear, as are the challenges that must be met in setting organizational goals. Effective goals, however, are only part of the solution. To maximize the overall impact of goals on organizational performance and to create a truly goal-based sport organization requires following the four guidelines shown below. To address this challenge, an organization such as the Virginia High School League (VHSL), the state association responsible for administering public high school athletics in that state, can incorporate the following steps to create a goal-based organization to address the issue of providing athletic participation opportunities for as many as possible, and to meet its stated mission of promoting "education, leadership, sportsmanship, character, and citizenship for students by establishing and maintaining high standards for school activities and competitions" ("Mission statement," 2012, p. 1).

Network

The concept of a network of goals suggests that specific end results should be identified for every department, team, and individual in a sport organization, and the desired results should contribute to meeting the organization's larger goals. In other words, the individual, department, team, and overall organization goals should build on one another, with the attainment of each goal moving the sport organization closer to achieving its purpose.

New York Times writer Jere Longman noted that opponents of the Virginia "Tebow Bill" made several arguments against the proposed law: that playing varsity sports is a privilege surrendered when students opt out of the public school system; that home-schoolers might take roster spots from public school students; and that it would be extremely difficult to apply the same academic, attendance, and discipline requirements to home-schooled students as to those who are monitored daily in public schools. To maintain varsity eligibility, the VHSL requires that member school students take five courses in the current semester and must have passed five in the previous semester. Home-schooled students have no such academic standard (Longman, 2012). "Every parent of every child … has a choice," said Virginia state Senator Richard Saslaw (D-Fairfax), who opposed the bill. "They know what the ramifications are [if they choose to home school their child]" (Kumar, 2012b, p. 1).

To address this issue of concerns about academic eligibility, the VHSL and an organization such as the HSLDA could cooperate to create a network of goals. Box 4.4 provides an example of such a network, with specific goals for various levels of management.

BOX 4.4 A PORTION OF A NETWORK OF GOALS

HSLDA   Goal = Obtain full participation for home-schooled students in Virginia; create a review system that monitors home-schooled student performance similar to that of the VHSL

VHSL   Goal = Serve all eligible state participants; provide HSLDA with guidance and assistance to create and monitor such a system

Public school Goal = Serve all eligible district residents; cooperate with
administrators VHSL and HSLDA in the creation of the eligibility system

---

The first requirement of a network of goals, then, is that the network be comprehensive, that there be specific goals for every unit and every position in the organization, and that all the goals in the network point in the same direction.

Prioritize among specific goals

A network or total system of goals would be easier to carry out if only one goal were identified for the entire sport organization and if individuals and departments each pursued only that goal. In today's complex and dynamic environment, however, most youth and school sport organizations must pursue multiple goals. To deal with multiple goals in the case of home-schooled children and athletic competition in Virginia, opponents, including many Democratic state legislators and some local school boards and parent groups, argue that not only would home-schooled participants not be required to meet the same academic criteria as public school athletes, but also that home-schooled participants might take team slots from enrolled public school participants. In addition, Republican lawmakers were looking to promote the measure, while Democrats were seeking to defeat it, based on the political agendas of each faction (Kumar, 2012a), since Democrats tend to have stronger support from teacher and educationally aligned union groups, which did not support the bill.

Because of this conflict – where all parents want either to obtain or to protect participation opportunities for their children – the VHSL must learn to prioritize these and must determine which goal is first in terms of importance, which is second, and so on. Multiple goals make the job of managing sport organizations much more complicated. But they are often unavoidable, even in the case of a potential collaboration between the VHSL and the HSLDA, and managers need to prioritize them if the organization is to be successful.

Benchmarking: set goals from the outside in

Benchmarking is the process of researching other sport organizations' goals and setting goals that match those of the best-managed organizations. With benchmarking, the search is on for role models. For many sport organizations, benchmarking is a simple process, because a competitive sport product will always be measured against other organizations. For every contest, there is a basic measurement tool – the scoreboard. The fact that the scoreboard gives a precise measurement on an organization's effectiveness is clear. However, although the teams that win usually score the most points (or, in sports such as cross country, the fewest), the score does not provide examples of how to achieve that measure of success. Other measurements are needed.

In the case of Virginia's home-schooled athlete debate, the HSLDA reports that 16 states permit home-schooled students to play sports at public schools, while nine others leave the decision to localities or have no laws prohibiting it (Kumar, 2012b). For example, in Louisiana, home-schooled students have the ability to participate on a public school sports team, if the principal of the local school approves, while in Montana, the state Supreme Court ruled that school district policies that keep non-public students from participating in sport programs were reasonable, because "the district's interest in developing full academic potential in each student outweighed the students' right to play sports" ("State laws," 2011, p. 2). The stakeholders and decision makers in the Virginia case can review all such state statutes as a basis for their goal formulation.

Build in flexibility

Some critics charge that commitment to specific goals results in sport organizations that are too rigid to respond to changes in their particular environments. A focus on specific goals, according to this view, restricts the ability of organizations to be flexible enough to take advantage of unexpected opportunities or unanticipated changes in their environment.

It is difficult to argue against the importance of flexibility. Speed and flexibility, as you recall from Chapter 1, are among the key emerging performance standards. But it is also difficult to argue against the effectiveness of goals in improving organizational performance. The solution to this dilemma is not to eliminate specific goals, but to ensure that the goal system includes the ability to review and revise goals in response to significant changes as they occur.

This kind of flexibility is an important element in the Virginia debate. If one or all of the organizational goals outlined above are not met, then the program managers would need to have meaningful steps in place to rectify the behaviors. We will examine such potential steps as part of performance motivation in Chapter 8.

Flexibility is an essential performance standard for sport organizations competing in the changing environment. The key to flexibility is not to eliminate goals, but to develop a system in which goals are continually reviewed to ensure they make sense in terms of the changing environment. The practice of creating goal networks, prioritizing among multiple goals, setting goals from the outside in, and building flexibility into the system are all essential elements of an effective goal-based management system. If well implemented, such a system makes possible the reconciliation of issues between all Virginia stakeholder groups, athletic managers, and other goal-based sport organizations.

EPILOGUE: VISION AGAIN, BUT THIS TIME WITH SOCCER

Building on the success of its boys' ice hockey player development model, Shattuck-St. Mary's has added a similar soccer development program. And it has been almost as successful. In 2010, ESPN reported that the SSM soccer program produced more recipients of NCAA Division I grant-in-aid offers than any other school in the U.S. The soccer program is one of three in the country (along with the IMG Academies (Bradenton, Florida) and St. Stephen's Episcopal (Austin, Texas)), but, notes *ESPN Rise* writer Sheldon Shealer, while all three focus on elite athlete development, only SSM combines its athletic and academic preparation at one site (IMG players attend local schools, while St. Stephen's players compete for outside local club teams) (Shealer, 2010).

The SSM soccer program began in 2005 with 34 student-athletes, and now has more than 100. As with the ice hockey programs, the soccer system fields several teams for both boys and girls. Over the past three years SSM sent male players – including Gideon Asante from Ghana to Old Dominion University in Richmond, Virginia – to play at the following schools: Boston University, Bradley University, Butler University, the University of Dayton, Furman University, Gonzaga University, Northern Illinois University, Southern Methodist University, the University of Hartford, the University of North Carolina-Asheville, the United States Military Academy, the University of Wisconsin, and Western Washington University. In 2012, female players opted to attend Creighton University, Drexel University, Johns Hopkins University, Marquette University, South Dakota State University, St. Lawrence University, and the University of Wisconsin – Green Bay. The school's most prominent product is Teal Bunbury, who attended the University of Akron and as a sophomore was named Player of the Year by several organizations in 2009. Bunbury was the fourth overall selection in the 2010 MLS Super Draft and is a member of the U.S. National Team and MLS' Sporting Kansas City ("Bunbury," 2010; Shealer, 2010; Quarstad, 2012).

So is this move toward the identification and cultivation of elite prospects in a combined academic–athletic residential model ("the SSM Model") the future for soccer (as well as all other high school and youth sports)? Tim Carter, SSM's director of soccer, puts it this way: "I think anybody and everybody would like to have the environment we can create here. The question always is going to be, 'How do you pay for it?'" Shealer notes that the tuition costs at SSM are covered by "families who can afford it or receive aid" (boarding tuition for the 2011–2012 academic year was just under $40,000, day tuition about $14,000 less). Carter does concede that "pro soccer and everyone else involved" is looking to create a "better environment for training, better environment for going to school, and a better environment for growing and less time in a car driving to and from," some of which are also significant concerns in terms of demand on the time and energy of parents and other family members (Shealer, 2010, p. 1).

Ultimately Carter feels more programs following "the SSM Model" will emerge because of a desire to emphasize the importance of the program's educational component, where a school can create an environment where students "have dedicated time for the development of the soccer player while making sure the kid gets a high school education rather than blowing it off" (Shealer, 2010, p. 1). SSM head of school Nicholas Stoneman described the soccer program in simple terms: "We built our soccer program exactly the same way [as hockey], and now we have a young man who's ready to sign with the Premiership in England" (Joyce, 2008, p. 85).

And maybe Stoneman and the SSM Model is right, since it is also employed by the European soccer club power Barcelona, which also houses and educates prospective players at a facility known as "La Masia." About 200 boys are enrolled in Barcelona's youth academy, and about half live in club facilities. Claudio Reyna, a former U.S. national team captain and current technical director for U.S. Soccer, says this about the system: "At Barcelona, they are about educating players, and winning takes care of itself. I believe it makes an impact when players can develop in a calm and proper environment" (Longman, 2011a, p. B13). So it seems likely that we will see much more of the SSM Model not only in the U.S. but throughout the world.

As discussed above, the need to compete and to excel in every segment of the sport industries mandates that organizational vision consist of a clearly defined, fully developed network of goals. Much progress has been made in our understanding and implementation of goal-based systems, but significant challenges remain. It is in finding effective responses to these remaining challenges that sport managers will fulfill what Peter Drucker defines as management's "first responsibility": give others vision and the ability to perform.

It is clear to most that school and youth sport programs, including the competitions run by school and non-school-based organizations, are usually run by responsible adults. However, competing values, such as the desire to win, often complicate the sense of vision for school and youth sports organizations. In his memoir of growing up in multi-racial Trinidad in the early part of the twentieth century, C.L.R. James had this to say about the power of school-based sport:

> [In classes], we lied and cheated without any sense of shame. I know I did ... but when we stepped on to the cricket or [soccer] field, all was changed. We were a motley crew. The children of some white officials and white businessmen, middle-class blacks and mulattos, Chinese boys, some of whose parents still spoke broken English, Indian boys, some of whose parents could speak no English at all, and some poor black boys ... Yet rapidly we learned to obey the umpire's decision without question, no matter how irrational it was. We learned to play with the team, which meant subordinating your personal inclinations, and even interests, to the good of the whole. We kept a stiff upper lip in that we did not complain about ill-fortune. We did not denounce failures, but "Well-tried" or "Hard luck" came easily to our lips. We were generous to our opponents and congratulated them on victories, even when we knew they did not deserve it. We lived in two worlds.
>
> (1993, p. 25)

The power of youth and school sports to educate, to create bonds, and to instill behaviors is neither new nor extinct, and it is the task of all managers of these programs to provide opportunities to learn what James did.

SUMMARY

The first responsibility of management is to give others vision and the ability to perform. Vision can be established by a total network of goals. Goals must satisfy several criteria to ensure that they provide individuals with the kind of focus, direction, and understanding they need to perform well. The acronym "S.M.A.R.T." identifies the key criteria for effective goals. Each should be specific enough for focus, meaningful enough to be accepted, realistic yet challenging, and time-framed.

Goals that are "S.M.A.R.T." provide for consistency throughout the organization and a blueprint for effectiveness. They ensure that individuals focus on achieving the organization's goals rather than their own. Effective goals provide a basis for cooperation and teamwork, ensure that the efforts of different departments are coordinated, and provide decision makers with the criteria for generating and evaluating options. In certain areas, defining specific goals is more difficult. In addition, goals that are too challenging can cause stress and burnout for participants.

To achieve the full impact of effective goal-based systems, goals must first be woven into a system or network. First, goals are most effective when they are defined for every task and area of the organization and where they all work to move the organization toward achieving its purpose. Second, goals must be prioritized. Organizations must have complex, sometime competing goals, and care must be taken to establish priorities, identifying which goals are more important. Third, benchmarking, or setting goals from the outside in, compares the goals of other sport organizations and mirroring what they do to improve performance. Finally, building flexibility into the goals system is essential. Goals must be reviewed and revised to ensure that they are right for the sport organization and its changing environment.

MANAGEMENT EXERCISE: LAND OF THE FREE (EXCEPT FOR YOUTH SOCCER PLAYERS)

Aside from the recent efforts of SSM outlined above, most Americans have yet to fall in love with the so-called "beautiful game" of soccer (known as "football" in most of the rest of the world). It is, however, undoubtedly growing in popularity in the U.S. At the youth level, more than 650,000 boys and girls ages 7 through 18 participated on more than 50,000 teams sanctioned by the American Youth Soccer Organization (AYSO). At the high school level, while over a million boys play football and 438,000 girls play basketball, nearly 400,000 boys and 360,000 girls play soccer ("2010–11 high school," 2011; "History of AYSO," 2011).

But this growing interest and participation has yielded varying levels of success at the professional and international levels. The American women's national teams generally do quite well at international tournaments (losing to an underdog Japan squad in the 2011 FIFA Women's World Cup and winning the gold medal in the 2012 Summer Olympics), but U.S. women's professional soccer is nearly non-existent. The men's teams have been less successful. In the 2010 FIFA World Cup in South Africa, the Americans tied perennial power England in the group stage, but lost to Ghana in the next round, and the men's team failed to qualify for the 2012 Summer Olympics. Major League Soccer (the U.S. men's pro league) has fared better than the various women's circuits that come and go, and while there is avid fan support in locations such as Seattle and Portland (Oregon), MLS is nowhere near as popular as the so-called "Big Four" pro sport leagues (MLB, NBA, NFL, NHL) or NCAA Division I football and men's basketball. The reasons U.S. men's soccer lags at the international level are multiple: a richer tradition and history in other countries, the competition from other sports in the U.S., the access to watch games from superior pro leagues around the world reflects poorly on the level of play in MLS, and the low-scoring and less-physical nature of the sport.

While each factor above contributes to the failure to perform on the international stage, the United States Soccer Federation (USSF), the USOC-sanctioned national federation for the sport, believes it has found a way to address the issue of poor on-field performance. In 2012, the USSF decreed that players on its top-level boys' teams – known as Development Academy teams, a system initiated in 2007 – must participate in nearly year-round team activities and would not be allowed to play for their local high school teams. The move, not surprisingly, stirred debate, as supporters praised the move as a necessary step in improving play, while detractors called the move overzealous and misguided. Steve Enna, a high school player from Kansas who also plays club soccer for the local academy team, also disagreed with the move. "You look at LeBron James – he played for his high school team and went pro. Why do we have to give it up?" Many coaches agree. Said one: "We should be in the business of letting kids be kids. Not forcing them into thinking they're going to be playing for [England Premier League clubs] Arsenal or Manchester United two years from now." Another coach put it this way: "There's about 3,000 kids on these [Academy] teams across the country, but there's not 3,000 future professionals out there. There's not 300 of them. So some of these kids and their parents are going to be misled" (Borden, 2012, p. Y2).

Tony Lepore, the director of scouting for the Academy program (which as of 2012 consisted of 78 clubs nationally), claims that the USSF model, which features a ten-month season and an enhanced focus on out-of-competition training, was the only way to promote excellence, and that losing players for several months a year while they played for their high schools was detrimental for their development. And while players practice up to 260 hours a year for their Academy teams, "they're probably

134

[practicing] closer to 600 hours a year in Spain or Holland," claimed Lepore. "We're not surprised by the reaction," he added. "High school sports are a big part of the culture [in the U.S.]. But when it comes to elite soccer players and their development, this change is optimal." Alex Frankenfeld, an Academy player in Texas, made the switch and says it was the right move. "I have goals and aspirations that I want to achieve," but he no longer attends games at his high school. "I'd see parents and teachers and students," he noted, "and they'd keep saying to me, 'Alex, why aren't you out there?'" (Borden, 2012, p. Y2).

QUESTIONS FOR YOU TO CONSIDER

1   Write a goal statement that helps the USSF address the issue of banning Development Academy players from participating on their high school teams. Review the statement to see if it is "S.M.A.R.T."
2   Assess your USSF goal statement against the four common problems associated with goal setting.
3   Using each of the guidelines for creating effective goals, list the three activities that might be undertaken to ensure that the USSF goal will be achieved.
4   Explain how Tony Lepore could get parents and other stakeholders to understand and to support the USSF Development Academy limited participation policy.
5   Based on elements of "the SSM Model," make a case based on mission and goals that the USSF should create for its own residential athletic/academic system.

CHAPTER 5

DECISION MAKING AND THE HEALTH AND FITNESS INDUSTRY

INTRODUCTION

In this chapter, students are introduced to the health and fitness sport industry segment, which includes not only health and fitness clubs, but also several health- and fitness-related services and spin-off products. Health and fitness clubs and programs can be found in a variety of settings, ranging from commercial chain clubs and corporate fitness clubs to non-profit wellness programs. Within this setting, we examine the managerial challenge of decision making. Sport managers make hundreds of decisions every day, and their actions not only affect individuals, but ultimately shape the organization and influence its ability to fulfill its mission and meet its goals.

Check the stats

Purpose
To promote health, physical fitness, and lifelong wellness and to heighten awareness of the benefits of exercise and healthy living.

Stakeholders
Clubs, professional organizations, member clients, personal trainers, club employees, equipment suppliers, media licensees, corporate partners, retailers, home fitness enthusiasts, medical community, and federal, state, and local government.

Size and scope
More than 29,000 health clubs in the U.S. including commercial and non-profit clubs. Clubs are also based in hospitals, military bases, resorts, living communities, educational institutions, and businesses ("IHRSA," 2012). Total number of

136

U.S. health club members reached 51.4 million in the U.S. in 2011 and industry revenues exceeded $21 billion ("IHRSA," 2012). In 2010, there were approximately 133,500 clubs worldwide in over 80 countries which served over 128 million members and reporting over $71 billion in revenue ("IHRSA," 2011).

Governance

Federal, state, and local government as well as professional organizations and trade groups including the IHRSA, American College of Sports Medicine, National Strength and Conditioning Association, International Association of Fitness Professionals, Aerobics and Fitness Association of America, and the National Athletic Trainers' Association.

Inside look: work it out

People around the world are joining fitness clubs as the message of the value of a healthy lifestyle is becoming more apparent. There are a wide variety of reasons that people are flocking to health clubs in record numbers including a better understanding of the value of exercise on overall well-being, the need to combat unhealthful behaviors such as sitting for hours at a desk or computer, and the fact that health clubs have become much better at marketing and delivering a wide variety of appealing programming in a high-quality setting.

There have never been more choices and types of health and fitness clubs than there are today. Some basic no-frills work-out places are still going strong; however, the clubs that are becoming the most popular, such as 24 Hour Fitness, are those that offer a wide variety of programming, flexible member access, health and fitness expertise, and spacious facilities in multiple locations. 24 Hour Fitness, one of the largest health club chains, started as one small local club in the United States, and currently has over 400 clubs. 24 Hour Fitness has served as a sponsor to the U.S. Olympic teams, co-sponsored a professional bicycle team, and worked with *NBC* to develop the reality show, *The Biggest Loser*. The chain is on Facebook and Twitter and YouTube. 24 Hour Fitness sponsors blogs and fitness forums and encourages members to engage in fitness on "your own terms" (Straff, 2012).

With multiple locations in the U.S., and some that remain open all day (the name would imply that all would be open all the time, but this is not the case), members can work out almost anytime and anywhere. The facilities are generally spacious and feature everything from high-intensity exercise classes, to core sculpting, to dance classes, along with strength and cardio equipment plus expert trainers and personal coaches. Other services include weight loss programming and customized work-outs along with creative programming such as Hot Hula (Straff, 2012).

For those consumers seeking a different approach to fitness, Equinox clubs combine high-end facilities with comprehensive programming in a spa-like atmosphere. Members can take classes that are tied to the latest advancements in sport medicine and sport psychology-based research. Classes might focus on topics such as mental engagement, movement quality, and breathing work. Personal fitness, wellness, and rejuvenation programs are offered, and group classes are also highlighted (Straff, 2012).

For millions of women, Curves is their fitness answer. The women-only club features circuit training delivered through a strength and cardio work-out in a 30-minute format. There are also a wide variety of educational and motivational materials and classes targeted at women who might not ordinarily join a gym (Straff, 2012). Curves franchise owners often sell Curves branded equipment, apparel, and supplements as well.

One of the most innovative health club options in this industry segment is typified by Mike Boyle Strength & Conditioning in Woburn, Massachusetts. Elite athletes from around the world come to this cutting-edge facility voted as one of America's top ten gyms by *Men's Health* magazine (Shakeshaft, 2012). This is a place for hardcore athletes who wish to focus on enhancing athletic performance by engaging in activities customized to sport-specific skills (Shakeshaft, 2012). Speed-, strength-, and agility-based programs are customized to the particular athlete, and expert trainers are actively engaged with members.

The health and fitness industry is far reaching and made up of a wide variety of fitness options targeted at very specific market segments with a full spectrum of health and fitness needs and preferences. From the serious athlete to the casual club user, today's health and fitness industry offers a facility and a program for everyone.

THE HEALTH AND FITNESS INDUSTRY

As outlined below in Table 5.1, the IHRSA divides health and fitness clubs into three distinct segments: commercial clubs, not-for-profit clubs, and miscellaneous for-profit health and fitness enterprises ("IHRSA," 2012).

Table 5.1 Types of health and fitness clubs

Segment	Examples of segment membership
Commercial clubs	Equinox, Gold's Gym, Planet Fitness, 24 Hour Fitness
Not-for-profit clubs	YMCA, Jewish community center, university or college health club, city community center, military base fitness club, hospital or rehabilitation center-based club
Miscellaneous other for-profit clubs	Corporate fitness center, hotel health club, resorts, spas, country clubs

Commercial clubs make up the clear majority of all health and fitness clubs. They consist of investor- or member-owned businesses that may be either individually owned entities or part of a larger fitness club chain. Commercially owned clubs operate as for-profit businesses. They may take the form of a locally owned business, a branded franchise, or a chain of multiple facilities. They pay taxes and may not collect charitable donations to enhance their own financial resources.

Not-for-profit clubs make up the second largest segment and consist of clubs that are owned and operated by non-profit organizations such as churches, educational groups, municipal entities, and the military. These clubs do not pay taxes but may conduct fundraising programs for their own benefit.

In the opinion of many in the health and fitness club industry, the non-profit status enjoyed by these clubs results in an unfair competitive advantage ("YMCAs," 2000). For example, suppose the local YMCA, a non-profit organization, is planning to construct a new strength and conditioning room. The YMCA is able to raise money through fundraising programs to pay for the construction. They are able to keep their existing membership price at the current level because fundraising provides needed revenue for construction. The local commercial fitness club decides to renovate its fitness center to compete with the new facility at the YMCA. The same project is more expensive for the commercial club (they have no tax-free status and must pay taxes on new equipment and materials purchased). The commercial club must bear the cost of the construction or pass the cost on to members in the form of higher membership fees. Additionally, the commercial club will pay property taxes based on the valuation of the property and building, whereas the YMCA, as a non-profit organization, is exempt from property taxes. Fitness club owners argue that the non-profit status of their competitors makes it increasingly difficult for the commercial club to compete.

The third group of health and fitness clubs, miscellaneous for-profit health/fitness enterprises, is made up of clubs that operate as an amenity or complementary part of a business. However, some of these organizations, such as Pilates or yoga studios, operate as specialized stand-alone businesses. Other health and fitness clubs that fall into this category are hotel and motel fitness centers, cruise ship fitness centers, resort-based clubs, apartment complex or condominium fitness centers, retirement community health clubs, and corporate health clubs.

Traditionally health and fitness clubs have been thought of as places where members and guests gather to engage in exercise activities that promote the general health and well-being of the individual. Club-based exercise programs and activities may be formal and structured (e.g. yoga class, supervised weight training, or spinning classes) or informal and unstructured (e.g. open swim time, walking on a treadmill, or using a rowing machine). Health and fitness clubs have greatly expanded their programs and services in the last decade to include new activities such as wall climbing, Zumba classes, nutrition classes, defense training, and targeted weight loss work-outs. Clubs recognize that to stay competitive and retain members, they need to offer new services and products. They may include things such as child-care programs and spa services such as message or hydrotherapy. They must also offer a full line of personal fitness products including the latest technology-based gadget to track diet, heart rate, calories burned, etc. Clubs are also embracing fitness apps for the smart phone, personalized fitness prescriptions designed by a personal trainer, and high-level amenities such as healthy food dining areas, laundry service, and well-appointed locker rooms.

To retain and grow market share, some clubs have adopted a clear differentiation strategy in which they have identified a particular market segment that they target. They work to establish a clear brand that will set them apart from others in the marketplace. Perhaps the most well-known specialized health and fitness club brand in the industry is Gold's Gym, which originally built its reputation by catering exclusively to the serious bodybuilder. The original Gold's Gym in Venice, California, came to be known as the mecca of bodybuilding, where club members were intensely committed to building bigger and better bodies and to competing in bodybuilding contests (Hoffman, 1998). The member base of Gold's Gym, however, has broadened in the last several decades to include more mainstream athletes such as professional, college, amateur, and recreational athletes who have joined the club to improve their general conditioning, appearance, and sport performance (Hoffman, 1998). The Gold's Gym concept may have served as the inspiration for the establishment of other clubs that target serious athletes. These types of gyms and clubs usually offer a high-tech and high-touch approach to providing sport science-based fitness programs for highly competitive athletes.

Some clubs emphasize the concept of wellness and focus on the development and general well-being of the entire person. These types of clubs are often community based, and their membership consists of individuals who are members of a particular organization or group. For example, a university fitness or wellness center devises programs and services targeted not only to students and faculty, but staff, alumni, and administration as well. A hospital-, senior-center-, or retirement-community-based health and fitness club would necessarily provide programming that would focus on rehabilitation, general health, or prevention of sickness or injury. Such a program would have a wellness focus and may also seek to teach members new skills, to develop community spirit among members, and to actively engage participants in social settings. For some of these programs, the provision of an opportunity for members to stay active and build relationships with one another is an important component. It is through daily engagement with other members that program directors can keep individuals from becoming depressed or socially isolated.

The corporate fitness center or municipal employee wellness club would provide activities designed to appeal to employees and encourage employee participation. Employers see these clubs and services as an investment in their organizations, as they recognize that healthy employees are more productive, less likely to be absent from work, and less likely to make sickness- or injury-related insurance claims. The corporate health and fitness center also encourages employee social interaction, a sense of community, employee loyalty, and team building. These clubs may also sponsor health improvement initiatives such as weight control, stress reduction, or smoking cessation programs, thereby improving the general health of the workforce.

Although health and fitness clubs are the primary component of the health and fitness industry, there are several other spin-off or ancillary organizations that by extension must be considered within the scope of this segment, as outlined in Box 5.1 below. Professional service providers such as personal trainers and instructors or fitness gurus (e.g. Billy Blanks (Tae Bo), Tony Horton (P90X), Alberto "Beto" Perez (Zumba), and Jillian Michaels (Biggest Loser)) and actor/fitness celebrities (e.g. Suzanne Somers, Daisy Fuentes, Chuck Norris, Jane Fonda, Dr. Oz) may be included in this segment. Health and fitness media aids such as digital video discs, television shows, magazines, books, and apps as well as products and supplement manufacturers and suppliers (e.g. GNC or Twin Labs) should also be included in this category.

BOX 5.1 SPIN-OFFS OR ANCILLARY HEALTH AND FITNESS SERVICES AND PRODUCTS

- Personal trainers, instructors, fitness gurus/celebrities
- Media products
- Equipment
- Supplements
- Products
- Specialty fitness apparel and footwear

Another large component of the ancillary services and products category is health and fitness equipment and its manufacturers and distributors. Companies such as Nautilus, NordicTrack, and Cybex provide related equipment to clubs and individual users. They also provide fitness equipment to retailers including sporting goods stores and discount chains for purchase for home use. There are millions of products on the market ranging from ankle weights to pedometers to free weights and stationary bicycles all designed and sold to support the health and fitness industry.

The growth of the industry to include these various ancillary products may be problematic. Some spin-off products, such as supplements and home equipment, may be predatory in that they are of little proven value and prey on the individual's hope to seek a quick remedy to their fitness challenge. Things like rolling contraptions with elastic resisting bands, mud wraps, weight loss magic pills, or super supplements and powders may be little more than scams or schemes designed to generate profit for the seller. Such products may be based on questionable science. Advertising for these products can be sensational and seeks to capitalize on consumers' naivety and desire for a quick solution to their fitness or wellness concerns. Consumers must carefully evaluate the claims made by various fitness product distributors and marketers. Fitness professionals generally agree that there is no quick fix.

Certainly, the sales and marketing of health/sport supplements have been very controversial and have generated heated debate in the U.S. and abroad. In some cases, products receive little federal review or approval. Long-term effects of product use may not be studied. As a result, several untested and potentially unsafe products are available to an unsuspecting consumer. Performance-enhancing supplements have come to market and athletes, seeking to gain an advantage over their competitors, have been quick to integrate these supplements into their training regimen. Doctors and fitness experts have given such products and supplements mixed reviews. Questions about product safety and effects of long-term use abound. Drug policy and testing in both amateur and professional sport continue to try to deter performance enhancement through chemical substances, yet some athletes and their trainers turn to performance-enhancement labs to help them utilize and then mask the use of prohibited performance-enhancing drugs.

The U.S. federal case involving BALCO Labs in California (see Chapter 2), the biographical expose by Major League Baseball player Jose Canseco, and the resultant U.S. Senate hearings about the use of steroids and human growth hormone in amateur and professional sport have raised public awareness of the use of performance-enhancing substances at every level of sport. As the government and professional and amateur sport governing bodies and unions continue to debate and analyze the realities and implications of the use of performance-enhancing drugs and supplements, the lesson for the average consumer is clear. Products that claim to help the user lose 20 pounds in two days, develop "six pack abs" overnight, or slow the aging process should be viewed with a great deal of skepticism. Not only may these products be ineffective, but they may also do the user great harm.

Health and fitness industry professionals have come to realize the popularity of these types of products and the power of what they promise to consumers. In response, health and fitness managers and practitioners have embraced the role of educator. They are committed to teaching the athlete and members of the general public to improve their personal fitness and wellness in a way that is both safe and effective. Their challenge is also to engage and motivate. Personal fitness and wellness takes a long-term commitment and in essence is a lifestyle change. For this reason, professional fitness club managers must continue to find ways to create meaningful programming combined with high levels of customer service to keep their members engaged and on track. This approach is not only good for the member but goes a long way to ensuring the organization's success.

Decision making in the sport organization

For health and fitness industry managers, the basic question of how to create a successful organization is at the core of every business decision. Once the organization has defined the goals that determine its direction, it is essential that the manager makes decisions that move the organization closer to its goals. We have defined management as the responsibility for an organization's achievement of its goals. Success in exercising this responsibility is determined to a large degree by the effectiveness of the manager's decisions.

Managers are charged with making important decisions every day. Some are small decisions that may be of small consequence and may be reviewed and reversed quickly and easily with little risk to the organization. Others may be much larger with organizational-wide, long-term importance and inherent high risk. For the fitness club manager, decisions might range from whether or not to extend hours of operation to a multi-million dollar buy-out of another fitness chain. Each decision must be made within the context of a broader vision of the organization and its goals. Decisions are what move the organization forward either closer to or further away from goal attainment. In effect, the sport manager is constantly engaged in the decision-making process, and his or her ability to make the right decisions determines the success of the organization.

THE DECISION-MAKING PROCESS

Decision making is the process of selecting and implementing alternatives consistent with a goal. It is a series of activities that begins with defining the purpose or goal of the decision, and then involves developing and evaluating alternatives, selecting an alternative, implementing the alternative, and monitoring the results to ensure that the decision goals are achieved. This entire process, from setting the decision goal to making sure the goal has been achieved, is called "decision making." There are a variety of ways to categorize the activities in the decision-making process. They can be reduced in number to three or four or increased to eight or

143

more individual activities or steps. Virtually every decision model, however, in one form or another, includes the activities or steps shown below in Box 5.2. Each of these phases of the decision process is worth considering in greater detail.

BOX 5.2 STEPS IN THE DECISION-MAKING PROCESS

1 Define the goals of the decision.
2 Gather relevant information.
3 Generate the broadest possible range of alternatives.
4 Evaluate the alternatives for strengths and weaknesses.
5 Select the optimal alternative.
6 Implement and monitor for effectiveness.

Six decision steps

Decision step 1: define the decision goals

The purpose of any management decision is to move the organization closer to the attainment of its goals. When we speak of the "goal of a decision," we mean that there needs to be established, in very specific terms, just what the decision is intended to accomplish. As we discussed in Chapter 4, goals that are specific provide a target to aim for and make feedback possible. In that sense, decision making is like any other activity. Performance is enhanced when the decision process itself is in pursuit of specific goals. When a goal is defined, decision making has the critical focus necessary to ensure that the decision will actually move the organization closer to attaining the goal(s). Also specific goals enable feedback to be provided in progress reports or annual performance reviews.

In addition to focus and feedback, there are benefits in defining specific goals that are unique to the decision process. Specific decision goals, for example, provide criteria for focusing the information search, determining which alternatives might be most relevant, and evaluating the relative strengths and weaknesses of each alternative. When a university fitness center set the goal of improving safety for students using free weights, this eliminated the alternative of leaving the fitness centers open 24 hours a day. It would be impossible due to budgetary considerations to provide 24-hour supervision of the area and the lifters, a condition that would be required to facilitate safe lifting. Specific decision goals not only help in evaluating alternatives but also provide the standards for evaluating the effectiveness of the decision itself once the selected alternative is actually implemented. Only with specific decision goals can the organization evaluate whether the decision is actually moving it closer to those goals. In this case, any decision regarding free-weight programming must clearly take into consideration the goal of the safety of lifters. Therefore, any and all subsequent decisions regarding the free-weight program such as setting standard qualifications of weight room staff and selecting the type and number of new free-weight benches all need to be made within the framework of the organization's goal to maximize lifter safety.

Decision step 2: gather information

Once the decision goals are clear, the next step is to gather as much information as possible relevant to the established goals. Clearly defined decision goals help focus the information search by defining which information is relevant. At the community senior center, the fitness club director was asked to provide aerobic exercise programming for the senior clients. The director needed to decide what types of classes to offer that would be most beneficial to the clients. It was important to provide aerobic activities that would be safe for seniors and appropriate to their abilities. The director began to search health and fitness programming resource guides and to network with peers in an attempt to generate programming ideas for consideration. The first resource guide book provided information about aerobic exercise alternatives such as step aerobics, kick boxing, and spinning. These options are all effective aerobic activities, but are these types of programs viable alternatives for the target population?

This is a very important point. The director needed to focus on information relevant to aerobic health and fitness programming for seniors. Goal-based decision making provides a critical advantage to the decision maker in that they focus information search. In an age when the amount of information available to management is expanding rapidly, clearly defined decision goals allow managers to set boundaries on their information search to target the most relevant or appropriate information. Although efficiency in gathering information is essential, it is important to gather as much information as possible before moving too quickly through the rest of the decision process. Quality decisions require quality information. Before the senior center's fitness club director can make a good decision, he or she must have good information about appropriate programming for seniors. A sense of the physical abilities of the clientele as well as a sense of their interests is equally important. Lastly, the director will need to be cognizant of available facilities, resources, and equipment. For example, the director might decide to begin a water aerobics class for senior clients that would be offered at 8:00 p.m. at the local community pool. A call to the municipal pool manager resulted in the director learning the high school swim team used the pool until 7:45 p.m. every evening. The pool was rented throughout the day to other organizations and, therefore, the 8:00 p.m. time slot was the only one available. Certainly, a water-based aerobics would be appropriate to the ability level of the group, but the program would be doomed to fail if seniors were uncomfortable with the hour, did not like to wear bathing suits, or were unable to secure transportation to the community pool. The director needed to gather more information about the lifestyles of the senior clients, their interests, and the availability of transportation.

If clients had been surveyed, information may have revealed that some clients have a fear of water, others are concerned with driving at night, and still others may even have a bedtime that precluded them from participation. The lesson of this example is clear; having the right information on which to base a decision is absolutely critical to the effectiveness of the decision. Too frequently, managers make decisions without the information they need or they make them on inaccurate information.

BARRIERS AND ONE SOLUTION

A variety of barriers can prevent management from having the information they need to make an effective decision. Managers often feel they lack the time to fully research important information. Some managers consciously try to avoid becoming overwhelmed by information, especially when a decision deadline is approaching. An example of this may be when a fitness club manager is asked to purchase new fitness equipment. There are several brands and types of equipment, and any manager could spend hundreds of hours researching different models and technology. The manager may be busy with daily operations of the club and may feel that he or she just does not have the time to read and learn about all the new equipment in the market or meet with every sales representative who wants to demonstrate a new exercise apparatus. The manager might also feel ill prepared to digest or interpret the available information about the equipment. As a result, the manager might tend not to ask others for information or recommendations for fear of appearing uninformed or not qualified to make a good decision. Another manager in a similar situation may just call one colleague and ask for a recommendation, thereby introducing potential external bias into the decision process.

The home user is faced with a similar challenge when gathering information about personal fitness equipment. One only need to go to a fitness equipment retail outlet or sporting goods store to examine the wide variety of options available to the home fitness enthusiast. There are literally hundreds of types of stationary bikes, treadmills, and stair climbers. The salesperson will be only too happy to give complete demonstrations of the equipment while pointing out the variety of features available on each model. Sales staff will share brochures, instruction sheets, DVDs, fitness equipment reviews, website information, and catalogs with consumers. The consumer, him or herself, is likely to do extensive independent research by reading fitness magazines and search on-line consumer review websites. Sometimes, what results is information overload. There is just too much information available to analyze and digest. It gets to the point where the consumer cannot remember everything that was said about a specific piece of equipment. Because our consumer is eager to start a home fitness program and feels overwhelmed by the amount of information available for each option, he or she may just buy the first available treadmill at the next store he or she visits. Whether or not the treadmill will serve

Decision making and the healthand fitness industry

the intended purpose or goal of the consumer becomes irrelevant and convenience becomes the primary motivator. This outcome is not unusual. Sometimes managers feel so overwhelmed by the breadth and depth of information available that they choose to disregard it all and make a decision based upon ease, comfort, or convenience. Frequently, these decisions result in less than optimal results.

One approach to overcoming these information barriers is called "management by walking (or wandering) around," or MBWA. Management theorists Tom Peters and Nancy Austin (1985) suggest that managers in effective companies get the information they need simply by walking around, getting out of their offices, out from behind their computer screens, and just talking with people – employees, suppliers, other managers, and customers. MBWA enables managers to avoid both appearing uninformed and having to frantically search out essential information when an unexpected decision suddenly needs to be made. Through MBWA, managers maintain a constant flow of useful information, and they keep that information continuously updated. Managers who engage in MBWA need to be good observers who know how to ask good questions. They need to understand the nature of their business and need to be open to discovery and feedback from a wide variety of stakeholders.

In the case of our fitness club manager who is faced with the task of purchasing new equipment, he or she might engage in MBWA by talking with clients and asking them what features they would like in new equipment. They might also talk with other club managers at professional meetings where she might also meet informally with suppliers and discuss new industry innovations. Our senior fitness club director might embrace the same approach. He or she could walk around the senior center, talk to clients about their programming interests, and, lastly, she could visit other senior fitness centers and watch and listen to what is happening there. Many managers admit that MBWA is not easy at first. It requires a commitment of time and a willingness to listen and learn. It also means that the manager must seek multiple sources of information over a longer period of time. In fact, MBWA amounts to an on-going leadership practice. But managers have also found that MBWA is a powerful tool in making sure that they are hearing what they need to hear and seeing what they need to see. It also helps to give managers multiple perspectives and multiple sources of information to consider without being bogged down by too much information or too narrow an information search.

Decision step 3: generate alternatives
In the third phase of decision making, the challenge is not to move too quickly to a consideration of only the obvious alternatives. In this era of accelerating change and global competition, the obvious alternatives, the traditional solutions to organizational challenges, have become increasingly ineffective. Innovative alternatives need to be generated, and as this need intensifies, creativity becomes an ever more critical ingredient in the decision-making process.

For the purpose of this discussion, creativity might be best described as the ability to think differently. The main barrier to creativity is our lack of flexibility in the way we view things. We tend to place the elements of our experience in fixed categories or frameworks. The longer we operate using these preconceptions, and the longer they work for us, the more difficult it is for us to see beyond them. If we place two elements in unrelated categories or within different frameworks, over time it becomes more and more difficult for us to relate them or apply them in new ways. For instance, consider the child-care challenge that faced many health and fitness clubs for many years. Mothers with young children often suggested that because of their role as primary caregiver, they were unable to utilize their membership fully. They explained that they were unable to leave their small children at home and go to the club to work out. It was often difficult to find a babysitter especially during school hours or weekday evenings when they hoped to use the club. As a result, many mothers with young children would use the facility only sporadically and might even allow their membership to lapse. In response, some club managers decided to not aggressively pursue this market for full memberships. Eventually, managers came to realize that they could capitalize on the situation not only by offering on-site quality child-care, but by introducing programs that catered to young children (e.g. toddler swimming lessons or gymnastics, mommy/daddy and baby fitness classes). For health club managers, they needed to see their businesses in a new way and to understand that child-care and programming involving young children with their parents was not beyond the scope of what they could do to retain and attract members.

Over the years, a number of techniques have emerged to help enhance creative capacity. The most familiar of these techniques is brainstorming. Brainstorming is a group technique for generating the broadest possible range of alternatives. The general rules for brainstorming are summarized below in Box 5.3.

BOX 5.3 RULES FOR BRAINSTORMING

- No judgments allowed.
- Go for quantity, not quality. The more ideas the better.
- Even wild ideas have value. The stranger, the better.
- Piggyback. Add to someone else's idea.
- Encourage all members of the group to contribute.

These rules reflect two basic realizations about the creative process. The first is that creativity is very often a synergistic process. One person's ideas can spark ideas in someone else's mind. The rules emphasizing quantity, strangeness, and piggybacking ideas are intended to encourage the synergistic potential of

148

a group. These rules also reflect the fact that judgment or criticism tends to restrict the flow of ideas. It takes courage to suggest an off-the-wall idea, especially in a group setting. That is why it is important to create a brainstorming environment that encourages participation of all group members and respects every idea. The knowledge that our ideas might be judged or criticized is usually enough to convince us not to risk sharing them. The no-judgments-allowed rule helps create a climate that enhances the willingness of group members to risk sharing their most outlandish ideas, again increasing their potential for developing innovative alternatives.

Decision step 4: evaluate alternatives

When the broadest possible range of realistic alternatives has been identified, the focus of the decision process shifts to evaluating those alternatives and identifying the strengths and weaknesses of each option. Perhaps no dimension of the decision-making process has been as well developed as the evaluation phase.

QUANTITATIVE APPROACHES FOR EVALUATING ALTERNATIVES

One set of methods used to evaluate decision alternatives has been found extremely useful in situations where all of the variables relative to the decision goals and alternatives can be expressed in numbers. These are called quantitative approaches because they use mathematical and statistical techniques to analyze the decision alternatives.

LINEAR PROGRAMMING

Linear programming is a decision sciences technique that allows the decision maker to use mathematical formulas to analyze and evaluate the full range of decision options before committing to one option. In the health and fitness industry, a club manager might use linear programming to decide how many staff members will be needed on a particular day, given the number of clients expected, the areas of the club to be utilized and the types of activities that will be held on a particular day.

BREAK-EVEN ANALYSIS

Another common quantitative evaluation technique is called break-even analysis. The technique is used to determine how many units of a product or service must be sold at what price for the producer or service provider to at least break even, given the cost of producing or providing that item or service. The break-even point occurs when revenues from the sale of a product or service exactly equal the cost of producing and selling it. For example, a club manager can decide exactly how many personal training sessions he must sell before he begins to make money. The break-even point for a product or service can be calculated whenever three things are known: fixed costs for operation, variable cost per unit, and the selling cost per unit, as described in Box 5.4. Break-even analysis allows the decision maker to clearly understand the financial impact of various alternatives before deciding which one to pursue.

BOX 5.4 DETERMINING COST PER SESSION FOR PERSONAL TRAINER USING BREAK-EVEN ANALYSIS

Fixed costs (fixed costs for operation: items such as rent, the cost of equipment, utilities, legal – costs that will be there whether one training session is produced/sold or 200 sessions are produced/sold)

Rent for new training room area	$6,000
Utilities	$1,000
Equipment and room renovation cost	$2,500
Legal/insurance	$500
Total fixed cost	$10,000

Variable costs (variable costs per unit/session, such as labor and material costs, that will vary depending on how many units/sessions are produced)

Trainer's salary	$20 per session
Supplies	$2 per session
Total cost	$22 per session

Selling price per unit/session
$50 per unit/half hour session

Break-even analysis

$$\frac{\text{Total fixed cost}}{\text{Selling price} - \text{variable cost per unit}} = \text{BEP (units/sessions)}$$

$$\frac{\$10,000}{\$50 - \$22} = 357 \text{ (units/sessions)*}$$

For the club owner to break even (where revenues equal costs) on personal training services, one would have to sell 357 sessions per year. To make a profit, one would have to produce/sell more than 357 sessions a year.

DECISION-TREE ANALYSIS

There is another technique for evaluating decision options, called the decision tree. There are some decisions where there is certain important information that cannot be known ahead of time. For example, the condominium association fitness club director is trying to select a date for the club's annual fun run. It is impossible to know for certain what the weather will be on any given day, so probability estimates about the likelihood of cold weather or rain can be made based on current forecasts and weather data from previous years. Decision-tree analysis uses probability estimates to help compare various alternatives.

Consider how a club manager trying to choose between the construction of a climbing wall or dedicated Pilates studio utilized decision-tree analysis in the decision-making process. Given the current design of the club facility, the Pilates studio would be less expensive to build and could be used by more people at a time. The manager must consider if it would generate as much revenue as a climbing wall. The manager has also decided that she will make either facility available to non-members for rental and plans to charge non-members a higher user fee than members. The manager would gather information from other clubs and talk to members in an attempt to appropriately estimate what percentage of the time each facility will be used and by whom. It is only by estimating patterns of use that the manager would be able to create a decision tree based on probability of use. With the tree she will be able to evaluate each alternative and attempt to determine which would be more profitable to the club. Of course, this kind of analysis is only as accurate as the probability estimates, which depend on the quality of research undertaken and the amount of experience the manager has had with the business that is being estimated. A manager that has had a great deal of experience with Pilates studios or climbing walls is in a much better position to make appropriate probability estimates of use than a manager who is unfamiliar with either facility. Nevertheless, quantifying expectations enables the manager to evaluate alternatives in a way that is extremely objective and that would not otherwise be possible.

THE T-CHART: A QUALITATIVE TECHNIQUE FOR EVALUATING ALTERNATIVES

Not all decisions involve factors that can be easily quantified or measured. For example, suppose a decision has to be made about which employee should be promoted to the position of fitness program director. Imagine that there are two excellent internal candidates for this job and that management needs to assess the strengths and weaknesses of both. When quantitative techniques seem inappropriate or non-applicable, the manager can employ a T-chart, one of the most widely used qualitative decision-making tools. The T-chart gets its name from the T-shaped format used to list and compare alternatives. A T-chart for the decision described previously is shown in Table 5.2.

151

Table 5.2 T-chart for use in hiring a fitness program director

	Candidate A	Candidate B
Time with company	Five years	Ten years
Education	Bachelor's degree	Master's degree
Interpersonal skills	Excellent	Good
Management skills	Weak organizer Excellent motivator	Strong planner Detail oriented
Knowledge of fitness	Extensive	Extensive
Certifications/professional organizations	CPR, IHRSA	CPR, ACSM, NASPE, IHRSA

The characteristics being compared in T-charts are not like costs or numbers of items that are typically part of quantitative decisions. They are more qualitative or subjective in nature. They might include communication and organizational skills, for example, which are not easily expressed in numbers. The value of the T-chart is that it puts on paper the qualitative considerations that otherwise would have to be juggled in the decision maker's brain. The T-chart registers all the factors the manager is attempting to consider in a decision and freezes action so that each factor can be considered carefully. In the example in Table 5.2, the T-chart allows the decision maker to compare the two job candidates on each factor that is relevant to the decision. As with the earlier phases of the decision process, the emphasis in the assessment phase is not on moving too quickly to selecting an alternative. Like the other phases, the evaluation phase is an attempt to impose a discipline on the decision maker to ensure that appropriate evaluation criteria are brought into focus and that each alternative is considered carefully.

Decision step 5: select the optimal alternative

The fifth phase of the decision process is to select the alternative that comes closest to satisfying the decision goal. Nobel laureate Herbert Simon was among the first to recognize that there is no such thing as a perfect decision. Simon (1957) uses the term bounded rationality to describe the fact that no matter how systematic the manager has been, in most cases it is impossible to have all of the relevant information, generate every possible alternative, or fully comprehend the advantages and disadvantages of each option. Furthermore, since most decisions are attempting to achieve a variety of goals, a single alternative will rarely satisfy all of them. These limitations of the decision process "bound" or reduce the rationality of the decision. Recognizing these realities about decision making, Simon coined the term "satisfice" to describe the way alternatives really are selected. According to Simon,

152

about the best we can do in making a decision is to select the best available alternative, recognizing our lack of time or complete information and the variety of goals most decisions are attempting to satisfy. Satisficing, says Simon, is the way most selections of alternatives are actually made.

Health and fitness instructors have found that their clients often satisfice when it comes to making decisions about their own health and fitness programs. A typical client has a variety of responsibilities including work, family, and social obligations. Consider the variety of personal and professional obligations facing Bill Durken on Friday. His calendar is filled with a late afternoon meeting at work, family events, and social obligations that all occur simultaneously, each involving separate goals (i.e. attend a late afternoon meeting with the university's marketing office to plan for a new recruitment brochure, cheer on his daughter at her first softball game, complete yard work in preparation for his in-laws' weekend visit, eat a healthy dinner, pick up his son at baseball camp, attend an evening retirement reception for a work associate, complete a scheduled 4:30 p.m. work-out with a personal trainer). Since it would be virtually impossible for Bill to achieve all of the desired outcomes, he will have to satisfice by selecting an alternative that is not ideal, but is the best one available. His decision might be to cancel the training session, reschedule the meeting, and put off the yard work in favor of picking up his son and then stopping for fast food on the way to his daughter's softball game before heading to the co-worker's retirement reception.

Bill's personal trainer recognizes that, for many of his clients, sticking to a health and fitness regime is often compromised as part of the process of satisficing. The optimal healthy alternative for Bill would be to work out with his trainer and avoid the fast food. Bill's trainer, like most health and fitness professionals, knows that clients often satisfice when it comes to personal fitness choices. They may pick a good alternative (working out two days a week) as opposed to selecting the optimal alternative (prescribed fitness regimen which includes some healthy activity every day). For that reason, health and fitness professionals have developed a variety of strategies to help counter the negative effects of satisficing when it comes to personal fitness. In an effort to address a client's lack of time, personal trainers might offer early morning or late evening sessions in an attempt to minimize work conflicts. Clubs are now open 24 hours a day, and offer 30-minute "come when you choose" work-out circuits. Trainers might also send clients daily healthful eating tips or text them reminders about class times or gym hours. All of these efforts can help to move the client closer to reaching his or her fitness goals. As a result of the new text message session reminders and information that the club recently sent him about eating healthy at fast food restaurants, Bill selects a healthy option at the burger chain and avoids the French fries. He also drops by the gym for a 20-minute workout on the treadmill after the retirement gathering. While Bill still has satisficed, his health and fitness club has helped him to make better, if not ideal, fitness decisions.

The challenge for Bill and for managers is not to compromise too easily, but to ensure that the alternative selected is truly the best available, given the bounded rationality of the decision-making situation. As Simon suggests, satisficing is not only how most decisions are truly made, but also is necessary given the reality of time and resources and information constraints.

Decision step 6: implement the decision and monitor for effectiveness

All too often, especially with difficult decisions, we tend to consider the decision process complete once we have selected the optimal alternative. There is often a definite sense of relief once the decision has been made. However, all the effort invested in the decision process will have been wasted unless the alternative selected is effectively put into action. A decision is just a choice until it is acted on. Once our fitness club director made the decision to go with the rock wall construction, a contractor needs to be selected, equipment companies would need to be consulted, and fees and operational policies and procedures would need to be set. The director will also need to create and distribute marketing materials, hire staff, update the website, and plan a grand opening. The decision is just the first step. Without a comprehensive implementation plan and execution, the decision is doomed to fail.

Effective implementation, however, does not complete the action phase of the decision-making process. Once the choice has been implemented, the decision must be monitored to ensure that the alternative put into action is in fact moving the organization closer to its goals. As we said at the beginning of the chapter, moving the organization closer to its goals is the ultimate purpose of every decision, and this cannot be assumed to be happening just because the decision has been implemented. An organization that attempts to improve performance by implementing a particular management approach needs to evaluate how well that approach is meeting the goals of the decision. Only when the monitoring and evaluation phase confirms that the decision goals have been achieved is the decision-making process finally complete.

The decision maker

As important as the decision process is, there is another key variable that determines the effectiveness of decisions: the decision maker. The decision maker is not a neutral factor. Decisions reflect the person making them as much as the process by which they are made. A number of dimensions of the decision maker are worth considering.

Intuition and the impact of experience on decisions

As part of his research on decision making, Simon studied chess masters to try to understand how they are able to consistently make high-quality decisions when there are so many variables and so little time. What Simon discovered is that chess masters do not use a purely logical or rational decision process of the type that has been presented. It would be nearly impossible for them to systematically evaluate the consequences of each of the available alternatives at every point in a match, especially in the very brief period allowed between moves in a chess match. Based on his observations, Simon concluded that it must be "intuition" that allows chess masters to select such effective alternatives in so little time. For Simon, however, intuition is not merely a "hunch" or "gut instinct"; it is ability based on extensive experience. Intuition based on years of experience in similar situations allows the chess master or veteran manager to select and implement the most appropriate course of action without exhaustively evaluating each alternative (Agor, 1986). In management, as in sports, the experienced player tends to make the better decisions.

Personality, values, and power

Like any behavior, a person's decision making reflects his or her personality, values, and power. Personality may be interpreted as the individual's consistent pattern of behavior. An aggressive personality, for example, on the other hand, shows a pattern of leaping to conclusions and preferring action to analysis (Etzioni, 1989).

We can reasonably expect that when confronted with all of the same goals and information, and even sharing all of the same experiences, each different personality might actually decide very differently. The aggressive personality might be expected to make decisions in ways that some might find argumentative or confrontational. The impulsive personality in decision making can minimize any negative effects a decision maker's personality might have on the effectiveness of the decision process.

Beyond personality, decisions tend also to reflect the values of the decision maker, those things that are personally most important to him or her in the decision context. A good example of this is the health and fitness club manager who is an active environmentalist and believes very strongly in being sure to consider the impact on the environment of every decision he makes. Therefore, he might be more likely to do business with an environmentally friendly or "green" vendor than another club manager who might be committed to environmental causes. Another example of how the values and beliefs of the decision maker influences the decision-making process may be found in the debate over the use of tanning beds. Where some clubs and personal trainers might refuse to sell or promote the use of tanning beds because of potential long-term negative effects of use, other clubs and individuals have chosen to continue to offer tanning services. As some club managers have decided not to offer tanning bed services based on their concerns that there is a connection between tanning bed use and skin cancer, other clubs have introduced spray tanning as a more healthful alternative. For each individual decision maker, personal values and beliefs strongly color and influence both the goals and outcomes of the decision process.

Finally, there is the issue of power. Some alternatives, including sometimes the best alternatives, are beyond the power of the decision maker to implement. Managers, especially team leaders and middle managers, often do not have the power to implement these changes. Unfortunately, experience has shown us that the managers with the best understanding of the situation and often the ability to devise the best course of action do not always have sufficient power to ensure that the best alternative is selected and implemented. Like experience, personality, and values, the power of the decision maker strongly influences the effectiveness of the decision-making process.

Consider the college student who has worked at the YMCA reception desk on nights and weekends for several years. Based upon her front-line experience and knowledge of members' concerns, she would like to institute a program where members needing squash partners register at the reception desk on a weekly basis. She would pair registered singles, set up matches, and then call each registrant to confirm the arrangements. She believes that this service would greatly benefit members and would give her something productive to do on Monday evenings when things are slow at the reception desk. She presents her idea to the manager who then tells her that he does not want her to do anything more than greet members, scan identification cards, and answer the phone during her shifts. While her idea may have great merit, she has no power to make a decision to implement the plan.

GROUPS AND DECISION MAKING

Organizations are built on the necessity for people to engage in cooperative efforts to get things done. Frequently, the effectiveness of decisions hinges not on the decision maker's ability to take direct action, but on how successfully he or she involves other people in making and implementing the decision. Typically, this includes both those whose input would improve the decision and those whose commitment is needed for the decision to be effectively implemented.

Decision making and the healthand fitness industry

Advantages and disadvantages of involving others

Although group involvement can improve the decision-making process, there are both advantages and disadvantages to group-based decisions. A summary of these is shown in Box 5.5.

BOX 5.5 ADVANTAGES AND DISADVANTAGES IN GROUP-BASED DECISION MAKING

Advantages of involving others in decisions:

- A better understanding of the reasons for the decision
- A greater commitment to making the decisions work
- Greater creative potential
- More careful evaluation of alternatives

Disadvantages of involving others in decisions:

- Increased time spent in discussion at each stage of the process
- Difficulty in reaching a consensus
- Creation of winners and losers as suggestions are reviewed and adopted
- Compromise rather than selection of the optimal alternative

---

There is no question that the involvement of others, no matter how great the potential benefits, complicates the decision-making process. Anyone who has ever been involved in a group project or committee has experienced firsthand the difficulty of actually making a group decision. On the other hand, the price of not involving others in decisions can also be high, particularly in terms of lack of valuable input, understanding, and commitment to the decision from them.

Levels of involvement in the decision-making process

Management theorist and consultant Victor Vroom and his associates have described five levels of involving others in decision making (Vroom and Yetton, 1973). These levels are shown below in Box 5.6.

In Vroom's model, a decision about what to include in a report summarizing a work group's activities for the year would require very little participation, if any. Participation is probably not essential for identifying the group's accomplishments, and there is little necessity of the group's commitment to the report. A decision on how to redesign the group's work area, on the other hand, would almost certainly benefit from a higher level of group participation. Both the group's input and its commitment would be essential to the success of the new design.

Vroom's point is that the same level of participation is not necessary in every decision. But the more important the group's acceptance of the decision is, or the more the decision might benefit from group input and ideas, the higher the level should be of individual and group participation, at least to the extent that time permits.

Interestingly, the amount of group-based decision making has increased significantly in recent years, as teamwork has become one of the key elements of the changing workplace. One of the defining characteristics of this trend has been the steadily increasing responsibility of teams for making many of their own decisions. Organizations now recognize that for them to compete in the changing environment, decisions must reflect the commitment, the expertise, and the creativity that can only come with highly participative decision making. For this reason, the challenge for managers is to improve not only their own skills as decision makers, but the decision-making skills of their teams as well.

Groupthink: a potential problem with group decisions

While group-based decision making unquestionably offers the potential for more effective decisions, it also has potential drawbacks, even beyond those mentioned earlier. One of the most serious is *groupthink*. Psychologist Irving Janis coined the term groupthink to describe the tendency of close-knit groups to lose their ability to function effectively in the decision-making process (Janis, 1982). In reviewing group decisions around famous events in recent history, Janis found that the more cohesive or unified a group was, the less willing the members were to present their own opinions, especially when they differed from the opinions of other group members. Instead of benefitting from the differing points of view of various group members, the decision-mkaing process in groups suffering from groupthink is unconsciously focused on not rocking the boat.

Recall the example of the seniors' fitness club introduced earlier in this chapter. Imagine that the manager decided to involve several staff members and club members in the decision-making process to create a new aerobic program for seniors. The unspoken desire to avoid creating conflict within the group might encourage group members to offer only traditional alternatives for aerobic programming. Alternatives offered might include bowling or walking clubs, but might not include more creative alternatives such as bicycling or line dancing. Individual members of the decision-making team may have creative suggestions or serious doubts about any one alternative, but when groupthink takes over, individuals never forcefully state their ideas or objections to the group. Instead, they just go along with the momentum, apparently for fear of being viewed as disloyal to the decision-making team. While the failure of a senior fitness club member to express her interest in line dancing doesn't seem to be earth shaking, the consequences of groupthink are always serious. Groupthink decisions are lacking both in terms of challenging the status quo and in critically evaluating the alternatives that are presented. For example, if the group seems satisfied with one member's interpretation of what a particular issue or problem is and how it should be addressed, not only are alternative points of view not raised, but suggested alternatives tend not to be very critically or carefully evaluated.

Janis describes a number of symptoms of groupthink, including self-censorship by members and the appearance of total agreement, even when consensus does not exist. Perhaps more importantly, he suggests strategies for avoiding groupthink. Some of these strategies are summarized in Box 5.7.

BOX 5.7 STRATEGIES FOR AVOIDING GROUPTHINK

- Assign the role of critical evaluator to every member of the group.
- The group leader should avoid stating preferences or positions early in the process.
- Encourage input from individuals and experts outside the group.
- Assign one member to play "devil's advocate" at each group meeting.
- Hold a "second chance" meeting to review the decision once a consensus has been reached.

159

With the trend toward more group- and team-based decisions, the tendency toward groupthink becomes an increasingly serious problem. By implementing Janis' strategies, groups can take much greater advantage of their potential for making higher-quality decisions.

ETHICS AND DECISION MAKING

As we discussed earlier in Chapter 2, ethical behavior continues to be a key challenge to management in an ever-changing sport world. Ethical behavior may be best defined as behavior that recognizes the difference between right and wrong, behavior that conforms to society's standards and expectations. Two easily justifiable moral standards might be honesty and fairness. We expect sports organizations to conduct themselves in a way that the average person might consider to be honest in terms of telling the truth, and fair in terms of how they equitably treat their customers or clients, employees, and society in general. In no area of organizational performance is ethical behavior more important than in decision making.

In sports organizations, ethics must matter. At the most basic level, our free market society is based on honesty and fair play. In the sports industry, our games and the operation of our organizations rely upon the integrity of individuals who participate in and manage the sport enterprise. In that sense, unfair and dishonest behavior threatens the very existence of not only the sport industry, but society as well. Every unethical act by organizations threatens the trust that is the foundation of a free society. At the industry level, there is a very real concern that a growing lack of trust in sport organizations may result in demands for additional legislation and regulation to control their operation. The fear is that such restrictions would not only make operations more difficult, but will further limit the ability of the sport organization to compete globally against businesses from other societies that operate without such regulations. Finally, unethical behavior of sport organizations, when discovered, invariably results in a loss of confidence in the organization by customers, investors, and employees. For example, many years ago during the first health and fitness club boom in the 1970s, many health and fitness club managers induced members to sign long-term contracts. These long-term membership contracts were expensive, yet seemed to offer members a much better deal than monthly renewal fees. Unfortunately, some of these clubs went out of business and literally shut down and moved in the middle of the night. Members were left with long-term memberships to non-existent clubs with no way to secure a refund. This pattern of ethical abuse of consumers put a black mark on the health and fitness club industry and left many consumers with doubts about the credibility and integrity of the fitness club business.

What this example suggests is that sport managers need to pay attention to the ethical dimensions of decision making. They must work to establish ethical organizational cultures that embrace ethics training, adherence to professional ethical codes and standards, internal ethics committees or teams, and outside review by professional organizations. The key to ethical decisions in organizations is the commitment to ethical behavior by top management. In order to avoid the making of unethical decisions, top management not only must support a system for dealing with ethical questions once they are raised, but they must actively encourage people to raise and discuss ethical concerns whenever they exist. Without that kind of managerial support, even the best internal ethics committees and organization systems and procedures are likely to be ineffective.

In other words, ethical decision making in an organization may have much more to do with the climate and standards that management creates than with the decision-making process itself. This means that if organizations are to achieve the goal of ethical decision making, they must commit themselves to creating an environment in which questions about ethics are a required part of the evaluation phase of every decision. Top managers must serve as ethical role models and must create an environment in which ethics is a key priority in every decision process. Management must insist that the question "Is this decision fair and honest?" be answered for all of the organization's decisions.

EPILOGUE: THE WALMART OF FITNESS CLUBS

As we have learned, the health and fitness industry is an extremely competitive environment in which organizations must battle for customers and market share. Unlike segments such as professional league sport (see Chapter 10), there are very few barriers to entry for those wishing to get into the health and fitness industry. Think back to all the various clubs and products outlined above, and this point becomes quite clear. All you need is an open site and a few cardio machines, free weights, and someone at the front desk to check people in and, *voilà*, you are a fitness club.

This open system means that there is room for entry for new products and services, and one such recent entry that has prospered is Planet Fitness (PF), a national franchised chain of clubs located in 48 states and Puerto Rico. You probably have seen their ads where they feature a character they call a "lunk." You probably know this guy or have seen him at a place where you work out – he's wearing a belt, he uses chalk for his hands, he wears a "shirt" that is really just a shredded tank-top, and quite possibly some combination of bandana and spandex shorts. This is the guy who is usually associated with the Gold's Gym, powerlifting-type clubs. In the ads, the lunk guy is discouraged from joining PF, because PF is a self-described "no judgment zone," where anyone can come to work out and not feel self-conscious about their body type or fitness level.

PF is hardly flashy, cool, or populated by supermodels or pro athletes. They have recently served as a sponsor for NBC TV's *The Biggest Loser* program. PF locations are mostly stocked with multiple cardio machines and weight machines. There are some free weights and benches, but no dumbbells over 75 pounds (to discourage lunks). PF bases its approach to reaching customers on the fact that most of us are not the guy described above, and targets mostly first-time gym joiners. If you have been to any PF location, you will notice a mix of people – men and women, older and younger, some folks who are struggling to get into shape, and others who are already in decent shape and seeking to maintain that level of fitness. Working out at PF, as described by one member, "is like going to Walmart."

And is this bad? Like Walmart, PF has also positioned itself as a cost-leader versus other clubs, featuring an initial fee of about $50, with a monthly cancel-at-any-time fee of $10, a total cost that is often half as much as similar commercial clubs. So while most of us have shopped at Walmart, most of us could probably meet our fitness needs and goals sufficiently working out at PF. Unless we are lunks. So in all likelihood, PF should continue to thrive in a hyper-competitive industry. As has Walmart.

SUMMARY

The health and fitness segment of the sport industry includes not only health and fitness clubs, but encompasses other spin-off or ancillary organizations including personal training businesses, fitness equipment companies, and nutritional supplement manufacturers. Health and fitness clubs can be considered to fit into one of three categories including commercial clubs, not-for-profit clubs, and miscellaneous for-profit health and fitness enterprises including hotel health clubs and corporate fitness programs.

Making effective decisions is a critical task of all sport managers. Only decisions that actually move the organization closer to its goals can be considered effective. Decision making must be viewed as a series of activities. These activities begin with an understanding of the decision goals followed by information gathering, generating and evaluating alternatives, selecting and implementing the optimal alternative, and concluding with the monitoring of the effectiveness of the decision. The decision process concludes only when the decision has actually achieved its goals. Management's responsibility is to ensure a decision process equal to this challenge. MBWA, creativity, and satisficing are all essential elements of effective decision making.

Besides recognizing the importance of an effective decision-making process, managers also need to recognize the importance of process itself and the influence of the decision maker on that process. The decision maker's intuition, if based on extensive experience, represents a significant asset in the decision process. The personality, values, and power of the decision-maker are likely to shape the decision process, and the decision itself.

There has been an increasing emphasis on involving others in the decision process. There are advantages and disadvantages to shared decision making and there are various degrees of group involvement. But clearly, the greater the value of group input or the more important the group's commitment to the decision, the greater the need for group involvement in the decision-making process.

However, with group decisions there is also the risk of groupthink, a decision process that reflects the group members' desire not to rock the boat that overrides the desire to achieve the actual decision goals. The challenge for management is to maximize the advantages of involving others in decisions, while managing that process to minimize the potential disadvantages. Finally, the decisions reached in the decision-making process must be ethical. Meeting this requirement begins with the development of a code of ethics. Managers must also establish a body to review questions of ethics in an organization and offer management training that includes instruction in ethical decision making. Ultimately, ethical decisions require a belief that pervades the organization from top to bottom that the decision process and all decisions must be both fair and honest and must move the organization closer to the realization of its goals.

MANAGEMENT EXERCISE: TEAMS AT MILE HIGH PERFORMANCE FITNESS CLUBS

You are a member of the management team at Mile High Performance Fitness Clubs (MHPFC), a fast-growing local specialty fitness organization made up of three clubs that serves the metropolitan region of Denver, Colorado. Because of their excellent reputation in working with professional athletes to improve speed, strength, and agility, the clubs receive clients from across the United States. In the last five years, the clubs have been working to increase the number of clients. As the result of the work MHPFC did with one professional hockey player recovering from a particularly violent check that sidelined him for six months, other similarly situated athletes with head or spinal cord injury have become clients of the clubs. This new group of members includes hockey players, soccer players, lacrosse players, baseball players, football players, race car drivers, and equestrians.

During the past year, MHPFC management has been experimenting with the creation of a sport-related spinal cord and neck injury program that would be managed utilizing a team-based approach. The professional staff had suggested that these particular sport members share unique emotional and physical needs and that a sport-related spinal and neck injury program could further enhance the clubs' reputation, attract top trainers and sport rehab specialists, and potentially provide the opportunity for a partnership with area hospitals. It had been agreed that the creation of such a program could result in immediate and long-term benefits for clients and their families. The experiment created a team of ten employees (four specialized personal trainers, two sport psychologists, two physical therapists, a program coordinator, and a certified athletic trainer). This team cares for only ten members who have a history of concussion or related head or spinal trauma. The rest of the MHPFC staff works with other members as they had in the past.

The team has been in operation for a full year and, as a member of MHPFC's management team, you are part of the group that will evaluate the success of this new program and this particular approach to working with these clients. The evaluation group will be meeting to prepare its recommendation later in the week, and you have begun to prepare for that meeting by utilizing decision-making skills and knowledge that you learned as part of your formal sport management education.

QUESTIONS FOR YOU TO CONSIDER

1 Define the goal(s) of the decision that MHPFC managers must make.
2 Identify and explain the financial information you would need to support the decision-making process.
3 Create T-charts to assist you in assessing the strengths and weaknesses of each of these options.
4 What recommendations might you make to the decision-making team during the meeting?
5 Identify and explain the marketing tools and strategies MHPFC management could use to build membership.

CHAPTER 6

STRATEGIC MANAGEMENT AND THE SPORT FACILITIES INDUSTRY

INTRODUCTION

This chapter introduces sport facility management, an important consideration for sport managers as well as a unique industry segment. The strategic management process is discussed within the framework of facility management. It is through this process that sport organizations define their mission and strategic goals, and analyze the environment and the organization's own strengths and weaknesses. Strategies to achieve the organization's goals are then developed. Operations management is the process by which these strategies are implemented. For the sport manager, operations management or operational planning is two-fold. The sport manager must be concerned with macro-level operations – how the strategic plan is put into action in the organization – and on the micro level – how individual events and activities are planned and executed on a daily basis. Techniques essential for effective strategic and operational planning such as SWOT analysis, management by objectives, and the Balanced Scorecard are introduced. Because game and event management is so critical to sport facilities management and because effective event management relies so completely on operational planning, we use this aspect of sport to illustrate operational planning and control in sport management.

Check the stats

Purpose
Sport facilities are designed and constructed to support particular sport, entertainment, or civic and private activities or programs. The sport facility is a critical resource that helps the organization to realize its mission and goals. It has been argued that sport facilities may anchor area development, particularly in urban areas, and will help to drive economic activity. It has also been argued that these

facilities, particularly those that require large public contribution, are detrimental to local communities and contribute little to the area's economy.

Stakeholders

Professional sport teams, tour events, sport and entertainment event rights owners, promoters, labor/trade/music unions, private facility management companies, food service companies, security companies, musicians, performers, athletes, guests, sponsors, media, community members, sport governing bodies/agencies, volunteers, vendors, suppliers, general public, and federal, state, and local government.

Size and scope

There are hundreds of thousands of sport facilities throughout the world ranging from stadiums and arenas to golf courses, water fronts, racetracks, ski resorts, cross country trails, bike paths, fitness trails, tennis courts, and multi-purpose grass fields. Convention centers, which feature ballrooms, meeting rooms, and exhibit halls, are often built in close proximity to a sport stadium or arena for the purpose of attracting visitors to the area and spurring economic activity.

Governance

▪ Federal, state and local regulation.
▪ Professional organizations, associations, and trade groups such as the International Association of Venue Managers (IAVM). Sport governing bodies such as the NCAA provide detailed specifications and requirements for facilities utilized by member sport organizations.

Inside look: can a minor league ballpark anchor a downtown renaissance?

Taking a lesson from major league cities such as Cleveland, Baltimore, Arlington, Texas, and Miami, smaller cities in the U.S. such as Lansing, Michigan, Harrisburg, Pennsylvania, Dayton, Ohio, Frisco, Texas, and Oklahoma City, Oklahoma, have built new minor league baseball stadiums to anchor downtown development projects or reenergize urban neighborhoods. These stadiums have been designed to fit naturally into the surrounding landscape so that any area visitor would suspect the park has been there for decades. These minor league ballparks are purposely designed to complement local architecture and existing structures. Architects want their designs to be a natural part of the existing landscape rather than to dominate the area. These new structures exude a simple charm and elegance and are combined with high-quality entertainment opportunities that encourage families to make a whole-day-out visit to the ballpark. These parks, which seat approximately 12,000–15,000 spectators, incorporate old-fashioned ballpark features with new technology and amenities that have proven to be very attractive to fans. In the last 20 years,

166

over 120 new minor league stadiums have been constructed throughout the U.S. as a result of the rising popularity of minor league baseball. Cities in Alabama, Florida, North Carolina, Oregon, South Carolina, Tennessee, Virginia, and Washington all have minor league ballpark projects in various stages of development.

Many minor league baseball parks, such as those in Dayton, Ohio, and in Memphis and Nashville, Tennessee, have been or are being constructed as part of larger downtown area development projects. While the 1970s and 1980s saw the exodus of retail, industry, and service businesses from downtown areas to suburban locations, the next three decades signaled renewed interest in rebuilding downtowns across the U.S. Minor league ballparks have become just one piece of the downtown revitalization puzzle. AutoZone Park, which opened in April 2000 in Memphis, was built as a cornerstone property designed to spur both public and private investment in the general area. Older buildings were renovated, and retail and residential space was created. An elementary school was built in the downtown area, and public works projects including a board walk and improved streets and lighting were completed. The ballpark itself is attached to the Toyota Center, a renovated 220,000-square foot office building that overlooks the field. The synergy created by the ballpark (whose main tenant is the Class AAA Pacific Coast League affiliate of the St. Louis Cardinals) and surrounding development was enough to create a spirit of excitement about the area and heightened demand for available properties. In fact, the Toyota Center office complex had commitments for all of its available space before construction began. Additional improvements were made to the Cook County Convention Center, and local business officials heightened their marketing efforts to promote tourism. Residents began to return to the downtown area, and retail, restaurant, and professional offices continued to follow.

In Dayton, a new minor league ballpark also served as a cornerstone for local area development. The stadium was designed not only to act as a magnet for business but to spur tourism as well. Through the incorporation of design elements such as picnic areas, playgrounds, and luxury suites and with promotional tie-ins to local restaurants, shopping, and hotels, the facility attracted visitors both during and beyond the baseball season. The new ballpark and baseball franchise, the Dayton Dragons (Class A Midwest League, affiliated with the Cincinnati Reds), is credited with breathing new life into downtown Dayton.

In Frisco, Texas, the new minor league ballpark for the Frisco RoughRiders, the Class AA Texas League affiliate of the Texas Rangers, became one of the first pieces of a sports complex that was designed to give the growing city an identity as a sport destination. Other facilities included in the complex include a brand new soccer stadium for FC Dallas of Major League Soccer, an ice arena, and youth sport fields. These sport facilities helped to anchor an urban development plan that included office and retail space, public park/walkway areas, and housing.

In Oklahoma City, a new $34 million Southwestern Bell Bricktown Ballpark, home of the Oklahoma City RedHawks (the Class AAA Pacific Coast League affiliate of the Houston Astros), served as a cornerstone of the city's metropolitan area project that also includes the construction of a downtown arena, performing arts center, river walk, and a renovated convention center. The park, which was part of a nine-piece urban revitalization project, was funded in part by a one-cent sales tax increase that was approved by voters. Surrounding shops, restaurants, hotels, and entertainment venues have turned the park and the Bricktown area into an entertainment destination for tourists and local residents as well, with visitor counts exceeding 4 million people a year.

Plans to build a new minor league stadium in Nashville, Tennessee, fell apart in 2007 but, despite several delays and failed financing attempts, plans were revived in November 2009. Three new sites have been selected (all in close proximity to the downtown area), and discussions continue. In 2012, the city of Pensacola, Florida, opened a new city park, complete with a minor league stadium on the city's waterfront. The project includes an amphitheater and the development of a maritime museum and other commercial development. Long-term plans include the development of a marina. The design of the ballpark takes advantage of the spectacular view of the Pensacola Bay and the breezes coming off the water, making the location one of the most fan-friendly minor league parks in the south.

Sport facility consultant Rick Horrow (2001) suggests that this trend in minor league baseball sheds light on the realities of sport facility construction both in minor and major league sports. Because of the rising costs of sport facility construction – many minor league ballparks carry $30+ million price tags, and professional stadiums and arenas have exceeded the $1 billion mark – facilities will need to be viewed within the context of the surrounding area and its contribution to the entire community. New facility construction must encompass creative, comprehensive, and integrative solutions, but these facilities, because of the high price tag, must be viewed as a broader asset to the community and must provide opportunities for year-round revenue development. Stadiums, arenas, and recreational sport complexes must be considered as community assets, rather than isolated private projects. They should be viewed as a valuable component and may often serve as the catalyst for the development or revitalization of entire metropolitan or suburban districts. For sport managers, the lesson is clear. Given the rising costs of sport facility construction and renovation coupled with the public's hesitancy to fund private development of facilities for professional sport teams, the successful park, arena, or stadium builder must position, present, and deliver a sport facility that will not only spur tangible area growth and economic development, but will complement the character of the surrounding area and contribute to the vitality of the community.

SPORT FACILITY MANAGEMENT

Sport facilities have existed for thousands of years. Ancient cultures, including the Egyptians, Greeks, Romans, and Chinese, invested in the creation of sport facilities that were used to promote sport for a variety of purposes including military readiness, entertainment, and physical wellness of their people (Fried, 2010). Contemporary sport managers agree that appropriate facilities are an important component of sport. Certainly, there are many examples of how the management of sport organizations is influenced by sport facilities. A professional sport team, for example, may be financially dependent upon a facility that not only provides the appropriate seating capacity, but also offers revenue generation opportunities such as luxury suites, club seating, retail space, and stadium restaurants. A high school that wishes to field swimming and diving teams may only do so if there is a regulation size competition pool with diving well available. Sport managers recognize that the sport facility is a critical resource for the organization.

Sport by nature depends on facilities. Just about every sporting activity requires a specific venue, playing surface, or area and most likely some type of equipment. Sport facilities may either be indoor or outdoor and may be naturally occurring – mountains, lakes, rivers, ponds – or manufactured – running tracks, bocce courts, golf course, or stadium. Regardless of the type, size, or number of facilities available to the sport organization, the sport manager is actively involved in planning, constructing, financing, maintaining, and operating these facilities.

Sport managers recognize that the facility impacts the organization in many ways. Certainly the number, type, and quality of sport programs and activities offered are directly influenced by available facilities. Second, the quality of the sports facility is a direct reflection of the organization and its programs. The facility contributes to the sport organization's brand. Facilities also play an important role in customer service. Third, the sport facility is a critical asset to the organization that can positively affect or negatively impact revenue generation.

Most sport management programs require students to take a specific course in sport facility management and event planning because of the broad recognition of the importance of facility management and operational planning to the sport organization. Sport professionals must master very specific issues, practices, and skills related to the management of the sport facility. The body of knowledge related to sport facility management encompasses such topical areas as planning, designing, financing, and construction of facilities as well as scheduling, budgeting, finance, marketing, operations management, box office management, maintenance, building systems operation, feasibility studies, economic impact, food service, security, risk management, loss prevention, inventory control, ticketing, sponsorship, and quality-control systems.

Managing the various types of sport facilities

The type of sport facility that people are most familiar with is a public assembly facility (PAF), a large structure created for the purpose of facilitating the gathering of large groups of people who come together for the purpose of viewing or participating in an event. Stadiums, arenas, and coliseums are categorized as public assembly facilities. Tiered seats, specialized playing or performance surfaces, spectator amenities such as rest rooms and food service areas, and performer amenities including locker rooms and training rooms usually characterize the PAF. These buildings host sporting and entertainment events such as concerts, pro sport team games, trade shows, and family shows (e.g. ice shows, circuses). They are usually designed to accommodate one or more sport team tenants that may include a professional sport team (major or minor league) or a top-level college team.

Convention centers, civic centers, auditoriums, exposition halls, theaters, and concert halls are also public assembly facilities. While the buildings may not be specifically designed to host sport activities, they are designed for public assembly and for the accommodation of entertainment, professional conferences, shows, and other performances or activities that provide entertainment or education for the community, enhance civic culture, generate tourism, and generally improve the quality of life for residents and visitors alike. Sport facility managers are often responsible for managing multi-building complexes that include any number of PAFs. However, one standard combination is the sport arena or civic center and the convention center.

Other sport facilities are designed primarily for the purpose of accommodating individual or smaller groups of users rather than large audiences of viewers. Such facilities might include a mountain ski resort, sports hall of fame, tennis court, golf course, gymnasium, municipal soccer field, state park, natatorium, equestrian course, or health and fitness club. This segment of the industry is clearly the largest, yet the larger public assembly facilities usually receive the most attention in the study of the sport facility industry. Stadiums, arenas, and convention centers, because of their affiliation with sport teams and the entertainment industry, capture public attention because they receive daily media coverage, while the smaller user-oriented facility operates in virtual obscurity. While there are thousands of public assembly facilities across the U.S., there are many smaller participant-oriented facilities. Virtually every state and town, high school, recreation department, college and university, military base, YMCA, and health and fitness club manages a variety of different sporting facilities and hosts numerous sport and entertainment events and activities at those facilities on a regular basis. While these facilities usually operate on a much smaller scale than the large public assembly facility, their managers are faced with similar responsibilities, issues, and challenges as the stadium or arena manager.

170

There are many different types of ownership and management of sport facilities. Some facilities are owned by governmental entities such as cities, towns, counties, states, or the federal government. Non-profit organizations or private interests such as private management companies, pro sports teams, individuals, or corporations own others. Sport facilities are not necessarily owner managed. Most facilities that are owned by a non-profit organization or a governmental entity such as the state or the city utilize some type of advisory board or commission to act as an agent or representative of ownership. The board or commission may serve as a policy-making body or may be responsible for oversight and control of the facility. The commission is ultimately responsible for selecting an appropriate management team to operate the facility.

Sport facilities may be owner managed. This model is often called *in-house management*. Historically, universities, states, and cities chose to manage their own buildings. However, when buildings fail to meet owner's expectations, other management alternatives have been considered. For some organizations, in-house management created a variety of problems related to inexperience; political patronage; burdensome public regulation and policies; and lack of resources to attract events, meet customers' needs, and purchase needed equipment, technology, or supplies. In these cases, owners have considered the private management alternative.

There are several private companies that specialize in the management of sport and allied facilities. These management groups promise to deliver more efficient operations and expect to reduce the facility's operating deficit. Relying on their expertise and connections within the sport, tourism, hospitality, recreation, and entertainment industries, they are usually able to create a more comprehensive and higher-quality schedule; hire more skilled managers; and negotiate better deals with sponsors, promoters, and suppliers. The facility owners will secure a private management company through a selection process that begins with a *request for proposal or RFP.* This comprehensive document provides an overview of the current state of the building and its operations, and details the owner's expectations for new management (Farmer *et al.*, 2001). The RFP is then sent to all major private management companies and a notice of the availability of the RFP is posted in trade publications. Interested parties will then express their interest in the facility by preparing a bid within the time limit specified in the RFP. Bidders are then provided with the opportunity to tour the facility and discuss the RFP with the facility's owner or governing body representatives. The private management company/bidder may then wish to review the RFP in more detail and are allowed to submit additional materials to supplement their original bid proposal. Once all proposals that have been received by the posted deadline are reviewed, finalists are chosen and are asked to do a personal presentation to the building owner or representatives. Once presentations are completed, a top choice is selected and both parties will enter into contract negotiations. The signing of the contract by both parties signals the official completion of the RFP process.

The RFP process is an important one to facility managers because many critical functions in the facility are outsourced through a similar process. Food service, security, maintenance, parking, and other functions can be outsourced. Utilizing private companies to provide these services allows the facility manager to acquire specialized expertise and is often seen as an efficient way to carry out functions that might otherwise be a very expensive and ineffective use of limited internal resources.

The role of the sport facility manager

Sport facility managers are essentially responsible for two functions: (1) the operation of the building itself, and (2) the planning and execution of events or programs within the building. Managerial tasks related to the operation of the building include facility systems management, maintenance, and the hiring of building administrative staff. A good sport facility manager has a working knowledge of the internal mechanical systems of the building including heating, ventilation and air conditioning, electrical, plumbing, and refrigeration. A facility manager must also be aware of issues related to building design and construction including weight-bearing capacity of the roof, accessibility, and building material composition. A facility manager must understand the building's structure and equipment and also is able to coordinate a maintenance plan that assures that the building is not only in top condition, but is safe for users, employees, and spectators alike. While the sport facility manager need not necessarily be an expert in mechanical engineering, it is important that he or she understands how the building works.

Other responsibilities that come under the heading of managing the building may include scheduling and booking events; marketing the facility to promoters, travel coordinators, and convention planners; budgeting; human resource management; public relations; marketing; and ticket, advertising, and sponsorship sales.

The second responsibility of the facility manager is event management. This function is commonly called operations, game operations, or "ops" management, but we use the term *event management* here to represent this function. Event management consists of the planning and execution of the wide variety of functions and activities that take place in a sport facility on a daily basis. Depending upon its size and accommodations, a large public assembly facility might host as many as 100 different events including concerts, family shows, meetings, and professional sport contests in one month. A local recreation sport complex may host a 30-game tournament, youth sport banquet, and instructional clinic in one weekend. A college field house may host a faculty reception, intramural floor hockey game, karate class, men's and women's basketball practice, cheerleading try-outs, and racquetball tournament in one evening. Regardless of the size or configuration of the sport facility, most front-line sport facility managers will suggest that the bulk of their time is spent on scheduling, planning, and executing events.

Most PAFs have an entire events management department or unit with an events manager or operations director who is designated to oversee this function. The operations director/event manager is responsible for the coordination of all needed services to support each event. They oversee the purchase of supplies, maintain equipment, and hire appropriate staff to guarantee that the event goes as planned. The event manager/operations director may direct laborers, stagehands, electricians, musicians, security, food service, customer service, medical staff, transportation, parking, ticket takers, concession workers, and other part-time workers. The event management function includes the management of the bulk of the behind-the-scenes staff who are responsible for planning and executing an event. Event staff work closely with event producers to ensure that all the physical requirements for the event are in place: that the equipment is available and functioning properly and that the building is configured and set up appropriately for the event. To summarize, the event management function encompasses preparing the building for each event according to specifications, ensuring the event goes off smoothly, and then cleaning up after the function.

For the purpose of our discussion, it is best to think of event management as micro-level operations management. That is the day-to-day activities of the building, carrying out its schedule of events, and hosting programs. This activity represents only one level of operations management within a sport facility. The other level of operations management takes place on a macro- or strategic organization-wide level. At this level, management translates its selected strategy into action steps or plans in each of the organization's key functional areas. This process is referred to as *operational planning.*

This distinction is an important one because operations management in sport facilities varies significantly from what is traditionally considered to be operations management in most businesses. For most non-sport organizations, operations management consists solely of what we refer to here as operational planning, by which strategy is translated into action across the organization. For sport facilities, the challenge is not only how to put the strategic plan into action, but how to plan and execute hundreds of events, programs, and activities every year. Sport facility management experts Peter Farmer, Aaron Mulrooney, and Rob Amon suggest that the difference is that "operations management in a sport facility focuses on *how* services are produced, rather than the production of those services ... this is the traditional definition of operations management" (Farmer *et al.*, 2001, p. 274, original emphasis).

For example, a sport business such as a professional sport team is interested in producing a high-quality team that wins championships. Their manager is focused on the game, the winning, and the team. A concert promoter is interested in securing talented performers who attract ticket buyers. In each case, management is focused on the product. The sport facility manager, however, has a different focus. He or she is keenly interested in how the game or concert is presented or produced. Pertinent issues for the sport facility manager include the sound system, the lighting, the cleanliness of the rest rooms, proper ordering and preparation of food, safe parking lots, clear walkways, and clean locker rooms.

To better understand the difference between the traditional definition of operations management and event/operations management in the sport facility business, it is important to understand the strategic management process.

THE STRATEGIC MANAGEMENT APPROACH TO PLANNING

The major components of the strategic management approach are summarized below in Box 6.1. Because the sports environment is continuously shifting and changing, strategic management must be an ongoing, continuous examination of how well sport organizations are aligned with that environment. In sport organizations, top-level managers such as CEOs, presidents, and commissioners are responsible for engaging the organization in strategic planning. Although responsibility for strategic management is increasingly shared through organizations, top-level managers must often serve as the directing impetus behind strategic planning.

A clear, compelling sense of direction is the starting point of the strategic management process; it is management's responsibility to give the organization this sense of its own enduring purpose (Carlson-Thomas, 1992). The most common way that organizations attempt to communicate this sense of purpose or direction is through a mission statement.

BOX 6.1 THE STRATEGIC MANAGEMENT PROCESS

- Develop mission and specific strategic goals
- Analyze environment
- Formulate strategy
- Implement strategy
- Strategic control

Step 1: establishing the organization's direction

The first responsibility of management is to provide vision. For example, consider the case of York University (U.K.) officials who sought to enhance their contribution to the health of the general public and create a positive relationship between the university and the community. Colin Smith, the university's director of physical recreation, believed that York had an excellent record of supporting the community through providing access to university sport facilities, yet had been limited in its effectiveness due to the lack of sufficient facilities (Patterson, 2006). Smith and university officials envisioned a versatile sport complex that would support a wide variety of community interests including football, indoor hockey, basketball, tennis, volleyball, badminton, netball, and martial arts. The university had already opened its doors to a community squash club, trampoline club, disabled cricket team, soccer teams, and youth sports instruction camps and clinics, yet had had to turn down community-use requests due to lack of availability and sufficient facilities (Patterson, 2006). A user-friendly, multi-sport facility was envisioned where a number of different activities could be run at the same time and where users would be provided with quality amenities.

In terms of strategic management, the vision of a dynamic, versatile sport facility that would play a critical role in enhancing university and community relationships while contributing to public health and quality of life was clearly articulated by top-level managers. They set this vision that would provide the organization with an immediate and enduring sense of purpose.

Mission statement

Vision serves as a starting point for the mission statement that is a written summary of what business the organization is in or seeks to be in. It often includes a statement of the organization's philosophy and values. The mission statement reveals an organization's long-term vision – what it wants to be and whom it wants to serve. An effective mission statement provides a sense of direction for every individual and group in the sport organization.

For sport organizations, it is important to define the business they are in. While some people may suggest that sport organizations are in the business of making money, simply defining an organization's mission in this way does not provide direction or keep the organization focused on its stakeholders. Rather, a mission statement should clearly answer the questions "What business are we in?" and "What business should we be in?" These questions must be answered in terms of customer needs and not in terms of the products or services the company currently offers (Abell, 1980; Collins and Porras, 1996; Collins, 1997). This emphasis on customer needs helps organizations avoid being left behind by changes in technology or consumer preferences and keeps them focused on developing strategies to support the mission. A sport facility's mission might suggest that it is in the business of "providing a high-quality entertainment experience to guests in a safe, comfortable, and friendly stadium environment." The statement clearly identifies the organization's business (provision of a high-quality entertainment experience) and addresses customer (guest) needs (high-quality entertainment experience in a safe, comfortable, and friendly stadium environment). By being very clear about its mission, the organization provides a foundation for strategy creation as well as a direction for developing new activities, programs, or amenities.

Beyond the business it is in or seeks to be, a mission statement should also articulate the organization's basic beliefs, values, and priorities. In the case of our facility mission statement, it is very clear that the organization is committed to quality, safety, comfort, and a friendly atmosphere. The mission suggests that the organization's top priority is the needs and satisfaction of its guests or patrons. This mission statement points to an organization that is customer centered, and one might expect that customer service is a critical element of organizational philosophy.

Step 2: analyzing the situation – comparing the organization to its environment

In terms of strategic planning, even organizations with clear missions often tend to get so caught up in day-to-day problems that they fail to recognize and respond to what's happening around them. For example, over the last few decades, lifestyles have changed. Many outdoor municipal pools have been replaced by water spray parks due to escalating costs of renovating older pools, the high overhead costs of operating a public pool, and the increasing number of other water-based recreation options including commercial water parks and well-developed lake and waterfront resorts. The availability of backyard pools, municipal budget cuts, as well as sport facility managers concerns over liability and rising costs of liability insurance for water-based attractions have all negatively affected the use of municipal outdoor pools and have forced some pool operators to scale back on hours and services (Ellerbrook, 2011). Additional pressures on pool operators come from government regulations which may stipulate number of showers and type of bathhouse facilities, ADA requirements, and supervision standards, all having affected the operation of large outdoor public pools (Cohen, 2006). For many sport facility managers in the public setting, public pool maintenance and operation have become prohibitive, and as a result pools may be closed and demolished, operate on a limited basis, or be replaced entirely by water spray features which are more efficient and cost effective (Ellerbrook, 2011). Clearly, environmental factors affect facility operation and have financial implications.

Sport managers must recognize that their organizations do not operate in a vacuum and that it is critically important to monitor changes and trends in their environment. In the strategic management view, before deciding on a plan of action, or a strategy to achieve a mission, the organization must analyze the situation carefully. Managers must understand the organization's strengths and weaknesses as well as those of its competitors. They must also recognize what is happening in the environment and then evaluate the organization in an environmental context. This process is called a situation analysis.

Situation analysis examines the complex set of interactions between factors both inside and outside the organization. It begins with a review of conditions in the environment to see if they pose opportunities or threats and then uses this review as a basis for assessing the organization itself for potential strengths and weaknesses. Box 6.2 details those factors that make up the general and the task environment. The general environment includes broad trends and conditions in society. These are factors that are outside the organization that tend to affect society at large and all organizations in general. The task or specific environment consists of individuals, groups, and organizations that directly affect a particular organization itself and specifically those dimensions of the organization that impact the organization's performance.

The first step in analyzing the organization's situation is to assess the environment for opportunities and threats. Two categories of environments must be monitored. They are the general environment that is shared by every organization in a society, and the task or specific environment, which is unique to a particular organization.

BOX 6.2 THE ORGANIZATION AND ITS ENVIRONMENT

- General environment: social, economic, political/legal, technological, global
- Task environment: customers, competitors, suppliers, regulators

---

General environment

As Box 6.2 shows, the general environment can be divided into five dimensions or subcategories of change: social, economic, political/legal, technological, and global.

Social change includes changes in social patterns, demographics, values, and institutions. In the case of our aquatic facility manager/pool operator, social changes may include a shift to a social norm where backyard built-in family pools are considered to be more desirable than the community pool.

Economic change refers to the overall status of the economy, which varies over time. In times of economic prosperity, demand for non-essential goods and services is high. Consumers, having high levels of disposable income, may seek out higher priced services or amenities and may be willing to travel greater distances to attain them. For the local aquatic facility manager, this may mean that local customers are more willing to travel further from home and may be willing to seek out premium entertainment options, forgoing the community facility. In times of economic difficulty, the reverse is true. Customers may be more willing to seek out affordable local options or they might completely abandon non-essential leisure, recreation, or sport spending.

Political and legal change includes the impact of governmental laws and the legal system, as well as the relationship between government and business. The sport manager must be aware of federal, state, and local laws and regulations that shape the operation of the sport organization. The Americans with Disabilities Act (ADA), as outlined in Chapter 2, has greatly influenced the design and operation of sport facilities, as sport managers have renovated or built facilities that must incorporate accessible seating and amenities, for example.

Technological change refers to the advances that create new products and new ways of producing goods and providing services. Technology has transformed every sports organization's environment with revolutions in manufacturing, communication, information processing, and shopping. Nearly every stadium and arena throughout the country has its own Internet website, where fans can access facility schedules, view virtual seat sight lines, and purchase event tickets. Sport facilities are now facing the challenge of providing wireless access to all patrons. High-tech scoreboards, communications equipment, and retail and food service ordering technologies are being incorporated in stadiums and arenas around the world at record pace.

Global change has been perhaps the most volatile recent environmental factor. International politics and economic conditions have been dramatically altered by the sudden shift of whole geographic regions to more capitalist economic systems from communist or totalitarian models, where governments planned and controlled the production and distribution of goods and services, and set prices. Political unrest also continues to shape the global sport environment as warring governments, religious and political factions, and individuals contribute to instability and unrest throughout the world. Additionally, technological developments in communication and transportation make it possible for sport organizations to operate in the global marketplace. In the sport facility industry, globalization has brought changes to the sport facility landscape as teams, leagues, and events move to more international venues.

Changes in the social, economic, political/legal, technological, and global environments, then, can have a dramatic effect on any organization. It is the responsibility of management to monitor continuously these key dimensions of the general environment to recognize as early as possible the changes that might impact the organization. This responsibility extends also to the task environment.

Task environment

The task, or immediate, environment includes the factors in the environment that directly impact a specific organization, and are the elements located closer to the organization. Like the general environment, the task environment consists of several dimensions. Among the most important are customers, competitors, suppliers, and regulators.

Customers are the individuals, groups, and other organizations that purchase the products and services an organization provides. Changes in customers' needs and priorities can have a significant effect on a sport facility. In the case of our aquatic facility, consumer interest in more amenities might require the facility manager to upgrade locker room and concession services.

Competitors are other organizations that vie for an organization's customers. In the aquatic facility environment, commercial water parks with high-tech entertainment features such as wave pools, cascading water falls, or towering water slides have been integrated with existing amusement parks. These new multi-faceted facilities have posed serious competition to community facilities.

Suppliers also can exert a strong outside influence on organizations. They may raise their prices, or the quality of their goods may become a problem. It is also important to note that labor supply may be limited in its skill or number, thus requiring the organization to train new hires or seek new sources of talent. Sport organizations view suppliers as potential sources of competitive advantage. Managers understand that relationships with potential suppliers can result in sponsorships, can support customer service initiatives, and contribute significantly to the quality of goods and services provided.

Regulators are the final component of the organization's task environment. These outside agencies have the ability to control or influence the internal working of the organization. For sport facility managers, government agencies influence facility design, construction, and operation through local building codes, health and safety codes, and other regulations. Governmental organizations and agencies are not the only groups that regulate sport organizations. Governing bodies and professional organizations can also influence an organization's policies and procedures. In intercollegiate athletics, organizations such as the National Collegiate Athletic Association (see Chapter 8) and individual conferences provide specific sport facility guidelines and requirements for some sport facilities and events. This was the case in 2010 when Northwestern University and the University of Illinois were slated for using Wrigley Field, home of MLB's Chicago Cubs, for their annual football game. Both teams were forced to run their offenses toward the west end zone due to safety concerns because the back line of the east end zone was only six inches from the famed Wrigley brick outfield wall. Big Ten Conference commissioner Jim Delaney said of the decision: "The health and safety of our student-athletes is of the utmost importance," and after reviewing the field, "all parties felt it was appropriate to adjust the rules" (Maynard, 2010, p. 1). Public interest groups also attempt to shape the operation of some sport organizations. When facility managers attempt to expand or build facilities, they often face scrutiny and in some cases outright opposition from local private interest groups who are against the organization's efforts to take land or use local tax revenues to finance construction. The result of such efforts can influence outcomes of public referenda on facility construction.

The purpose in studying the general and task environments is to identify trends and conditions that represent opportunities or threats to the organization's ability to achieve its goals. The process of monitoring and evaluating puts the organization in a proactive rather than reactive position and reduces the likelihood of being caught off guard by shifts in the environment. This phase of the strategic management process can be thought of as a kind of early warning system that allows management to take the initiative either to maximize the opportunity or to minimize the corresponding threat resulting from environmental change.

Once the sport manager understands the environment, he or she must clearly understand the organization's competencies and then must be able to see links between organizational competencies and environmental conditions. The manager must begin by doing a thorough evaluation of the organization. A checklist of key areas of organizational competency might include the following.

MANAGEMENT

Does the organization possess the management skill and experience necessary to address potential threats or pursue potential opportunity? What management systems, processes, experience, and resources are available? For example, is the current management structure appropriate to move the organization in directions that the environment demands?

CORPORATE CULTURE AND VALUES

Is the value system or the organization consistent with the demands of the environment? Does the organization value or exhibit behaviors or operational standards that will support functioning in a way that the environment demands? For example, does the organization embrace conservative thinking when the environment calls for risk-taking initiatives?

HUMAN RESOURCES

Do the organization's employees have the skills necessary to respond effectively to changes in the environment? As technology becomes more complex, does the organization have the people it needs to manage technological innovation? On a global basis, does the organization have the people with the language skills and cultural understanding necessary to compete?

OPERATIONAL SYSTEMS

Does the organization possess, or can it develop, the systems necessary to succeed? Does the organization have the necessary equipment, processes, and policies to conduct business in ways that the environment demands? For example, as more sport organizations seek to conduct business on-line, do they have the necessary knowledge, systems, and equipment to conduct transactions effectively and efficiently in cyberspace?

MARKETING

Does the organization have the ability to evaluate customer needs and to price, promote, and advertise its products and services effectively? Is the organization able to deliver high-quality customer service and meet ever-changing market demands for speed, flexibility, technology, and quality?

FINANCIAL RESOURCES

Does the organization have access to the financial resources necessary to respond effectively to the environment? Can it afford the management, human resources, technology, research, and marketing that will allow it to compete as the environment demands?

SWOT analysis

Only with an understanding of all of its competencies can the organization begin the next step of determining its strategic strengths and weaknesses and then determine how these competencies align with environmental conditions. This process of considering an organization's competencies in terms of changes in the environment is called a SWOT analysis (Andrews, 1971; Schendel and Hofer, 1979). SWOT stands for the **s**trengths and **w**eaknesses of the organization and **o**pportunities and threats in the environment. A SWOT analysis for a sport facility organization might identify a long-term prime tenant relationship as a strength and a lack of club seating as a weakness. The construction of a new on-campus arena at a local university could be perceived as a threat and the expansion of a regional semi-professional arena football league could be viewed as an opportunity. Once a SWOT analysis has identified strengths and weaknesses in the context of opportunities and threats in the environment, an organization can begin to develop strategic alternatives for achieving its goals.

Step 3: developing strategy

The term strategy comes from the Greek term meaning "to lead an army." In that sense, a strategy is a kind of battle plan. In strategic management terms, strategy is the course of action an organization selects to minimize threats and maximize opportunities that emerge in the environment. The strategies an organization selects must reflect its mission, the opportunities, and threats in the environment, and its own strengths and weaknesses. The process of developing strategy helps the organization find its best fit among the three sets of forces.

Developing strategic alternatives

Strategic alternatives are the options that management can select as the possible courses of action for obtaining its goals. The different levels of strategic alternatives are listed in Box 6.3.

BOX 6.3 DIFFERENT LEVELS OF STRATEGIC ALTERNATIVES

Corporate level   *Strategies pertaining to companies that conduct business across several industries or several markets.*

Business level   *Strategies for companies operating in a single industry.*

Functional level   *Strategies for the organization's functional areas or departments.*

Corporate-level strategy

This level deals with the alternatives a company or organization explores as it conducts business across several industries or markets. At the corporate level, strategy deals with an organization's decision about either expanding or retreating in general or from industry to industry. It is useful to think of corporate-level strategy in two distinct terms: either getting bigger or getting smaller.

MERGER AND ACQUISITION

These strategies represent the organization's intent to grow or "get bigger." An organization adopts these strategies to either offset threats in its own environment and/or take advantage of opportunities in the environment of another industry. This strategy might also be designed to develop new organizational competencies. A merger with another organization or an acquisition/purchase of another company can expand the organization's resources and/or expertise. In the sport facility industry, a stadium management company might choose to

182

acquire a food service company for the purpose of expanding its expertise in concessions management. This strategy of moving food service "in house" might have the additional benefits of allowing the sport facility company to capture all associated food service revenue.

RETRENCHMENT

When an organization is not competing effectively, retrenchment, or turn-around, strategies are often needed. One retrenchment option involves divesting or selling off divisions in industries an organization no longer wants to compete in. For example, a sport facility management company may choose to divest itself of its building security division that for a variety of reasons has become unprofitable and unwieldy to manage. The other retrenchment strategy involves downsizing, which typically involves a significant reduction in the size of an organization and the number of employees working for it. In the sport facility business, a manager might decide to downsize his operational staff by eliminating several full-time box office positions and moving toward more on-line ticketing. These strategies may be viewed as helping the organization to "get smaller" for the purpose of running more efficiently by eliminating divisions or areas that have become ineffective or unnecessary. It is important to remember that corporate-level strategies are based not only on current information about the organization and environmental conditions, but also on forecasted conditions of tomorrow. For example, in the sport facility business there has been a great deal of discussion of a trend toward more on-line ticketing and the possible influence that virtual ticketing is having on walk-up gate. Some managers suggest that while some facilities currently employ several game-day box office personnel to handle walk-up sales, computerized ticketing may eventually eliminate the need for day-of-game sales.

Business-level strategy

The second level of strategy deals with an organization or corporate business unit operating in a single industry. The purpose of defining a business-level strategy is to give the organization an advantage over its competition in the same industry. At the business level are three approaches for achieving a competitive advantage: differentiation, cost leader, and focus (Porter, 1985).

DIFFERENTIATION

When an organization attempts to gain a competitive advantage through a differentiation strategy, it strives to be unique in its industry or market segment by designing product characteristics to satisfy customer needs in ways that competitors find difficult to match. This uniqueness may come from physical characteristics of the product, such as quality or reliability, or it may lie in the product's appeal to customers' psychological needs. Consider venerable ballparks such as Fenway Park and Wrigley Field. Each of these facilities offer unique physical attributes and boast a history of baseball tradition. To capitalize on fan interest, these parks have clearly differentiated themselves as one-of-a-kind historical facilities.

COST LEADER

An alternative to differentiation is the cost-leader strategy. Companies that strive to produce goods or services at the lowest cost in the industry, thereby enabling them to offer the lowest prices, pursue a cost-leader strategy. It is important to recognize that low cost does not mean cheap or inferior. For example, some minor league teams and sport facilities have assumed a cost-leader strategy by marketing themselves as high-quality affordable family entertainment.

FOCUS

In the focus strategy, an organization targets a particular customer or geographic market or follows a focus strategy that specializes in some way. Some sport facilities, such as an upscale private golf course, for example, have chosen to focus on affluent consumers. To carry out this strategy, the facility might feature upscale amenities such as fine-dining restaurants, luxury suites, spas, priority parking, cigar clubs, in-stadium art galleries, and the like.

Functional-level strategy

Functional-level strategies deal with plans that must be developed in each organization's key areas of functioning to support and implement corporate-level and business-level strategies. For example, a typical sport facility might have separate functional areas such as finance, marketing, human resources, public relations, event operations, box office, food service, security, parking, etc. The public relations office would play an important role in media relations, community relations, customer service, and marketing. Each individual unit or department would implement functional area strategies designed to support the achievement of organizational goals. Functional-level strategies must link across departments and units. For example, in the sport facility public relations office, strategies such as the enhancement of the current website might link to marketing strategies in the area of sponsorship, ticket sales, and merchandise sales.

Step 4: implementing strategy

As important as it is to develop strategy at the corporate, business, and functional levels, for strategies to be effective they must be translated into action. In step 4, strategies are implemented in a process called *operational planning*. As you recall

184

from the beginning of the chapter, strategy implementation takes place at the macro level, where the strategy is executed within an organizational context, and at the micro level, where individual events and activities are executed on a daily basis.

Once a strategy is formulated or chosen, it must be translated into terms that can be understood and acted upon at the operational level. As shown in Figure 6.1, on the macro level, operational planning is part of the implementation stage of the strategic management process.

Contrast this macro-level approach of operational planning with event management in the sport facility industry in Box 6.4. As discussed earlier in the chapter, operations, event, or game management is cross-functional strategy implementation on the micro level. The sport manager must consider a broad variety of functional considerations in event management. They include marketing, sales, logistics, maintenance, facility preparation, food service, staffing, risk management, hospitality advertising, etc. To illustrate this point more clearly, consider another example from the sport facility industry. A golf course operations manager is responsible for overseeing the production of various events and programs at the course. He or she might be responsible for coordinating tee times, scheduling tournaments or league play, marketing events, preparing advertising materials, reporting scores to the media, calculating handicaps, selling merchandise, hiring staff, and providing high-quality customer service. For a sport organization to meet its goals and carry out its strategy, operational planning must be carried out effectively at both the macro and micro level.

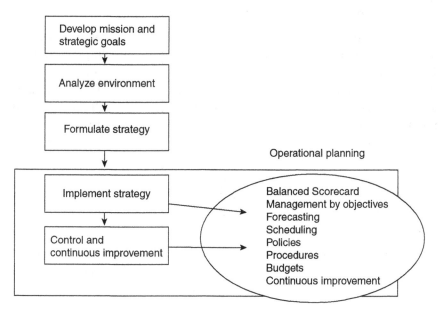

Figure 6.1 The relationship of operational planning to the strategic management process and the event management process (macro level)

Operational planning

Operational plans differ from strategic plans in several ways. First, operational plans tend to be drawn for a shorter period than strategic plans. For example, the strategy for providing wireless technology throughout the stadium may be a three-year plan. In contrast, the integration of wireless technology into food service for luxury suite customers might be a six-week project.

Another distinction is that operational plans focus more on the organization than on the external environment. As discussed earlier in the chapter, strategic plans are developed based on projected societal trends, national and regional economic forecasts, and technological factors, for example. The owner of the sport facility that seeks to diversify the food service menu by offering vegan, gluten-free, and sugar-free menu items is seeking not only to provide a better service to customers but he or she is seeking to capitalize on forecasted trends that the popularity of healthy eating will continue. The stadium manager decides that in addition to adding new items to existing menus that the stadium should create several new small healthy-eating dining areas or mini food courts throughout the stadium. This strategic initiative is clearly based on societal trends within the environment and an expectation that such expansion will be profitable for the organization.

Operational plans, on the other hand, are internally based and involve keeping the company running efficiently. Because the focus is on internal operations, planning techniques such as management by objectives and the Balanced Scorecard, forecasting, scheduling, policies, procedures, and budgets ensure that every department's actions mesh with the larger strategies of the organization. In the case of the construction of new mini healthy food court areas within the stadium, operational-level planning would involve the coordination of the construction projects, creation of marketing and sales materials, the development of an advertising campaign, the hiring of the staff to work in these areas, and the ordering and purchase of necessary supplies and equipment to set up and maintain these areas. Techniques utilized in operational planning at both the macro and micro level are the topic of the next section.

Management by objectives and the Balanced Scorecard

Peter Drucker (1954) developed the concept of management by objectives (MBO) as a system of goal setting and planning to help individuals and departments be more productive, and it proved to be the first framework for converting intangible mission statements into a unified system of interrelated performance measurements. A sport facility's mission of providing high-quality entertainment experiences is intangible. However, tallying the level of customer satisfaction is by no means intangible and can be measured easily based on surveys and the number of fans' visits.

The MBO approach involves sequential steps and starts with top managers identifying their objectives. Through negotiation and agreement, unit heads then establish objectives for their units. A cascading of objectives takes place as the process moves down the line to subordinates. Action plans are defined, and performance reviews are conducted at agreed-upon intervals. Although MBO remains a popular management technique for linking management and subordinate objectives, the concept of the "Balanced Scorecard" is designed to take this one step further and create strategy-focused organizations (Kaplan and Norton, 1993, 1996). The Balanced Scorecard is a framework where groups and individuals develop and closely monitor performance based on customer measures, internal processes, human resource measures, and financial measures – all tied directly to a specific strategic objective. The Balanced Scorecard framework consists of four steps or processes that separately and in combination contribute to linking strategic objectives with operational actions.

1   *Translate the vision*: despite the best intentions of those creating the organization's mission or vision, statements to deliver "quality entertainment" or "the best sports arena in its class" do not translate easily into operational terms. Like MBO, for people to act on words in mission and strategy statements, top management must agree on the specific objectives and measures that will be the drivers of success. Typically, these are the larger financial and customer objectives.

2   *Communicate and link the objectives to the next levels in the organization*: although the first process ensures that ten or so individuals in the organization

now understand the strategy better than ever before, it is critical that the next levels of subordinates formulate the internal-business process and human resource or employee learning objectives. For example, if satisfying customer expectations for immediate access to event tickets via a smartphone app, a major company objective identified by top management, the next levels of subordinates would identify several internal-business processes (such as installing new equipment, conducting training sessions, constructing new order processing forms, and establishing guidelines for order preparation), in which the company has to excel. This may involve retraining front-line employees and improving information systems available to them. The group sets up performance measures for these critical processes and measures for staff and systems capabilities.

3   *Business planning*: some organizations develop a strategic plan and then separately create their budgets for each year. Which document is discussed at monthly and quarterly meetings? Usually, it is only the budget, because a comparison of actual to budgeted figures is based on specific items, such as supplies, cost of goods sold, etc. The strategic plan is often only discussed or reviewed closely when the next major strategic planning effort occurs. Integrating these two important planning tools (strategy and budgets) is the purpose of this phase of the Balanced Scorecard approach. The budget's short-term financial framework is not changed; however, those developing it now allocate resources based on objectives and plans that are linked to the organization's larger strategies.

4   *Feedback and learning*: this aspect of the process enables companies to engage in strategic learning, much like a learning organization. With the Balanced Scorecard and the company's strategy at the center of its management systems, employees can monitor or control short-term results from the perspectives of financial performance, customers, internal business processes, and human relations. Because of this feedback, companies can modify strategies to reflect real-time learning.

In summary, although the Balanced Scorecard approach, as outlined in Figure 6.2, has many characteristics similar to MBO, it requires managers, teams, and individuals to develop and closely monitor performance based on customer measures, internal processes, human resource measures, and financial measures that are all tied directly to a specific strategic objective. This deliberate linkage of strategic objectives with operational actions distinguishes the approach from its older cousin, MBO, and is designed to build a strategy-focused organization.

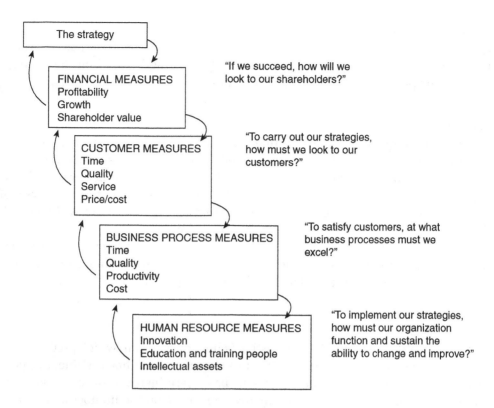

Figure 6.2 Strategy-driven Balanced Scorecard

Forecasting

To utilize the Scorecard approach effectively, it is important to develop accurate forecasts. Forecasts are predictions, projections, or estimates about future events that are the basis for determining the levels of business in each department. To illustrate, if the manager of an arena projects that the "Stars on Ice" show will sell out weekend evening performances, but not afternoon matinees, this forecast would form the basis for the number of concessions stands opened, employees hired, and level of spending for a marketing campaign.

Forecasts typically fall into two categories: quantitative and qualitative or judgmental. Although these forecasting techniques are described separately below, managers often use a combination of both quantitative and qualitative forecasts to help predict future events.

Quantitative forecasts

Quantitative forecasts use numerical data and mathematical formulas to project information about future events. This type of forecasting is based on the assumption that the past is a good predictor of the future.

TIME SERIES ANALYSIS

One method of quantitative forecasting using a historical approach is time series analysis, which estimates future values based on a sequence of statistical data. For example, organizations often base their sales forecasts on how much was sold during a similar period in the past. Figure 6.3 (below) shows a time series analysis of merchandise sold by an arena retail shop. Assuming that the future will be much like the past, the forecast in Figure 6.3 is that sales are expected to increase 17.5 percent in 2013 over 2014 (40,000 to 47,000). Based on this method of predicting future sales, an organization implementing a growth strategy would be able to plan at what rate to hire more workers, to order supplies, or to expand the retail shop.

LINEAR REGRESSION

Another quantitative method of forecasting is linear regression, which predicts how changes in one variable might be related to changes in another variable. Suppose that a private facility management company has determined that sales of beer at the stadiums and arenas it manages are highly dependent on the number and type of events scheduled at the facility and the demographics of fans attending the events. Using a mathematical equation and sales information from various facilities, managers can forecast sales at a new building based on the number and type of events scheduled for the facility and the demographic profiles of fans for each event.

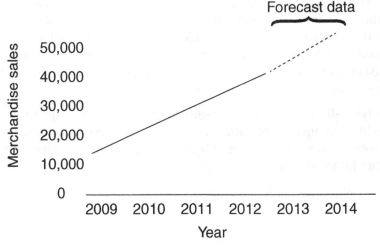

Figure 6.3 Time series analysis

Qualitative forecasts

Qualitative methods of forecasting consist mainly of subjective conclusions. For example, an experienced sport facility executive might predict that the previous year's winning season by the facility's prime tenant will create greater demand for luxury and club seating. These predictions rely more on individual or group judgment or opinion to predict future events, rather than on mathematical or statistical analysis.

DELPHI METHOD

The Delphi Method is one such qualitative technique. In the Delphi Method, input is solicited from a variety of experts who provide opinions on an individual basis. Their separate opinions are then gathered, evaluated, and summarized to form the basis of a forecast. Suppose a college is planning to build a new on-campus ice arena. It is likely that funding for the building will be secured within five years. The athletic facility manager is interested in building a state-of-the-art arena, but is unsure of what technology will be available in five years and what players and fans will expect in terms of locker rooms, training facilities, and scoreboard. The sport facility manager is interested in forecasting what new technologies will be available and should be integrated into design and construction plans. For this situation, participants in the Delphi forecast might include experts in refrigeration and scoreboard technology, sport facility architects, executives in the hockey industry, and market researchers. The experts are asked anonymously to predict what the hockey rink of the future will be like and when new technologies will become available. Persons coordinating the Delphi group collect the responses, average them, and ask for another opinion. Those experts who provide predictions in the first round that are significantly different from the others are asked to justify them. When the predictions get more and more similar, the average prediction is taken and becomes the group's forecast.

OPINION AND METHOD FEEDBACKS

Other qualitative techniques for forecasting future events include opinion surveys of executives, sales force feedback, and information from consumers. In each case, individual judgments are combined to generate information about the timing and other details of future events, and about conditions in the environment essential to the organization's strategy.

As noted earlier, frequently qualitative and quantitative forecasts are combined. When this occurs, forecasting begins with a quantitative prediction, which provides basic data about a future trend. Next, the qualitative forecast is added to the quantitative forecast, as a validity check. Then, the quantitative forecast is adjusted according to the subjective data. Whether companies rely more on quantitative, qualitative, or a combination of both types of forecasts, the challenge is to develop approaches that are continuously monitored by management to determine if improvements are necessary (Fisher *et al.*, 1994).

Scheduling

Scheduling is the process of formulating a detailed charting of activities that must be accomplished to attain objectives with timetables for completing the activities. A visit to a company organized around a Balanced Scorecard process would reveal these charts tacked on walls so that functional departments, teams, and individuals can closely monitor the progress of scheduled projects. One might also expect to see this chart in event management offices, where sport facility event managers and their teams carefully plan and execute literally hundreds of events and activities every year.

In the sport facility industry segment, scheduling also refers to the creation of a calendar of activities or events for the building or facility. For example, a political breakfast might take place on Friday morning in the exhibition hall, a rehearsal for a dance competition might take place on the arena floor on Saturday afternoon, a basketball game will be played on Saturday evening, and the circus might begin to move in and set up on Sunday morning for a Wednesday opening performance. Similarly, a university sport facility operations director would schedule activities for space within the building by allocating and reserving appropriate time and space for each program or event while also creating a master schedule of games and practices for all of the college's sports teams. Sport facility managers create either manual or computerized schedules for all sport facilities and available spaces. It is not unusual for a PAF to maintain a five–ten-year working calendar. Specialized computer software programs for sport facility scheduling help personnel manage the complex task of coordinating multiple events that take place in multiple spaces on a daily basis.

It is important to remember that not only must the manager consider the time and space requirements of the event, but he or she must also consider set-up and breakdown time as well. Facility managers must plan for building changeovers and must provide appropriate labor and equipment to ensure that the appropriate building configuration is achieved for each event. Building changeovers – especially those that involve a new playing surface, e.g. basketball court to ice surface or a new seating configuration – and addition of floor or end-zone seats require careful planning and coordination to achieve the changeover in a timely manner. The goal for the facility manager is to create and maintain a schedule that maximizes the use of the facility while avoiding logistical conflicts between events.

The *booking* process is different than scheduling. Booking involves negotiating terms and conditions for the use of the facility on an individual event basis. Booking involves signing a contract that details all event requirements and the guidelines, policies, and procedures for using the facility. Therefore, a facility manager would book individual events to create a schedule or calendar of events for the facility.

Once the calendar is created, the event or project manager would need to create a plan for executing all activities needed to produce the event. This event schedule serves as a critical tool for the operations/event director. It helps him or her to ensure that there is a timely and coordinated plan for carrying out all of the activities needed to ensure the event goes off as planned. For example, an event manager planning for a weekend flower shower recognizes that there are literally thousands of tasks associated with the event ranging from show set-up, electrical and water hook-ups, printing of the event program, coordinating media coverage, arranging for food service, and distributing VIP passes. Each event represents thousands of details that must be identified, delegated to appropriate staff members, coordinated, executed, and controlled.

Three popular techniques for scheduling and tracking activities in the sport facility business are Gantt charts, program evaluation and review technique (PERT) charts, and the event script.

GANTT CHARTS

Gantt charts are one of the most commonly used graphic scheduling tools. Developed by Henry Gantt, these charts show the significant activities required to meet an objective or to complete a project, with the events arranged in chronological order and the amount of time allotted for each activity. Gantt charts are particularly important in event management because of the myriad tasks involved in event preparation and the very specific time frame in which the sport manager must prepare in order for the event to be hosted successfully.

Although simple in concept and appearance, Gantt charts are used widely, from coordinating large projects to scheduling everyday activities. Table 6.1 shows a sample Gantt chart for a tennis complex hosting a local youth tournament. The tasks indicated by an X represent parts or steps of completed activities, and managers can use Gantt charts for progress reports. In Table 6.1, note that steps 8 through 10 are yet to be finished. These charts require analytical thinking, as they reduce projects or jobs to separate steps. They have the additional advantage of allowing planners to specify the time to be spent on each activity and are especially useful for scheduling activities that happen sequentially.

PERT CHARTS

The main weakness of the Gantt chart is that it does not contain information about the interrelationship of tasks to be performed. There is no way of telling if one task must be performed before another. The PERT chart (program evaluation and review technique) does not have this drawback and instead is designed to show the interrelationship of large and complex projects.

Table 6.1 Gantt chart for tennis tournament

	September			
	Week 1	Week 2	Week 3	Week 4
ACTIVITIES	1 2 3 4 5	8 9 10 11 12	15 16 17 18 19	22 23 24 25 26
1. Invite players	x x			
2. Establish brackets	x x x x	x x x x x	x	x x x
3. Press releases	x x			
4. Secure sponsors		x x x x x		
5. Order/ equipment		x x x x x		
6. Arrange security			x x x x x	
7. Staffing plan			x x x	
8. Print program				x x x / /
9. Set up stands/ tents				x x x / /
10. Set up courts				x x x / /

x completed
/ planned

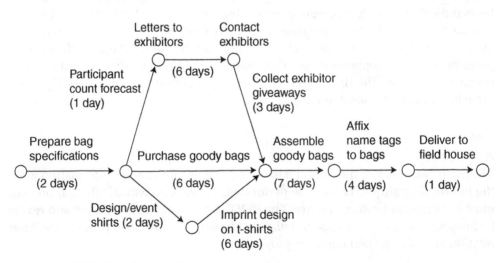

Figure 6.4 PERT chart for creation of event participant goody bags

Strategic management andthe sport facilities industry

Figure 6.4 displays the activities involved in the creation of goody bags for participants in a college fun fest held at the campus field house using a PERT chart. Note that there are time estimates for each PERT activity. Planners pinpoint the critical path, or most time-consuming chain of activities and events in the network. The longest path is the most critical because any delays will cause a delay of the entire project. In Figure 6.4, the longest path is 24 days. Any delays in that path will affect the scheduled completion date of the project. This example is intentionally simplified for instruction purposes. PERT charts are actually most often utilized for projects with numerous activities. The charts allow managers, teams, and individuals to predict resource needs, identify potential problem areas, and assess the impact of delays to the overall project completion time. In this way, they provide valuable information about whether objectives will be achieved and what modifications may be necessary.

EVENT SCRIPTS

Event scripts are one of the most important tools available to sport facility managers. Event scripts provide an outline of every activity that occurs in the production of a particular event much as a script details the dialog of a play. The event script usually begins to detail event activity about three hours before the event and then concludes with the completion of the event. The script provides timed direction to all the event staff participating in the production of the event. For example, the script will detail when the doors of the facility open, what music is played at one time, what the announcer will say, when the teams will be announced, etc. The script provides an outline for what will happen during every step of the event. It not only helps the manager plan out in detail how the event will be executed and what will be needed to ensure that the event runs smoothly, but it also keeps the staff informed and prepared for what will happen next. A sample of a portion of an abbreviated event script is presented in Box 6.5.

Guidelines for operational planning

Organizations frequently have guidelines for ensuring that actions will be consistent with organizational objectives. For example, an organizational policy relating to human resources might be that the organization "strives to recruit only the most talented employees." This policy statement is very broad, giving managers a general idea of what to do in the area of recruitment. Nonetheless, the policy emphasizes the importance attached to hiring competent employees, and it provides a framework for developing actions and plans that support the organization's strategy.

195

5:30	Gates open.
5:45–6:30	Pre-game warm ups – teams on field.
6:20	Color guard and band assemble in south end zone.
6:30	Teams return to locker rooms.
6:45	Band and color guard march to center of field. Cheerleaders form tunnel at home team entrance.
6:47	Teams return to field. Visitor enters first (north-west entrance). Home enters second (north-east entrance).
6:50	Officials move to center of field for coin toss. Announcer: *Good evening, football fans, and welcome to Eagles Stadium for tonight's conference matchup featuring our guests, the Littleton High School Golden Bears, and your Argyle Eagles! Please direct your attention to the center of the field for the pre-game coin toss.*
6:53	Presentation of colors. Announcer: *Fans, please welcome the District 5 color guard and the Argyle High School Band as they present our nation's colors.* Announcer: *And now, we invite you to rise as we honor America with our national anthem.*
6:54	Sound technician: switch sound feed to field microphone. Return to booth microphone when anthem complete.
6:55	Sound technician: play "Jump Around" – fade as officials move to field; switch sound system feed #2 to official's microphone.

Policies

Policies serve two purposes. One is that decisions in the organization are consistent with the organization's strategic objectives. Strategies heading in one direction, when combined with decisions reflecting a different course, are a disaster for an organization. For example, private sport facility management companies support their strategy of developing highly committed facility management experts by moving employees into increasing positions of responsibility and authority in different buildings managed by the company. In this way, they know that their executives will be placed in situations where they can learn all aspects of the business in different settings and can develop mentor relationships with other employees. This policy allows the company to achieve their strategic objective of a highly committed and expert team of facility management experts.

The other purpose of policies is to ensure a reasonable degree of consistency throughout the organization in the ways decisions are made. Decisions tend to reflect the personality, values, and experience level of the decision maker. Policies can offset this built-in idiosyncratic tendency by establishing guidelines to ensure consistency regardless of who is making the decision. Policies increase the likelihood that decisions will reflect the larger strategic objective of the organization, rather than just the personality or individual objectives of the decision maker. For example, sport facilities will provide detailed policy statements about ticketing. One common policy is that lost tickets will not be replaced. While this policy ensures that all ticket buyers are treated fairly, it also supports the facility's goal to eliminate problems associated with having two different groups of people showing up to an event holding tickets for the same seats. This policy also helps to deter the illegal sale of tickets when one ticket holder sells his or her first set of tickets and then seeks to replace them claiming that they were stolen.

Another policy that most sport fans are familiar with is the policy at professional baseball parks that any fan entering the playing field will be ejected. This policy guarantees uniform treatment for unruly fans, helps to deter inappropriate behavior, and supports the organization's larger goals of protecting both the spectators and the game participants.

Procedures

Procedures are guidelines for how tasks in the organization are to be performed. In general, procedures outline more specific actions than policies do. A well-developed set of work procedures can serve as a kind of road map guiding the efforts of individuals throughout the organization. Concession workers, for example, follow a specific set of procedures in serving alcoholic beverages at a sport facility. Workers receive vigorous training in alcohol service and often participate in formal alcohol service training programs such as TEAM or Techniques for Effective Alcohol Management. These programs help workers to understand alcohol service procedures so that they might not only become more efficient servers, but can help to protect the safety of the patron and limit the liability of the facility. Alcohol-service procedures might include having the server check the patrons' identification or requiring patrons to secure a plastic wrist bracelet at an identification checking station.

Although policies and procedures or work rules and guidelines point managers and employees in the right direction, they should leave room for creativity and judgment in terms of the details of how to get there.

Budgets

Budgets are guidelines indicating how an organization intends to allocate its financial resources. One technique used to ensure that budgets reflect the most current strategic objectives is called zero-based budgeting. In the traditional approach to budgeting for an upcoming year, managers begin with the existing budget, justify any changes that might be needed, and then add or subtract from the existing budget amounts. In zero-based budgeting, on the other hand, managers start each year from zero and justify each expense based on Balanced Scorecard measures from the customer, internal processes, and human resource perspectives.

The budgeting process involves keeping track of revenues and expenses and then comparing them in a summary statement. Box 6.6 shows this type of statement for a hypothetical sport event. Although this statement shows budgeted and actual figures at the end of the event, it is not unusual to list actual figures against budgeted figures on a daily, weekly, or monthly basis to identify expense overruns or revenue shortages early in the operation.

BOX 6.6 STATEMENT OF REVENUES AND EXPENSES FOR SPORTS EXPO

Statement as of December 31, 2012

Revenues	Budget	Actual
Admission	$120,000	$72,000
Booth sales	$120,000	$82,000
Goods sold inside	$270,000	$162,000
On-line sales	$2,500	(a)
	$512,500	$316,000
Expenses		
Rental	$40,000	$40,000
Labor (security)	$2,500	$2,500
Production	$18,000	$30,000
Cost of booth sales	$62,500	$77,500
Cost of selling goods inside	$135,000	$81,000
Talent	0	$8,000
Marketing	$80,000	$137,000
	$338,000	$376,000
Surplus (deficit)	$174,500	($60,000)

(a) On-line sales were not offered as intended due to insufficient technology.

This hypothetical example shows an extreme condition. As can be seen from Box 6.6, budgeted revenues were forecasted higher in every category. Reasons for the shortfall in revenues can be overoptimistic forecasting or unforeseen circumstances such as severe weather conditions that typically cause less attendance than expected. Also, ticket prices may have been set too high. In the expense area, marketing spent over four times the budgeted amount, and this was the primary expense causing the $60,000 deficit for the event.

Step 5: The control function

Traditionally, control has been defined as the process of ensuring that actual performance and results are consistent with performance goals. Control is the process of monitoring performance to ensure that performance goals are being achieved. The steps of the control process are shown in Box 6.7. Each of these steps represents a challenge to the sport organization as it seeks to ensure that performance is on target.

BOX 6.7 STEPS IN THE TRADITIONAL CONTROL PROCESS

- Establish/identify performance goals or standards.
- Monitor performance.
- Compare actual performance to the standard or goal.
- Take corrective action.

Establish performance standards

Clearly defined goals of the kind described in Chapter 4 are the first step in the control process. Besides serving as a target for performance, every type of goal within the organization – from strategic to operational goals, from benchmarks to budgets, from team to individual performance goals – also becomes a standard against which performance can be measured.

For example, a box office manager may set the goal of providing high-quality service to all patrons utilizing the facility. The manager may believe that quality service is tied to the amount of time it takes to process one order and sets the goal of processing ticket orders from walk-up patrons in three minutes or fewer. While this goal sets a target for ticket window staff, it also provides a standard by which the performance of each ticket seller can be measured.

DIFFICULTIES WITH ESTABLISHING STANDARDS

The problems with establishing performance standards are the same as the problems with defining effective goals. Obviously, the standards cannot be vague or general; they must be specific enough to be measurable. This presents a special challenge to sport organizations and performance units involved with providing services rather than products. The initial goal of high-quality patron service is too broad. It leads to the immediate issue of what is the standard for good box office service. Even if a ticket window representative is able to process the patron's order in three minutes, does this mean the patron received good service or was satisfied with the transaction? It is likely that quality box office service is tied to more than speed.

Establishing clear and appropriate standards, then, is the first step in the control process. Without clear standards there is nothing against which to measure performance, no well-defined basis for determining whether existing levels of performance are acceptable. Our box office manager might expand the performance goals to include 20 fewer complaints a month and decrease processing errors by five percent.

Monitor performance

Once performance standards are set, management must gather data over time to determine the actual level of performance. Management must continuously track performance so that accurate information is available about what is being accomplished. The performance standards that are defined in the first step of the control process determine which factors or variables will be measured. If standards are set in terms of quality, cost, and speed, for example, then those are the variables that will be monitored and measured. The key decisions of the second stage of the control process involve not which areas of performance will be monitored, but when, where, and how often to inspect or monitor key performance areas. For example, if a facility concessions manager is interested in decreasing waste by ten percent, he or she must then determine how and when to monitor progress toward these goals. Should individual concession stands be monitored or should all concession stands be treated as one unit? Should evaluation be completed on a by-event basis, weekly basis, or monthly basis? Should all stands be inspected or should just a random sample of stands be checked? Facility managers who are interested in effectively monitoring performance do so by creating well thought out and systematic evaluation methods. The performance data that is collected is only as good as the evaluation process employed by the manager.

Compare performance to the standards

The third step in the control process involves an evaluation of actual performance against the goal or standard. Performance goals are set, performance is monitored or measured, and now it must be determined whether a significant gap exists between the goal and the reality.

An important concept in the evaluation stage is the issue of critical deviations. Critical deviations are any gaps or differences between goals or standards and actual performance that critically impact the success of the process. For example, suppose a sport facility sets the staffing goal or standard of eight security personnel per entry gate. Let's assume that the national average of coverage for facilities and events of this type and size is ten security officers. The facility then monitors its own actual staffing levels and discovers that it employs seven security personnel members per gate, a rate that is 30 percent lower than the benchmark national average. This gap between the goal of ten and the actual level of seven represents a critical deviation in management's judgment. The 30 percent deviation suggests that the gate may be understaffed, which may in turn result in unnecessary risks to patrons and to the facility itself.

Defining which performance deviations are critical to the overall success of a process or to the success of the organization is an essential task for managers. Even in small organizations, there will be numerous deviations or gaps between actual performance and the goal or standard. If management attempted to respond to every performance deviation, there would be little time left to do anything else. The manager's task is to determine which performance deviations are genuinely critical and to focus on these.

One strategy for focusing management energy and attention is to identify and focus on a limited number of goals or standards. Limiting the number of critical goals not only facilitates the control process, but also tends to focus the attention and effort of everyone involved in pursuing those goals, which in turn tends to improve performance.

Take corrective action
If the level of actual performance reveals that performance standards are being met, the organization knows enough to continue what it is doing, because it is working. If performance is not at a level consistent with goals, and if this gap represents a critical deviation, the organization knows that it needs to take action to improve performance. This is called corrective action.

For some sport facilities that are municipally owned, the decision to seek private management is a corrective action. Particularly those facilities that are running large deficits, falling into disrepair, failing to attract a prime tenant, and remaining vacant or "dark" for too many days of the year, the decision to secure private management brings venture capital, managerial expertise, and professional clout that can be helpful in securing events and sponsorships.

Regardless of the form it takes, corrective action is the action management takes to put performance back on track in terms of meeting goals and performance standards.

CONTINUOUS IMPROVEMENT

There has been a dramatic shift in recent years in the focus and scope of the control process. It is no longer enough merely to find and fix problems that occur. To compete effectively where quality, innovation, and service are important, the focus of control must extend beyond merely monitoring performance, finding mistakes, and taking corrective action. In a world where everyone is looking for a competitive advantage, control is increasingly becoming the process not just of problem solving around critical deviations, but also of learning how to continuously improve performance even when there are no problems.

The search for never-ending improvements involves a "plan–do–check–act" circular cycle (Sashkin and Kiser, 1993) shown in Figure 6.5. Management, teams, and individuals plan a change, make the change, check the results, and, depending on the outcome, standardize the change or begin the cycle of improvement again with the new information. The improvement process also involves considering how things would be done if one were to start all over from scratch. The term reengineering has been applied to this process of improvement (Hammer and Champy, 1993). Reengineering means that management, teams, and individuals rethink and redesign operations that have become antiquated and do not add value. For example, a university soccer field has been used for over ten years for local youth soccer games on Sundays. The grounds crew and maintenance staff members have been awarded an hour overtime each week to prepare the field for use by the youth group. The maintenance team has traditionally limed the field, set up additional goals, and set up eight additional sets of portable bleachers that are then removed on Monday mornings. The facility manager, who was recently hired and has a daughter old enough to participate in the league, attends the weekend games and learns that, during the course of the season, only three sets of bleachers are

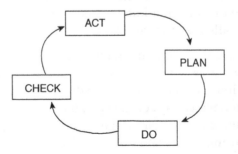

Figure 6.5 The "plan–do–check–act" cycle of continuous improvement

used, the extra soccer goals are never used, and the soccer league relines the field to accommodate its own rules and field specifications. The facility manager recognizes that the university's grounds crew's preparations are no longer effective and do not serve the purpose of the league. For the facility manager, continuous improvement means rethinking the field preparation process for the Sunday youth league games. The manager may now call together his grounds team, plan a new preparation process, carry out the process, check to see that the new preparation plan is meeting the needs of the league, and then act on any changes that need to be made.

Like the other responsibilities of management, controlling and managing continuous improvement are demanding tasks but are essential to the success of the organization. An effective control process ensures that critical deviations in performance are identified and responded to well before they threaten the organization's ability to achieve its goals and mission. An effective process of continuous improvement ensures that the organization will continue to satisfy the expectations of its customers and keep pace with competition.

Service quality

Sport facility owners and managers agree that at the heart of the facility's ability to succeed is the organization's commitment to continuous improvement and to service quality. In fact, Global Spectrum, considered to be one of the premier private sport facility management companies in the world, suggests that they have successfully turned around under-performing buildings because they operate facilities as entrepreneurial businesses that focus on the best interests of their clients and communities. Global Spectrum emphasizes improving operational efficiency, operating cash flow and fiscal accountability while delivering innovative solutions, high-quality event activity, and high levels of customer service. Global Spectrum, which operates over 100 distinct building operations including stadiums and arenas around the world, has articulated a corporate philosophy that states that successful facility operation and financial performance are linked directly to top-quality experienced management, rock-solid industry relationships, effective marketing, and customer service.

Sport facility managers understand that their business is highly dependent on their ability to attract and retain customers. While offering a schedule of attractive events and activities is certainly an important factor in filling the building night after night, there is a broader recognition of the importance of how events are presented and how fans are treated. Customers are likely to return when they are pleased by their experience at the facility. Therefore, stadium, park, and arena managers must constantly focus on finding new ways to delight their customers. Sport facilities of today are designed and constructed with the users in mind. Prime tenants and

203

performers are considered in the design of locker rooms, meeting rooms, training facilities, dressing areas, media and production space, loading docks, private visitor and family lounges, etc. Spectators are considered in myriad ways ranging from the design of the seats (padded with cup holders), to unobstructed sight lines, to handicapped accessible seating areas, to plush luxury and club areas, to a wide array of food offerings and technology interface. A visit to any stadium or arena or to a major facility website illustrates the lengths to which designers are willing to go to attract and keep fans. Today's facilities are entertainment complexes where it is not unusual to find an art gallery, retail store, upscale restaurant, concourse games, museum, picnic area, children's playground, or sports bar integrated into the stadium or arena design.

Amenities, however, are only one piece of the service quality puzzle. Sport facility managers recognize that they must emphasize service excellence in order to create loyal fans who will return to the building for event after event. Customer service programs within the sport facility industry are supported through employee training programs, guest or patron relations areas, concierge stations, and technology-based customer service applications.

Management theorist and author Ken Blanchard (1993) supports this approach to service quality. For Blanchard, having satisfied customers is not enough: the successful organization must deliver exceptional customer service in order to create "raving fans" whose unwavering loyalty will result in astounding bottom-line results. The sport facility business is above all else a service-oriented enterprise. Managers must not only provide a high-quality product supported by creative, interesting, and attractive amenities, but they must constantly strive in the spirit of continuous improvement to find new and better ways to delight and surprise their spending customers.

SUMMARY

This chapter focuses on strategic management and the sport facility industry. The concepts of environmental analysis, situational analysis, and SWOT analysis are introduced. Operations planning as it pertains to the sport industry takes place on two levels: a micro level that involves the management of events that are conducted within the facility, and a macro level where the organization's strategy is translated into action. Operational plans are different from strategic plans in two ways: they cover shorter time periods and are, for the most part, internally focused.

The Balanced Scorecard, which is a current version of management by objectives (MBO), is a system of setting objectives and identifying measures within four categories or perspectives. Managers, teams, and individuals develop and closely monitor performance based on customer measures, internal processes, human resource measures, and financial measures all tied directly to a specific strategic objective. This deliberate linkage of strategic objectives with operational actions distinguishes the approach from its older cousin, MBO, and is designed to build a strategy-focused organization.

To create the specific measures and objectives required by the Balanced Scorecard approach, forecasting and scheduling become critical activities for understanding and planning the conditions and activities necessary for implementing strategy. Forecasting generates predictions and projections that form the basis for determining the levels of business in each department. Scheduling ensures the effective identification and sequencing of key activities within the organization.

Policies, procedures, and budgets are important tools for ensuring that behavior throughout the organization is consistent with the organization's mission and strategies. Policies are guidelines for decisions; procedures are guidelines for action; and budgets are guidelines for the allocation of financial resources.

Control is the process of ensuring that actual performance is consistent with the organization's goals and standards. Performance must be monitored to ensure that progress is on track, and action must be taken to solve performance problems and to continuously improve performance.

The sport facility business is above all else a service-oriented enterprise. Managers must provide a high-quality product supported by a wide variety of amenities in an environment where the fans are treated as guests rather than customers. The organization must be imbued with a spirit of continuous improvement combined with a commitment to excellent service quality.

MANAGEMENT EXERCISE: HOOP HYSTERIA

The Sport Management Association at your school has decided that a campus-wide three-on-three basketball tournament would be a good way to raise funds to support the club's activities. Taking on a project of this magnitude would also allow sport management students to gain hands-on experience in sport event management.

1 Identify and explain which operational planning tools would be most helpful in planning the event.
2 Identify and explain the information, resources, and authorizations you will need on your campus to proceed with planning and executing the event.
3 Explain how you will break down the work that needs to be done, how you will structure your management team/organizing committee, and create templates or examples of important operational planning documents.
4 Explain how you will market this event on campus.
5 Develop a budget for this event based on a grant of $500 to run the tournament. Once your budget is developed, what steps will you take to control expenses and maximize profit?

CHAPTER 7

DESIGNING THE ORGANIZATION AND THE SPORT AGENCY INDUSTRY

INTRODUCTION

This chapter describes the creation and coordination of the various work units necessary to implement sport agency organizational strategies, including the various departments necessary to do the work these organizations perform – player representation and player marketing, for example. The chapter also discusses in detail the elements of these organizational design responsibilities and traces how sport organizations in general and sport agency organizations in particular have sought to design their structures in response to the continually emerging performance challenges they face.

Check the stats

Purpose
To help clients find the best outlet for their talent and to help them derive the greatest financial and life benefits from their professional relationships.

Stakeholders
Professional athletes, agents, player unions, coaches, individual franchise management personnel, individual franchise employees, franchise owners, league management personnel, league employees, tour management personnel, tour employees, intercollegiate athletes, intercollegiate athletic management personnel, broadcast networks, franchise, league, and tour sponsors, franchise, league, and tour advertisers, sport broadcast, print, and on-line media, fans.

Size and scope

- In 1967, the average salary in Major League Baseball was $19,000, and the league minimum was $12,000. In 2012, the average had ballooned by 178.5 times to $3.4 million, and the minimum was $480,000. By comparison, the average U.S. household income in 2010 was just under $52,000 (Blum, 2001; "Frequently asked," 2012; Nightengale, 2012; "USA quickfacts," 2012).
- Here is a quick look at the growth in average player salaries in U.S. professional league sport since 1976:

League	1976	1986	1996	2006	2012
NFL	$47,500	$244,700	$787,000	$1.7M	$1.9M
MLB	$52,300	$402,579	$1.1M	$2.85M	$3.4M
NHL	$85,000	$159,000	$892,000	$1.5M	$2.4M
NBA	$130,000	$382,000	$2M	$5M	$5.15M

(Hoffer, 2006; Dorish, 2011)

- As of 2011, the average salary of a Division I Bowl Subdivision football head coach was $1.47 million (up 55 percent from $950,000 in 2006). At least 64 of these coaches made $1 million, 32 made at least $2 million, nine made more than $3 million, and three made more than $4 million. University of Texas head coach Mack Brown topped the list, earning over $5 million (Brady *et al.*, 2011).
- In 2011, Eldrick "Tiger" Woods was again the top-earning American professional athlete, garnering nearly $2.3 million in salary and prize winnings and another $60 million in endorsements. The rest of the top ten Americans: Phil Mickelson ($61 million), LeBron James ($44.5 million), Payton Manning ($38 million), Alex Rodriguez ($36 million), Kobe Bryant ($34.8 million), Kevin Garnett ($32.8 million), Matt Ryan ($32.7 million), Tom Brady ($30 million), and Dwight Howard ($28.6 million) (Freedman, 2012a).
- The top ten international earners in 2011 were Roger Federer (tennis, Switzerland; $52.7 million), Manny Pacquiao (boxing, Philippines; $52.5 million), Fernando Alonso (auto racing, Spain; $45 million), Lionel Messi (soccer, Argentina; $43.8 million), Cristiano Ronaldo (soccer, Portugal; $38.8 million), Yao Ming (basketball, China; $35.6 million), Rafael Nadal (tennis, Spain; $31.5 million), Valentino Rossi (motor sports, Italy; $30 million), Wayne Rooney (soccer, Great Britain; $29.2 million), and Ricardo Kaká (soccer, Brazil; $27.3 million) (Freedman, 2012b).

Governance

Player unions certify all player agents, as do many individual states. Unions also serve to negotiate basic agreements with leagues, limit the percentage of compensation that agents can charge for contract negotiation, and help players and agents access information that will aid them in preparing for negotiations. Courts and arbitrators also serve to regulate agents by voiding contracts that are illegal or unfair.

Inside look: knocking on heaven's door

The income data for pro athletes outlined above can be mind-boggling. Check the numbers again. How can Tiger Woods earn $60 million in endorsements when his game failed him due to injuries and his notorious personal issues? How can LeBron James make $30 million in endorsements after he so famously announced that he would take his talents to South Beach, left the Cleveland Cavaliers in the lurch, claimed he and his new teammates would win multiple championships, and along the way became to many the most loathed player in the National Basketball Association? And many Americans wonder who Fernando Aloso is, and why is anyone giving him $45 million to do anything? Whether you feel these athletes have earned it or not, the fact is that professional athletes have the potential to earn significant levels of income during their peak performance years. And if someone was willing to pay you Tiger Woods' money to perform a task, would you refuse it?

But for every Tiger and LeBron, every Fernando, Lionel, and Valentino, there are hundreds of thousands of other athletes in nearly every sport imaginable who are struggling to make ends meet as they pursue their professional aspirations. Consider the case of minor league baseball players in America. While A-Rod, Ichiro Suzuki ($24 million), CC Sabathia ($23.8 million, $23 million in salary) and Joe Mauer ($23.7 million, $23 million in salary) are doing quite well (as is the average major leaguer as outlined above), each Major League Baseball club has about 125 other players in addition to their 25-player major league roster. While some minor leaguers have been able through the efforts of their agents to negotiate signing bonuses that could reach several million dollars (for example, in 2011 the top pick in the MLB amateur draft, Gerrit Cole – a pitcher from the University of California-Los Angeles (UCLA) – got $8 million from the Pittsburgh Pirates, while the last pick in the first round – Kevin Matthews, a high school pitcher from Georgia – got $936,000 from the Texas Rangers ("2011 MLB," 2011)), the rest lack the bargaining power to command such a bonus (after all, there could be as many as 50 rounds in the MLB draft, meaning that upwards of 1,500 players could be drafted annually) and must survive on far more modest means. For example, the pay structure of minor league baseball players is organized between three minor league farm systems, and the current salary system for the minor leagues is listed below in Box 7.1:

Negotiating signing bonuses in the MLB is now becoming a more nuanced enterprise. In 2012, new draft signing bonus rules were in place due to changes in the collective bargaining agreement (CBA) MLB negotiated with the Players' Association. The CBA now sets a limited pool of bonus money for teams to spend on selections in the first ten rounds, and limits teams from spending over $100,000 on players taken after the tenth round (the excess on any late round bonuses will count against the bonus pool). The penalties for exceeding the pool are: (1) if exceeded by zero to five percent, the club will be charged a 75 percent tax on the excess; (2) if exceeded by five to ten percent, it will pay the same tax and will also lose its first round pick next season; (3) if exceeded by 10 to 15 percent, the club will be charged a 100 percent tax on the excess and lose its first and second round picks next season; and (4) if exceeded by more than 15 percent, a 100 percent tax on the excess is charged and the club will lose its next two first round picks. According to writer Mike Andrews, "these are obviously harsh penalties, and it's unlikely that many teams will test the waters by going more than five percent over the pool limit" (2012, p. 1).

In addition, another new rule cites that if a team fails to sign a pick in the top ten rounds, it loses its slot allocation for that round, so its draft pool would be reduced by the amount of the slot recommendation for the particular draft slot. For example, let's say the Miami Marlins are able to sign their first round pick (No. 24 overall) for $1,000,000 (which is $750,000 under the slot price); the Marlins would be able to allocate that $750,000 to its other picks in the draft. So, says Mike Andrews, "it wouldn't be surprising to see some clubs target easy signs in the supplemental to 4th round area in the hopes of using any excess bonus money elsewhere" (2012, p. 1).

210

So let's consider the players at the far end of the monetary spectrum, players who can't demand significant signing bonuses and are earning subsistence wages in minor league ballparks across the U.S. These are guys such as Peter Bergeron, Doug Clark, Randy Ruiz, and Charlie Zink. Heard of them? Probably not. These are players who have labored in the minors for years, and maybe got a brief stay in the big leagues (the proverbial "cup of coffee," as the old timers might call it). Most of them are like Zink, who went undrafted after a college career at Savannah (Georgia) College of Art and Design, an NCAA Division III program, and got nothing – that's $0 – to sign (Dobrow, 2011).

Who represents guys such as Charlie Zink, who reinvented himself as a knuckleball pitcher soon after joining the minors? One of the industry heavy hitters such as Scott Boras, Peter Greenberg, the Hendricks Brothers, Seth Levison, or Arn Tellem? Firms such as Creative Artists Agency, IMG, or Octagon? One of the lesser-known yet still influential figures such as John Boggs, Casey Close, or Adam Katz? Or one of the thousands of other men, and, yes, a few women, with a handful of little-known minor leaguers hoping to make it big with that one prospect who can help them step up into "The Show"? Bergeron, Clark, Ruiz, and Zink are represented by DiaMMond Management, which is run by Jim Masteralexis, Lisa Pike Masteralexis, and Steve McKelvey. All three are lawyers and sport management professors. Jim and Lisa are married to each other, and do most of the player acquisition and contract negotiating. Steve works mostly on securing DiaMMond clients endorsement and other marketing opportunities. They are a small shop in comparison to some of the industry heavyweights, and generally focus on representing clients from the six-state New England region, which lags far behind the hotbeds of California, Florida, and Texas in terms of generating future MLB stars (Dobrow, 2011).

DiaMMond has had a handful of clients make it to the majors for an extended period (players such as Manny Delcarmen and Tomo Ohka), but few have made it and struck it rich with a big free agency signing. This can hurt small firms such as DiaMMond, and point to one of the many ugly realities of the sport agency business. Players, especially those with promise, are always under siege from predatory agents, telling them what they can do for them, sowing seeds of doubt about the abilities of their current representation. They'll be told that they shouldn't risk their futures with a firm that is inexperienced in salary arbitration or has never had a player make it to free agency. Poaching agents will whisper that a player will be better off with someone with experience. Lots of guys listen, and lots of guys jump, firing their agents with a phone call, e-mail, or text, cutting their ties with the ones who courted them before they were pros, helped them find apartments and equipment deals, buy rings for their fiancées, or, in the case of Jim and Lisa, drive all of Tomo Ohka's furniture and clothes from Ohka's apartment in Rhode Island to Canada when he was traded and had to relocate (Dobrow, 2011).

These are the realities of the sport agency business. Player salaries are the most significant expense for professional sport organizations, and have steadily, and in some cases dramatically, increased since the 1970s. So what sparked these increases? Much of this increase came with the advent of free agency following the Andy Messersmith arbitration ruling in 1975 (see below). Marvin Miller, executive director of the MLB Players' Association during this time, viewed that event in these terms: "Qualified people have told me that decision and the labor agreement which was signed the following summer resulted in more money changing hands from an owner group to an employee group than any other decision or negotiation in history" (Bodley, 2000, p. 10C). This includes not just sport labor history, but the history of all labor negotiations everywhere. The advent of free agency, spurred by strong labor unions and an ever-increasing appetite for sport consumption from fans, has created an atmosphere in many sport organizations where there was plenty of money to be had, and the negotiating expertise of a skilled agent could secure it.

As the sport and entertainment industry has grown, so too has the sport agency segment. As we see in this chapter, the individual negotiating skills of a single agent are only part of the sport agency business. There is also the dimension of sport agency that deals with extensive and lucrative product and service endorsement agreements and has meant great wealth for many players and coaches. However, these benefits have come at a cost. The expectations of managing and investing this wealth, negotiating contracts, and securing endorsement deals pose significant managerial challenges for one single sport agent. In response to industry growth, all sport organizations have sought to improve performance by improving the definition and coordination of the units that do the work necessary for organizational success. We examine the most recent efforts of sport agency organizations to organize for performance, but first some background information is necessary.

SPORT AGENCY DEFINED

There is an unquestionable lure to being a sports agent. Why? Is it the desire for big money? For fame? For power? To be like Scott Boras? A former St. Louis Cardinals minor leaguer, Boras was responsible for negotiating in 2000 arguably the most celebrated American professional sports contract of all time, when Alex Rodriguez signed a ten-year, $250 million deal with the Texas Rangers. Later, after the Rangers shipped A-Rod to the New York Yankees after the 2003 season (but agreed to pay the majority of his salary), Boras famously announced during the 2007 post-season that Rodriguez would opt out of the deal and elect for free agency. Rodriguez later said the announcement was a "mistake that was handled extremely poorly. It was a huge debacle," he said, calling the timing "distasteful and very inappropriate." After hearing from Boras that the Yankees were not interested in resigning him, since the opt-out would mean that the significant portion of the payments covered by the Rangers would end, Rodriguez approached the club without Boras (the agent described by former client Gary Sheffield as having "an ego the size of L.A."). The sides worked out a new $275 million, ten-year deal without the super-agent to stay with the Yankees. "Within two conversations we got a deal done," Rodriguez said (Crasnick, 2005, p. 177; "Rodriguez finalizes," 2007, p. 1).

Nonetheless, Boras, of whom a former MLB Players Association official said, "If I had a son and he was [sic] a premier high school player, I'd pick Scott Boras to represent him" (Crasnick, 2005, p. 188), continues to be the preeminent MLB player agent, representing young stars such as Robinson Cano, Jacoby Ellsbury, Bryce Harper, and Stephen Strasburg, as well as veteran standouts like Adrian Beltre, Prince Fielder, Matt Holliday, and Jayson Werth. Other industry big guns include Tom Condon, who heads the football division for Creative Artists Agency (CAA) (representing a cadre of top NFL quarterbacks including Drew Brees, Peyton Manning, Matthew Stafford, and Matt Ryan), and Arn Tellem of Wasserman Management Group (WMG) (who represents NBA stars Pau Gasol, Joe Johnson, and Derrick Rose).

But make no mistake, regardless of whether you're Scott Boras or DiaMMond, the agency business is cutthroat and competitive. The big-name firms have the lion's share of the players. For example, similar to all unions that certify agents, the National Football League Players' Association (NFLPA) has certified over a thousand agents, with several hundred applying for status each year. To become certified by the NFLPA, all one needs is to have paid a non-refundable application fee of $2,500, obtained an undergraduate and post-graduate degree (Master's or J.D.) from an accredited college or university, given authorization for a background investigation, attended a two-day seminar in Washington, DC, successfully completed a written proctored examination, and have provided a valid e-mail address ("Agent regulations," 2012).

There is also the issue of what it takes to be an agent. A student like you reading this text as you prepare for class could be an agent right now, because essentially all you need to be an agent is a client. Many individual states have certain certification standards that seek to curb aggressive recruiting of college players, such as giving them cash and thus threatening their amateur status, but there is no uniform nationally approved certification (although each players' association has some requirements).

So money, power, and fame and the desire to make the big deals. And what's even more alluring about this job is that it could really happen right now. But that's also the problem with the sport agency business. The competition for clients is fierce. Lots of people believe *they* can be the next Boras, Condon, or Tellem – they just need to find the next A-Rod, Peyton, or D-Rose. It is a wide open market, but that also means the competition is virtually unlimited and can come from anywhere and at any time.

The job of a sport agent is certainly high profile, but what precisely does he or she do? A sport agent is a personal manager/representative who finds the best outlet for a client's, also referred to as a principal's, talent. Agents also provide their expertise so athletes can focus on their game performance without distractions. A sports agent's biggest responsibility is negotiating contracts, those agreements between players and coaches and sports and business organizations, as described in Box 7.2.

BOX 7.2 AGENCY LAW AND CONTRACTS

Under the tenets of agency law, an agent acts on the behalf of a principal (the player or coach) to achieve a specified accomplishment. In an agency agreement, responsibilities known as fiduciary duties are required of both sides. The principal must comply with the terms of a contract, compensate the agent, and reimburse for expenses. The agent has a duty to obey the wishes of the principal, to remain loyal, to notify, and to show reasonable care (Yasser et al., 2011).

At the heart of nearly every financial relationship is a *contract*. A contract is defined as a written or oral agreement between parties that is enforceable under the law, which must contain a promise to do something in the future. A contract typically consists of the following elements:

1   An *offer* – A conditional promise where one party agrees to act if the other also acts.
2   *Acceptance* – The agreement to the promise on the part of the party to whom the offer is made.
3   *Consideration* – The concept of the exchange of value, that one party must give something in return for the other's doing the same.

Contracts are not valid if they are illegal (for example, if they include the promise for an act that is illegal, such as murder), or if the party to whom the offer is made lacks the *capacity* to understand the contract due to impairments, or is under age 18. The failure to perform a duty imposed under the contract is referred to as a *breach of contract*. The remedies for a contractual breach are monetary compensation, or specific performance, which means that the party responsible for the breach performs the duties the contract stipulates (Berry and Wong, 1993).

The contract elements that can be negotiated include salary, guaranteed income, bonuses, and the length of the agreement. For example, in Rodriguez's initial landmark deal, Boras negotiated a $10 million signing bonus, the right for Rodriguez to terminate the contract after the 2007, 2008, or 2009 seasons, an escalator clause that

214

specified Rodriguez must receive an increase in 2009 or 2010 by the higher of $5 million or $1 million greater than the average annual value of the non-pitcher with the highest annual average value, a no-trade clause, and various award bonuses, including $500,000 for a first MVP, $1 million for a second, and $1.5 million for any subsequent MVP awards. When Rodriguez was traded from the Rangers to the New York Yankees in 2003, several changes were negotiated into the new contract. Specifically, all the money listed in the initial contract as deferred money from the Rangers – $36 million – was now set to be paid from the Rangers in installments with interest (1.75 percent) from 2016 to 2025. The new contract also stipulated that Rodriguez would be booked into a hotel suite for all road trips, and that his own personal website be linked directly to that of the Yankees. To take on the contract, the Yankees also negotiated that the Rangers would pay $43 million of Rodriguez's remaining guaranteed money. The 2007 contract with the Yankees allowed Rodriguez to earn $30 million more for achieving historic milestones, and provided a $10 million signing bonus, of which $2 million was payable upon approval, and $1 million each January 15 from 2009–2013 and $3 million on January 15, 2014. Rodriguez could receive an additional $6 million each for five milestones that the team designates as historic achievements: tying the home run levels of Willie Mays (660), Babe Ruth (714), and Hank Aaron (755), as well as tying and breaking the home run mark set by Barry Bonds (762) (Hawkins, 2000; Foster et al., 2006; "Rodriguez finalizes," 2007).

As noted above, contracts and negotiated clauses for college coaches have also become quite lucrative. Much of the growth for coach compensation is due to the impact of agents in the negotiating process, with half of the coaches in the so-called "big time" NCAA Division I conferences employing agents. Agents usually take three to five percent of the contract value as their commission, and are generally unapologetic for the increases their efforts have generated. Says Jimmy Sexton of Athletic Resource Management, who represents Steve Spurrier of the University of South Carolina and Frank Beamer of Virginia Polytechnic University: "We are responsible for driving up prices. What else are we supposed to do? Drive them down?" Coaches such as the University of Iowa's Kirk Ferentz say they need the expertise of agents such as Sexton and Neil Cornrich (who represents Ferentz, Bob Stoops of the University of Oklahoma, and Bo Pelini of the University of Nebraska) because, as Ferentz stated: "All I know is football ... I have zero knowledge when it comes to the business aspect of things" (McCarthy and Wieberg, 2006, p. 15C). However, lawyer Raymond Cotton says coaches "are much more business-oriented than the schools," are in search of "cold, hard cash," and "that attitude is paying off for them." Says Cornrich of the efforts of agents: "Clearly, knowing the market leads to a fair result to both sides" (Sander and Fain, 2009, p. A24).

Not only do coaches receive salaries, their contracts usually provide for other perks. In the case of Louisiana State University (LSU) head football coach Les

Miles, his agent, George Bass, had negotiated escalator clauses (specific language in a contract that provides the coach with salary increases based on the salaries of other coaches) in Miles' contract that required LSU to make Miles at least the fifth-highest paid coach in the Southeastern Conference (SEC) if his team won ten games in a season, third-highest if the Tigers won the SEC championship, and third-highest in the nation if LSU won the Bowl Subdivision national championship. When hired by the University of Alabama in 2007, Nick Saban (who had coached previously at Michigan State, LSU, and the NFL's Miami Dolphins), thanks to his agent Jimmy Sexton, was able to ink an eight-year, $32 million deal that includes 25 hours of use of the school's private jet, two cars, a country club membership, total control of the football program in the areas of recruiting and hiring, and can leave the school at any time without incurring a financial penalty. In 2011, new University of Arizona head football coach Rich Rodriguez negotiated a five-year contract, starting with a base salary of $1.45 million. Rodriguez will earn an additional $300,000 per year from outside income, paid by Nike and IMG. The base salary escalates to $1.5 million in the second year, and then to $1.6 million, $1.7 million, and $1.8 million in subsequent years. The five-year base salary total is $8,050,000, which rises to $9,550,000 with the additional outside income. His bonuses include $150,000 for playing in the national title game, $100,000 for any other Bowl Championship Series (BCS) game, $75,000 for earning the Pac-12 South championship, $75,000 for winning the Pac-12 championship, and $75,000 for earning a bid to a non-BCS bowl game (Wieberg, 2006; Wieberg and Upton, 2007; Burke, 2008; Gimino, 2011).

After the terms of the contract are finalized, agents must then make sure that all terms and payments are upheld (Lester, 1990; Greenberg, 1993). The next most important duty for sport agents is marketing the athlete or coach and helping the principal secure endorsement and sponsorship agreements. This is a key factor for both agents and principals, because it is an additional and potentially significant source of additional income, as outlined above, especially in the case of performers such as Tiger Woods, for whom in 2011 nearly 97 percent of his $62 million income came from endorsements.

The final important duty is assistance with financial planning, which should not be overlooked. In none of the big four American pro sport leagues is the average career length of players longer than six years, which means that the peak earning window for the majority of players is a small one. As recently as 2009, *Sports Illustrated* estimated that even though salaries had risen steadily in the previous three decades, 78 percent of former NFL players have gone bankrupt or are under financial stress because of joblessness or divorce within two years of retirement, and 60 percent of former NBA players are broke within five years of retirement (Torre, 2009).

In addition, many pro athletes often succumb to individuals touting risky investments. According to Pablo Torre of *Sports Illustrated*, "athletes are often uninterested in either conservative spending or the stock market ... Inventions, nightclubs, car dealerships and T-shirt companies have an advantage: the thrill of tangibility. Many players, consequently, are financial prey." "Disreputable people see athletes' money as very easy to get to," says Steven Baker, an agent who represents 20 NFL players. For example, Detroit Tigers outfielder Torii Hunter recently invested almost $70,000 in an invention – an inflatable raft that would sit under furniture in high-rainfall areas so that consumers could pump up the device and allow items to float and remain dry during floods. "The guy I invested with came back and wanted me to put in more, about $500,000," Hunter says. "Then I met [financial advisor Ed] Butowsky, who just said, 'Hell no!' I wound up never seeing that guy – or any of my money – again." "It's always so predictable," said Butowsky, a managing partner at Chapwood Investments, a wealth management firm located in Dallas. "Everyone wants to be the next Magic Johnson." According to Torre, Johnson "is the rare, luminous exception of tangibility gone right." In 1994, Johnson started a chain of inner-city movie theaters. Today Magic Johnson Enterprises includes partnerships with Starbucks, 24 Hour Fitness, Aetna, and Best Buy, and its capital management division has invested over a billion dollars in urban communities (Torre, 2009, p. 2).

Agents usually make more money when their clients make more money, because most agents earn income based on the percentage of their clients' income. Other methods of earning income include working for a flat fee or an hourly rate (McAleenan, 1990). The risk in the percentage approach is that there is no guarantee of what the agent will make. It is contingent on what he or she can negotiate on behalf of the client, and the agent can't get paid until the client gets paid. In professional league sports, agents are limited by the unions on what percentages they can charge, which is no more than six percent (Greenberg, 1993). And the agent is paid this percentage only on the amount over which the contract exceeds the league minimum. However, agents can earn more when negotiating contracts for endorsements and other agreements and for coaches and non-unionized clients, because these are not subject to union oversight. Most firms have standard percentages for marketing services, the highest reaching the 30 percent range.

But what an agent does is mostly sales. The key in this selling process, according to one agent specializing in golf representation, is

> doing things the right way, having good values, treating your clients the way they deserve to be treated, creating profitable business relationships, and doing it the honest and respectable way. Agents are portrayed as evil, money-sucking scumbags. That's a tough reputation to get away from. Part of what an agent does is look after the best interests of their clients. That can mean anything. Trying to find them the right team to play for, trying to get them more money under a certain contract to help them provide for their family. One of my main responsibilities is to find marketing opportunities for them, to create endorsement relationships, sponsorship agreements, to

217

put money in their pockets. My division is not going to be profitable unless I make money for our golfers, and we get paid for doing it.

But selling can be tough. "There's nothing worse than having a client you can't provide for, but sometimes that's the reality of the situation," says the golf agent. "Sometimes your players lose their marketability. They might fall out of favor with the public, or they're just not playing at a level where they're going to command endorsement dollars."

But the good agents, that is, the ones who make money for their clients, are often painted as greedy and fingered as the cause for decay in sport. Some in management say that agents catering to a player's needs creates a dependency. One former MLB general manager put it this way:

> They don't want the players to be able to think for themselves ... "You call me before you buy a car. You call me before you buy a house. You call me on the mortgage. You call me." A lot of the things that normal people do in the course of life, [players] never experience because they have somebody doing it for them.
>
> (Crasnick, 2005, pp. 28–29)

Nonetheless, sport agency is about selling. An agent must sell to the client, whether that client is a player, a team, or a potential sponsor. The products vary, but the premise is the same. Competition is fierce, but the potential payoffs are great. It's not for the faint of heart.

Historical influences

Although the history of sport in North America is replete with astute businesspeople, colorful promoters, and dubious hucksters alike, three key figures stand out as having exhibited particular influence on the development of the sport agency business: Charles C. Pyle, Christy Walsh, and Mark McCormack. Pyle, also known as "Cash and Carry," was a theater owner and stage producer when he met University of Illinois running back Harold "Red" Grange, the "Galloping Ghost," in 1925. Pyle became Grange's manager, negotiated his professional contract with the Chicago Bears of the fledgling NFL (which stipulated that Grange receive 50 percent of the Bears' home game ticket revenues – of which Pyle got half), and organized many of Grange's endorsement deals and post-season barnstorming tours. Grange's drawing power was so strong that he is credited with saving the inchoate NFL, although Pyle and Grange also organized a short-lived competitor league in the late 1920s (Carroll, 1999).

Sportswriter Christy Walsh served as agent and representative for two of the early twentieth century's sport colossi, New York Yankees outfielder Babe Ruth and University of Notre Dame head football coach Knute Rockne. Like Pyle, Walsh

Designing the organization and the sport agency industry

negotiated barnstorming tours and endorsements for Ruth, and lucrative deals for ghostwritten syndicated newspaper columns, endorsements for coaching schools and sporting goods, and speaking engagements for Rockne. Ruth had no real contract bargaining power with the Yankees due to the reserve clause (see below), but Rockne faced no such restrictions. Walsh also helped Rockne use job offers from schools such as Columbia, Loyola Marymount, and Southern California to leverage substantial salary raises and football facility construction and improvements from Notre Dame. At the height of his popularity before his death in a plane crash in 1931 en route to California (to make a film of his life story, for which he was to be paid $50,000), Walsh helped Rockne earn $75,000 a year, a sum that would not be reached by another coach until the 1970s (Sperber, 1993).

Mark McCormack established the basis for the modern sport agency and marketing firm in the early 1960s when he secured endorsement deals for golfing legend Arnold Palmer. McCormack used these skills to found the International Management Group (IMG) in 1960, which remains one of the most powerful agency and event marketing firms in sport. Since the formation of IMG, other firms have moved into prominence, such as CAA and Octagon, and large firms have come to dominate the sport agency business.

Although there are numerous examples of such changes impacting professional leagues, the most significant is probably the gradual dismantling of the reserve clause. Professional baseball's National League initiated the reserve clause in 1879 to reduce player salaries, the most significant expenditure for professional teams. Before this, players would often leave teams in mid-season for better offers from other teams. It was the functional equivalent of Adrian Gonzalez choosing to leave the Los Angeles Dodgers in mid-July if the San Francisco Giants offered him just a dollar more over the $21 million his contract stipulated.

At first, teams reserved five players who were not permitted to sign with other teams. Other teams effectively bound those players to that club by agreeing not to sign them away. This also meant that teams could then trade and sell players under contract as well. Eventually a clause, Paragraph 10A, was inserted into the Uniform Players Contract stipulating that clubs had the right to renew a signed contract for a period of one year on the same terms (Helyar, 1994).

Players and rival leagues made a few attempts at destroying this system. The formation of the Brotherhood of Professional Baseball Players, led by John Montgomery Ward, a player for the then-New York Giants, led to the formation of the Players League (PL) in 1890. The Players League, formed on a profit-sharing model in conjunction with owner-investors, lured away many of the game's best players, but through the efforts of Albert Spalding and other National League owners and facing first-year financial peril, the Players League owners sold their franchise interests to the NL owners, killing the PL and reinstating the reserve system (Lowenfish, 1980).

Another competitor league, the Federal League (FL), challenged the reserve system of the then-established American and National Leagues in 1914–1915, but the FL met the same fate as the Players League when owners were bought out or co-opted, except for the owners of the Baltimore franchise. In response, they sued the established leagues, claiming the reserve system was an antitrust violation that kept them from acquiring the talent necessary to compete equally. In 1922, the U.S. Supreme Court ruled against the Baltimore franchise, stating, somewhat curiously, that professional baseball did not qualify as interstate commerce, so the reserve clause could stand (White, 1996).

The clause withstood several challenges over the next fifty years, including another unsuccessful Supreme Court decision on a claim initiated by former St. Louis Cardinals outfielder Curt Flood, who challenged the right of the Cardinals to trade him to the Philadelphia Phillies in exchange for slugging first baseman Dick Allen. The Court used the 1922 decision as a precedent in ruling against Flood, and it recommended that any change in professional baseball's antitrust exemption be addressed by the U.S. Congress (Lowenfish, 1980).

The reserve clause effectively ended not from a court decision but from a salary arbitration hearing. In the 1960s and 1970s, the emergence of a more powerful and united MLB Players' Association, under the leadership of Marvin Miller, negotiated an agreement with MLB owners that many disputes between players and clubs be adjudicated not by the commissioner, an employee of the owners, but by an independent arbitrator whose decision both sides were bound to follow.

The hearing that broke the stranglehold of the reserve clause occurred just before Christmas 1974. Because of a protracted salary dispute with Los Angeles Dodgers' management, star pitcher Andy Messersmith played the entire year without signing a contract. The arbitrator, Peter Seitz, ruled that although Messersmith had been renewed automatically by the Dodgers as permitted under Paragraph 10A of the Uniform Player Contract, the fact that he had not signed a contract in 1974 meant the one-year renewal clause had expired. Therefore, Seitz decreed that Messersmith was no longer contractually bound to the Dodgers and was free to sign with whatever team he chose. The current system of salary arbitration after three years of major-league service and free agency after six years was then negotiated and agreed to by the union and ownership. The first agent to take advantage of the new labor landscape was Jerry Kapstein, a former ABC Sports statistician who introduced such fare as the time-of-possession tabulation. Kapstein got his start when a friend introduced him to three members of the Baltimore Orioles, and since he excelled at negotiation and statistical evaluation, he was able to win big awards for his players in salary arbitration hearings. During the 1976–1977 offseason, Kapstein represented 60 percent of MLB's free agents (Helyar, 1994; Crasnick, 2005).

Other such significant legal changes can come from other leagues' cases. In 1982, the union for the now-defunct North American Soccer League won a suit that permitted union access to all player salary data. The NFL's players union used this case so their players could compare salaries. Before that, Tommy Kramer, the starting QB for the Minnesota Vikings who threw for 3,912 yards in 1981, made $100,000; Guy Benjamin, the backup for the San Francisco 49ers who threw for 171 yards, made $30,000 more. Dick Berthelsen, the NFL's general counsel who won the case, underscored the ruling's significance: "What it did was make sure that false information was no longer being passed around. Players felt they would get in trouble if they talked about salaries" (Forbes, 2001, p. 14C).

Ethics and sport agency

In the sport agency business, there are few restrictions as to who can become an agent. This lack of formalized approval and the significant closeness and potential dependence between players and agents mean that this segment is particularly vulnerable to unethical, illegal, and dishonest actions by agents. Sadly, there are scores of examples of clients taken by their agents. One notable case involved hockey great Bobby Orr, who had wanted to end his career with the Boston Bruins, the team he broke in with in 1967. However, his agent, Alan Eagleson, had a personal relationship with the owner of the Chicago Blackhawks, and disregarded an offer from the Bruins that would have made Orr a part owner of the Bruins to accept a deal with Chicago. Eagleson was later convicted of defrauding many of his clients (Conway, 1995).

Perhaps the most well-known case demonstrating this problem involved sport agent William H. "Tank" Black. Black, who had a tryout with the Atlanta Falcons in 1979, was a former assistant football coach at the University of South Carolina in the late 1980s. According to a former colleague, Black left to become a sport agent because he wanted the opportunity to make big money. By 1999, Black's firm, Professional Marketing Inc. (PMI), represented more than 35 NFL players, including running back Fred Taylor (who called Black "Pops" and described him as his second dad), wide receiver Ike Hilliard, and defensive end Jevon Kearse, as well as the NBA's Vince Carter. Black attracted these talents to PMI because he would call his clients at all hours, express care and concern, and give them expensive gifts. The firm grew by developing a system of runners on college campuses and paying prospective clients. Black offered under-the-table payments to University of Florida players in 1999, such as $600 a month for Johnny Rutledge; and he leased a $133,500 Mercedes S600V for Kearse, in violation of NCAA amateurism rules and the many state agent regulations. But as Black got more capital, he spent more on recruiting. The more he invested in recruiting, the more players he landed, and the more players he landed, the more capital he had at his disposal (Wertheim *et al.*, 2000).

221

However, in 2000 federal investigators from the Securities and Exchange Commission claimed Black was involved in the biggest case of agent fraud in the history of sport. Black was accused of defrauding clients and mismanaging approximately $15 million. Fred Taylor lost his entire $3.6 million signing bonus, which Black had invested in a pyramid scheme that promised a 36 percent annual return on loans made to people who used their car titles as collateral. Black actually promised 20 percent and skimmed 16 percent for himself, and he charged an additional fee for administering the funds. Some players liquidated legitimate stock portfolios to invest in this, although Black was never licensed as an investment adviser. He also encouraged his clients to invest stock in a company that Black himself had ties to, received a consulting salary, sold them shares they were supposed to receive free, and charged them a commission for it. Black also allegedly laundered millions of dollars for a Detroit drug trafficking ring through an offshore account in the Cayman Islands, with connections in Colombia, for which he made a 25 percent commission (Wertheim *et al.*, 2000).

Black thrived on his clients' lack of knowledge of fiscal and financial matters, and instead of educating them, he exploited this lack of knowledge. His PMI brochure actually read: "A successful athlete simply does not have time to research, study, compare, and negotiate every opportunity that arises. Too often the result is a missed opportunity or a hasty decision that results in a less than fair deal" (Wertheim *et al.*, 2000, p. 69). This example of agent fraud and exploitation illustrates for clients the importance of choosing an agent and staying informed on the agent's dealings. The design and structures of sport agency firms also impact their overall efficiency and effectiveness. The better the design and oversight in a firm, and the more attention on the part of the client, the less opportunity for Black-like misdealings.

Another ethical issue facing sport agency is the phenomenon of players leaving agents for other representation. It is something that the emerging agencies such as DiaMMond face all the time. DiaMMond had worked closely with University of Massachusetts pitching prospect Matt Torra (for whom DiaMMond would eventually negotiate a signing bonus just over $1 million) prior to the 2005 draft, but because of amateurism rules Torra could not yet sign with any agent. This made him fair game for another to come in and potentially woo him away to his/her firm. Such a scenario occurred at one game at UMass, when Jim got a call from an MLB scout who said: "You better get over here fast. There's a Scott Boras representative who is all over Mr. and Mrs. Torra." The agent in question had actually just struck out on his own and was looking to boost his credentials. Panicked, Jim called Lisa, who got to the field in time and intervened between the agent and the flustered Torras, and possibly preserving Matt's future with DiaMMond (Dobrow, 2011, p. 124).

And this mindset is also a problem for teams, as described by one MLB GM: "When a player jumps from one agent to the next, he's jumping based on a set of promises that he's been given, or something he feels he's entitled to. Now there's this attitude of, 'What's in it for me?' Or, 'How does that benefit me?" (Crasnick, 2005, p. 30). And it's not just an issue in MLB. NFL running back Peyton Hillis used three different agents in 2011 alone, and switched to a fourth in 2012 after parting ways with agent Kennard McGuire. According to writer Gregg Rosenthal, "the Madden cover subject consistently overvalued himself last year, which is why he felt the need to keep firing agents ... Hillis likely keeps changing agents because he wants more money than the agents think he's worth" (2012, p. 1). It is easy to see why such behavior could be detrimental to team performance.

ORGANIZATIONAL DESIGN AND SPORT AGENCY

It is the choice of whether to sign with a large sport agency firm or to sign with an individual sport agent that is the key decision for emerging professional athletes. Their choice is not a simple one. This section outlines the essential elements of organizational design and how they impact these two basic models of the sport agency business.

The essential elements in organizational design

Edgar Schein (1985), a prominent organizational theorist, suggests that four essential elements must be present for an organization to function effectively: common goals, division of work, coordination of effort, and authority structure. According to Schein's model, if any of these elements are missing or poorly designed, the organization is likely to be unsuccessful in implementing its strategies and pursuing its mission.

Common goals

Common goals, as we saw in Chapter 4, provide the sense of direction, the target to aim for, and the basis of cooperation that are critical for the success of any organization. The concept of using academic achievement to determine interscholastic athletic eligibility is implemented to encourage academic performance. Without goals as a focus for its efforts, the energy of the organization would be wasted on random activities toward no particular end. The emphasis on academic performance sends the message that schools place primary importance on educational activities.

Recall from Chapter 6 that planning is the process of developing goals and strategies to achieve the organization's mission. Schein's point is that you have to know where you are going (as defined through an organization's mission and goals) and how you're going to get there (using what strategy) before you can design a structure to take you there. So under agency law, the agent is bound to represent the client's wishes. In the case of the sport agency industry segment, a client is seeking an agent who can represent his or her interests the most effectively. A prospective agent, therefore, must show that he or she has the ability to produce a plan for clients to achieve their financial, professional, and personal goals. But the goals of the client also impact the goals of the agent.

The organizational design, therefore, must enable the agent to serve the client in the most effective manner and must aid the agent in serving the best interests of the client. Thus, the first essential element in designing an effective organization is shared or common goals – from mission to strategic goals to policies and procedures. In the case of sport agency organizations, this means a mission, strategic goals, policies, and procedures consistent with the goals of the athletes the agencies seek to serve.

Division of work

Common goals alone, however, are not enough. Once the organization's mission and strategic and operational goals are clear, the work necessary to achieve those goals must be divided up in the most productive way possible. Sport agency managers have struggled with this question of how to group and divide the tasks of negotiating contracts, securing endorsements and sponsorship agreements, and producing plans for clients to achieve financial goals. Following this overview of Schein's four key elements of organizational design, much of this chapter focuses on how organizations in the sport agency segment have chosen to divide up work for maximum effectiveness.

Coordination of effort

Logically speaking, if the work of an organization is divided among separate units or departments, coordination is critical to ensure that the work being done within each unit is consistent with the overall goals of the organization. Also, these units must not work at cross-purposes with one another. Consider a sport agency organization with a mission to provide clients with financial stability combined with a consideration for a client's personal values. The contract department focuses on negotiating the highest rate of compensation regardless of the location of employment, but the client might be content with less money if he or she could be located in an area closer to home and family. The sponsorship unit might be seeking only the most lucrative endorsement agreements, but the client might be unwilling to represent certain products that he or she doesn't use or feels are unhealthy or destructive (such as alcohol). In essence, these units are working at cross-purposes and need better coordination to ensure the organization's mission is achieved and the organization satisfies the client's goals.

As we will see, these factors are complicated in larger sport agency firms. A comprehensive network of goals serves as a starting point for this type of coordination, but goals are not enough. A steady flow of communication among the various units of an organization ensures that the coordination of efforts is continuous and effective. We discuss how sport agency firms attempt to achieve and maintain effective coordination later in the chapter.

Authority structure

The fourth of Schein's elements of effective organizational design is authority structure. *Authority* is often defined as the right to guide the actions of others (Weber, 1947). Organizations, as we have said, are collections of individuals who share common goals. However, sharing common goals does not mean they will also agree on what must be done to achieve these goals or on who must do what. For this reason, authority – the right to direct the actions of others – is a key element in designing the organization. For an organization to succeed there must be an authority structure, what Henri Fayol would call a "chain of command," to define the goals, to divide the work, and to require coordination to the extent that others will accept and follow this direction. An organization without an effective authority structure is like an individual without discipline or an agent who does not follow the rules of agency law: the goals and plans may be clear and in place, but without the ability to require action, the desired actions will not be performed.

For most of the last century, authority was assumed to be most effective when it rested in the hands of managers at the top of the organization, the so-called executives. It was assumed that only the people at the highest levels of the organization had the education and information necessary to exercise authority responsibly.

DECENTRALIZATION

The overall trend in organizations has been toward greater decentralization: authority to make decisions is distributed throughout the organization so decisions can be made more quickly and with more focus. Management thinkers David Conklin and Lawrence Tapp (2000) refer to the organizational structures that are emerging in response to decentralization as creative webs, because changing environments and technological innovations require "that all parties interact on an ongoing, extended basis ... If there is a free exchange of information and communication, all parties benefit" (p. 221). The creative web focuses on creating change, continual collaboration, and ongoing mutual dependence. Such webs may be created between separate organizations as well.

Another expert, Mick Carney (1998), points out that today's organizational structures need to achieve trust while undergoing decentralization and diffusing power. Trust and communication are especially key factors in the agent–client relationship and must be emphasized in any sport agency firm. The firms that emphasize these aspects must cede to their individual agents the authority to make decisions in the best interests of their clients in today's heightened atmosphere of real-time communication.

225

From the perspective of clients, communication and related services are critically important. As we have seen in the case of DiaMMond, once many of their players begin to have success in the minors, other better-known agents begin to try and woo them away.

So how does such a change, going from a small, baseball-only firm like DiaMMond to a firm like Wasserman Media Group (WMG), whose team sports representation division is headed by Arn Tellem, impact clients in meeting their own personal goals? Does it mean that a client will no longer get the direct service from his agent now that he's part of a much larger organization with many more clients, and with potential conflicts in communication, coordination of effort, and common goals? To serve all clients, WMG must address design issues such as decentralization effectively. However, decentralization can pose challenges in the areas of coordination and consistency. In response to this challenge, many organizations are highly centralized in setting goals for the organization's many units, but decentralized when it comes to deciding how these goals are achieved (Peters and Waterman, 1982). The key to developing an effective authority structure is balance: authority must be centralized enough to ensure consistency and coordination and decentralized enough to provide for timely and focused decisions and action by managers in the various units of the organization. In sport agency organizations, this means it is management's responsibility in designing the organization to ensure that this balance in terms of authority is effectively achieved and maintained.

A fifth element of design: structure follows strategy
Clearly, Schein's four elements of organizational design are essential for the success of an organization. Without common goals, effective division of work, coordination of effort, and authority structure, an organization is unlikely to achieve its purpose. In a sense, Schein's elements are like a chain that is only as strong as its weakest link.

So while these four elements are essential, more is needed to ensure that the design of an organization will be effective. Based on his study of successful U.S. corporations, management historian Alfred Chandler suggests what might be termed a fifth element of effective organizational design: structure follows strategy. Chandler (1962) found that successful organizations were designed by management to pursue specific strategies, and when they changed their strategies they also changed their structures.

Structure follows strategy in sport agency
A few large firms represent the bulk of professional athletes. But what does this mean, this distinction between large and small firms? According to Berry (1990), three basic organizational design models operate in the sport agency business: the freestanding sport management firm, the law practice, and the law firm/sport management firm affiliation. Each of these designs also has a strategic advantage.

226

The large freestanding sport management firm such as WMG offers a wide range of services to athletes. These firms serve their players' needs in the areas discussed earlier, but also serve corporate clients interested in sport-related sponsorships and managing sport-related events. Firms designed in this way can offer advantages for clients who can benefit from these various activities. These firms seek to serve all the clients' needs in these areas and can make more money from these services, which increases potential revenue sources. The larger firms are also usually more established and have a higher profile because of their other prominent clients. For example, WMG's Team Sports arm represents many star athletes in a number of sports, including football (such as 2012 top NFL draft pick Andrew Luck) and basketball (such as 2012 top NBA draft pick Anthony Davis). This can help generate positive influence by association for an up-and-coming player. WMG is also a presence in other sport industry segments. In 2012, WMG created an action sports and Olympics division to specialize in representing athletes, properties, and corporate sponsors active in those sports. The move sought to expand business opportunities WMG offered in terms of social media and branding to these athletes, and begin pushing into Olympic corporate and property consulting and sales. Steve Astephen, President of the Action Sports & Olympics Division, said: "There's great Olympic consulting groups. There's great athlete management groups. But I don't think you can say there's a group that does everything. We are that in our space [of action sports] and we're going to add that in the Olympics." On the consulting side, the agency has worked on social media and marketing with brands ranging from Puma to Sunoco Fuel, and oversees sponsorship sales for USA Cycling (Mickle, 2012, p. 1). WMG also negotiated the 20-year deal with MetLife to secure the naming rights to the New Meadowlands Stadium. The net worth of the firm is valued at $250 million (Atkinson, 2012).

Larger firms also can benefit clients because of the resources that can be expended more broadly. For example, in addition to its developmental "academies" for youth sports hopefuls (see Chapter 4), IMG runs a predraft "performance institute" for their NFL prospects in Bradenton, Florida, where players train and are coached by former NFL staffers to increase their draft value through improved performance in the predraft combine work-outs. Former NFL top draft pick Cam Newton described the experience this way: "You're down here ... and it's like 485 acres of just straight work, basically ... You've got every opportunity to be successful ... You don't have any media out here to critique everything you do" ("NFL combine," 2012, p. 1).

But size and growth can be problematic. When compared to the industry giants, DiaMMond's strategic advantage is a competitive advantage: they can't outspend the industry giants, so they would focus on the personal touch. Jim, while hardly a seasoned outdoorsman, goes deer hunting with prospective clients. Lisa connects with prospects' mothers and can identify with their concerns about protecting their sons' well-being. Would Scott Boras do this? Does he even have to? Heightened levels of attention and personal service are generally recognized as the major benefits of the small firm's organizational structure. Jim summarizes it this way: "[The big agents] won't spend the time with you when you're nobody. But when you become a prospect, they decide to get off their ass and pretend they care about you" (Dobrow, 2011, p. 124).

So to Schein's four elements of effective organizational design, we add a fifth: to be effective, organizations must be structured to implement their strategies. The relationship between structure and strategy can be thought of this way: structure *follows* strategy, structure *reflects* strategy, structure *implements* strategy, structure *supports* strategy. We next consider the model of organizational design consistent with these five elements.

Traditional models of organizational design

Functional structure

Like many organizational changes, the next major advance in the design of organizations came in response to the changes in the internal and external environment. Remember, most large organizations at the beginning of the twentieth century were business organizations involved with some form of mass production. Typically, this involved the operation of a large facility filled with a variety of machines, employing large numbers of people to perform many specific and relatively simple tasks. To ensure that a steady flow of products from these factories was being matched by a steady supply of customers, sales became an important function. Sales work was different from manufacturing, and yet the sales tasks were essential to the success of the organization.

"Sales are important in the sport agency business," says a golf agent. He continues:

> I wish I had more practice in college. I wish I had known I was going to need to do it. I always told myself, "I don't want to be in sales." Well, I've got news for you. I'm in sales in a big way, whether it's selling one of my athletes to a company that we're trying to create a relationship with, whether it's trying to sell my firm to a client we're trying to recruit, whether it's me trying to sell myself to my bosses. I'm constantly selling. I'm selling what I believe in, my thoughts, and my ideas. I'm always selling.

A similar pattern of specialization can be seen for marketing, for accounting and finance, and for the other kinds of work that become essential in all agency organizations.

But no individual or group of individuals could be expected to perform all the different kinds of work that needs to be done in all organizations. Different people now

228

specialize in specific areas. The organizational structure that emerged to implement this specialization strategy is called the *functional structure*. Under this framework, the organization is divided into units, with each unit performing one of the specialized functions essential to the operation of the business.

Organizational structures are usually shown on organizational charts. The chart of a sport agency organization designed according to the functional model is shown in Figure 7.1. The functional model is most effective for organizations producing a single product for a single market, and, in the case of sport agencies, the basic units of the organization are contract negotiation, athlete marketing, and financial planning.

Although functional structures have an ever-increasing number of units as organizations become more complex, the basis for dividing the work remains the same: a separate unit or department of specialists is created to perform each function essential for achieving the organization's goals.

Division structure

In the *division structure*, the work of the organization is divided according to the kind of products or services being provided, the type of customer being served, or the geographic area in which the organization competes. Firms such as WMG have separate divisions for each sport. For many large and complex sport agency firms, which provide a wider range of financial and marketing services for clients, an organization's structure might actually combine the functional and divisional models. Separate divisions are created to focus on the organization's different types of customers or products, and functional departments provide services to these various divisions.

In each of the preceding examples we see a common thread: the organization is divided into separate units to focus more effectively on the factor most essential to the organization's success. The divisional model allows the agency organization to respond more effectively to the special needs and requirements of different kinds of clients or markets, whichever of these factors is the focus of its strategy.

Figure 7.1 Functional structure of a player representation agency

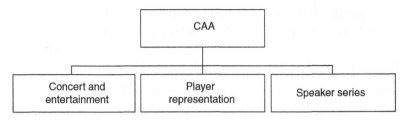

Figure 7.2 Conglomerate structure of CAA

Conglomerate structure

The 1980s saw a significant increase in what came to be known as the conglomerate structure. As shown in Figure 7.2, organizations with a conglomerate structure have separate divisions operating in entirely different industries. Creative Artists Agency (CAA), which represents numerous music and entertainment acts (including AC/DC, Justin Bieber, Cee Lo Green, Ed Helms, Kraftwerk, Pitbull, Radiohead, Sarah Silverman, and Sugarland), as well as its sport agency business, fits this type of description. The conglomerate structure allows organizations such as CAA to expand into many types of entertainment activities, and it uses these separate yet similar divisional operations to the benefit of the company. In the case of CAA, the expertise used in representing athletes can translate into running concerts and other performances.

Problems with traditional models of organizational design

Virtually every successful organization that emerged during the twentieth century was bureaucratic in design. Whether the design of the organization was functional, divisional, conglomerate, or some combination of all three, the model was organization by rules with a fully developed chain of command (authority structure) to ensure that the organization's decisions followed the rules, which is exactly what is meant by the term bureaucratic. And for most of the twentieth century, bureaucratic organizations, because of these qualities, were impressive in terms of their efficiency and effectiveness.

Recently, however, the bureaucratic design has begun to show signs of ineffectiveness. The bureaucratic model seems to work well when the environment changes very slowly, because the rules can be gradually modified to reflect these changes. As the rate of change begins to speed up, however, changes in rules begin to fall behind changes in technology, the competition, and customer demands. At some point, the rules and structure intended to make the organization more efficient become obstacles that impede the organization.

Recall endorsements, the important source of revenue for athletes and agents. Endorsements are complicated by three factors that are notoriously unpredictable

Designing the organization and the sport agency industry

and uncontrollable: injuries, performance, and personal behavior. Companies seek to sign athletes who embody the personal skills and abilities that potential customers admire so the company will benefit from the endorsement association, but these can be blunted or obliterated when an athlete gets hurt, plays poorly, gets arrested, or some combination of the three. Examples of these situations are numerous, with a most recent and lurid example involving Tiger Woods, his late-night car accident while fleeing from his club-wielding, since-estranged wife, and subsequent revelations concerning his numerous extra-marital affairs.

To be responsive to these kinds of sudden, uncontrollable changes, according to Rosabeth Moss Kanter and John Buck (1985), leading management scholars and consultants, "The organizations now emerging as successful will be, above all, flexible" (p. 6). To be effective in the changing environment, organizations must now satisfy an additional requirement for effective organizational design. In addition to common goals, division of work, coordination of effort, and authority structure, the design of the organization must also be flexible. A structure that enables an agency firm to react quickly and to deal with the changes in the environment described here, and to respond rapidly to new opportunities, is a requirement of organizational design.

Flexible models of organizational design

Matrix structure

One of the earliest forms of flexible models of organizational design was the *matrix structure*, in which specialists are assigned to a specific project or product or customer account. In a traditional agency organization, for example, marketing specialists work only with other specialists in their own department. In a matrix agency organization, these specialists work directly with specialists from other areas such as event management as part of an on-going group or team assigned to a long-term project or to develop a new project. Table 7.1 shows a matrix structure for CAA:

Table 7.1 Matrix structure for CAA

	Athlete/talent representation	Athlete/talent marketing	Venue management	Event management
Spike Lee (celebrity speaker)	Agents	Sales staff	Operations staff	Operations staff
"So you think you can dance" tour	Agents	Sales staff	Operations staff	Operations staff
Katy Perry (concert performer)	Agents	Sales staff	Operations staff	Operations staff

231

One such new project area in the agency segment, as targeted by WMG, is in the area of Olympic sports. Given the four-year cycle of the games, there is a period of planning in the intervening years that allows firms to focus on which athletes might work as endorsers. For the 2008 Summer Olympics in Beijing, the anointed figure was swimmer Michael Phelps. For 2012, it was swimmer Ryan Lochte, described by *New York Times* writer Melena Ryzik as possessing a "muscle-bound 6-foot-2 frame and sculptured abs ... [and] twinkling blue eyes, [an] aquiline nose and dimpled smile." Lochte was groomed to be a breakout Olympic superstar (he won four medals (two gold, two bronze) in Beijing, compared to eight golds for Phelps), with millions in corporate sponsorships to match his athletic accomplishments. Prior to the 2012 Games he was featured in ad campaigns for Gatorade, Gillette, and Nissan. And all this before the final squad bound for London had even been finalized (Ryzik, 2012, p. 1).

"We always sort of internally refer to him as the rock star of the swimming community," said Katie Malone, the director of marketing at Speedo, which has sponsored him since 2006 and has him under contract through 2016. Malone added that Lochte was not typical of the swimmers, who often do little but train. "If someone's zigging left, he's zagging right," she said. "He wants to stand out." While serving as a strong image force for Speedo, a swimming products brand, is one thing, being able to reach a broader mainstream market and its consumers is quite another. But industry experts are bullish. "We're a little Phelps'd out," said one. As a brand, Lochte's appeal is "through the roof," he added. "He has potential for winning golds, and then just the fact that he's so damn good-looking. If he can't beat Michael Phelps in anything else, he can beat him in that category" (Ryzik, 2012, p. 1).

These emerging market opportunities mean that matrix agency firms with specialists from each functional area can focus their expertise on a specific project or product area, such as the emerging endorsement market for female athletes. Another advantage is that it facilitates communication and coordination among specialists. Instead of having to communicate through channels, specialists communicate directly with each other, dramatically increasing their ability to respond quickly to challenges and opportunities.

Finally, a matrix structure has the potential to increase an organization's flexibility and speed by allowing it to create a new group of specialists drawn from existing departments to respond to a crisis or to a rapidly developing opportunity. For example, after the world championships in Shanghai in 2011, Ryan Lochte cut ties with Octagon, his former agent firm (and who represents Phelps and other top swimmers), and signed instead with Erika Wright and Shawn Zenga, who, according to *New York Times* writer Karen Crouse, showed up at one of Lochte's meets "wearing jeans, high heels, and black leather jackets with 'Team Lochte' emblazoned on the back. Nobody was going to confuse them with the buttoned-down management at Octagon." "That's what I like about them," Lochte said. "They're different, like me.

232

They make my life 10 times easier," Lochte said of the agents, who spend time pursuing deals and monitoring Lochte's Facebook fan page and blocking women who send inappropriate photographs or messages. "I know absolutely nothing about swimming," said Wright, "but what I could tell from the first time I met Ryan is he's marketable. He has such an ability to reach people, to touch people, to get into people's hearts because of his nature." Gregg Troy, Lochte's longtime coach, noted that: "I'm dealing with a 27-year-old man who lives on the edge a little bit. If you do anything other than allow him to be himself, he's not going to be the same athlete" (Crouse, 2011, p. 1).

A project group made up of specialists from all the functional areas may have enabled Octagon to maximize the expertise and coordination around Lochte and his personality to target the optimum client–company endorsement match with maximum speed in this fast-moving and highly competitive field. For whatever reason, Lochte failed to see this from Octagon and fired the agency. But one weakness of matrix organizations is that the authority structure can be confusing. Most who work in a matrix organization have two managers to answer to, instead of the one superior prescribed by Henri Fayol's unity of command principle described in Chapter 1. Workers are then responsible both to the manager of their functional department (accounting, sales and marketing, finance, etc.) and to the group manager in the area or project to which they are assigned. When an individual's managers fail to communicate and coordinate with one another, it can lead to conflicting demands being made on the worker and can leave the worker in the middle, not knowing which manager's directions to follow. One of the keys to an effective matrix structure in sport agency firms, then, is to train managers in effective communication and coordination skills, so important in dealing with relaying information to clients, to enhance their ability to provide clear and unified direction to workers in the firm.

Network structure

A second design option for meeting the organization's need for speed and flexibility is the network structure (Snow *et al.*, 1992). The *network structure* is a temporary alliance of organizations that come together to take advantage of a strategic opportunity. Most organizations do not have all of the in-house expertise needed to respond to every opportunity and challenge – and by the time they develop the necessary expertise, it may be too late to take advantage of the opportunity. The network organization brings together independent companies with different areas of expertise to function as non-permanent organizations.

Many large sport agency firms that also perform event management functions often work in a network with companies that seek to create brand identity and sales opportunities. When ESPN created "B³, the Bikes, Blades, and Boards Tour" as an action-sports broadcast complement to their X Games competition, they employed Octagon to run the competition and sell sponsorships while

ESPN handled all the broadcast elements. Octagon, in turn, employed several other smaller companies to run certain aspects of the actual sport competitions (Covell, 1999). ESPN eventually expanded to take over all aspects of the event, but Octagon was then able to take its expertise gained from B³ to combine with new partner NBC and produce the Gravity Games, a competition similar to the X Games. Octagon later left the partnership with NBC and created the Mountain Dew Action Sports Tour.

In 2012, the event – now known as "the Dew Tour" – was connected with Alli Sports, a division of the NBC Sports Group, which sought to rebrand the Dew Tour into three large-scale events. In 2011, the NBC Sports Group acquired 100 percent of Alli Sports, which manages more than 40 events including the Red Bull Signature Series and Lucas Oil Pro Motocross Championships. The new format created the "Beach," "City," and "Mountain" tour model, which managers hoped would be aided by expanded television programming and digital strategy across NBC, NBC Sports Network, nbcsports.com, and allisports.com, as well as local promotional and programming opportunities through the NBC Sports Group's owned stations and regional sport networks. "The action sports landscape has grown and changed dramatically since we launched the Dew Tour in 2005," stated Wade Martin, President and CEO of Alli Sports. "The multi-stop series format was what the industry wanted and needed then ... The new Dew Tour, which will include three major events across Beach, City and Mountain venues, represents what the athletes and industry want and need today. We believe our partnership with Mountain Dew represents one of the most unique, integrated relationships between brand and property in all of sports" ("Alli Sports," 2012, p. 1; Stanger, 2012).

Soon thereafter, Alli Sports announced a partnership with on-line retailer Dogfunk. Alli Sports' Martin describes the rationale for the move this way:

> We tried to launch its own on-line shop [shop.allisports.com] two years ago. In 2010, we purchased standardboardshop.com, and converted it to an Alli branded ecommerce site that included products for not just Alli branded events, but also featured products from brands like Vans, DC, Volcom and more ... But when we originally launched, we underestimated what it took to be a really good on-line retailer ... We think Dogfunk is the best in the business in terms of their scalable operation. We were really impressed with their management and what they have done with other brands as well as how big their growth potential is.
>
> (Stanger, 2012, p. 1)

Figure 7.3 shows a network structure where organizations come together for a specific project.

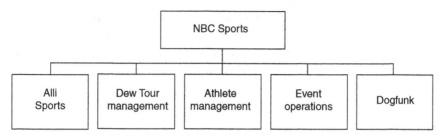

Figure 7.3 Network organization for NBC Sports and the Dew Tour

The potential weaknesses of the network model of organizational design are in three of the areas identified by Schein: common goals, coordination of effort, and authority structure. Obviously, in an organization consisting of several different independent companies, the management will have to take great care to define common goals and an authority structure, and to develop effective means of coordination. And even if all these challenges can be worked out, there is still an increased number of handoffs and consequently increased potential for disconnects when more than one company is involved in manufacturing a product or providing a service.

Still, it is clear that, when managed effectively, network organizations give their constituent organizations more speed, expertise, and flexibility than each possess individually. For the Dew Tour property, NBC Sports provides significant expertise in broadcast production and access to media outlets. For NBC Sports, Alli Sports provided knowledge of the action-sports segment, access to potential sponsors, and a demonstrated ability to pull off such an event. In terms of the new version of the Dew Tour, managers understand the power of such organization. "We're always evaluating the industry and the other events out there and really felt it was best to do less [sic] events but have them be bigger, better events," said Chris Prybylo, general manager of the Dew Tour.

> A lot of the athletes feel that way, and a lot has changed in the seven years since we launched ... We'll be uplifting everything from the television production to the competition courses and really looking to take an approach to develop great individual events with unique, distinct identities, and really continue to progress action sports ... we're also going to be adding some new disciplines to the mix at each event, so that each locale will really stand out and have its own feel and personality.
>
> (Bane, 2012, p. 1)

With such success stories, one can expect a steady increase in the number and variety of sport organizations moving into network structures.

235

While organizational design is a significant challenge for firms involved in sport agency, the reliance on cooperation between individuals means an increased reliance on teamwork. The remainder of the chapter will focus on understanding the nature and importance of teamwork in sport agency firms.

TEAMWORK

Chances are you have been on a sports team, or you may be on one currently. Think about this for a moment – what was the team supposed to do? At some point when your team was in trouble or struggling, you may have heard someone – a player, a coach – shout at the group, "Hey, we have to start playing like a team." Well, that may be true, but that's not the goal. The goal is for a team to be successful and to achieve a goal – namely, winning a game. And for this you need a team, because seldom is a single person good enough to achieve a goal alone. A full complement of participants is needed, all functioning at full capacity in their specific roles, to get the job done. And if the other team is more proficient at working together, they will probably be the ones celebrating at the end of the game.

In sport organizations off the field, we find teams everywhere. A work team is a designed group of individuals who together are responsible for a significant unit of work – a product or service that is delivered to a customer either inside or outside an organization. Work teams are known by various other names, including autonomous work groups and self-managing teams. Work teams are more like departments than they are like project teams, because the members of the teams work together on a long-term, day-to-day basis. In its most advanced form, the work team essentially replaces the manager by taking on responsibility for most of the tasks traditionally performed by management: planning and scheduling the work, hiring and training team members, and providing discipline and resolving conflicts among team members or work teams. The move toward increasing work teams in sport organization has been prompted by the competitive requirements of speed and flexibility, as outlined in Chapter 1.

While effective teams are powerful tools for improving performance, teamwork is not necessarily the right work design in every situation. For tasks in which individual talent, insight, or intuition is the most important element, a team-based work design might only complicate or undermine the effort. The task of sport managers is to recognize the kind of work that can best be done by teams, and in those situations to create and to support the conditions necessary for teams to be effective.

In terms of the sport agency business, many firms refer to themselves as "teams" in an effort to convey to clients the fact that they work with them to achieve their personal and financial goals. The best agents not only convey the message effectively, but also follow through on the promise. But how do these teams become effective?

Conditions for effective teams

As team-based work designs have become more and more widely adopted through-out the sport industries, important lessons have been learned about how to make teams work and how to ensure that team-based work is as productive as possible. Katzenbach and Smith (2003) studied the differences between high and low performing teams by interviewing hundreds of people on 50 different teams in 30 different organizations. Based on their research, Katzenbach and Smith composed the following definition of a high-performance team:

> A team is a small number of people with complementary skills who are com-mitted to a common purpose, a set of performance goals, and an approach for which they hold themselves mutually accountable.

> (p. 45)

The six characteristics identified by Katzenbach and Smith are summarized in Box 7.3 below. We will consider each in detail in terms of whether they can be identified at DiaMMond.

BOX 7.3 CONDITIONS FOR EFFECTIVE TEAMWORK

Small number of people	Three to eight members, no more than 40
Complementary skills	Each team member contributes some of the skills necessary for the team's success
Common purpose	The team commits to a shared mission or purpose
Performance goal	The team sets specific targets for its performance
Common approach	Teams need to agree on the best approach to reach their goals
Mutual accountability	The team has a sense of shared responsibility for the team and its work

---

Small number
The first lesson noted by Katzenbach and Smith is the importance of keeping teams small in terms of the number of people who are members. They suggest that small can be as few as three, to as many as 40. Their point is that there appears to be limits to the number of people who can maintain the level of communication and coordi-nation necessary to operate as an effective team. The larger the team, the more effort management and team members must exert in ensuring that the requisite levels

of communication and coordination exist. If the team size exceeds 40, the performance of the team begins to suffer.

These numbers would seem to favor not the industry conglomerates but rather the small- and medium-sized firm approach of DiaMMond. But with only three people on board, is DiaMMond too small to work as an effective team? Possibly, and their focus on one specific region of the country may hamper the firm's ability to grow.

Complementary skills

As discussed earlier, any successful on-field team needs members with a variety of different skills. Just watch a National League game where pitchers have to hit, and you'll understand this concept immediately. Katzenbach and Smith point out that team efforts are likely to be most effective when members possess complementary skills – that is, when each team member contributes some of the skills necessary for the team to achieve success. Work teams benefit when team members possess different skills, which could be technical or functional expertise, problem-solving and decision-making skills, or interpersonal skills, all of which complement those possessed by others. It isn't essential that each team member possess all the skills required (again, think of that pitcher, or any MLB pitcher, trying to hit), but rather it is critical that the team as a whole possess all the skills required to perform.

In the case of DiaMMond, some of the complementary skills needed have to do with personalities. As noted above, Jim and Lisa have different approaches in dealing with clients. Lisa connects with prospects' mothers and can identify with their concerns about protecting their sons' well-being, while Jim takes the lead in dealing with scouts and player development personnel. This two-fold approach can work to their advantage. As writer Marty Dobrow observed, with Lisa

> it's not all nurturing nice-nice ... As the daughter of a union carpenter, she has been a tough fighter in negotiations, sometimes even surprising Jim with her even-tempered fierceness. "I get a kick out of the reaction on the other side of the table," she says. "They don't know quite what to do with me. They try to clean up their language. It kind of throws them off."
>
> (2011, p. 128)

Also, Jim grew up close to Boston dreaming of playing for the Red Sox at Fenway Park, while Lisa was raised in Western Massachusetts as a New York Yankees fan. If two people from these opposite fan camps can work together and capitalize on complementary skills, anything is possible.

Common purpose

The third key ingredient for successful teamwork is the commitment of team members to a common purpose. Without this shared commitment, work groups are likely to be little more than collections of individuals each performing independently.

238

With a shared commitment to a common purpose, work groups become genuine teams. Shared commitment requires a purpose all team members can believe in, much like the sense of organizational mission outlined in Chapter 6. Katzenbach and Smith suggest that the sense of common purpose is most powerful when it raises the sights of team members, that team purposes that truly motivate often have to do with winning, with being first, or with being on the cutting edge.

Much of what we have been discussing relating to the sport agency business has been an explanation of how the business works, but we haven't delved much into why those in this highly volatile business choose to be in it. Jim, Lisa, and Steve chose to pursue agency because it allows them to chase their personal goals and dreams. They know that, like their players, they can make it big with the signing of the right clients. But to be successful, they will have to make sure they perform for their clients, and that means making them money, either through contract negotiations or endorsements.

Performance goals

The right size, complementary skills, and strong commitment to a meaningful common purpose are the critical starting point for effective teams. Not surprisingly, the best teams are also able to translate their common purpose into specific goals. The common purpose for DiaMMond is to perform for their clients, but is that specific enough? DiaMMond's performance, indeed their long-term viability, will ultimately be measured by how much money they can make for their clients through contracts, endorsements, and prudent financial planning.

As we discussed in Chapter 4, such specific goals provide a clear target to aim for as well as for the possibility of feedback, but common purpose alone is not sufficient. It's the combination of shared purpose and clear performance goals that is essential, for, according to Katzenbach and Smith, "specific performance goals help a team track progress and hold itself accountable; the broader, even nobler aspirations in a team's purpose supply both meaning and emotional energy" (2003, p. 55).

Committed to a common approach

Katzenbach and Smith define "common approach" as the way teams will work together to accomplish their purpose, which includes agreeing on which team members will do what jobs. In addition, they found that effective teams have members who assume important social as well as leadership roles such as challenging, interpreting, supporting, integrating, remembering, and summarizing. These roles, they conclude, help promote the mutual trust and constructive conflict necessary to the team's success. What is established, they state, is "a social contract among members that relates to their purpose, and guides and obligates how they must work together" (2003, p. 59).

In many ways, this commitment is connected to the aspect of complementary skills outlined previously, but translates more into what tasks agents actually execute. In working on behalf of their client Matt Torra prior to the 2005 draft, Jim handled the negotiations with interested clubs. Draft gurus had predicted Torra could go as high as twenty-first overall, but if he were to slide to later in the first round, it would mean hundreds of thousands of dollars lost for agents and client (DiaMMond's commission was four percent of the signing bonus). Scouts and teams kept calling to gauge Torra's "signability," asking if Torra was going to be a "hard sign." Jim would respond cagily, staking out his negotiating position: "He really likes UMass and he'd like to get his degree, but the kid wants to play. We're just looking for a fair offer" (Dobrow, 2011, p. 126).

Mutual accountability

The final component in the establishment of an effective team is a shared sense of responsibility for the team and its work. In the highest performing teams, members hold themselves individually and collectively accountable for the team's performance. They may receive their initial direction from management, but the most effective teams eventually define their own purpose and their own goals, and hold themselves responsible for achieving them. According to Katzenbach and Smith, this sense of shared responsibility produces a unique satisfaction for team members. We have defined management as responsibility for performance, so it is no surprise that the most effective teams are self-managing – that is, they take responsibility for their own performance. DiaMMond's long-term success is dependent on just this sort of self-management.

The challenge of converting to team-based work

The potential effectiveness of the team-based work design is clear. It is equally clear that making such a team work effectively can be a challenging task for sport managers. In Chapter 10, we will discuss in detail the natural human resistance to change. As with any work redesign, the move to team-based work may represent a significant change in the way people are asked to perform their daily tasks. As a result, not everyone makes this sort of change willingly. This can be especially problematic in the agency business, when individual risk and personal effort are what gets most agents to the top of their firms. And it is also likely that many agents are likely to share similar skill sets and personality types, therefore making the composing of teams with members with complementary skills and a commitment to a common approach more problematic.

One strategy for reducing resistance to team-based work is training. If people feel they possess the skills to be successful in a new team environment, they are more likely to follow through on the transition to teams. On the other hand, it is important to realize that, even with training, some workers will be unable to make the transition. Even with an effective campaign of worker education and training, a period of time will likely be required for any sport organization to allow less willing employees to leave and to recruit new workers who are more comfortable with the demands of working in teams.

It is also important to realize that individual workers are not the only source of resistance to work team design. The large firms such as CAA, WMG, and Octagon, designed around highly managed departments of experts, can have great difficulty learning how to function as self-managing teams. Issues of chain of command (who reports to whom) and channels of information (who tells what to whom) take time to refine. These agency firms, like many individuals, often require training and education to work effectively through teams.

Teamwork: the bottom line

As Katzenbach and Smith summarize it: "Focusing on performance – not chemistry or togetherness or good communications or good feelings – shapes a team more than anything else" (2003, p. 61). Once again, the goal is not to play as a team, but to achieve the team's goal. To this end, teams enhance the speed of work processes in all sport organizations; they have the potential to increase quality and productivity. Where workers are motivated by growth needs, teamwork can increase job satisfaction. However, the barriers to effective teamwork are also apparent. They include the natural human resistance to major change, the inherent difficulty of organizations learning to operate in new ways, and the need for work teams to develop the skills necessary to manage themselves effectively. It is the task of sport managers to have the patience and commitment necessary to meet these challenges to improve overall organizational performance.

EPILOGUE: NICE GUYS FINISH ...

Former agent Jeff Moorad (also a former GM of the Arizona Diamondbacks and minority owner and vice chairman of the San Diego Padres), who negotiated multiple multi-million dollar contracts for pro players such as Manny Ramirez and Steve Young, says this about sport agency: "It's not a profession for nice guys" (Crasnick, 2005, p. 150). Therein lies the challenge for DiaMMond Management: can they be ethical and still do business in a cutthroat industry? Can they keep holding out for that breakthrough client, the mega-star that can bump them into the upper echelon, Scott Boras-level of business? The firm has had a few players make it into arbitration and free agency, while others, such as Doug Clark in Korea, made decent money playing for a few years overseas (Dobrow, 2011).

But many others have fallen by the wayside. Brad Baker, a high school star from Western Massachusetts who was the fortieth pick in the draft by his favorite club, the Boston Red Sox, is now a security guard at a nuclear power plant in Vermont. After the draft, Ray Fagnant, the scout assigned to negotiate his signing bonus, offered $600,000 during a negotiating session with Baker and Jim Masteralexis. According to Baker, Fagnant "sold the dream" of playing in Fenway Park for the team he grew up rooting for as a kid. "Are you fucking kidding me?" responded Jim, and countered with a figure of $1.1 million. "You do want to play, don't you?" said Fagnant to Baker. Later, another Sox staffer, Wayne Britton, spoke to Jim about Baker: "How long have you been in the business?" Britton queried to Jim. "Seven years," Jim replied. "I've been in this business for thirty years," said Britton, and proceeded to rant to Jim about how agents were ruining the game, running up bonuses and salaries for players. "When's it going to stop, Jim? Where's it going to stop?" After nearly two months of negotiating, Jim and the Red Sox reached a compromise on the bonus figure: $832,500. Baker was now a pro and would head south to join other Red Sox minor leaguers in Florida (Dobrow, 2011, pp. 27–28).

Did the Red Sox waste nearly a million on Baker, who never pitched an inning in the majors? The Sox eventually traded Baker in a deal that brought back left-handed reliever Alan Embree, who was a solid member of the Sox's bullpen in their 2004 championship season. Do they win that first World Series in 86 years without Embree, who was on the mound to get the final out of Game 7 of the American League Championship Series against the Yankees? What about DiaMMond? DiaMMond worked for years to cultivate another Western Massachusetts product, Scott Barnes. Barnes had been selected in the 43rd round by the Washington Nationals, and DiaMMond advised him not to sign and to go to college. Barnes did – matriculating to St. John's University in Queens, New York – and DiaMMond kept working with him to prepare him for the next time he would be eligible for the draft (after his junior year). But shortly before that draft, Barnes signed with another agent, Barry Meister, a mid-level guy who has represented numerous major leaguers, including Roy Oswalt, Edgar Renteria, and Tim Wakefield. "The term we use is 'big league,'" says Steve McKelvey. "When they start to believe it, then everything's out the window, all loyalty." DiaMMond's clients were always susceptible to poaching from other firms, and Steve knew that DiaMMond didn't "do it the right way – which is the wrong way." In his lowest moments, Steve doubts the wisdom of chasing the dream and working with ungrateful clients. "That's not what I want to do with the rest of my life," he says (Dobrow, 2011, p. 286). So DiaMMond is selling, selling their clients to prospective teams and for potential endorsement dollars, selling themselves to new clients, and selling themselves to keep current clients. Selling every day.

242

SUMMARY

The organizing responsibility for sport agency firm managers is to implement the company's strategic direction effectively. The design of a sport agency's structure is a critical factor in how effectively it will achieve its strategic goals and satisfy its various clients.

Edgar Schein has suggested four elements that must be present for the design of an organization to be effective: common goals, division of work, coordination of effort, and authority structure. The careful development of each of these elements is essential for the organization to function effectively.

A number of models for designing organizations have emerged since the late nineteenth century. Each of these models is bureaucratic in the sense that each is designed around rules, plans, and policies to ensure efficiency and objectivity in decision making. The functional, divisional, and conglomerate models are all bureaucratic, and each has specific advantages.

As the rate of change has accelerated in sport agencies, firm managers have been challenged to develop organizational designs that are faster to respond and more flexible than the traditional bureaucratic models. Firm structures based primarily on plans and policies can be slow to adapt to rapidly developing threats and opportunities in the environment. Matrix and network structures have emerged to give sport agency organizations greater flexibility for adapting to the realities of changing environments.

It is highly unlikely that the bureaucratic organizational structure will ever disappear. Within every sport organization there are difficult tensions. On the one hand, there is the need for the kind of rules and clear authority structure that bureaucracy provides. On the other, there is the need for speed and flexibility. It is management's responsibility to recognize both these needs and to exercise creativity and judgment in structuring the organization for optimum performance and for effective response to change.

The growing emphasis on teamwork in sport organizations has meant an increasing need for sport managers to understand the conditions for effective teamwork. Research has shown that complementary skills, a commonly shared purpose, specific performance goals, a commonality in the approach to work, and a sense of mutual responsibility are essential for team-based efforts to be successful.

MANAGEMENT EXERCISE: GOLF'S MR. 100

The life of a professional athlete is seen by many as glamorous, full of adulation from fans, and an extravagant lifestyle paid for by endorsements and lucrative contracts. How great it must be, we think, to do something you love and get paid for it. Hell, we think, we'd do it for nothing. Well, if you did happen to be good enough to play any sport professionally, you should expect to be paid for it. You would be

243

one of the tops in your chosen field, why shouldn't you be compensated? And if Tiger Woods can earn over $60 million a year, doesn't he deserve it? There are no guaranteed contracts in golf, so anything Woods gets he has to earn on the course (and to keep his endorsement deals). Golfers also have to cover their own expenses as they work their way across the world playing tournaments – no team-chartered jets and equipment guys taking care of their luggage. Golfers also have to take care of their caddies. One golf agent describes the world of golf this way:

> Golf is unique. There are no guaranteed contracts, there's no draft. If you're out there on the PGA Tour, it's because you earned it. You didn't come out of high school drafted by the NBA and get a guaranteed fat contract regardless of how you play. If you go out there [in golf] and have a bad year, you're probably not going to be out there the following year. The professional golfer has to pay for his taxi to the airport. He has to pay for his flight to California to play at Pebble Beach. He has to pay for his hotel, pay for his caddie. I would estimate the cost of a single guy traveling on the PGA Tour for a full season would be close to $100,000.

PGA Tour member Dudley Hart (with career earnings of nearly $12.5 million) put it this way when asked why he didn't stay at the pricey Four Seasons like some other pros during a tour stop in Dallas: "Five hundred dollars a night there, one hundred dollars a night [at the Marriott]. No problem for me deciding where to stay" (Hoffer, 2006, p. 59; "Dudley Hart," 2012).

And then, players have to go out and actually play well to earn their money. Said one agent:

> If you have a couple of million dollars in endorsements waiting for you, there's pressure to show that you're earning those endorsements, but that's a little bit different pressure than knowing that if you don't make the cut this week, you might not be able to afford taking a flight out to your next week's event. That's the harsh reality of golf: you're not getting paid unless you're earning it.

But below the big-name, high-earners such as Woods and Mickelson, newcomers such as Bubba Watson and Hunter Mahan, women's players such as Stacey Lewis and Yani Tseng, and Champions Tour players such as Bernhard Langer toil the vast majority of golfers. Consider the case of Briny Baird, who ranked one-hundreth on the tour money list in 2011, with winnings of $942,285.75. Baird was born in 1972 in Miami Beach, Florida, and attended Valdosta (Georgia) State University. He turned pro in 1999, and in 2011 he played in 19 events (one major – the U.S. Open at Congressional Country Club – where he missed the cut), missed the cut seven other times, and finished in the top ten at events three times. His highest finish in 2011 was second at the Frys.com Open in San Martin, California, where he lost in a six-hole playoff to Bryce Molder, but took home $540,000, the majority of his revenue for the season. The previous week he had finished fortieth at the Justin Timberlake Shriners Hospital for Children Open in Las Vegas, winning $15,200. He has played in nearly 400 PGA Tour events – winning none – but has earned over $12.5 million based on his tournament finishes in his career ("Briny Baird," 2012).

Baird, like the majority of the players on the golf and tennis tours, must earn his living every time he goes out, with nothing guaranteed. To help him capitalize on the final years of his PGA Tour career, Baird is looking to earn as much as he can from endorsements and sponsorships as his ability to earn from tournament winnings may begin to flag. He has been working on his own to secure these revenue streams, but is now thinking about hiring an agent for those duties instead. That's where you come in.

QUESTIONS FOR YOU TO CONSIDER

1   Baird has asked you to advise him on his choice of representation. He is considering golf agent industry leader IMG, Steve Loy of Gaylord Sports Management (who represents golfers Phil Mickelson and Nick Watney, as well as MLB players Bronson Arroyo, Alex Rodriguez, and Dan Uggla), and Wasserman Media Group, which is looking to expand its golf representation client base. Explain to him Schein's four elements of an effective organization and how each of these three choices might exhibit these elements.
2   Explain to Baird how the bureaucratic structure of these firms will protect him from the abuses similar to those experienced by Tank Black's clients.
3   Explain to Baird how these firms exemplify functional, divisional, and conglomerate structures, and why it is important for him to understand these distinctions.
4   Outline for Baird the component elements of effective teams, and which firm is most likely to possess the elements outlined by Katzenbach and Smith.
5   Finally, using all this information, along with the concept of structure follows strategy, explain which of the three choices would be best for Baird in terms of securing future sponsorship and endorsement deals.

245

CHAPTER 8

MOTIVATION AND LEADERSHIP AND INTERCOLLEGIATE ATHLETICS

INTRODUCTION

This chapter focuses on the indispensable role of leadership and the function of performance motivation within the rubric of intercollegiate athletics. The chapter reviews the evolution of leadership theory and the increasing importance of more recent leadership forms, as well as the critical act of motivating personnel to make these organizations as successful as possible within the framework of a highly competitive and unique business and organizational environment. Communication, perhaps the most essential component for effective leadership, is also discussed, along with the dynamic of leadership in the team context.

Check the stats

Purpose
To provide opportunities for college students to engage in athletic activities designed to enhance the educational experience and character development of participants; to generate visibility and to enhance the reputation of sponsoring institutions; to attract support to the sponsoring institution; to create community identity; and to communicate messages to aligned stakeholder groups.

Stakeholders
Participants, parents, students, coaches, athletic department managerial personnel, conference managerial personnel, faculty, staff, and administrators of host institutions, institutional alumni, national governing bodies (e.g. the National Collegiate Athletic Association (NCAA)), corporate sponsors and advertisers, sport broadcast, print, and on-line media, fans, and local, state, and federal taxpayers.

246

Size and scope

The NCAA has evolved into the preeminent intercollegiate athletics national governing body in the U.S. The NCAA is a voluntary association – meaning members choose to join – consisting of more than 1,000 institutions, conferences, organizations, and individuals. Because of its significant role, much of the discussions in this chapter will focus on issues within the NCAA.

Other national governing bodies include the National Association of Intercollegiate Athletics (NAIA) and the National Junior College Athletic Association (NJCAA). The NAIA, its establishment connected to a 1937 national basketball tournament formed by Dr. James Naismith, the inventor of the sport, claims nearly 300 member institutions from the U.S. and Canada. The NAIA is headquartered in Kansas City, Missouri, and its membership is divided into 14 regions. The NAIA serves 50,000 student-athletes, and offers 23 championships in 13 sports (with two divisions each for men's and women's basketball). Its current president and CEO is Jim Carr.

The NJCAA also traces its roots back to 1937, when a handful of California-based junior college representatives met to organize an association to promote and supervise nationally intercollegiate athletic activities for two-year schools. The NJCAA currently has a membership of over 500, divided into 24 geographic regions across the country (except in California, whose two-year schools have formed their own governing body). The NJCAA sponsors championships in 13 men's sports and 13 women's sports, some of which offer competitions in three separate divisions (which are defined based on the amount of athletically related financial aid schools can award: Division I schools can provide tuition and room and board, Division II schools can provide tuition only, and Division III schools can award no athletically related aid). The current executive director of the NJCAA is Mary Ellen Leicht.

Governance

The NCAA, founded in 1905, is organized into three divisional classifications based on the stated philosophical direction of each school's intercollegiate athletic program. The organization provides the definition of its basic purpose as part of its fundamental policy under Article 1 of its Constitution, codified as "the competitive athletics programs of member institutions [that] are designed to be a vital part of the educational system. A basic purpose of this Association is to maintain intercollegiate athletics as an integral part of the educational program and the athlete as an integral part of the student body and, by so doing, retain a clear line of distinction between intercollegiate athletics and professional sports" (*2011–2012 NCAA Division I Manual*, 2011, p. 1).

As outlined above, the purposes stated in Article 1 of the NCAA Constitution relate to general areas of managerial operations such as recruiting, eligibility, and playing and practice seasons. These are codified operationally in 16 principles of

247

conduct in Article 2 of the Constitution. This article attempts to convey the rationale behind all association rules so that the membership can better understand how to operate its programs in compliance with NCAA guidelines and objectives. The guiding premise that underscores each of the 16 principles is the fact that all legislation enacted by the NCAA be designed to advance one or more of these basic principles.

The NCAA's separate three-tier divisional classification system, established in 1973, acknowledged the existing disparity in institutional missions and goals relating to intercollegiate athletics. The separation created an opportunity for regular and post-season competition against schools with comparable missions, and established a more stratified approach to the awarding of athletically related financial assistance.

A key difference amongst members is the right to vote on all Association legislation. This legislative process reveals that all the rules in each of the divisional manuals are enacted because member schools and conferences have approved them. This is outlined under Article 5 of the Constitution, which explains that "all legislation of the Association that governs the conduct of intercollegiate athletics programs of its member institutions shall be adopted by the membership in Convention assembled, or by the presidential administrative groups and the divisional management councils [see below]." When issues are voted upon at the Annual Convention, and at specially convened meetings, the legislative rules specify that each member with voting privileges has only one vote, and the individual selected to cast that vote must be properly certified (*2011–2012 NCAA Division I Manual*, 2011, p. 29). The restructuring of the Association's organization and legislative process, voted upon and approved at the 1996 NCAA Convention and taking effect in August 1997, gave the NCAA a structure with more focus on divisional issues controlled by members affiliated with that division.

From 1951 to 1987, the NCAA was headed by Walter Byers, who was responsible for much of the growth of the Association through the development of television rights fees first from football and later from the Division I men's basketball tournament. Byers' successors were, in order, Richard Schultz, Cedric Dempsey, and Myles Brand. Mark Emmert, former president of the University of Washington, took over as President in 2010.

Inside look: is the BCS "Fiesta" over?

In March 2011, the non-profit organization that operates the Fiesta Bowl post-season college football game fired long-time Chief Executive John Junker. According to writers from the *Arizona Republic* newspaper in Phoenix, Junker was bowl's "public face" and "corporate face" (and, according to *Sports Illustrated*, one of the

Motivation and leadership and intercollegiate athletics

top ten most powerful people in college football), along with other bowl personnel. The writers were summarizing a 276-page report, commissioned by a special bowl committee in October 2010, which detailed

> a culture of excessive spending on bowl employees, politicians, and business associates despite rules barring it from using its money to benefit individuals; a system of campaign contributions that could run afoul of state and federal campaign laws; and accounts of efforts by bowl staffers to mislead government investigators.
>
> (Harris and Wagner, 2011a, p. 1)

While the paper credits Junker for "transforming the bowl into a major player in college football," the transformation came at a price – literally: Junker was reimbursed nearly $5 million for his expenses over a ten-year period ending in March 2010. Among the reimbursed expenses included four golf club memberships, including one in Oklahoma and one in Oregon. Junker told investigators that the Oklahoma membership (Karsten Creek in Stillwater, at $2,078 a year) was purchased at the suggestion of a former Big 12 (Conference) commissioner "'primarily to support Oklahoma State University golf' and show visible support for a Big 12 school" (Harris and Wagner, 2011a, p. 1). The investigative report noted, wrote the *Republic*:

> Junker said those benefits were meant to win favor with bigwigs who could provide helpful legislation, secure a new stadium, or ensure network contracts. However, the report says he spoke at length about questionable contracts, travel, game tickets, and other expensive gifts given to politicians, TV executives, and college administrators. When the Fiesta Bowl's top administrator was confronted about lavish spending and political lobbying under his watch, he intermittently wept with sorrow, touted his accomplishments, and justified his expense reports, according to interview reports written afterward.
>
> (Harris and Wagner, 2011a, p. 1)

Additional reimbursements were equally damning: a visit to a high-end Phoenix strip club ($1,241), of which Junker said in the report: "We are in the business where big strong athletes are known to attend these types of establishments. It was important for us to visit and we certainly conducted business." Also cited was the bowl's footing the $33,188 bill for Junker's fiftieth birthday party bash – a four-day "bacchanal" at the renowned Pebble Beach golf course, of which one attendee said had "absolutely no business purpose." Of the debacle, Fiesta Bowl chairman Duane Woods said: "The cover-up was worse than the crime" (Murphy and McKnight, 2011, p. 1).

After these and other revelations broke, the NCAA released a statement that it could revoke the Fiesta Bowl's certification license, while Bowl Championship Series (BCS) Executive Director Bill Hancock stated the Fiesta Bowl could lose its coveted

BCS slot, even though the bowl had a three-year contract to remain in the cartel. "If the bowl does remain a BCS bowl, its handling of things will be closely monitored going forward," said Hancock (Harris, 2011a, p. 1), who heads the organization which is managed by the commissioners of the 11 NCAA Division I Football Bowl Subdivision (FBS) conferences, along with University of Notre Dame's athletic director, and representatives of the four BCS games – Orange, Fiesta, Rose, and Sugar. Fiesta Bowl officials traveled to meetings in Chicago and New Orleans soon after Junker's ousting to lobby to save the bowl's slot. "They clearly are taking every step possible to regain the trust of people internally and externally. They have conveyed a strong willingness to be open and transparent," said Nick Carparelli, Jr., chairman of the NCAA Postseason Bowl Licensing Subcommittee (Harris, 2011b, p. 1).

The bowl did retain its BCS slot for the time being, albeit after paying $1 million in fines (considered to be a slap on the wrist, since the bowl has $15 million cash on hand). But the bowl's contract with the BCS expires after the 2012–2013 season (which some speculated as the reason Junker was spreading the cash – to keep the game in the BCS mix). And other problems are still looming. An op-ed piece in the *Arizona Republic* worried that the Fiesta Bowl still had to deal with separate investigations from the county and state Attorneys General, and that the Internal Revenue Service was investigating whether the bowl could keep its tax-exempt, non-profit status, a critical factor in the bowl's viability. As a result, the bowl must try and recoup the monetary value for all the free tickets and donations dispersed to local and state politicians (Zidich, 2011a, 2011b). County attorneys were mulling on whether to bring forward civil or criminal charges or both against the politicians (Harris and Rough, 2011).

In addition, Tostitos, the snack chip brand owned by Frito-Lay North America, a division of PespsiCo Inc., and some other major sponsors of the Fiesta Bowl considered ending contacts with the bowl after what Tostitos deemed "potentially illegal conduct among its employees." Tostitos has been the title sponsor of the Fiesta Bowl for 16 years, and had not confirmed whether the company would continue its naming rights sponsorship (Randazzo, 2011, p. 1).

And then, on May 4, 2011, the United States Justice Department's antitrust chief, Christine Varney, announced plans to contact NCAA President Mark Emmert seeking answers as to why no playoff system exists at the Division I FBS level. Had the Fiesta Bowl scandal triggered the action, and was it possible that the events in Phoenix were set to influence the greater landscape of Bowl Subdivision football? Varney's action was prompted in part by the intention of Utah Attorney General Mark Shurtleff to file an antitrust suit against the BCS. The suit accused the BCS of being an illegal monopoly and sought damages for schools that claim they have lost millions of dollars because the existing system keeps non-preferred conferences at a competitive disadvantage. It was also noted in several media outlets that U.S. President Barack Obama was in favor of a playoff system at this level, and that he had said he intended "to throw my weight around a little bit" to achieve the goal ("Justice Department," 2011, p. 2; Wharton, 2011).

It is no surprise that a Utah official sought to attack the BCS, since Brigham Young University, located in Provo, Utah, formerly of the Mountain West Conference in football and now an independent, has likely prompted Shurtleff into action. This pressure was probably increased when the University of Utah was part of the "non-preffered" group, but now that Utah is part of the newly expanded Pac-12 Conference (see below), they would be looking for past damages only (and might be looking to have AG drop the inquiry to protect their new-found conference cohorts). Hancock of the BCS met with Justice Department officers in late June 2011, after which Hancock stated:

> I went into [the meeting] confident that the BCS complies with the law, and I left the meeting even more confident ... We had an opportunity to explain what we do and why it doesn't pose any antitrust concerns ... Obviously the next step is up to them.
>
> (Wieberg, 2011, p. 1)

This dispute between the BCS, possibly prompted by the Fiesta Bowl's troubles (ultimately Junker, as well as another former Fiesta Bowl officer and a current high-ranking bowl employee, pleaded guilty to the charges against them, and Junker pleaded guilty to one Class 4 felony on soliciting a fraudulent scheme, in which fellow employees at the Fiesta Bowl made political contributions that were funded by the bowl's money (Harris, 2012)), questions the entire bowl game system, which in many ways is a microcosm of the evolution of intercollegiate athletics in general, and FBS football specifically. The very first intercollegiate athletic event, which involved rowing teams from Harvard University and Yale University on Lake Winnipesaukee in New Hampshire in 1852, was essentially a bowl-game model, where two opposing sides were brought to a neutral location to perform and compete for the purpose of generating a crowd at the neutral site for the benefit of the sponsors (in the case of Harvard–Yale rowing, it was the Boston, Concord, and Montreal Railroad Company, who believed that spectators keen on watching such a race would secure passage on the train to the site, so the company paid for the travel and week's lodging for the two teams) (Smith, 1988). Once football emerged as the dominant offering of college programs (a position it maintains today), the bowl system flowered with the blooming of the Rose Bowl, leading to the creation of a phenomenon that grew mostly untended by college leaders and administrators, and thrived because of extraordinary support from the general public.

But will an agency of the federal government act to change an entrenched model of the intercollegiate athletics industry segment? It seems unlikely, because the system works well for so many of the parties involved. Colleges and universities must attract resources to survive, like any other organization. If they can do so through the bowl game system, they will. If not, they won't. If the combined forces outlined above make the bowl system untenable, it will go away. Its disappearance seems unlikely, however, as evidenced by the comments of University of Notre Dame Athletics Director (and BCS management team member) Jack Swarbrick:

> College football is the engine that drives collegiate athletics, and that is built not around the post-season but the vibrancy of the regular season. Those of us in the industry will do anything we can to protect the regular season because it's so important to the overall enterprise. If I'm going to give student-athletes an opportunity [to compete] in 26 sports, I have to have a vibrant regular season in football.
>
> (Carey, 2011, p. 1)

Swarbrick also said preserving the integrity of the regular season and keeping the bowl system in place are reasons to push for the continuation of the BCS, even if it means fighting against the U.S. Justice Department. In support of this notion, NCAA VP of Communications Bob Williams stated: "It should be noted that President Emmert consistently has said ... that the NCAA is willing to help create a playoff format for Football Bowl Subdivision football *if* the FBS membership makes that decision" (original emphasis) ("NCAA statement," 2011, p. 1).

So where does all this leave the Fiesta Bowl? To replace the disgraced Junker, the bowl hired former University Arizona President Robert Shelton to its executive direc-tor post in July 2011. The move was called "unprecedented" for a college president, but Shelton (described as "a consummate academic" by a presidential colleague) was under fire at Arizona over several issues, including conflicts with state lawmakers on funding, as well as Shelton's public political support for President Obama. Shelton, a Phoenix native, had never attended a Fiesta Bowl game, but is a former member of the Presidential Oversight Committee of the BCS. Duane Woods of the Fiesta Bowl was surprised to learn of the 62-year-old Shelton's interest, but Shelton stated:

> I really viewed the Fiesta Bowl more as an opportunity that came to me out of the blue, rather than I felt pressured [to leave the University of Arizona] ... One thing that attracted me was that college athletics are playing such a huge role in college now.
>
> (Ashburn, 2011, p. A11)

While it is obvious to most that intercollegiate athletics have always played an important role in the operation and management of colleges and universities, Shelton is certainly correct in his observations. In noting all the factors cited in the case of the Fiesta Bowl and the BCS, the challenges for the college presidents, ath-letic directors, bowl officials, conference commissioners, and the NCAA leadership will be to reconstruct a high-performance environment in which all factions are

Motivation and leadership and intercollegiate athletics

motivated to perform at levels that allow them to succeed personally while allowing the alliances that bind them together to prosper as well. Creating this kind of workforce has become an essential management responsibility. However, the task is neither simple nor easy. The BCS was created to keep the bowl game system alive even as fans and other stakeholder groups clamor for a playoff system that crowns a real rather than mythical national champion. As a result, even the most carefully developed strategies and structure are not enough to make intercollegiate athletics organizations competitive unless its people are highly motivated to perform. This chapter will examine performance motivation and leadership at various levels of intercollegiate athletics throughout to understand its critical organizational impact.

THE INTERCOLLEGIATE ATHLETICS SPORT INDUSTRY SEGMENT

Establishment and evolution

From before the inception of intercollegiate athletics, and since the very first contest between teams from different schools, the appropriate role of athletics in higher education has been actively debated. While students first initiated and organized athletic programs for health and fitness reasons, the focus quickly shifted away from participation-based programs toward institution-maintained programs that sought to achieve primacy over rival institutions. Proponents of the development of "big-time" athletic programs, as embodied today by those at many NCAA Division I institutions, cite the ability of these programs to create a sense of community among campus constituencies and to promote the institution in general, while critics note that academic integrity is often sacrificed in the pursuit to athletic success, and that institutional resources are misdirected away from academics to support athletics. Whatever your point of view, it is clear that intercollegiate athletics in the U.S. has evolved to mean different things to different stakeholder groups: students, faculty, administrators, coaches, parents, boosters, alumni, and the general public. These diverse collections seek varied outcomes from intercollegiate athletics, including entertainment, a way to create bonds with the institution, a chance for physical activity, and an opportunity for professional advancement.

What makes the management of intercollegiate athletics programs so challenging is that, regardless of the size of the school and the number and success level of programs, most institutions expect that their athletic programs meet the expectations of all stakeholders and all anticipated outcomes. Part of what we will seek to understand in this chapter is how the system was created and evolved in light of these expectations, and how those who work in the segment can understand how the unique qualities that characterized the formation of the intercollegiate athletics enterprise impact and influence performance motivation and leadership.

253

From its earliest inception at Harvard College (now University, located in Cambridge, Massachusetts), American institutions of higher education have sought to integrate all facets of life into the collegiate experience. Turner (1984) found that Harvard's founders intentionally chose the English collegiate system where students and masters lived, ate, studied, worshipped, and played together, rather than the European or Scottish model where students lived and boarded in the community and not on a single unified campus. This choice was based first on academic and religious principles to form a sense of community within the school. In much the same manner, intercollegiate athletics would later be used to build and promote school loyalties. This institutionalizing of non-academic student life would inevitably give rise to the college's involvement in sponsoring, at least by virtue of its responsibility of *in loco parentis*, the extra-cirriculum, those non-academic activities that were emerging on college campuses.

Nearly a century before the advent of intercollegiate athletics, students formed literary societies, Greek-letter fraternal organizations, and organized on-campus "intramural" athletics. However, faculty usually decried athletics. Smith (2011, p. 17) points out that colleges had always "had lists of things forbidden ... refusing a variety of activities thought to be harmful to moral character, learning or safety," including "card playing, drinking, smoking" and sports. But students persisted for the most part because, as one Amherst (Massachusetts) College student of the day noted, such activities "served to vary the monotony, and relieve the dryness of college duties" (Smith, 1988, p. 15). Students participated in exercise regimens as a precipitate of the gymnasium movement of the 1820s, with colleges opting then to formally incorporate such programs by mid-century. Amherst was the first school to add a Department of Hygiene and Physical Education in 1860, in hopes to channel student activity to these areas. By 1870, Sheldon (1969, p. 195) reported: "Athletics had won a recognized place in college life," and by 1900

> a greater portion of the public know[s] a college almost exclusively through its athletic records, for three fourths of the news items concerning student life deal with sport ... intercollegiate contests play by far the largest part in the daily life and talk [of undergraduates].
>
> (p. 230)

Student-run organizations still operated athletic programs well into the early twentieth century, paying for programs through dues-assessing athletic associations, fundraising drives, alumni donations, and gate receipts. The games on the field were still run by team captains, increasingly with support and direction from paid or unpaid coaches, and the off-field managerial aspects were still run by students. In the 1860s and 1870s, faculty would only impose their will on athletic programs when they perceived athletic matters were infringing upon students' academic activities. By 1881, Princeton formed the first faculty committee to gain control of college athletics from students (Smith, 1988). The era of student-run teams and

Motivation and leadership and intercollegiate athletics

programs was coming to an end as well, beginning with Yale's hiring of the first professional coach in 1864. William Wood, a New York City gymnastics and physical education instructor, was brought to New Haven to train the school's crew team. The move to professional coaches helped Yale become the dominant athletic power in many sports well into the twentieth century, although Cornell University crew coach Charles Courtney and Harvard football coach Bill Reid were other early notables, some earning more than the highest paid professors at their schools and becoming better known than their school's president (Smith, 1988).

By the end of the nineteenth century, football had become the dominant sport on college campuses. Annual contests such as "Bloody Monday" at Harvard, a soccer-like melee that was in reality nothing more than an opportunity for upperclassmen to haze freshmen, evolved into intercollegiate contests, the first of which involved teams from Princeton and Rutgers University in 1869, with Rutgers prevailing, 6–4. A version of the game closer to rugby emerged at Harvard, with rules allowing players to carry the ball rather than just kick or punch it. The Harvard version eventually won converts at Princeton and Yale and, by 1876, the three schools, along with Columbia University (located in New York City), formed the Intercollegiate Football Association (IFA) to adopt standard rules. The IFA's annual Thanksgiving Day championship game became the seminal event toward launching the sport into the nation's consciousness, drawing tens of thousands of fans to the contests held in New York City (Smith, 1988).

The resulting developments related to the rise in the popularity of football were identified by Michael Oriard, a historian and former football player at the University of Notre Dame, in his book, *King football: Sport and spectacle in the golden age of radio and newsreels, movies and magazines, the weekly and the daily press*. Oriard concludes that:

> From the initial discovery, in the 1880s and 1890s, that college football games could attract thousands of spectators with no direct connection to the competing universities, football served disparate interests. For many university officials, building a big-time football program meant a Faustian bargain: prestige and growth in return for surrendering control of the sport to the demands of popular entertainment.
>
> (2001, p. 67)

One of the elements that proved difficult to control was on-field, in-game violence. At the turn of the twentieth century, such violence seriously threatened the existence of college football. Contributing factors were dangerous game tactics. These included momentum plays such as the flying wedge and lineman lining up in the backfield, and mass plays where teammates pushed and pulled a ballcarrier down the field (even picking up and hurling one through the air was legal), the lack of the forward pass, and rules that called for ballcarriers to verbally call themselves "down," allowing defenders to pile on until the "down" call was made. Complicating matters was the inability or unwillingness of the sport's power programs and managers to curb or alter these tactics. As a result, severe injuries were frequent and fatalities common (in 1905, at least three men died and 168 were seriously injured playing college football, although some contemporary press reports put the death toll at 25), so much so that in October of that year, U.S. President Theodore Roosevelt, a Harvard grad and parent of a son who suffered a broken nose during a frosh game at his alma mater that year, summoned coaches from Harvard, Princeton, and Yale to the White House to lobby these leading programs to reform the sport. Notwithstanding Roosevelt's efforts (he ultimately had no power to compel changes in the game), the death of Union College player Harold Moore by cerebral hemorrhage after making a tackle in a November game against New York University (NYU) would prove to be a seminal occurrence (Yaeger, 1991; Gems, 2000; Watterson, 2000).

In response to Moore's death, NYU Chancellor Henry McCracken, who had witnessed the incident, sought to convene a meeting of school leaders to discuss the reform of the sport. The so-called "McCracken Group" met twice in New York City the next month, with 13 schools represented on the 9th, then with 68 on the 29th. In a letter to a colleague, Nicholas Butler, president of Columbia, stated that the efforts were "the first step in a general overhauling of the whole athletic situation in American colleges." The conference delegates would later name their conclave to reflect these lofty aims: the Inter Collegiate Athletic Association of the United States (ICAAUS). The ICAAUS would be renamed the National Collegiate Athletic Association in 1910. Eventually, rules changes were instituted that allowed for the forward pass, a neutral zone at the line of scrimmage with a minimum of seven men required on the line, and the elimination of mass (pushing and pulling ballcarries) and momentum (e.g. the flying wedge) plays. These alterations helped create a more exciting game and to usher in decades of growing popularity for college football (Smith, 1988; Gems, 2000; Watterson, 2000).

However, the popularity of intercollegiate athletics did not come without costs. Sperber indicated that

> toward the end of the nineteenth century, two conflicting trends occurred: colleges and universities began to raise their academic standards, and the proponents of college sports increasingly demanded winning teams, [and] athletes who could perform at the highest possible level and beat their opponents. The search for the scholar athletes began.
>
> (1998, p. 11)

The emergence of the land-grant college (those schools founded soon after the Civil War with public funds as decreed under federal law to provide greater access to higher education – initially, mostly in agricultural and technical studies programs)

Motivation and leadership and intercollegiate athletics

coincided with the increasing acceptance and proliferation of intercollegiate athletics, and that "both were in a sense manifestations of democratic trends in nineteenth century American education," and that land-grant schools were "probably the greatest beneficiaries of the sports movement," as they "could compete in these areas as equals with the traditional colleges" (Turner, 1984, pp. 158–160). A school need not acquire the strongest faculty nor the most pristine and agreeable campus and grounds to conjure up a litany of athletic successes. A school needs only the chance for its students (not necessarily undergraduates or apt scholars) to knock heads against those from another institution.

The land-grant movement also diminished the air of privilege that had permeated most campuses, which helped change attitudes around athletic excellence and professionalism. Industrial expansion, changing demographics, and expanding cities also created markets and demand for leisure and entertainment opportunities. Both professional and intercollegiate athletics filled these needs nicely. Many institutions were founded by towns in the Midwest and West in the nineteenth century to promote emigration and local development. As a result, as noted with the linkage of the land-grant ideal and athletics, in 1924 six of the top nine schools in football attendance were non-Eastern schools (Notre Dame, Michigan, the University of California-Berkeley, Ohio State University, the University of Chicago, the University of Illinois). Ninety thousand patrons witnessed that year's California-Stanford University grid battle, and in 1928 over 120,000 fans – still the largest college football crowd ever – packed Chicago's Soldier Field for the game between Notre Dame and the University of Southern California. From 1924 to 1940, four Eastern teams and 37 non-Eastern teams were considered as possible football national champions (Sperber, 1998; Lester, 1995; Sack and Staurowsky, 1998).

Presidents at some of these new powers actively promoted athletics as a vehicle to promote the institution at large when competing for students and donations amongst the burgeoning ranks of higher education institutions. William Harper at the University of Chicago (later to be undone under the tenure of Robert Hutchins), John Hannah at Michigan State University, H.C. "Curly" Byrd at the University of Maryland (who once served as the school's head football coach), and Herman Lee Donovan at the University of Kentucky are four notable cases (Lawson and Ingham, 1980; Shapiro, 1983; Thelin, 1996; Sperber, 1998).

The NCAA's membership has since established thousands upon thousands of rules pertaining to the administration of intercollegiate athletics, most of which focus on setting policy relating to and curbing abuses and perceived unfair institutional advantages in recruiting, financial aid, and issues of amateurism. The NCAA assumed slowly the role of arbiter for initial eligibility academic requirements, with the primary goal of such a system to ensure that all institutions used the same minimum academic standards by which to assess prospective student-athletes in determining athletic eligibility, and, in some cases, the appropriate financial aid award.

257

The NCAA began to develop significant powers in 1952, when the association negotiated the first college football television contract with NBC for a total rights fee of just over $1 million for 12 games. Sixty-one such schools coalesced in 1976 to form the College Football Association (CFA), whose members would threaten to leave the NCAA entirely over the TV issue, but eventually opted to challenge the NCAA in court for the right to sell their own games for broadcast. In 1984, the United States Supreme Court found for the CFA on antitrust grounds, decreeing that the NCAA limited the output of games to raise prices, that the games were the property of the schools (Covell and Barr, 2010).

The early decades of intercollegiate athletics were mostly the preserve of affluent white males. By 1920, however, nearly half of all college students were women, but while the number of women on campus was significant, their opportunities to participate in intercollegiate athletics were both far fewer and far more restrictive. The growth of women's programs was aided in large part by the passage of Title IX of the Education Amendments of 1972, a federal law that sought to increase equity for women in federally funded educational programs. The AIAW permitted athletic scholarships in 1973 to keep members from moving to the NCAA but, in 1980, the NCAA began holding championships in women's sports, with the membership voting to expand committees and allocate positions to women. As European minority groups slowly gained admittance to higher education institutions, their influence was soon felt in intercollegiate athletics, as was that of Native and African Americans (Covell and Barr, 2010).

Smith (1971) stated that as student bodies approached heterogeneity, "the sole community of interest began to reside in attendance at sporting events and a few other social pastimes" (p. 65). Handlin and Handlin (1970) noted that "the athletic contest was a great ritual event which drew together students and alumni and, in the zest of the effort to beat the other side, developed a consciousness of their identity" (p. 59). Said Higgs (1995): "the sporting spirit became virtually synonymous with the college spirit, in a mixture of competition, achievement, and leadership" (p. 102). Said Smith (1971): "By the mid 1920s, the foundations of intercollegiate athletics as they exist today has been cemented" (p. 70). Simon (1991) argues that it is not necessary for universities and colleges to host intercollegiate athletic programs, and that "scholarship can proceed quite well without having athletic departments, football weekends, the NCAA basketball tournament, or baseball games with a crosstown rival" (p. 48). These are the realities that make American intercollegiate athletics what they are, and serve as a framework for the motivation and leadership challenges facing intercollegiate athletic managers.

UNDERSTANDING PERFORMANCE MOTIVATION

For several decades, scientists, researchers, and theorists, primarily in the fields of psychology and organizational behavior, have worked to develop a clearer understanding of the factors that influence and shape individual and group performance. The combination of these factors is called performance motivation. The results of these efforts strongly support the view that human performance reflects a highly complex set of dynamics, involving people's needs and goals, their skills and abilities, and the demands and challenges of the task itself.

In this section we consider four different models or theories of performance motivation. Although each of these theories differs in emphasis, each makes an important contribution to our understanding of how to improve human performance in pursuit of the organization's goals.

Goal theory

As we discussed in Chapter 4, the power of goals is to enhance organizational performance. Effectively defined goals are no less important for individual and team performance. SMART goals provide direction, the basis for decisions on where to invest energy and effort, and the basis for feedback. Each is a key element in performance motivation. On the playing field or in the arena, specific goals are a natural part of the environment. Competitive or recreational sports almost always include a goal or target outcome.

Throughout the chapter we will look to examples from throughout the intercollegiate athletics segment. The first specific example is Trinity College's men's squash program and its relation to goal theory. Trinity, a small (enrollment 2,200), private liberal arts school located in Hartford, Connecticut, is home to the country's best squash team. In 2011, the program notched its thirteenth straight undefeated season (244 straight match wins) and captured its thirteenth straight National Championship. According to the school's website, it is "the longest winning streak in the history of intercollegiate varsity sports" ("Trinity men's," 2011, p. 1). It began the 2011–2012 season ranked number one, with the team's top players including internationals Antonio Diaz (from Mexico City, Mexico), Johan Detter (Malmo, Sweden), Reinhold Hergeth (Bloemfontein, South Africa), Elroy Leong (Selangor, Malaysia), and Vikram Malhotra (Mumbai, India).

So what? It's squash, you say. Who cares? And who the heck has even played squash (an indoor racquet sport like racquetball, only with a much less lively ball)? So why does Trinity pursue excellence in squash? According to coaches, student-athletes, and administrators at Trinity, in the mid-1990s former school president

Evan Dobelle charged the then-recently hired head coach Paul Assaiante with building a program good enough to take on the then-dominant Ivy League programs at Harvard, Princeton, and Yale. Assaiante recalled the meeting with his president when the goal was made clear:

> Evan called me into his office and he said, "Coach, here's the deal. I noticed that the squash team plays the highest caliber of institutions in competition. You play Dartmouth and Pennsylvania and Yale, whereas your tennis team plays Williams and Middlebury and Bowdoin – and that's all great. But I need to be able to walk into boardrooms and raise money and get people excited, because I'm trying to give this school a facelift and a morale boost. And the fact that you're competing with those schools is very important to me. And my question to you is how do we take it to the next level in that pond? Because if the tennis team wins the Division III national championship, that's great, and we can promote it. But if the squash team wins the national championship against a Princeton or a Harvard or a Yale, that's *very* compelling."
>
> (Lincoln, 2004, pp. 196–197; author's emphasis)

Dobelle was also facing the fact that a major problem in attracting students to Trinity was the Frog Hollow neighborhood in which the school was situated, described as "crime-ridden" and "blighted," so Dobelle sought to renew the area through a partnership between public and private entities to the tune of $225 million (Wachter, 2011, p. 37). For this, fundraising was key, and squash became a key to help access such funds.

As Dobelle alludes, the college squash world is different from the vast majority of American intercollegiate sports. The NCAA does not hold a squash championship (it is organized by United States Squash Federation), and most collegiate programs are housed at a handful of highly selective Northeastern colleges and universities. This is why Trinity competes against Ivy League schools, even though Trinity belongs to the Division III New England Small College Athletic Conference (NESCAC), whose membership consists of Trinity, Amherst College, Bowdoin College, Williams College, and seven other similarly situated institutions.

Assaiante, who grew up in the South Bronx section of New York City and didn't pick up a squash racquet until he was 27, was able to create a squash juggernaut by recruiting international players. He told Dobelle at that same meeting: "The best squash is not being played in this country. I coached the U.S. team in Cairo. We had our best finish in a decade: we finished seventeenth. So you've gotta let us begin looking in different ponds" (Lincoln, 2004, p. 197).

This approach was not a new one, since American intercollegiate squash has been dominated by foreign players for years, but Yale coach Dave Talbott questioned the academic merits of Trinity's players. Assaiante describes the reaction to his success

Motivation and leadership and intercollegiate athletics

by the squash community this way: "Trinity? How the hell can it be Trinity? How dare you?" (Beech, 2004, p. 30), even though the international players were stronger academically than the domestic players Trinity used to attract (Lincoln, 2004).

Trinity was able to attract good international players in part because Dobelle encouraged international recruiting trips by coaches, and pushed squash prospects with demonstrated financial need to the top of the school's financial aid priority list. In addition to their travels, coaches worked hard to use alumni contacts and Dobelle himself in the recruiting process. Dobelle was able to convince Marcus Cowie, a player from Norwich, England, to come to Trinity by saying: "You know, Marcus, we don't really want to lose to Harvard anymore. You could be a big part of that." His first year, Cowie led the Bantams to a 6–3 win over Harvard, the first-ever win for Trinity over the Crimson. Now, according to another English player who attended Trinity:

> There's huge pressure to go professional and play professionally. But going pro and going to school is impossible ... So the U.S. offers a chance to do them together, and it makes more sense ... [and] It's sort of known in England that if you wanted to play squash [in America], you go to Trinity.
>
> (Lincoln, 2004, pp. 203, 207–208)

In the case of the goal of creating a squash power, Trinity's administration identified a sport in which it can compete against the best programs at the most prestigious schools in the country, in part because there is far less competition for squash prospects than for those in, say, football or basketball, where there are many more programs competing to attract the best players. Trinity, which as a Division III school is not allowed to provide athletically related aid, can also compete on this level against the Ivies, which under conference rules also do not permit such aid. Finally, Trinity seeks to measure itself against institutions such as the Ivies in terms of competing for faculty, students, and donations, so demonstrating the ability to compete against and to defeat the Ivies gives the appearance that Trinity is a peer of their more prestigious counterparts.

Trinity is also able to admit prospects that competitor schools don't, because Trinity's admissions acceptance rate is 65 percent – compared to 20 percent for NESCAC rivals Amherst and Williams. In 1996, when Trinity landed Cowie, its first significant international recruit, it was because he had been denied admission at Harvard, and Harvard's then-head coach, Bill Doyle, a Trinity alum, put Cowie in touch with Assaiante. "'Trinity made a tremendous pitch,' said Cowie ... he met with Dobelle and was courted by Luke Terry, a Trinity graduate who served at Credit Suisse's London offices" (Wachter, 2011, p. 38). *New York Times Magazine* writer Paul Wachter states that: "Trinity does enjoy one significant recruiting advantage: lower admission standards. 'The kids that play squash for Trinity could not get into Williams [and Harvard, Yale, and Princeton]' according to Zafi Levy, head coach at

Williams. Wachter also states that "Trinity's admissions office, with support from the president [currently James Jones, Jr.], is able to give more slots to squash players than its competitors do. As Yale's Talbott puts it, 'At Yale, where sports aren't the emphasis, the president isn't going to put that much focus on any sport'" (Wachter, 2011, p. 39).

Assaiante, who claims to have no recruiting budget, works the phones and the Internet to keep the international pipeline open. He is also the school's men's tennis coach, still drives the team van to away matches, shares a room with two players in $100-a-night motels, and hosts at his home during school breaks his international players who can't afford to travel home. His dedication to the sport, he tells his players, cost him two marriages. He also tells them about his oldest son, a heroin addict who is in prison for armed robbery. "I love the guy. We play for him," said Baset Chaudhry, the Bantams' number one player in 2010, who is also a former professional player who was deemed eligible to play collegiately because he could prove he spent more in expenses than he earned in prize money (Bamberger, 2008, p. 64).

However, the program received a dose of negative attention in February 2010, when Trinity's Chaudhry was caught on video screaming in the face of an opponent, Kenneth Chan of Yale, at the end of a match won by Chaudhry which earned Trinity its twelfth national title. Even though there had been taunting both ways throughout the match, Chaudhry's actions were shown throughout the national media and on YouTube. As a result, Chaudhry withdrew from the national singles championship, and issued an apology to Chan and the Yale team ("Trinity squash," 2010). For acts such as this, and for its years of dominance, the Harvard student newspaper dubbed the Trinity program "The Evil Empire," a reference from the *Star Wars* series of films, which was also notably applied in an American sport setting by Boston Red Sox President and CEO Larry Lucchino to long-time rivals the New York Yankees. The phrase also pulls into focus that the program's success was built almost exclusively through non-American players, giving Trinity the look of a domineering, globe-straddling colossus.

Given these factors, Trinity and every sport organization must face challenges that can be addressed through goal theory. This is a goal that is specific, meaningful, and challenging, to say the least. For Trinity, squash has become the school's signature program as well as the best college program in the U.S. The task for Dobelle and Assaiante was to create a climate in which they could attract the talent sufficient to achieve the goal of squash dominance, that it was realistic enough for the school to accept the goal fully and to put forth all the work and effort that winning would require.

However, in 2012 the vaunted Bantams fell to Yale University, 5–4, ending its dual match unbeaten streak at 225. The win for Yale was hardly an upset, as the Elis had lost 5–4 to Trinity in last season's national championship, and Trinity had lost its top four players to graduation. Assaiante was somewhat gracious in defeat, commenting that "there's a lot more parity, and four or five schools have a shot at the championship this year" (Wachter, 2012, pp. B10, B12).

Yale and others have caught the Bantams by copying them: that is, by recruiting foreign players. Yale head coach Dave Talbott noted that of the 18 players in their match, only four were American (three from Yale). The message from goal theory is that, to enhance motivation, sport managers must establish goals that engage and challenge their people to achieve the levels of performance needed for the organization to compete and succeed. There is no doubt that Trinity has met the goals Dobelle set.

Reinforcement theory

A second lens through which to bring performance motivation into focus is reinforcement theory: all behavior is shaped by the consequences of that behavior. Consequences are what happen as a result of that behavior. B.F. Skinner (1953, 1972), perhaps the most prominent reinforcement theorist, describes the four types of consequences, what happens after people perform, shown in Box 8.1.

BOX 8.1 TYPES OF CONSEQUENCES IN REINFORCEMENT THEORY

Consequences that strengthen behavior
Positive reinforcement = behavior + positive consequence
Negative reinforcement = behavior + avoidance of negative consequence

Consequences that weaken behavior
Punishment = behavior + negative consequence
Extinction = behavior + no consequence

The pressure to win in intercollegiate athletics, regardless of the level of competition, is a significant motivating force, and the positive reinforcers are obvious: the reward of celebrating a win over a long-time rival, a conference championship, or a post-season victory, as well as the potential for increased financial payoffs in terms of salary, bonuses, and endorsement deals for coaches and future professional contracts for players.

The lure of these positive reinforcers has, however, led many programs and schools to seek competitive advantages by skirting established recruiting and eligibility rules. It is through efforts to ensure compliance with conference and nationally installed rules by organizations such as the NCAA, and a system to penalize those institutions that choose to ignore them through a system of enforcement, that intercollegiate athletic governing bodies seek to maintain the concept of the level playing field, where all programs and all schools are theoretically given an equal opportunity to be successful through the maintenance of operational guidelines. The enforcement of these rules can also lead to punishment (behavior + negative consequence) and negative reinforcement (behavior + avoidance of negative consequence).

The most significant example of a school violating rules to gain a competitive advantage and subsequent punishment came to a head in the 1980s in the case of cash payments to football players at Southern Methodist University (SMU), a private, four-year NCAA Division I institution located in Dallas, Texas. Over the course of more than a decade beginning in the 1970s, boosters, coaches, and school administrators – including board of trustees head and future Texas Governor Bill Clements – conspired to create an intricate system of paying star players. At the time, SMU football was riding high as one of the power teams in the country. Led by future Pro Football Hall of Fame running back Eric Dickerson, the Mustangs finished second in national polls in 1982. This success was attributable in part to the payments delivered to recruits and players by the Mustang Club boosters. Head coach Ron Meyer, who came to the school in 1976, would meet with high school prospects, "pull out a plump money clip and peel off a hundred-dollar bill. He would get up, walk to a nearby bulletin board, pin up the C-note, and announce: 'Young man, this is my calling card'" (Byers, 1995, p. 19).

In 1985, SMU's program was placed on NCAA probation for the fourth time in 11 years because of cash payments (with monthly disbursements ranging from $85 to $750), gifts, cars, and no-show jobs provided to football players. But the payments continued to the tune of $61,000 over the next 18 months, mostly because the program had done such a good job in developing the system that those involved could wean neither the boosters nor the players from the financial relations. In 1987, NCAA investigators, faced with additional reams of damning evidence and institutional intransigence and intractability, leveled what a later SMU football coach called "the atomic bomb," but what is most often referred to as "the death penalty": already on probation from the NCAA for major violations due to similar payments, the NCAA ruled that SMU could play no games at all in 1987, and could play only seven games (all away from home) in 1988 (SMU would later opt to cancel the 1988 games on its own). The rationale, stated the NCAA's Committee on Infractions, was due to SMU's repeat offender status, but also because "its past record of violations is nothing short of abysmal" (Whitford, 1989, pp. 200–201). When SMU's football program returned, it was with severe restrictions on recruiting and grants-in-aid (Byers, 1995; Layden, 2002).

The punishments for SMU were clear, and the long-term ramifications were significant. In the aftermath of the "death penalty," SMU's football program languished for nearly three decades. From its return in 1989, the team went 62–163–3. From 1980 to 1986, 28 SMU players were drafted by the National Football League; since then, only seven have. The program operated without a full complement of athletic grants-in-aid (commonly referred to as "scholarships") until 1992. Nearly a year after the sanctions were announced, newly hired head coach Forrest Gregg (SMU Class of 1956 and a former NFL star player and head coach) was asked by a fellow alumnus at his introductory press conference: "How many years before the Mustangs return to the Cotton Bowl? Five? Ten?" "A lot less than ten," said Gregg, and "the room erupted in cheers" (Whitford, 1989, p. 212). SMU appeared in a bowl game for the first time since 1984 in 2009, defeating the University of Nevada in the Hawaii Bowl, 45–10. The Mustangs followed that up with a 16–14 loss to the United States Military Academy in the Armed Forces Bowl in 2010, and a 28–6 win over the University of Pittsburgh in the BBVA Compass Bowl after the 2011 season, but SMU's Cotton Bowl drought is now close to three decades. The devastating impact of the "death penalty" for SMU has meant that it has not been leveled again by the NCAA, in part because of negative reinforcement: schools are loath to risk the severity of the sanctions endured by SMU by acting similarly, so rather they behave in a manner to avoid negative consequences.

The final aspect of reinforcement theory is extinction, when no reinforcement, neither positive nor negative, is forthcoming after performance. Skinner predicts that, without reinforcement, organization members will not maintain high levels of performance. One significant recent incident of rules violations occurred at the University of Southern California (USC), a private, four-year NCAA Division I institution located in Los Angeles, and the actions surrounding the recruitment of O.J. Mayo, who played at the school for only one season (2007–2008) before leaving to play professionally in the National Basketball Association. According to USC officials, Mayo was involved with a booster who helped steer him to the school, and former head coach Tim Floyd gave the booster $1,000 to funnel to Mayo. Others have alleged that the booster had funneled hundreds of thousands to Mayo on behalf of a sport agency firm. As a result, USC announced it would not participate in any post-season tournaments in 2010, reduce grants-in-aid and off-campus recruiting by coaches through 2011, return to the NCAA money earned through its 2008 Division I tournament appearance, and vacate all 21 victories earned while Mayo was on the squad ("USC announces," 2010). Members of the 2009–2010 men's squad called the sanctions "unfair," as evidenced by the comments of senior guard Dwight Lewis: "We did feel like we had a chance to be in the NCAA tournament ... To have that taken away, it was hard." Forward Kasey Cunningham, out because of a season-ending knee injury, succinctly summarized the team's perspective: "This sucks" (Holmes, 2010, pp. 1–2). After the sanctions were announced, Mayo's agent denied that the player had received any gifts or money during his recruitment by or playing for USC. Floyd also denied any wrongdoing (Pugmire, 2010).

Meanwhile, USC was enmeshed in similar problems with the case of football running back Reggie Bush. In 2006, Bush left USC after his junior year and was selected second overall in that year's NFL draft by the New Orleans Saints, signing a contract that would guarantee him more than $26 million. According to various reports, while a student-athlete at USC, Bush and his family allegedly received cash and gifts totaling close to $300,000 from a prospective sport marketing agency, New Era Sports & Entertainment, formed in San Diego (Bush's hometown) by Lloyd Lake, Michael Michaels, and LaMar Griffin (Bush's stepfather). In November 2004, Bush met with Michaels and Lake at a TGIFriday's restaurant in San Diego, and confirmed his commitment to become the nascent firm's first client. At about this time, Bush allegedly asked for a $3,000 a month payment from the firm in living expenses as an advance on the firm's future income from Bush's contracts. Over the next several months, Bush was paid $13,000 for the sale of a 1996 Chevrolet Impala SS (although Bush instructed that the payments go to his stepfather), and Michaels purchased for Bush's parents a 3,000-square-foot home at 9715 Apple Street in San Diego for $757,500, with a down payment of $36,000, under the terms that they would purchase the home from Lake and Michaels once Bush declared for the draft. They later asked for over $13,000 for furniture and appliances for the house. Another individual, Mike Ornstein, is also alleged to have given cash and gifts to Bush and his family while Bush was still enrolled at USC. Bush's ties to Ornstein began when he served as an intern in Ornstein's office in the summer of 2005 (Yaeger, 2008).

After declaring for the draft, Bush hired Ornstein as his marketing agent, and Joel Segal to represent him in his future contract negotiations. The move was not a surprise, because during a meeting the previous December between Lake and LaMar Griffin, Griffin told Lake: "I said it's going to be his decision. And no matter what his word said, you're talking to a 22-year-old kid that's looking at the opportunity of a lifetime. He's the best player in college football. And I got to tell you, he's got to look at all avenues" (Yaeger, 2008, p. 139). Soon thereafter, Lake and Michaels sought to file suit against Bush, claiming that Bush and his parents defrauded them out of $3.2 million in what was termed lost business capital and monies given to Bush and his family.

Those involved with these machinations believed that officials at USC, including head football coach Pete Carroll and assistant coach Todd McNair, knew about the

266

payments to Bush. Lake and Michaels have stated that they not only attended USC home games but also had access to the Trojan locker room after games (Yaeger, 2008). Following a disappointing 2009 season, Carroll left USC to return to the NFL as head coach of the Seattle Seahawks.

On June 9, 2010, news reports cited that after an NCAA investigation, USC would suffer a two-year bowl game ban and lose 20 grants-in-aid ("NCAA sanctions," 2010). Of the sanctions, outgoing USC President Steven Sample said: "We will accept some of the penalties imposed … and will appeal those penalties that are excessive … The process of self-scrutiny must [ask]: What went wrong? What should we do differently?" Pete Carroll denied responsibility, stating: "The university didn't know. We didn't know." Reggie Bush commented: "I am disappointed by today's decision and disagree with the NCAA's findings" ("What they're," 2010).

As a result, USC did not renew the contract of running backs coach Todd McNair, which expired on June 30, 2010. The NCAA's Committee on Infractions report noted that McNair "knew or should have known" that Reggie Bush and two would-be sports marketers from the San Diego area "were engaged in violations that negatively affected" Bush's amateur status, and determined that McNair "provided false and misleading information to the enforcement staff" and "violated NCAA legislation by signing a document certifying that he had no knowledge of NCAA violations" (Klein, 2010, p. 1). Soon thereafter, USC AD Mike Garrett was fired. Former Trojan QB Pat Haden replaced Garrett (himself a former USC football star and the school's first Heisman Trophy winner), who had been in the post since 1993. Incoming school president Max Nikias also announced that the school would return the school's Reggie Bush Heisman Trophy statue to the Downtown Athletic Club, and take down all displays featuring Bush and O.J. Mayo in and around campus (Klein and Dwyre, 2010, p. 1). A week after Garrett's firing, officials from the newly christened Pac-12 Conference were in New York City announcing the conference's addition of two new members (the University of Colorado and the University of Utah) and intentions for the formation of a new television network. Scott had to acknowledge the issues with USC, commenting: "No one likes to see sanctions, especially the magnitude that have been handed down," but Scott tried to be upbeat: "In the long term, USC is still USC" (Thamel, 2010f, p. B11).

If no actions had been taken by USC to discipline its programs and terminate the contracts of managers in charge during these violations, there would have been no reason to expect that these behaviors would have changed. It could also be argued that if USC continued to reward coaches and programs in which violations had occurred, the violating behaviors would have almost certainly continued. The message from reinforcement theory for sport managers is that to build high levels of performance motivation, positive performance must be shaped by a carefully selected set of consequences that reinforce and strengthen that performance.

267

Needs theory

A third perspective on performance motivation is provided by needs theory, which suggests that all human behavior, including behavior in organizations, is an effort to satisfy the individual's needs. In other words, people work and perform at a level that will allow them to satisfy their needs. Some of the most important contributions to our understanding of human needs have come from psychologist Abraham Maslow (1970), who concluded that most of our needs can be grouped into five categories and arranged in levels, as shown in Box 8.2.

BOX 8.2 MASLOW'S HIERARCHY OF NEEDS

Self-actualization: the need for the feeling or sense that you are achieving your full potential as a human being.

Esteem: the need for the sense of respect first from others and then self-respect.

Social: the need for the sense of belongingness and acceptance by others.

Security: the need for those things that will allow us to feel physically and psychologically safe.

Physiological: the need for those things that will keep us alive and functioning physiologically.

Maslow suggested a number of interesting elements about human needs. He began with the assumption that in any given situation human behavior or performance tends to reflect the particular need level of an individual in a particular situation. For example, Maslow states that different individuals in exactly similar situations might behave or perform in totally different ways depending on their needs at the time. Someone at the esteem-needs level, for example, might work extremely hard to receive recognition. Someone at the social-needs level might only work hard enough to be accepted by the group in which he or she is working. And someone at the security-needs level might purposely perform only well enough to keep his or her job and seek to avoid any attention at all. The message from needs theory is that sport managers must recognize and understand the need levels of employees and create opportunities for them to pursue the satisfaction of these needs through what they do.

An examination of various positions within intercollegiate athletic departments provides an excellent illustration of Maslow's hierarchy of needs in action. For Division I head football coaches, strict physiological and security needs can be met at lucrative levels. The average compensation for NCAA Division I head football coaches in 2011 was $1.47 million, a jump of nearly 55 percent in six seasons. That same season at least 64 coaches made more than $1 million. Of those, 32 were paid more than $2 million, nine made more than $3 million, and three made more than $4 million. Mack Brown of the University of Texas topped the list at more than $5 million. Mississippi State University head coach Dan Mullen got the season's second-biggest raise – $1 million. Mullen earned $1.2 million in his first season at the school in 2009, got a $300,000 raise for his second year, and the latest raise bumped his pay to $2.5 million. In 2010, he led the Bulldogs to a 9–4 record, their best since 1999, and a victory against the University of Michigan in the 2011 Gator Bowl. "It's all market-driven," Mississippi State athletic director Scott Stricklin says, adding:

> When we hired Dan, we paid him $600,000 less than our previous coach … with the understanding that you know when you do that, you're saving money today but if he's successful you're going to catch him up to where the market is. All of us are paid based on what our value is within the context of the job we do. You can make a lot of comments about society and what football coaches get paid, but the fact of the matter is it's a highly valued position.
>
> (Brady *et al.*, 2011, p. 1)

While the lower-level needs are certainly critical, from a needs theory perspective the intensity of these upper-level needs can help determine the level of performance achieved by an organization. What about the "walk-ons," those student-athletes at Division I and II programs who don't start or even receive much, if any, playing time, and are receiving no athletically related financial aid for their efforts? What is it they get out of the intercollegiate athletic experience? They work just as hard, get up just as early, and deal with all the same time demands. Consider the case of Stephen Duckett and Joe Hughes, members of the perennially strong men's basketball program at Xavier University, a private Catholic, Jesuit-affiliated school with 4,000 undergrads located in Cincinnati, Ohio, and a member of the Division I Atlantic 10 Conference. Both Duckett and Hughes had been good high school players, but neither received any Division I grant-in-aid offers, so they became "walk-ons" at Xavier, meaning they receive no athletically related aid. And from their first practice at Xavier, they knew why. Said Duckett: "Physically, there was no comparison. It was like, Wow, I couldn't believe their speed and size. I'm looking at myself, 6-foot-4, 190 pounds. I'm like, What am *I* gonna do?" (Wolverton, 2008b, pp. A1, A7; author's emphasis).

What they do is serve as subjects to prepare their teammates for games, and spend time watching game films of opponents and trying to mimic them in practice. "You have to know your role," said Duckett. "You can't come in here thinking you're gonna be a big shot." During games, their job is simple. "Keep morale high," said Hughes. "Make some noise." At timeouts they're first off the bench to encourage teammates, and scream and cheer throughout the game. They only get to play when, according to Hughes, "we're beating the crap out of some team." And for this privilege, they still have the same time demands and expectations as their more celebrated teammates. But there is some small measure of glory for Duckett and Hughes. Late in games, if Xavier has a big lead, fans will chant their names hoping they will get into the game, and erupt in cheers when they do. And if they don't get in the game? "It's OK," says Hughes. "We had the best seats in the house" (Wolverton, 2008b, p. A7).

Based on their responses, both Hughes and Duckett are achieving social benefits from being part of a high-performing team, and both are achieving esteem by gaining the sense of respect first from their coaches, teammates, and fans, which in turn trigger self-respect. Finally, the pair has reached self-actualization by understanding that while they may not be as gifted as many of their teammates, they realize they are still achieving their full potential. With these factors in place for all team members, even those who don't bask in the limelight, it is clear that such a program can hope to achieve success on and off the court.

Expectancy theory

Developed by Victor Vroom (1964), expectancy theory suggests that the level of effort an individual puts into a task depends on three factors:

1   The strength of the individual's expectation that he or she is able to perform at a level that will result in success. According to Vroom, the more positive the expectation, the greater the likely effort.
2   The strength of the individual's expectation that success will result in reward. Some rewards are extrinsic (e.g. money, recognition, a promotion); others are intrinsic (e.g. learning new skills, sense of personal satisfaction). However, for motivation to be positive, the expectation must be positive that success on a task will result in reward.
3   The valence of the reward, or how much the reward for success is valued by the individual. Just having a reward is not enough. For motivation to be positive, the reward for success must be something valued by the individual.

According to expectancy theory, each of these conditions must be met to ensure a high level of performance motivation. But in the case of many student-athletes, the time demands and expectations inherent in combining athletic participation and pursuing a degree can be daunting and can serve as an illustrative example of the application of the tenets of expectancy theory. Consider the daily schedule of Stephanie Campbell, a field hockey player at Villanova University, a private Catholic institution with just over 6,000 undergraduates located in suburban Philadelphia, Pennsylvania, and member of the Division I Big East conference. Stephanie begins classes at 7 a.m. each day so she can be in the locker room by noon in preparation for four hours of weightlifting and on-field practice. Travel to away games forces her to miss classes and exams, and most evenings she has mandatory team meetings and study halls, in addition to weekend practices. She spends weekend nights in her room trying to catch up on sleep (Pennington, 2008).

These experiences are the rule, not the exception, with most Division I student-athletes reporting that they devote at least four hours a day to their sport, not counting injury treatment, games, or travel, with classes scheduled in the mornings to leave time each afternoon for practices and games. Then there are often team dinners and mandatory meetings and study halls after that. A recent NCAA study of 21,000 student-athletes supports this, with one in five noting that their sport participation has prevented them from choosing the academic major they wanted. Division I football players reported spending almost 45 hours a week on activities related to their sport, with golfers and baseball and softball players reporting similar time spent, even though NCAA bylaws permit only 20 hours a week be spent on in-season activities (Wolverton, 2008a).

The question here, in terms of expectancy theory, is how should athletic department managers respond? Are the time demands too great for student-athletes? The lesson from expectancy theory is the importance of creating strong links between success and rewards that people value, and of creating the strongest possible expectations that high levels of effort will lead to performance. In the case of the vast majority of all student-athletes, who will not be pursuing a professional on-field sport career, that means communicating that personal performance is critical in ensuring the organizational and personal success. During her first year, when Stephanie Campbell struggled with the time demands, her mother put the experience in perspective, telling her:

> Villanova costs more than $40,000 a year to attend. They're paying you $19,000 to play field hockey. At your age, there's no one out there anywhere who is going to pay you that kind of money to do anything. And that's how you have to look at this: it's a job, but it's a great job.
>
> (Pennington, 2008, pp. C15, C18)

Campbell kept at it for four years, became a team captain as a senior, majored in marketing, and graduated in 2008. The spring of her senior year, she admitted:

> Receiving an athletic scholarship is a wonderful thing, but most of us only know what we're getting, not what we're getting into ... I know a lot of people who would have loved to trade places with me. But I'd still say Division I athletics is not meant for everybody. Nobody tells you that.
>
> (Pennington, 2008, pp. C15, C18)

For programs to be effective under expectancy theory, therefore, managers must, like Ms. Campbell's mother, make explicit each of the three factors.

THEORY INTO PRACTICE: CREATING A HIGH-PERFORMANCE WORK ENVIRONMENT

The true value of performance motivation theories is that, taken together, they provide a clear direction on how to structure the work environment for high levels of performance. Four key factors – goals, training, incentives, and involving employees – help support performance motivation to contribute to the achievement of organizational success.

Engaging, challenging goals

High levels of performance motivation clearly begin with a set of fully developed goals and standards that define exactly the performance target. These goals and standards provide the basis for focus, challenge, and feedback, all essential for high performance. Any athletic department, program, coach, and collection of student-athletes may have the goal of winning a rivalry game, a conference championship, or a national title, the latter of which is unquestionably a challenge, and one that would only be met if all organizational members found it sufficiently engaging.

But what about conference management? Nearly every college or university has membership in an intercollegiate athletic conference. Intercollegiate athletic conferences, described by Bowen and Levin (2003) as "orbits of competition," were developed primarily for the formulation and enforcement of rules governing student-athlete eligibility, ease and convenience of travel and scheduling, and "lifting some of the political burden away from the individual member institutions" (Quarterman, 1994, p. 129). To support this, Thelin states that:

> The conference is the crucial unit in shaping and regulating intercollegiate athletics because it can have more impact on shaping athletic policies than the NCAA ... [and] is the locus where a small group of institutions in voluntary association agree to work together, to compete while showing some sign of mutual respect and comparable academic standards.
>
> (1996, p. 129)

But conferences, these so-called competitive orbits that operate between the like-minded for the betterment of all members, also demonstrate that participating schools must simultaneously cooperate and compete. Member schools come together and cooperate in the ways described above, but they also compete. They

272

compete for wins in games, for media attention, for prospective student-athletes and coaching personnel, and for revenues and resources to run their programs. It is this competition that can be a potential source of conflict between schools.

In his discussion of the role of athletic conferences at the intercollegiate level, Sweitzer (2009) noted that these organizations have "meaning that extends beyond the playing field. Institutions generally desire to compete against others that are similar in profile, including their approach to athletics" (p. 55). Sweitzer continues that given similarities in mission and geographic proximity,

> institutions within conferences typically compete in areas outside athletics, whether in recruiting students, hiring and retaining faculty, or attracting research funding. The commonalities between and among institutions in a conference create a peer group useful in benchmarking, one that might even heighten competition between and among members.
>
> (p. 55)

Intraconference competition also serves as a measuring stick. When one school in the conference wins, it comes at the expense of another conference member. Steven Lewis, Jr., former president of Carleton College, a private school with 2,000 undergraduates located in Northfield, Minnesota, and a member of the NCAA Division III Minnesota Intercollegiate Athletic Conference, expressed this concerning the role of conferences:

> In athletics ... students don't just compete against a standard of excellence as they might in music or theater. They compete against teams from other schools. Therefore ... we need to act in concert with other colleges whose goals and values are similar.
>
> (2001, p. 9)

Lewis' comment expresses the realities of intercollegiate athletic management as schools look to coordinate programs beyond the boundaries of their own teams and departments. The intercollegiate landscape is segmented distinctly by discrete groupings of peer institutions that operate to manage these like-minded spheres of competition.

So who controls and operates these conferences? In most cases a commissioner fulfills the role of COO. While the commissioner is an employee of the member schools, it is his or her responsibility to manage functional operational areas such as rules compliance, negotiating broadcast and sponsorship agreements, and managing conflicts amongst members. Conference commissioners also work amongst themselves to manage relations and competitions between conferences, the most notable such arrangement being the NCAA Division I football Bowl Championship Series (see above).

But not all managerial issues impact each conference to the same degree. Because of stated divisional and philosophical guidelines, personnel associated with NCAA Division II and III conferences will not deal with the same types of managerial challenges as do their Division I colleagues. But even within Division I, differences exist among conferences in terms of managerial operations. There are numerous so-called "mid-major" conferences, those that include Division I institutions but lack the level of popular support from fans and alumni that garner it the degree of notoriety entertained by the so-called "big-time" collections such as the Atlantic Coast Conference, the Big Ten Conference, the Pac-12 Conference, and the Southeastern Conference. One such "mid-major" conference is the Horizon League, founded in 1979 as the Midwestern Collegiate Conference, with nine member schools located in the Midwest in four of the top 35 U.S. media markets (Chicago, Cleveland, Detroit, Milwaukee). The league sponsors competition in 19 sports, and receives automatic bids to NCAA championships in baseball, men's and women's basketball, men's golf, men's and women's soccer, softball, men's and women's tennis, and women's volleyball. The league is headquartered in Indianapolis, Indiana, and is governed by a board of directors comprised of the ten member schools' chief executive officers ("About us," 2012), as shown in Box 8.3.

BOX 8.3 HORIZON LEAGUE MEMBERSHIP

Cleveland State University
Loyola University Chicago
University of Detroit Mercy
University of Illinois – Chicago
University of Wisconsin – Green Bay
University of Wisconsin – Milwaukee
Valparaiso (IN) University
Wright State University (Dayton, OH)
Youngstown (OH) University

Training

High levels of performance motivation also require high levels of skill. Expectancy theory makes clear that workers must be confident that the skills they possess will allow them to achieve the performance goals. Training is the critical means for ensuring that people have the skills they need to meet the performance challenge. As we show in Chapter 9, training – effectively provided and continuously

274

updated – is essential for ensuring the levels of confidence and competence necessary for high levels of performance motivation.

To learn more about the importance of training, let's continue to examine the example of the Horizon League and commissioner, Jonathan B. (Jon) LeCrone. Training is a significant part of the background for any manager. In preparation for his Horizon League leadership post, LeCrone earned his B.A. in English from Wake Forest University in 1976, and his Masters in sports administration from Ohio University in 1978. He has been in his current post since 1992, prior to which he garnered significant work experiences, spending nine years as assistant commissioner in the Atlantic Coast Conference (ACC), where he was responsible for projects relating to television, marketing, revenue generation, and public relations. Prior to his ACC work, McCrone was Assistant AD at ACC-member Wake Forest University, and was also business manager for the Wichita Cubs, the then-AAA minor league affiliate of Major League Baseball's Chicago Cubs. In addition to his commissioner's job, McCrone has also served on the NCAA Division I Leadership Council, the NCAA Division I Men's Basketball Committee, and the NCAA Division I Men's Soccer Committee (three years as chair). As of 2012, LeCrone is the fifth-longest serving commissioner amongst the 31 multi-sport Division I conferences ("Commissioner LeCrone," 2012).

Of his background and the importance of training, LeCrone says this:

> You have to be able to read, to comprehend, and to understand. You have to be able to communicate effectively, be it speaking or writing. You have to be able to communicate effectively in meetings. A graduate degree is absolutely essential. A focused graduate degree in either education or business would be excellent. Any practical experience you can get in coaching is helpful. If you have the ability to get a Ph.D. or a J.D., that can't hurt you.
>
> You have to get practical work experience in any way you can while you're on your college campus. That might mean volunteering and showing up and saying, "I'm here, I'd like to work."
>
> (Covell and Barr, 2010, p. 93)

The message here is that training, the type that is correct and focused, will contribute to organizational success, and LeCrone has trained in various important roles and positions prior to running the Horizon League.

Performance incentives: creating a stake in achieving success

A third key element in creating a high-performance environment is rewards, also known as incentives. Both expectancy theory and reinforcement theory emphasize creating a clear link between high levels of performance and incentives or rewards for achieving performance goals. Needs theory helps the manager understand the needs level of his or her people and also helps determine the types of incentives that will be most valued.

In the case of the Horizon League and organizational success, Jon LeCrone must perform his duties to benefit the operations of member conferences. In terms of referring to the Horizon League as a "mid-major" conference, which some might view as denigrating his organization, LeCrone expresses no such concern about such perceptions, and does not believe this status affects his ability to meet conference goals. "We're only limited by what we think of ourselves," he says. "We're not limited by what other people think or say about us" (Covell and Barr, 2010, p. 92). LeCrone continues to outline what incentives impact his job and the performance of his membership:

> I would not be successful in this job if I try to take the approach for success the ACC has, even though that's the conference I came from. I understand that level and how the ACC operates. If I came here and tried to replicate that approach, I would miss a lot of points ... The successful commissioner tries to create successful approaches based upon the conference and what those in the conference hold as believable, conceivable, and achievable.
>
> So can the Horizon League have eight teams in the men's basketball tournament and four teams in the Final Four every year? That's probably not believable, conceivable and achievable ... The successful commissioner needs to think about their own definition of success and pursue that, rather than have some other group – colleagues, conferences – define success for them. And that's what we have tried to do.
>
> (Covell and Barr, 2010, p. 92)

So in terms of incentives, LeCrone first must help his members understand what types of goals are realistically achieved before they can be pursued. Thus, a third key element in creating a high-performance work environment is a clear link between achieving performance goals and the assurance of highly valued rewards for pursuing and achieving those goals.

Involving employees: sharing responsibility for performance

A fourth key element is directly involving employees in problem solving and decision making. This strategy of employee involvement has most recently been called employee empowerment (Conger and Kanungo, 1988; Manz, 1992). Even the most effective goal and incentive systems are almost always part of an overall management effort to more fully involve people in the responsibility for their own performance. Empowerment strategies are certainly consistent with needs theory. More specifically,

Motivation and leadership and intercollegiate athletics

sharing responsibility for performance responds directly to people's esteem and self-actualization needs. Empowerment represents a significant form of recognition of employees' judgment and skills, as well as an opportunity for employees to test and develop their own potential. This combination of recognition and opportunity for development results in an enhanced level of performance motivation.

In the case of the Horizon League, Jon LeCrone is an employee of the member schools, but as commissioner must provide leadership by engaging conference members. Says LeCrone:

> Commissioners need to say to their members, "Listen, I'd like to propose to you my definition of success. But I've gotten a definition of success by talking with you, and thinking about and vetting what I've heard. Do you think that if this is our approach, we could be successful? Could we all agree to this? Is it believable, conceivable, and achievable? And can we pay for it?" Here are our measures, and by our measures we were very successful this year. These are the places we did well, these are the places where we've continued to improve, and here's where we're headed.
>
> (Covell and Barr, 2010, p. 93)

In addition, LeCrone believes there is great value in involving member schools in the problem-solving and decision-making processes, commenting that "philosophically, I'm not sure concentrated power in one area is good for any organization" (Covell and Barr, 2010, p. 92). He continues:

> I like the fact that conference offices are structured where the commissioner reports to a board of presidents. This works best because there is a level of oversight. Everything that works top-down is not necessarily best for our business, because we are managing groups of schools that are competing with one another. There is natural tension because they are not always pulling in the same direction ... I think a shared governance structure works best rather than a military structure where what the general says goes.
>
> (Covell and Barr, 2010, p. 92)

But conference commissioners must always be looking ahead to the next big challenge, which for LeCrone is connected to the recent spate of NCAA Division I conference realignment moves (see below). Butler University, whose men's basketball program made it to the national championship final game in 2010 and 2011, jumped from the Horizon League to the Atlantic-10 Conference in 2012 (and may yet move again to a join the seven former Big East Conference Catholic schools in a new configuration). Of the switch, LeCrone acknowledged that "lots of this stuff is kind of a national phenomenon ... Some of it's sensible, some not very sensible" (Woods, 2012, p. 1). LeCrone and the rest of the Horizon League membership will need to consider how to replace Butler and attempt to continue its men's basketball success.

277

THE LEADERSHIP FACTOR

In managing intercollegiate athletic conferences, commissioners such as Jon LeCrone are most effective when they engage performance motivation theories such as goals, training, incentives, and involving employees. But these individuals also serve as organizational leaders. Leadership has emerged as one of the most critical ingredients for success in all organizations, not just in sport organizations. All organizations are in a seemingly never-ending quest to define leadership and to seek those with the abilities to lead effectively. A quick check of the business and management sections in any local bookstore or on-line seller will reveal hundreds of titles devoted to the study of leadership in organizations. One such book, *Leaders*, by Warren Bennis and Burt Nanus, emphasizes the crucial importance of leadership: "A business short on capital can borrow money, and one with a poor location can move. But a business short of leadership has little chance of survival" (2003, p. 20).

Think about this: are the definitions for the terms "manager" and "leader" interchangeable? Do we expect managers to be leaders? Most of us probably do. However, management scholar John Kotter identified an important distinction:

> Management is about coping with complexity ... Leadership, by contrast, is about coping with change. Part of the reason [leadership] has become so important in recent years is that the business world has become more competitive and more volatile. More change always demands more leadership.
>
> (1998, pp. 37–38)

Because of this element of change (especially as sport organizations look toward international expansion), leadership is a crucial component for every kind of organization. Leadership in organizations is the process of directing and supporting others in the pursuit of the organization's mission and goals. From this perspective, leadership is as much every team member's responsibility as it is the highest-level managers' and CEO's responsibility. Everyone is a potential leader, capable of contributing to the direction and support of others as he or she pursues the mission and goals of the organization.

The question for all sport organizations is how best to provide the kind of direction and support people need to be productive. The answer to the question is not a simple one. It has been evolving and ever changing as research reveals more about the leadership process, and the very nature of leadership has altered to meet the realities of the contemporary workplace. Our discussion of leadership begins with a review of some research and theories, which focus on the personality and characteristics of effective leaders, and then highlights how individual leaders, namely coaches, athletic directors, school presidents, and national governing body personnel, influenced the development of the intercollegiate athletics enterprise.

The psychology of the leader

The early research on leadership focused on the leader as a person, on the personality traits of the effective leader, on the leader's attitudes and assumptions, and on leaders' expectations of their followers. The underlying assumption was that if research could determine the kind of person who would be an effective leader, organizations might be better able to identify and select people with the greatest leadership potential.

Leadership and personality

The initial leadership research focused on determining whether there might be specific personality traits that are common to effective leaders. For many years, the results from this research did not substantiate that premise, and little or no evidence supported the concept of a particular leadership personality. By the 1980s, however, expanded research identified at least five personality traits consistently associated with effective leaders (Kirkpatrick and Locke, 1991). The personalities of those considered effective as leaders might vary in other ways – whether they were shy as opposed to outgoing, for example, or reflective versus immediately reactive. But the most effective leaders were found to possess many of the five traits listed in Box 8.4.

BOX 8.4 PERSONALITY TRAITS OF EFFECTIVE LEADERS

- Drive, ambition, energy, tenacity, initiative
- Desire to lead
- Honesty and integrity
- Self-confidence
- Intelligence

Recognizing the key personality characteristics of effective leaders can assist organizational efforts to identify potential leaders. It can also aid in efforts to develop leadership potential among employees who are not yet in leadership positions. An individual who possesses drive and initiative, for example, as well as the traits of desire to lead, honesty, and integrity, might be provided specific training and assignments to improve self-confidence, which is also associated with effective leadership.

In the intercollegiate athletics industry segment, ultimate leadership is often said to rest at the feet of the head of the NCAA. Throughout its history, the actions of the NCAA have been shaped by its leadership, specifically those individuals who have served in the post of president (formerly "executive director"). From 1951 to 1987, the association was headed by Walter Byers, who was responsible for much of the growth of the association. Early on, Byers was also involved in establishing the association's enforcement capabilities as well as negotiating TV rights fees, an area in which Byers excelled. According to Dave Gavitt, a former Division I head basketball coach and the first commissioner of the Big East Conference, Byers was not afraid to take a hard line in talks, as was the case in 1981 when executives from the NBC TV network were trying to finalize a deal to keep the rights to the Division I men's basketball tournament. Said Gavitt, who was part of the committee reviewing the bids:

> [NBC's negotiators] came in and basically tried to poor-mouth what was going on. They were saying it's hard to sell, hard to clear, blah blah blah. It wasn't where we thought we were. We thought [the tournament] had wings for the future. The meeting was classic Byers. He stood up and closed his notebook, and he said to them, "I want to apologize to my colleagues who I brought in from around the country to listen to that. This meeting is over".
>
> (Davis, 2009, p. 244)

Byers' abruptness was not just a negotiating ploy, as it led to an opening of the bidding to other networks. CBS was quick to offer $48 million over the next three years (a 60 percent increase over the previous deal with NBC). The next time around CBS kept NBC out of the bidding entirely by re-upping for another three years for $96 million – double the value of its previous deal (Davis, 2009).

But Byers could also be aptly described as a micro-manager, as he crafted organizational policies that specified that each employee had to be at his or her desk before 8:30 a.m. (or risk being marked tardy), and could not leave until 5 p.m., at which time all desks had to be cleared and window drapes drawn. Drinks were not allowed at desks, nor were personal items such as photographs. Former NCAA investigation staff member Curt Hamakawa, now a sport management faculty member at Western New England University in Springfield, Massachusetts, related that if a staffer brought in an unauthorized picture or wall decoration, it would disappear overnight, its whereabouts unknown, with no explanation given as to why it was removed.

During Byers' time the association was also criticized for overzealous enforcement efforts in some cases, most notably a years-long investigation surrounding the men's basketball program at the University of Nevada-Las Vegas and its infamous and successful head coach, Jerry Tarkanian. Of these criticisms, Byers responded in 1986: "We have more investigators than ever before. But you cannot police college athletics properly unless the universities are going to make a solid effort to apply and enforce the rules. That's the only way the system will work, if the [presidents] give hands-on administration" (Selcraig *et al.*, 1986, pp. 2–4, 9, 12).

Although Byers' management style was idiosyncratic to say the least (with others describing him as reclusive and paranoid, since he often registered at hotels under pseudonyms and instructed family members and staffers not to alert others of his whereabouts at certain times, and once told a reporter that "any administrator is going to self-destroy if he becomes totally oriented to his public image"), many staffers at the time respected his ability to think creatively. Said one during Byers' tenure:

> The thing that really intrigues me about [Byers] is that he continues to be more imaginative than anyone on the NCAA staff. He's been in this job for 35 years and, still, he's always looking for a new and better way of doing something.

Former Big Ten Commissioner Wayne Duke summarized Byers' influence over the NCAA this way: "The NCAA prospered, in my opinion, because of three factors: enforcement, football on television and the [Division I men's] basketball tournament. And Walter was the architect of all three." Donna Lopiano, former women's AD at the University of Texas and later head of the Women's Sports Foundation, who opposed Byers while she headed the Association of Intercollegiate Athletics for Women, asserted that: "The NCAA was nothing until Walter Byers" (Selcraig *et al.*, 1986, pp. 2–4).

The power of expectations

Research on the leader as an individual also suggests a strong direct relationship between the leader's level of expectations and followers' level of performance (Single, 1980). According to this research, not only must the leader's assumptions about followers be accurate, but the leader's expectations as to what the followers are capable of achieving must be as positive as possible.

In studying the reasons for strong links between leader expectations and follower performance, researchers discovered that leaders with positive expectations provide their followers with significantly more direction and supervision than leaders with less positive expectations about their followers with:

1   a greater degree of challenge
2   more direction on how to complete the tasks
3   greater feedback on how to improve performance
4   in general, a more positive work climate.

In other words, high expectation leaders provide much more leadership.

This pattern of effective leaders working hard to help their people succeed is an example of a self-fulfilling prophecy. Positive examples of this pattern can be found in every type of sport organization. The leadership lesson of the self-fulfilling prophecy is this: to influence the performance of their followers positively, leaders must expect the best of them. Only a leader with high expectations is likely to provide the amount and quality of direction and support that his or her followers need to achieve the highest levels of performance.

In terms of the progression of NCAA leadership, Byers was replaced in 1987 by Richard Schultz, who had been AD at the University of Virginia after stints at Cornell University and the University of Iowa, and had served on several high-level NCAA committees. Schultz was forced to resign in 1993 after it was revealed that NCAA violations pertaining to improper loans made to student-athletes occurred while he was at Virginia, about some of which he knew. Cedric Dempsey headed the organization from 1994 to 2002, moving to the NCAA from the AD position at the University of Arizona. Dempsey created a more informal working environment, which included eradicating the association's dress code (which, as outlined in the association's office conduct sections of its 100-page *Office Policies and Procedures*, required that male administrators wear "suits or sport coats and slacks, shirts and ties," and that female administrators and non-administrative employees "wear dresses, suits, skirts or slacks and blouses," and that all such blouses "cover the waistline and below at all times") (Rushin, 1997, p. 4).

Dr. Myles Brand, a former college president who served in that role at both the University of Oregon (where he had also served as a philosophy professor and provost) and Indiana University, served as NCAA president from 2003 until his death from pancreatic cancer in 2009. He was the first former college president to serve as the head of the association. According to Brand, many ADs were wary of him because of his background as a college president and not as an AD (Nethery, 2004). This was compounded by the fact that while president at Indiana, Brand fired legendary men's basketball coach Bob Knight after Knight committed a series of on- and off-court transgressions.

While many view the NCAA as an omnipotent force within intercollegiate athletics, they might also conclude that it is the one in charge who wields all the power. In fact, while the President does sit on the Association's Executive Council, he or she has no opportunity to vote on the matters before it. Big Ten Conference commissioner James Delany describes the exercising of power in the NCAA this way:

> There are a lot of checks and balances in the NCAA … when it comes to the actual authority to change policy, or to right a wrong, or to deal with systematic problems, no one really has that authority … at the end of the day, [a president] can't do any more or less than what the schools are willing to do collectively.
>
> (Nethery, 2004, p. 28)

282

When Brand assumed the president's mantle, many familiar with the intercollegiate athletics enterprise noted that his experiences at Indiana and Oregon would work in his favor within the newly constructed governance and legislative NCAA organization to deal with the major issues facing the association. These issues included:

■ The relative absence of African–American football coaches

■ Control of athletics by school presidents

■ The quandary surrounding the Bowl Championship Series in Division I football

■ The ever-expanding expenses associated with the enterprise.

(Lapointe, 2003; Wieberg, 2003a)

It was in the area of expanding expenses that Brand chose to take on as a key area of emphasis early in his tenure, which he chose to bolster through the NCAA's periodic collection of financial data coordinated by Daniel Fulks, professor of accounting and faculty athletics representative at Transylvania (Kentucky) University. The report noted that athletic spending had increased in Division I since 1997, that these increases were leading to a growing gap between the schools already investing heavily in their athletic programs and those who were not, and that these increased investments were not yielding high returns. In response to the report, Brand noted that if schools value the experiences that intercollegiate athletics can bring, then he suggested that schools should fund intercollegiate athletics programs like any other institutional department, with the same degree of budgetary oversight, and with less concern for profit. Said Brand:

> We have to bring [intercollegiate athletics] into the university. If you want to bring it into the university, you have to think about it in a different way, and that includes how you budget it ... Presidents and others have to examine the rate at which they want to expend their funds for athletics [and] they have to weigh that against the fact that the vast majority of them are going to operate in the red. They can't recapture, even [at Division I schools with Bowl Subdivision football programs], for the most part, the amounts of money they're spending. Those are hard priority decisions.
>
> (Wieberg, 2003b, p. 11C; 2003c, p. 1C)

Two years after taking office, Brand launched a campaign for fiscal responsibility at the Annual Convention, because, as he observed in a convention address, "the spending spiral has not abated." Brand expressed particular concern with the justification for athletics facility projects, where schools are looking to have facilities that outdo those of pro league franchises. He then qualified his stance, stating:

283

I'm not talking about cutbacks. I'm not even talking about staying at the same level. I expect there to be growth in athletic budgets just as there is growth in the rest of the university. What I'm talking about is the rate of growth and whether the rate of growth is justified. The rate of expenditure being higher than the university on average ... is not a sustainable business plan.

(Wieberg, 2005, pp. 1–2)

Leadership behavior

A second major focus of the research on leadership has been on the behaviors of the effective leader. In addition to studying the leader's personality, assumptions, and expectations, researchers have attempted to analyze and understand what the effective leader actually does.

In some of the initial work on leader behavior, researchers suggested that leadership could be defined as a combination of two different kinds of behavior: task behavior and relations behavior (Katz *et al.*, 1950; Fleishman *et al.*, 1955). Task behavior is defined as leader behavior focusing on the design and completion of a specific task. It includes setting goals and establishing priorities, providing direction and instruction, and supervising and monitoring tasks to completion. In contrast, relations behavior focuses on satisfying the needs of the people performing the task and includes providing support and encouragement, answering questions, and problem solving with followers. A more complete comparison of task and relations behaviors is shown in Box 8.5.

BOX 8.5 DIFFERENCES BETWEEN LEADER TASK AND LEADER RELATIONS BEHAVIOR

Task behavior	Relations behavior
■ Goal setting	■ Giving support
■ Organizing	■ Communicating
■ Establishing time lines	■ Facilitating interactions
■ Directing	■ Active listening
■ Controlling	■ Providing feedback

These studies defined leadership as various combinations of these two kinds of behaviors. The different combinations of leader behaviors are often called leadership styles. Defining leadership in these terms was important in that research on leadership could now concentrate on identifying which combination of leader task and relations behaviors, or which leadership style, resulted in the most effective leadership.

284

Styles of leadership

Robert Blake and Jane Mouton (1982, 1985) created the "Leadership Grid" to present in graphic form the leadership styles possible from integrating task and relations behavior. They call the task behavior dimension "concern for production" and the relations behavior dimension "concern for people." Based on an extensive review of the leadership research then available, Blake and Mouton concluded that the most effective pattern or style of leadership combines high levels of concern both for people and production. They termed this high task/high relations behavior approach the team management style of leadership. According to Blake and Mouton, team management was the leadership style used in over 60 percent of situations reported in the research.

From the Blake and Mouton Leadership Grid point of view, the task of management is to ensure that leaders have the skills necessary to implement the team management approach to leadership effectively. To develop these team management skills, training is the key. Individuals being prepared for leadership positions must be provided with training and work experiences that will enable them to be both high task and high relations in their leadership behavior.

In the case of both Byers and Brand, each faced challenges relating to finances and how best to manage these challenges to benefit all association members. The work of Blake and Mouton seemed to have answered the question of which pattern of leader behavior is effective in *most* situations, but the challenges encountered by the NCAA in other areas raises an even more difficult question: how to determine which leader behavior pattern might be most effective in a *particular* situation.

Contingency leadership

The contingency theory of leadership claims there is no "one best way" to lead or influence people, and that leadership style depends on the situation. Supporters of the contingency view point out that the team management approach represents only 60 percent of the success stories in the research on leadership styles. They say that many situations require leaders who are high-involvement team manager types, similar to the NCAA in the 1960s and 1970s under Byers. Other situations may require a leader who encourages greater participation by followers in establishing goals and direction, such as Brand. The new head of the NCAA, Dr. Mark Emmert, named to the post in October 2010, will require these skills to face an ever-emerging set of issues.

According to the contingency theory of leadership, different leadership styles are effective in different situations, and there are a number of situational or contingency models of leadership. In the situational leadership model, developed by Paul Hersey and Ken Blanchard (1982), the key situational variables for a leader to consider are the competency and commitment of his or her followers. The leader must first determine the level of training, education, and experience of the followers (*competency*), as well as their level of motivation and confidence (*commitment*) to perform the task. These two variables together they called the *readiness level* of the followers. The leader must then match his or her style of leadership to these key follower variables. Hersey and Blanchard's four options in terms of leadership style and the matching degrees of follower readiness are shown in Box 8.6.

Regardless of the specific aspects on which the situation is focused, all of the contingency models emphasize that different styles of leadership are required for different kinds of situations. The challenge for the sport manager is to be flexible in his or her approach to providing the support and direction needed for high performance.

Transformational leadership

Most of the research on leadership, including the models described in the previous section, has focused on the leadership of organizations. The emphasis has been on how managers influence subordinates to perform well. Historian James McGregor Burns, in his efforts to understand the essence of effective leadership, took a different approach. Burns reviewed and analyzed the actions of important political and social leaders such as Jesus Christ, Mahatma Ghandi, and Franklin D. Roosevelt. Based on his research, Burns (1978) coined the term transformational leadership in relation to those leaders who actually transform or change the beliefs, attitudes, and needs of followers. Traditional models of leadership, as we have said, have been concerned with directing and supporting the performance of followers. These are what have been called transactional leadership, because the leader provides rewards, recognition, support, and direction as a part of an exchange for follower performance consistent with the organization's goals.

BOX 8.6 HERSEY AND BLANCHARD'S FOUR LEADERSHIP STYLES

Relationship behavior (supportive behavior)	Leader behavior	
	Share ideas and facilitate in decision making PARTICIPATING	Explain decisions and provide opportunity for clarification SELLING
	DELEGATING Turn over responsibility for decisions and implementation	TELLING Provide specific instructions and closely supervise performance
	Task behavior (guidance)	

Motivation and leadership and intercollegiate athletics

In recent years, as interest in achieving continually higher levels of performance has increased dramatically, a number of researchers and theorists have focused their efforts on identifying what the essential elements of transformational leadership might be. Researchers James Kouzes and Barry Posner (1987, 1990) identified five behaviors common to transformational leaders (see Box 8.7).

BOX 8.7 CHARACTERISTICS OF A TRANSFORMATIONAL LEADER

- *They inspire a shared vision.* They have a mission in which they passionately believe, and they tirelessly enlist others to share in that mission and to help make it happen.
- *They challenge the process.* They are unwilling to accept things as they are, they push for change, and they risk mistakes to find better solutions.
- *They enable others to act.* They emphasize cooperation and collaboration. They build teams and empower their followers.
- *They model the way.* They live their beliefs. They communicate their vision through the consistency of their actions.
- *They encourage the heart.* They dramatize encouragement, reward performance, and celebrate winning. They love their people, their customers, their products, and their work.

The transformational leader, in contrast, endeavors to transform the belief system of his or her followers to enable them to achieve new and significantly higher levels of performance. Each of the NCAA's heads have made successful transactional leadership moves, some of which have been outlined above. As to what the new president Mark Emmert faces, one conference commissioner noted that the job has become more attractive to prospective replacements because it has "more teeth," but that it is also more challenging than when Brand took office in 2003 because the financial issues facing the membership are more complex (Smith, 2009, p. 25). When asked by *Street & Smith's SportsBusiness Journal* writer Michael Smith to identify the other pressing issues the next president will need to take on, NCAA executives, media rights holders, conference commissioners, and ADs listed fiscal responsibility, the revenue disparity amongst Division I schools due to Bowl Championship Series affiliation, a possible playoff to replace the bowls in the Football Bowl Subdivision (FBS), and diversity in hiring head coaches at FBS schools. Interestingly, this list differed little from what Myles Brand faced when he took over in 2003, suggesting that the issues are deep-seated and will require extensive effort to tackle (Smith, 2009).

Part of what will enable new NCAA head Mark Emmert to guide the association through this rocky period will be explained by his embodiment of the five transformational

287

leadership traits identified by Kouzes and Posner. To inspire a shared vision to take up the issue of how to control spending, a major issue championed by his predecessor (two years after taking office, Brand launched a campaign for fiscal responsibility at the annual convention, because, as he observed in a convention address, "the spending spiral has not abated"), many ADs expressed doubt over whether the NCAA could impact the trend. Said University of Texas AD DeLoss Dodds: "The presidents, I guess, could agree in principle that they want to [rein in spending], but in practicality I don't know how it happens" (Wieberg, 2005, p. 2).

Brand had looked to his former presidential colleagues to advance his vision for the future of college sports, as evidenced by *The second-century imperatives: Presidential leadership – institutional accountability*, a report released in 2006 by the NCAA's Presidential Task Force on the Future of Division I Athletics. The task force, comprised of sitting and former school presidents, compiled the report in response to NCAA data that indicated that intercollegiate athletics costs were indeed rising at a rate that was, as pointed out by Brand in the report's introduction, "not sustainable ... and has been growing at a rate two to three times faster than the rest of higher education over the last decade." In addition, data showed that in spending to improve athletics facilities, many institutions held mortgages that represented, in Brand's words, "on average 20 percent of intercollegiate athletics spending. This factor puts institutions at risk over decades of time if the popularity of college sports wanes" ("NCAA Presidential Task Force," 2006, p. 4). Although the report stated and restated numerous times that no financial crisis was imminent, these factors, admitted Brand, when combined with what he identified as "the popularity of intercollegiate athletics to media and marketing," as well as increased pressures to win and generate revenue, created an atmosphere where "avid fans or trustees" interfered with presidential authority, and where "the integration of athletics within the academy ... and the primacy of education in the student-athlete experience have all been threatened" ("NCAA Presidential Task Force," 2006, p. 4).

In addressing the financial crisis issue, Emmert stated simply that "there are more collisions between the collegiate and the commercial models than ever before ... the whole environment right now is very challenging" (Brennan, 2012, p. 1). Figures show that all NCAA institutions spend approximately $7.75 billion a year on athletic programs, slightly less than the $7.8 billion in revenues generated. The largest and fastest-growing expense for Division I programs are the expenses for coaches and support staff salaries. The median salary for head football coaches grew 47 percent between 2004 and 2006, rising from $582,000 to $855,000, while the median salary for head men's basketball coaches rose 15 percent, to $611,900. Athletic aid and salaries combined for at least 50 percent of D-I expenses (Wolverton, 2006; Kelderman, 2008).

288

There is specific information from other sources, moreover, that indicates the degree to which there is a significant gap in profits and revenues among D-I programs. According to data from the United States Department of Education based on the fiscal year ending June 30, 2006, the University of Notre Dame's athletic department's revenues exceeded expenses by $22.7 million, the largest departmental differential that year. The other most profitable programs were at the University of Georgia ($20.5 million), the University of Central Florida ($19.5 million), and the University of Michigan ($17.5 million). Schools that endured low revenues and either lost money or broke even included the Virginia Military Institute ($5.5 million in revenues, and a loss of $30,000), the University of Louisiana-Monroe (which broke even on $7.2 million in revenue), and the University of Louisiana-Lafayette ($8 million in revenue, also breaking even).

The ultimate rationale behind these increases in expenditures is, according to Todd Diacon, vice provost for academic operations and the faculty athletics representative at the University of Tennessee, the concept that has schools thinking, "if you field a team, you ought to be able to compete to win," which has meant an increased pressure to spend heavily even on sports that don't generate revenue. "Even if we win the NCAA championship in swimming, that's not going to pay for the pool" the school just built, said Diacon (Kelderman, 2008, p. A15). The pool is only part of a construction binge on the Tennessee campus that includes a new softball stadium, a new soccer stadium, and plans for new facilities for golf, volleyball, and an indoor track (Kelderman, 2008).

So it is clear that athletic spending is increasing, and it may also be true that while the *Second-century imperatives* report indicated that no crisis was imminent, there was legitimate reason for concern. Schools seem to be willing to lose money on athletics programs because, as pointed out by Darin Spease, president of the College Athletic Business Management Association, there is increasing pressure to keep up with the spending of schools such as Tennessee, even at schools in other conferences and in the other divisional classifications. Said Spease, a senior associate AD at the University of North Carolina-Charlotte: "As long as there is an elite group of schools with generous alums, I don't see that it ends. I don't know how the rank-and-file schools compete" (Kelderman, 2008, p. A15). Stephen Trachtenberg, president of George Washington University, defends such expansionary actions this way: "I think it's very hard to say you're committed to excellence if you're prepared to deny excellence in a very conspicuous and public aspect of your enterprise" (Schoenfeld, 2006, p. 29).

The issue Emmert must deal with, therefore, is the long-standing paradox facing intercollegiate athletic managers, specifically the fact that some believe that intercollegiate athletics is not part of the educational experience, and should not be drawing resources away from the institution. Under this line of thinking, intercollegiate athletics departments should be self-supporting and look to generate revenues in whatever way it can. But, as departments and programs begin to focus too extensively on profits, and the wins needed to generate them, these departments are then seen as deviating from the educational mission of the institution. Therefore, others argue that to integrate athletics into the institution, the institution must be prepared to pay for it and not expect athletic departments to become commercialized entities, the very pressure point Emmert identifies above.

In this vein, Emmert will need to challenge the process by thinking about new ways for the association and its members to deal with other challenges to the issue of finances. In 2012, ESPN.com's Eamonn Brennan put this question to Emmert: "Why can't college athletes be paid? Or, why is it the position of the NCAA that college athletes shouldn't be paid?" Emmert responded:

> Because this is about a model completely different than professional athletics. College athletics has always been about college students who happen to be athletes … The whole notion is that these are young men and young women who come to universities, who play athletics vocationally and represent their schools. When you convert those student-athletes into professional athletes, then they're virtually no different than NBA and NFL or MLB.
>
> (Brennan, 2012, p. 1)

The challenge for Emmert in communicating this, however, is that many fans and stakeholder groups see little to distinguish between the game product and presentation of the NCAA Division I men's basketball tournament, where the participants are not compensated monetarily, and the NBA playoffs, where the participants are compensated handsomely.

When asked whether Emmert and the NCAA could address this double-standard perception through the adoption of what Brennan described as an "Olympics-style model, where amateurism still exists in some form but athletes are allowed to go outside and secure endorsements," Emmert responded:

> The problem is the analogy doesn't work … When a young man or woman is trying out for the Olympic rowing team, the Swedes aren't over here recruiting them. If they're an American, they're an American. They row for America. That's that. Imagine if you were going to have sponsorships in oh, let's just say, the state of Alabama. Do you think there might be competition between sponsorships between Auburn and Alabama? Or between Michigan and Ohio State? Or between Texas and Oklahoma? You would immediately convert it into a professional model, with students going to the highest bidder. And then they're no longer student-athletes, they're professionals.
>
> (Brennan, 2012, p. 1)

While Emmert raises points that are logical in theory – and acknowledges the significant stakes in the recruiting battles between rival schools – his response doesn't seem to address the root problem and contradictions voiced by fans and stakeholders. To address this problem, Emmert will need to model the way and communicate a vision of stakeholder financial fairness. Recently Emmert expressed discomfort over his own annual seven-figure salary, and when asked by an interviewer on the PBS program *Frontline*, "I wonder why you're so sensitive about your remuneration here at the NCAA," Emmert retorted, "I'm not sensitive about it. I simply don't talk about it" ("Interview," 2011, p. 1).

Finally, Emmert will need to encourage the hearts of all stakeholders on the issue of financial equity, especially Division I men's basketball and football participants, since these are the two sports from which significant revenues are generated. But on this score as well Emmert has staked out a potentially unpopular stance when he told PBS' *Frontline* that it "would be utterly unacceptable ... to convert students into employees. We don't pay our student-athletes." Emmert justified his position this way:

> We provide them with remarkable opportunities to get an education at the finest universities on earth – that's American universities and colleges – to gain access to the best coaches and the best trainers, to develop their skills and abilities, so if they have the potential, that small proportion, to go on and play in professional sports, we're helping them develop those skills, and they can go do it.
>
> If they choose to not go on, or if they don't have those skills or abilities, then they get to go on in life and be successful as a young man or a young woman. I find that to be a perfectly appropriate balance. And indeed, most people in the world do, because there are many, many, many students around the world who would love nothing more than to be able to come to an American university and gain access to American intercollegiate athletics, because it's such a great place to develop skill and to have that great experience.
>
> ("Interview," 2011, p. 1)

Again, while Emmert's position may have validity (but may also be sending a mixed message of the primary importance of pursuing an education undercut by the fact that the NCAA is also a training ground for some to pursue athletic careers after college), he and other Division I intercollegiate athletic managers must continue to deal with the perceptions of financial inequities between him, ADs, and coaches who earn multi-million dollar salaries, and certain student-athletes who are seen as the real producers of the revenues that pay these salaries but who themselves prosper comparatively very little from it. If Emmert and the NCAA enterprise is to continue to meet its stated goals and missions, he will need to continue to strive to become a transformational leader and transform the belief system of interested stakeholders.

Leadership and communication

Effective leadership requires effective communication. Virtually all the leader behaviors, practices, and skills presented in this chapter involve communication. Every leadership task – from providing direction, support, and encouragement to providing inspiration and meaning – can be accomplished only through effective communication.

The conditions for effective communication

Scholar Howard Gardner (Gardner with Laskin, 1996) took an approach similar to Burns in seeking to understand the nature of leadership. In studying significant social, political, religious, and business leaders, Gardner identified four factors that he cites as crucial to the practice of effective leadership, each of which relates to the key function of communication. As noted above, Emmert will face the dual tests of building on the successes of his predecessors and identifying new challenges as they emerge, and his success in this endeavor will be partly determined by Gardner's factors.

A tie to followers. Gardner states that the relationship between leaders and followers must be on-going, active, and dynamic, and leaders and followers must take cues from each other. Leaders and followers, says Gardner, must work together to build organizations that embody their common values. This type of connection and collaboration cannot occur without communication. As noted above, Emmert's ties to the college climate are strong, as he has been a college president at both the University of Washington and Louisiana State University, both members of the NCAA's Division I classification, and has also served as an administrator at several other NCAA D-I schools, including the University of Colorado and the University of Connecticut.

A certain rhythm of life. Gardner states that a leader must be in regular contact with his or her followers while maintaining a sense of his or her own mind, thoughts, values, and strategies. This will be a particular challenge for Emmert, who like all NCAA heads will be challenged to meet these expectations, keeping contact with the many stakeholder groups while sustaining his own individual concepts of what is important for the successful operation of the NCAA. In a recent interview with ESPN, Emmert admitted that

> there has historically been an impression that the NCAA is sort of a black box and impermeable. I want to make sure that we're being as transparent and as open as we can about what we do, why we do it, and how we're doing it.
>
> (Brennan, 2012, p. 1)

Communication with these groups will be critical to maintaining this regular and constant contact.

An evident relation between stories and embodiments. Gardner argues that leaders exercise their influence through the stories and messages they communicate and through the traits they embody. To Gardner, these stories grow out of life experiences and are naturally embodied in the presentation of the self. Before Emmert was hired, a poll of more than 1,100 senior industry executives indicated that 29 percent thought that Myles Brand's replacement should also have been a college president, 26 percent felt he or she should have been a college AD, and 17 percent listed professional sports property executive as the most important qualification. The fact that Emmert had only one of those criteria on his resume and all his other significant work experience had been in higher education administrative roles means that to meet the challenges facing the association Emmert will need to overcome those who might doubt his abilities and knowledge relating to intercollegiate athletics.

The centrality of choice. To Gardner, effective leaders are those who are chosen by followers, rather than those who take power by means of brute force. Media reports noted that Emmert was selected over at least three other finalists, which included U.S. Senator Evan Bayh (whose father Birch, also a former U.S. Senator, was a key architect of the 1972 federal law that included passage of Title IX), Lt. Gen. Franklin "Buster" Hagenbeck, superintendent of the United States Military Academy, and Beth Brooke, a global vice chairman with the accounting firm Ernst & Young (Brooke played basketball at Purdue University and, according to media reports, is consistently ranked by *Forbes* magazine as one of the "world's 100 most powerful women") (Wieberg, 2010, p. 1).

Steve Wieberg of *USA Today* stated that over 100 candidates emerged during the search that started in October 2009. The NCAA's top-level executive committee, chaired by Oregon State University President Ed Ray, made the decision, but Wieberg stated that the selection of Emmert, a middle-aged white male, "may disappoint activists who expressed hope at the start that a female or minority administrator could wind up leading the NCAA for the first time" (2010, p. 1).

Others were critical of the hire for reasons connected to Emmert's job performance at Washington. "I wondered how the hell the NCAA saw him fit to be interviewed, much less hired, as its president," said author Derek Johnson. "Since a NCAA president oversees the nation's Division I athletic programs ... the [University of Washington (UW)] football program under Emmert should have been looked to as a predictor of his performance as NCAA president." Johnson notes that while Emmert was president at Washington, the program lost 76 percent of its games while the number of season ticket holders dropped by 20,000. "The NCAA presumably wanted a strong leader," posits Johnson, "instead, they hired a man who failed to investigate the reasons behind [former UW football coach] Tyrone Willingham's notorious firing from [his former post at the University of] Notre Dame." Johnson purports that if Emmert had "conducted due diligence and talked to people from Notre Dame, he would have heard stories of an arrogant and incompetent coach who exerted little effort in recruiting and golfed multiple times a week during the football season" (Johnson, 2011, p. 1).

Johnson also blames Emmert for retaining Willingham "despite the fact his coach was mismanaging the program and was loathed by most of his players," and that athletic department employees "were apologizing repeatedly to the players for having to endure Willingham's arrogant and surly behavior." Johnson also claims that "one of Emmert's first big decisions" at Washington was the hiring of former Vanderbilt University AD Todd Turner as athletic director. "Over the next four years," Johnson asserts, "Turner would fail miserably as a fundraiser and constantly respond to his critics with contempt by accusing them of overvaluing wins and losses" (Johnson, 2011, p. 1).

Although Emmert was chosen by the leadership of the NCAA in accord with its stated processes, it seems that that might not be enough to convince many stakeholders of the correctness of the decision.

SUMMARY

Creating a high-performance work force has become an essential management responsibility, particularly with the increased level and intensity of global competition that sport organizations face. Four theories help managers understand the factors that influence and shape individual and group performance. First, goals provide the direction and feedback to engage and to challenge people toward high levels of performance. Second, reinforcement theory provides the basis for shaping behavior through a carefully selected set of consequences. Next, needs theory suggests that managers must understand the needs level of employees and create opportunities for them to pursue the satisfaction of their needs in the workplace. Lastly, expectancy theory emphasizes the links between success and the rewards that people value.

Reflecting ideas from this range of theories, sport organizations increasingly are focusing their efforts in four areas: (1) defining tasks in the most challenging and specific terms possible; (2) providing continuous training to ensure the competence and confidence required for high performance; (3) empowering employees by sharing responsibility with them for decisions and problem solving around their own performance; and (4) providing employees a stake in the success of the organization, a reason to pursue high performance.

Leadership is the process of directing and supporting others in pursuit of the organization's missions and goals. With the competitive pressure of the changing international sport environment, leadership is more important than ever as sport organizations seek to develop high-performance work forces.

294

One focus of the research on leadership has been on the leader as a person, on the psychology of the leader. This research has resulted in identifying a number of personality traits that are associated with effective leaders. Additionally, in terms of the psychology of the leader, the importance of leader expectations has been documented.

Research has also examined the behaviors of effective leaders. Initially the focus was on identifying the one most effective leadership style. Subsequent research resulted in developing contingency models of leadership that emphasize the importance of matching leadership style to the needs or demands of the situation. Most recently there has been interest in the transformational leader, the leader who succeeds in changing the beliefs and attitudes of followers to enable them to achieve unprecedented levels of performance.

Communication is the tool through which the leader provides support and direction. Effective communication requires an understanding on the manager's part of followers' needs and concerns. For this reason, effective communication relies on a leader's tie to followers as each takes cues from the other, a certain rhythm of life where leaders stay in regular contact with followers, an evident relation between stories and embodiments, and the centrality of choice.

The leadership responsibility in all sport organizations is a critical one. In many ways, leadership represents the connection between the sport organization and its people. Understanding how to develop most effectively and to maintain the leadership connection is a significant challenge, to say the least. Intercollegiate athletic managers met different aspects of this challenge, proving that high performance is a difficult goal to achieve in such a complex set of organizational relationships, but possible when the leadership connection works.

MANAGEMENT EXERCISE: PAC-10 + 2 + ? = >?

On July 1, 2011, Pac-12 Conference Commissioner Larry Scott was making the rounds in San Francisco, going from meeting to meeting at downtown restaurants. Scott had been busy that day, since the conference had formally introduced its two new members, the University of Colorado and the University of Utah. According to Antonio Gonzales of the *Arizona Republic* newspaper, Scott "does not waste a moment. There's a network to launch, marketing opportunities to pursue, and a host of other issues to capitalize on with the momentum behind the league's growing national spotlight" (2011, p. 1). But Scott is no stranger to innovation, having served as the chairman of the Women's Tennis Association (WTA) and working to force Grand Slam tournament events to give women prize money equal to that given to men. Of his time at the WTA, a former staffer said of Scott: "He has tremendous vision in marketing the game, in thinking forward." Of his own career path, Scott said: "I have this entrepreneurial bug about me. For me, my satisfaction has to come from if I'm motivated or excited or do I see another hill to climb" (Gonzales, 2011, p. 1).

Gonzales notes that when Scott took over in 2009, the then Pac-10 Conference provided more than a significant hill for Scott to climb. The affiliation (the University of Arizona, Arizona State University, the University of California-Los Angeles, the University of Southern California, Stanford University, the University of California-Berkeley, the University of Oregon, Oregon State University, the University of Washington, and Washington State University) "was stuck in neutral" (2011, p. 1) and was in need of Scott's abilities. At that time, speculation was running high over the possible shifting of as many as a dozen schools among the existing NCAA Division I Football Bowl Championship conferences. Driving these changes, wrote Pete Thamel of *The New York Times*, was "television money ... the biggest consideration [with] little regard being given to geography or tradition" of the existing conference configurations (2010b, p. D2). As noted by many, the Pac-10 expansion was motivated by the creation of its own TV network, especially since the creation of the Big Ten Network was so lucrative to that grouping (now up to 12 schools with the recent addition of the University of Nebraska). At the time, its football broadcast deals with ESPN and Fox Sports Net were worth $222 million. At the very least, a Pac-10 expansion could provide increased leverage in negotiations with traditional broadcast outlets. A post-season football championship game, which requires 12 members to be instituted, was also an important motivator for the Pac-10.

Thamel wrote that these moves were a significant managerial departure for the Pac-10, founded in 1915 by Cal-Berkeley, Washington, Oregon, and Oregon State, had "always clung to their traditional roots with white-knuckle fervor," but that the potential for increased revenues had "dramatically transformed" it "from staid traditionalists to potential homewreckers" (2010a, p. B9). But Western Athletic Conference commissioner Karl Benson defended the approach of commissioner Scott: "He's done what he was hired to do. That's to change the way the Pac-10 has done business in the past ... In light of the economic crisis in higher education and intercollegiate athletics, conferences are being looked at and expected by our membership to maximize revenues. This is all about maximizing revenues at the top" (Thamel, 2010e, p. B12).

On June 10, 2010, a day before Nebraska's board of regents was set to vote on its school's athletic future in moving to the Big Ten, Thamel also reported that Big 12 commissioner Dan Beebe was laboring to save the conference. Said Beebe: "It's certainly been the most challenging time of my career ... There's no stone left unturned or bullet in the chamber. I'm doing everything I can." A Big 12 AD said: "I think people realize that there's something still viable, whether it remains at 11 or 10 or whether we look to expand back to 12 to keep this going" (Thamel, 2010c, p. B14). On D-Day 2010 (June 11), Colorado did indeed jump to the Pac-10. Colorado AD

Mike Bohn acknowledged that many details still needed to be ironed out concerning the Buffs' move to the Pac-10, noting: "There are numerous issues. The faster we can resolve those issues, it will allow a lot of people to plan and move forward" (Moss, 2010, p. 1). According to Irv Moss of *The Denver Post*, Colorado faced an approximately $10 million buyout to leave the Big 12 after the 2011 season, but it is not clear how big the penalty would be if the school left after the 2010 season.

Utah became the final piece for the Pac-10 when it agreed to leave the Mountain West Conference, reducing that grouping to nine. On July 3, the school officially announced the move, which occured fully in 2011. Utah president Michael Young said: "We are thrilled and delighted with this invitation," and Utah Governor Gary Herbert, who attended Brigham Young University, called it a "red-letter day ... Today, the university is Utah's university" (Wodraska, 2010, p. 1). Lya Wodraska of the *Salt Lake Tribune* commented: "With the move comes more exposure, more money, and yes, more pressure to prove it belongs in the big leagues." According to Utah AD Chris Hill, the school wouldn't begin to share conference revenues immediately, but commented: "When you compete for championships in the Pac-10, you compete for national championships." Head football coach Kyle Whittingham said of the move: "It's a win–win for us. No question about it. It's a win–win for the university" (Wodraska, 2010, p. 1).

But soon thereafter speculation was already beginning on the results of these changes. Syracuse University AD Jake Crouthamel (whose school was spurned by the Atlantic Coast Conference (ACC) a decade ago and by the Big Ten in 2010, but finally got the nod from the ACC in 2012) believed the moves were a prelude to something much bigger: "I see this coming down to four major conferences ... The presidents sit back there and they say that we'd like to have similar academic institutions and research institutions and it's bull ... The motivator is money and the issue is TV" (Thamel, 2010c, pp. B9, B14). Thamel commented that these four superconferences could form an alliance and secede from the NCAA. This is something that those who follow intercollegiate athletics know is a move that has been long predicted, and opined that the Pac-10's Scott would go hard after other teams from the Big 12, such as the University of Oklahoma, Oklahoma State University, the University of Texas, and Texas A&M University, with Texas as the key factor. The moves would give the Pac-10 entrée into two more top-20 TV markets (Dallas and Houston). An unnamed Big 12 "athletic official" commented that "Texas is the linchpin" (Thamel, 2010b, p. D2), meaning that if Texas were to go, others would be sure to follow.

So is this conference shifting over, or is the ever-entrepreneurial Larry Scott and the Pac-12 looking to become even bigger through adding the likes of Texas, among others, to get to 16? As we noted earlier, in supporting high-performance work teams, the focus of the leader's energy and activities shifts to members of the organization – both at the individual school level as well as the conference level. Larry Scott's

297

task is to reduce or eliminate the barriers and interference that might hinder performance and to assist in securing the resources member schools need to achieve their goals. What barriers and interference? What resources?

QUESTIONS FOR YOU TO CONSIDER

1   Can Scott's behaviors in response to shifting conference alignments influence the performance of followers and other stakeholder groups? How might he affect them positively? How might he affect them negatively? What specific leader behaviors would you recommend to solve Scott's challenge? Cite models or concepts from this chapter to support your recommendations.

2   How can Scott become a transformational leader for the Pac-12 as it looks to capitalize on additional expansion opportunities?

3   Which of the performance motivation theories can Scott adopt to promote the Pac-12's entrée into new forms of digital media and expanded media outlets?

4   Given what you have read concerning the Pac-12 and associated moves, how should Jon LeCrone of the Horizon League proceed given that Butler University is considering a jump to the Atlantic 10?

CHAPTER 9

HUMAN RESOURCE MANAGEMENT AND THE TOUR SPORT INDUSTRY

INTRODUCTION

Human resources are considered to be the sport organization's most important asset. People, in essence, are the organization. Their skills, their knowledge, and their abilities dramatically shape the organization and have a critical impact on the organization's ability to carry out its mission and achieve its goals. In this chapter, the reader will be introduced to the human resource function through an examination of the tour sport industry. Students will consider the human resource function within the sport organization from the perspective of both potential employee and manager within the organization who is responsible for the staffing function.

Check the stats

Purpose
To present and promote sport competition through single events and series.

Stakeholders
Tour athletes, tour facilities, facility designers and managers, maintenance and equipment providers, host communities, spectators, sponsors, media, sport governing bodies/agencies, volunteers, media, general public, and federal, state, and local government.

Size and scope
The tour sport industry consists of thousands of professional and amateur sport events and series, such as traditional tour sports, outdoor adventure/extreme sports, and sport entertainment enterprises.

Governance

Federal, state, and local regulation. Professional organizations, associations, and trade groups such as the United States Golf Association, Professional Golf Association, International Tennis Federation, International Dragon Boat Federation, Professional Rodeo Cowboys Association, Action Sports World Tour, Ultimate Fighting Championship, Professional Bull Riders Circuit, Bass Anglers Sportsman Society, and National Association for Stock Car Auto Racing.

Inside look: can Stephen get a job?

Stephen Paul had just completed his senior year in college and was planning to graduate in two weeks. Stephen has been an avid golfer all his life. He had received his first set of clubs from his parents for his fifth birthday and had hung out at his local golf course about every spare moment since then. Stephen read everything he could about golf and the golf business. He watched the Golf Channel every day and subscribed to several golf magazines. He secured his first part-time job at the course on the grounds maintenance staff when he was 14. For the next eight years, Stephen spent summer vacations, holidays, weekends, and after-school time working at the course in a variety of capacities. He worked in the pro shop, at the snack bar, at tournaments, and on the course itself. Stephen was eager to learn everything he could about the golf business and was happy to take on any job that came his way. Stephen scheduled tee-times, took inventory in the pro shop, resolved customer complaints, met with golf equipment sales representatives, assisted the pro with junior lessons, helped with landscaping, and even cleaned carts.

During Stephen's college years, he participated on the university golf team and, as part of his sport management curriculum, completed an internship with Titleist. He also volunteered at several annual charity golf tournaments, assisted with the intramural golf program, and worked three nights a week as an assistant manager of the golf department at a large retail sporting goods store. Stephen also volunteered to help with the university athletic department golf tournament. He coordinated student volunteers and managed golfer registration. At the tournament, Stephen was able to work directly with corporate sponsors and had the opportunity to meet and become friends with many of the university alumni including several alumni who work in the golf industry. In fact, it was through one of these contacts that Stephen was able to secure the internship at Titleist. At Titleist, Stephen was invited to attend several Professional Golf Association (PGA) and Ladies Professional Golf Association (LPGA) tournaments. At each event, Stephen effectively networked as his supervisor introduced him to PGA and LPGA officials, golf course managers, sponsors, members of the media, and some players. Stephen began following some of the top golf reporters on Twitter and made it a point to check golf business websites daily. His supervisor gave Stephen various golf trade papers and insider newsletters to read. At the end of his internship, Stephen felt a new enthusiasm for his major and felt for the first time that he really had a good idea of what he wanted to do with his passion for golf.

As the last few months of his undergraduate program and his final season of collegiate golf began to wind down, Stephen scheduled an appointment with his college advisor to discuss his post-college plans. He knew he wanted to work in the golf industry and was particularly interested in tour events. He was eager to explore his options. What should he do? Where should he look? How should he start? Looking over the résumé he developed with the university's placement counselor, Stephen felt good about both his experience and his education. He knew he was ready to start his professional career and fully expected to realize his life-long dream of working in tour sport. More than anything else, Stephen wanted a job that involved professional golf.

THE TOUR SPORT INDUSTRY SEGMENT

The tour sport industry consists of those sport organizations that sponsor and participate in sport competitions at various tour event site locales throughout their season. It may be useful to look at the tour sport industry as consisting of three specific segments: traditional tour sports (e.g. golf, tennis, auto racing), outdoor adventure or action sports (e.g. skateboarding, BMX, fishing, surfing, mountain climbing, log rolling), and commercial sport entertainment (e.g. WWE and Harlem Globetrotters). See Table 9.1 below for an overview.

The typical tour sport event usually features a number of individuals or teams that compete in a tournament-type format. Results of individual events may or may not be compiled and recorded as part of a tour series with individual contestants or teams competing for points toward a tour season championship. Such events can take place on a single day or may be held over a period of days. Among the sports currently being offered through the tour sport system are tennis, golf, auto racing, rodeo, volleyball, speed boating, mountain biking, mixed martial arts, running, bicycling, skiing, motor cross, skateboarding, kayaking, fishing, and white water rafting.

Table 9.1 Tour sport industry segments

Categories	Examples of sport organizations
Traditional tour sports	PGA, LPGA, ATP, NASCAR
Outdoor adventure/action sports	Summer and Winter X Games, Cross Endurance Games, Association of Surfing Professionals (ASP) World Tour
Sport entertainment	Harlem Globetrotters, World Wrestling Entertainment (WWE)

Those activities classified as traditional tour sports are those that are usually more mainstream sports and have a significant history. Examples include professional golf, tennis, and auto racing. These traditional-type sport tours have a set series or calendar of events for a given season. Event sites frequently vary and may be local, regional, national, or even international. In some cases, tours or series are set up geographically or by competitor classification; for example, in professional golf there are European, Canadian, American, Korean, and Australian tours as well as women's tours, men's tours, amateur tours, and seniors or champions tours.

The second category of tour sport includes outdoor adventure or action sports. These activities may also be called extreme, endurance, or free sport. These events often feature an amalgamation of competition or contests. This type of tour series encompasses those activities that are seen as being non-traditional in nature. They are characterized as being high-risk and dangerous activities that often involve intense levels of physical exertion or endurance. These sports usually present unique challenges related to speed and height as well as environmental conditions. Action sport athletes pride themselves on pushing the limits of human performance and skill as they attempt to jump higher, go faster, and add new twists and elements that have never been done before. Extreme sport athletes are also aware that uncontrollable conditions including wind, water, and weather conditions may have a significant impact on the individual's performance and safety. Participation in extreme sport events requires a high level of skill and a willingness to push both the human body and the sport equipment to the limit. These types of sports are usually individual rather than team based. Action sport events feature competition in sports such as motocross, freestyle skiing, surfing, base jumping, hang gliding, kayaking, and skateboarding. Where traditional sports are typically assessed on standard quantitative performance metrics such as time, score, order of finish, and distance, extreme sport athletes may additionally be evaluated on more subjective metrics such as aesthetics of skill demonstration and the judge's perceived difficulty of a particular trick or move.

Action sports have historically been identified with younger athletes who have created the extreme sport culture to counter what they have viewed as a conservative and excessively commercial traditional sport industry. In addition to being aligned with a certain demographic, these sports are also seen as being connected to a certain lifestyle, personality, or individual identity. The profile of these competitors and their fans contains words such as trendsetters, edgy, risk takers, non-traditional, free spirited, cool, and rebellious. Interestingly enough, it may be argued that in the creation of these extreme sport tours and competitions, extreme athletes and their fans have begun to adopt some of the trappings of highly organized traditional sports (corporate sponsorship, endorsements, television deals) that this counterculture sport previously criticized. In effect, these events that had been considered fringe have come into the mainstream through the formal organization of tour events, inclusion in the Olympic Games, and the subsequent popularization of extreme or action sport competition.

Other tour sport events in this category offer unique outdoor adventure activities rather than extreme sports. These events may include boating, hunting, fishing, target sports, timber sports, and sporting dogs. The Lumberjack World Championships, which is held annually in the United States, attracts lumberjacks from around the world to compete in events such as chopping, pole climbing, sawing, boom running, and log rolling. Over 100 male and female lumberjacks from countries such as Australia, Canada, and the Czech Republic demonstrate their speed, agility, and strength in front of thousands of spectators in an event that is considered to be a premier timber sports competition ("Welcome," 2012).

The third category of tour sports may be defined as sport entertainment. Sport entertainment events are highly commercial in nature and may have a predetermined outcome. The sport event is often tightly scripted and comedy or drama is played out within a sport context. The most well-known examples of sport entertainment include the Harlem Globetrotters and World Wrestling Entertainment (WWE). Both of these sport organizations offer sport entertainment as part of a tour or series and have been very successful in playing to full arenas throughout the country. Some tour sport entertainment teams, such as the King and His Court softball team, which disbanded in 2011, travel from city to city and often arrange to play a home team made up of local all-stars or celebrities as an exhibition or fund-raising event. Exhibition-type sport contests such as a tour of figure skating or gymnastic champions may be included in this category. A portion of the proceeds of these sport entertainment events may be designated to a local charity or the sponsoring organization. It is not unusual for these athletes to engage in community service activities while visiting the host city.

Another interesting feature of the tour sport industry is its dependence on sponsorship. Most tour sports are dependent on sponsorship because of the high cost involved in putting on these events. Partnerships with corporations, media, or businesses may bring a host of benefits to the event including equipment, volunteers, operations capital, media opportunities, and prize money. ESPN has actually created tour events as a way to develop compelling programming and attracting specific target audiences.

Sponsors may be secured on the tour series level, the individual event level, and on the athlete level. For example, NASCAR's championship series is known as the *Sprint* Cup Series. Western clothing manufacturer Wrangler is the title sponsor of the professional rodeo tour. One of the best examples of individual event sponsorship is the professional golf tour where events often carry title sponsors such as the *Farmers Insurance* Open, *Barclays* Golf Tournament, or the *FedEx* Championship Cup.

As noted in Chapter 7, individual athletes who participate in the tour sport system also often rely upon sponsorship. Recall that golfers, tennis players, cyclists, skateboarders, runners, surfers, and drivers often utilize corporate partnerships to help pay for entry fees, travel, equipment, lodging, food, clothing, and living expenses. Tennis players or golfers, for example, may sign a deal with a footwear, clothing, or equipment manufacturer. They may agree to use the particular brand of equipment in competition in return for free equipment or cash. A sponsor need not necessarily be obviously related to the particular sport. However, the corporate sponsor always seeks an appropriate fit with the property (series, event, or athlete) and the fan base. Each of these corporations utilize their association with the athlete and tour event to reach a wide variety of marketing goals including accessing specific target markets, increasing sales share, and enhancing brand recognition. Tour sport organizations and athletes ranging from horse racing, to speed boat racing, to bull riding have all utilized sponsorship to support their operation.

Certainly, auto racing and motor sports have deservedly received recognition as some of the most effective and efficient organizations and athletes in utilizing corporate sponsorship in the tour sport industry. Most tour series have a title sponsor as do individual races. Drivers and race teams have successfully leveraged sponsorships on the tour, series, event, and athlete level as well. The fact is that fans and media alike refer to cars not solely in terms of their drivers or race team, but also in conjunction with the car's main sponsor. It isn't NASCAR driver Jeff Gordon's #24 car or Hendrick Motor Sports #24 car, it's Jeff Gordon's #24 DuPont Chevrolet Impala. DuPont spends millions of dollars annually for the prominent hood, rear quarter panel, and back panel locations and the de facto naming rights for the car.

In 2010, DuPont extended its sponsorship of Gordon through the 2013 season and extended one of NASCAR's longest sponsor-driver relationships which began in 1992 (Murphy, 2010). DuPont and other makers or sellers of non-automotive products and services such as Home Depot, Lowe's, Go Daddy, McDonald's, Bass Pro Shops, Best Buy, Coors, and 5-Hour Energy Drink, along with companies that make automotive products such as Citgo, Interstate Batteries, and Pennzoil, make these investments because they know that fans identify strongly with the drivers. They also know that fans can identify and recall their sponsorship activities, and that they make purchasing decisions in part based on these sponsorships. Three-quarters of NASCAR fans buy products to support their favorite drivers (Hagstrom, 1998). Simply put, if a fan likes a driver who is sponsored by a particular beer company, then the fan is nearly 75 percent more likely to buy that brand of beer.

However, tough economic times have resulted in some NASCAR sponsors such as General Mills and UPS lessening their sponsorship while others including Red Bull have pulled out entirely. There also seems to be a shift in the cost of sponsorship. Ten years ago, a full sponsorship was commonly thought to cost anywhere between $20

Human resource managementand the tour sport industry

and $30 million depending on the driver, while today NASCAR insiders suggest that a good full sponsorship ranges between $13 and $15 million (Bernstein, 2012).

Despite economic uncertainty, tour sport organizations will continue to seek out sponsorship support. It is likely that new and emerging companies will seek out sponsorship benefits that may not have been previously available to them as they had been priced out of the market. As more and more tour sport organizations and athletes seek limited sponsor dollars, they will need to become increasingly creative in developing mutually beneficial sponsorship packages and delivering value to corporate partners.

HUMAN RESOURCES IN SPORT ORGANIZATIONS

The challenge of securing a position in the sport industry can be daunting to any graduating sport management student. While competition for jobs in sport is intense, there are many opportunities available to a skilled student who is willing to work hard, be persistent, and consider the full spectrum of segments that make up the sport industry. For students seeking to secure a job in sport, it is important to understand how the human resource function works in sport.

There really are two different tracks or types of human resource development in sport organizations. One is the athlete, performer, or talent track. It may be useful to think of this track as being the on-field side of human resource management. It is the means by which sport organizations secure athletes or other highly skilled specialty performers for their organization. In professional sport, for example, this track of human resource management is called player development. The player or talent development side of the sport business is distinct in that there are a variety of unique systems and practices that have been developed to ensure that the organization is able to find, develop, and secure players.

Components of this system are controlled on the league level for the express purpose of managing the on-field side of human resources. For example, league rules set forth the terms and conditions for acquiring players either through the draft or by trades. Through basic labor agreements with player unions, leagues may also set minimum salaries, requirements for free agency, and other important policies and guidelines for the management of player talent. Leagues, owners, and player unions have a vested interest in influencing how player talent is managed. Leagues and owners are particularly interested in the distribution and management of player talent and its effect on league operations. For example, the draft system has been seen as a mechanism by which competitive balance among teams can be created – teams that have finished poorly in any year have better draft positions and theoretically are able to improve their teams by bringing in new young talent. Player unions are focused on establishing and protecting players' interests, and influencing policies and procedures related to the treatment of players through the collective bargaining process.

There are a variety of systems related to player development. They include scouting, drafts, developmental leagues, coaches, trainers, and instructional leagues. Sport organizations that are dependent on the performance of player talent create divisions or departments that focus specifically on player development. The player development division, for example, is likely to include player talent specialists including scouts and instructors, whose sole focus is on the identification, evaluation, and acquisition of appropriate player talent. On the university or collegiate level, the player development function rests within the athletic department, and specifically with the individual sport program. Coaches and their staffs are responsible for identifying, recruiting, and developing player personnel. In university or college sport, player development is controlled not only through institutional oversight, but through the National Collegiate Athletic Association (NCAA) or other governing bodies that establish rules and guidelines pertaining to the recruitment and treatment of the student-athlete.

This first track of human resource management in sports includes coaches as well as players. Coaches are, in fact, the second critical component of the on-field talent equation. They are an important asset because of the unique abilities, personality, and skills they bring to the sport organization. The professional team sport coach (and, in the United States, the Division I high-profile head coach) has risen to celebrity status. Some sport organizations view the acquisition of a marquee coach as being more important than the acquisition of a star player. Because of the coach's role in managing player talent, his or her network, ability to handle the press, and relate with stakeholders, the head coach position is vital to the performance of the sport organization.

While this first track of human resource management in sport organizations has predominantly come to mean players and coaches as the on-field talent, this track also includes top-level sport broadcasters in the sport media industry segment. These broadcasters are those performers who work in the high-profile, on-air environment. For example, sport media personalities such as college basketball analyst Dick Vitale, ESPN's Michael Wilbon, and FoxSports' Erin Andrews are distinct talents who are unique assets to their sport organizations. They fall into this first track of human resource management because, like coaches and players, they are specialty talents. They are highly skilled and have reached the highest level of success within their profession. Like the player and coach, they provide the talent that directly shapes the sport organization's product and, ultimately, its success. Those jobs that comprise this first track of human resource management in sports are highly specialized, require distinct and unique talents, demand the very highest of salaries, and often represent complicated and complex negotiations and compensation packages.

Relatively few segments of the sport industry are extensively involved in on-field human resource management. On-field personnel management is, in fact, a specialty of human resource management in sport. Those few students who pursue careers in sport that involve the on-field side of human resource management can build on their academic preparation in the specialty of player development or scouting through targeted coursework, an appropriate internship, and professional experience in that area.

For those students who are interested in working in the on-field personnel area such as scouting or player talent evaluation, related opportunities in agency, scouting, coaching, and recruiting may be considered. Individuals who wish to pursue these careers must have knowledge in the areas of labor law, contract negotiation, agency, drafts, salary cap management, player talent evaluation tools including analytics, and collective bargaining. While some of these issues are addressed in other chapters throughout the text and to a limited degree in this chapter, it is important that any student interested in working with player personnel development be well versed in sport law and labor relations.

The second track of human resource management in sports may be best described as the off-field, front-office, or business side. This area deals with those employees who are not athlete performers, coaches, or media personalities, but are administrative or managerial. These jobs represent the business side of the organization. For example, where professional athletes and coaches provide the on-field talent, the concessions manager, marketing director, arena manager, fitness instructor, and ticket taker are the other half of the human resource equation for sport organizations.

In this chapter, emphasis is placed on the front-office, off-field, or business track because the majority of human resource management in the sport industry occurs in this area. For students studying sport management, a general understanding of human resource practices for the business side of sport is most important. Because students themselves are potential front-office and front-line employees and because they are likely to be involved in managing and hiring others, an understanding of this human resource management track is most relevant. Clearly, the majority of sport management students will pursue careers in sport that focus primarily on working within the business side of sport rather than becoming a professional athlete or media personality.

As students begin their job search in sport, they are often most concerned with personal issues. How does my résumé look? Who would hire me? What do I want to do? How much will I be paid? What type of benefits can I expect? Where do I want to live? Am I qualified for a job in this industry? What can I expect in an interview? While all of these questions are important to the job seeker, it is also very valuable to look at the job search from the sport organization's perspective as well. What is the sport organization looking for? Where will they find good candidates? How will they know that they are hiring the right person for the job? By looking at the human resource function in sport organizations from management's perspective, sport management students can not only gain insight into the job-seeking process, but can also develop critical knowledge and skills that they can then put to good use as employees of a sport organization.

The importance of human resource management

The sport industry is a growing enterprise that requires sport managers to find and develop the right people with the right skills to move their organization forward. Clearly, the success of the organization hinges on management's ability to secure the necessary human resources. In this way, sport organizations are not all that different from other non-sport organizations. In order for the organization to succeed, they must be able to attract and retain high-performing employees.

For much of the twentieth century, whether the job involved processing paperwork or producing products, most work was organized in an assembly-line approach. Each worker was responsible for performing fairly simple tasks and for then passing the work on to the next person to continue the process until the job was completed. Training for this kind of work was fairly simple and long lasting, with the technology involved in performing these tasks changing very little over the years. In this approach, the worker is really just an element in the production process and, with just basic education and a good work ethic, could perform the typical job quite well.

During the past 30 years, however, all of that has changed dramatically. The work to be done has become progressively more complex and demanding. Teamwork is now the basic approach, requiring interpersonal and problem-solving skills that simply weren't necessary on the product or paperwork assembly line. Competency in computer and other information technologies is essential and, increasingly, individuals and teams share in the responsibility for managing performance and promoting and sustaining quality throughout the organization. Ensuring that the organization is attracting and holding onto people with the right attitudes and the right skills is the challenge of human resource management.

The function of human resource management is to work closely with executive management to implement a wide array of activities and processes related to the strategic engagement of employees for the purpose of supporting the organization in meeting its goals. Activities may include recruiting and developing staff, evaluating employee performance, and managing tasks related to the employee including payroll and benefits administration. Human resource managers also oversee work environment, employee assistance, and health and wellness programs. While some sport organizations have their own human resources department or staff, other smaller organizations often rely on executive management to carry out this function.

Some sport enterprises, including many tour sport organizations, have the complex human resource challenge of not only working with paid staff, but also many volunteers. Volunteers can be a critical resource for many sport organizations, particularly those that require a great deal of manpower to carry out their activities. For example, in Australia, sport and physical recreation organizations attracted over 2.3 million people in 2010 ("Volunteers," 2011). Volunteers work for thousands of tour sport organizations every year. They serve as hosts, course marshals, parking attendants, concessions workers, members of the set-up and clean-up crew, etc.

Other sport organizations need volunteer coaches, field maintenance staff, game officials, and scorekeepers. The list of possible event jobs is endless, and event organizers and sport programmers readily admit their reliance on volunteer assistance. The effective performance of volunteers is frequently an important component of successful sport events or sport programs. For this reason, sport managers often also have the responsibility of identifying, training, and managing volunteers.

Human resource management systems

Successful sport organizations treat all employees as valuable resources. The process of providing appropriate human resources for the organization involves a series of areas or systems that are essential to the development and support of the human resources necessary for developing and supporting a high-performance workforce. These HRM systems are shown in Box 9.1. With these systems in place, management can recruit, develop, and retain the highly skilled people needed for an organization to pursue and achieve its goals.

BOX 9.1 A GENERAL MODEL FOR HUMAN RESOURCE MANAGEMENT

Human resource planning
Staffing
Training and development
Performance evaluation
Compensation
Employee wellness
Employee relations

HUMAN RESOURCE PLANNING

As with nearly all of the management responsibilities, the human resource management process begins with human resource planning. The human resource planning process actually flows naturally from the strategic management process. Once the organization is clear on its mission and on its strategy for pursuing that mission – whether it's a growth or a retrenchment strategy – it becomes essential to develop a plan to ensure that the organization has the right number of people with the right skills to accomplish the work necessary for the organization to achieve its strategic goals. For example, at a golf club that hosts an annual PGA Tour event, managers might set forth very specific goals for each year in the areas of administration, accounting, golf course maintenance, golf shop and outside operations, food and beverage, marketing, and tennis and pool based upon their mission and strategy (see Box 9.2). These goals are then analyzed on the basis of staffing needs and requirements in order to achieve the goals.

Job analysis: assessing current capabilities

Once the manager has determined human resource needs by examining the strategic plan and reviewing goals for the organization, the next task is to look closely at what the organization is currently doing and how this work is being carried out. At this point, the manager should have a thorough understanding of what type of work is required for the organization to achieve its goals. He or she must assess current capabilities against these needs in order to construct a human resource plan.

Good managers recognize that an effective human resource plan begins with a clear and comprehensive understanding of all of the types of work the organization is currently capable of performing. Job analysis is the process of determining the skill and other requirements of each of the jobs performed in the organization. Typically, this analysis is performed by individuals who are specifically trained in evaluating and categorizing the range of skills and personal characteristics required for effective performance in each job.

Position descriptions

The product of this job analysis process is a job or position description, which is a clear and concise summary of responsibilities, skills, and other key elements required in each job. Box 9.3 provides a sample job description for the position of a banquet manager for a sport facility that sponsors recreational play and hosts a tour sport event.

311

Beach Tennis Club food service division, maintenance division, accounting division, security division, and marketing and member service division. Responsibilities may include, but are not limited to, the following:

- Gives tours of the banquet facility with prospective clients;
- Establishes room layouts for various types of functions;
- Establishes and reviews informational packet for clients;
- Maintains schedule for banquet facilities;
- Handles contracts for sales, clients, bartenders, cleaning services, and other outside contractors as necessary;
- Collects deposits and balances due from clients and patrons at each function, coordinating financial management with the accounting division;
- Schedules and hires all necessary event staff;
- Orders all necessary supplies and materials for functions;
- Maintains accurate inventory;
- Develops equipment and facility maintenance schedule with the maintenance division;
- Serves as liaison with outside tour event management and staff in the area of hospitality;
- Carries out other related duties as assigned.

The North Beach Tennis Club Banquet Manager will have demonstrated expertise in the area of food service and event management. The individual will need to have the ability to plan, organize, and execute high-quality events that are in keeping with the mission and goals of the club. The Banquet Manager must demonstrate excellent communication skills, as the Banquet Manager will be required to represent the club before community groups, private clients, media, members, and other key constituents. A high level of professionalism is expected of the Banquet Manager at all times. A bachelor's degree in hospitality management, sport management, or related field is required, and five years' progressive experience is highly desirable.

In many ways, the position description provides the foundation on which much of the rest of the human resource management process is built. The position description plays a major role in shaping the staffing, training and development, performance evaluation, and compensation elements of that process.

Understanding strategic requirements

Once the organization is clear on its current capabilities, the next task is to compare the current level of human resource capabilities with the demands of the organization's strategy. As sport organizations increasingly attempt to adapt themselves to the Internet and other information-based technologies, for example, they may require a level of capability – in terms of both numbers of people and their level of expertise – beyond what is currently available in the organization.

The same would be true in a case where changes in strategy require changes of levels in capability in areas such as business analytics, social media marketing, finance, customer service, or even human resource management itself. The development of position descriptions allows the manager to look at all of the jobs currently being performed and the required skill and expertise within the context of the entire organization. In this way, the manager can see what existing workers have to offer. Once the manager has assessed the skills of existing employees, he or she is ready to identify and understand any gaps in terms of human resource requirements that now exist because of changes in the organization's strategy.

For example, recall the position description for the Banquet Manager of the North Beach Tennis Club. Let's assume that an outside company had previously handled the food service function at the club. Club trustees decided to adopt a growth strategy by taking over their own food service, thereby entering an industry that they had previously not competed in. The club chose not to renew their contract with the private food service company and then built a new food service building complete with snack bar and banquet facility. It was their plan to provide all elements of club food service. The club's general manager was then faced with the challenge of staffing the facility. In writing position descriptions for food service employees, he was able to identify what skills, experience, and expertise would be needed for the club to carry out its strategy. In Box 9.3 above, the manager set out the responsibilities and qualifications for a banquet manager. Once the manager examined the requirements for this new position in the context of existing positions and their requirements, he recognized that these skills were not available within the organization. The manager realized that it would be necessary to do something to bring the requisite skills to the organization to successfully move forward with the new strategy.

Formulating and implementing the human resource management strategy

It is at this point that the club's general manager must devise a strategy to ensure that the organization's human resource needs are met. The goal of this phase of the human resource planning process is to ensure that effective systems are in place to support a high level of performance by current employees, and to recruit and select new employees with the skills and other characteristics needed to achieve the organization's strategic goals.

At the North Beach Tennis Club, the general manager was faced with an important decision. Once he had determined that the skills, experience, and expertise needed to manage the new banquet facility were not currently available to him through the existing staff, he identified two alternatives for securing the skills needed to run a new banquet facility. He realized that he could either train an existing employee to fill the new position or he could conduct a search to hire someone who already possessed the requisite skills needed to manage the banquet facility.

Once a manager has developed and examined position descriptions and reviewed the available human resources within the organization, the next task is to formulate and implement a strategy not only for filling positions but for developing systems, policies, and procedures that will facilitate optimal performance by employees.

STAFFING

The process by which an organization brings new employees into the organization is called the staffing process. In recent years, this process has become increasingly challenging. As the workplace requires ever-increasing ranges and levels of skills, and as economic growth has resulted in ever-greater competition for people with the right skills, the task of staffing has become significantly more difficult. In the sport industry, one of the major challenges for sport managers is to sift through the ever-increasing numbers of applicants for jobs to find the individual who has the right skills and personal attributes that will allow them to contribute to the success of the organization.

Sport jobs often attract hundreds of applicants who believe that, because of their interest in a particular sport, knowledge of relevant sport statistics, or they have either played or followed the sport all their lives, they would be perfect for the job. Sport managers are not unfamiliar with candidates who profess their love for the game, their status as a die-hard fan, and their reputation as being people oriented. While these personal attributes may be interesting to a particular sport employer, they are not always significant. Sport managers generally assume that *all* candidates will have knowledge of the game, will enjoy the sport or activity, and possess people skills. What they are really interested in are individual skills, experiences, ideas, and personal abilities that will benefit the organization. Prospective employees of sport organizations should think about what makes them stand out from the crowd of literally hundreds of applicants for any sport position. What value do they bring to the organization?

Recruiting new employees

Once it is clear what the needs are in terms of additional employees to implement the organization's strategy, the first step in the staffing process is to notify potential employees of job openings and encourage them to apply. This is called recruiting. In the past, most sport organizations recruited new employees primarily by means of word-of-mouth (employees telling colleagues, associates, family, and friends about job openings) or industry or trade paper advertising. Historically, the word-of-mouth approach in sport organizations led to patterns of nepotism and/or political hiring in sport. Critics still suggest that there is an old-boy or old-girl network in sports that dictates hiring of friends, associates, and/or colleagues. Several sport career specialty websites emphasize the value of networking in the sport industry ("Why should I," 2012).

While a candidate may learn of a job through a colleague or friend, there are several trade or industry magazines and websites that are used for the placement of sport job advertising. For example, many jobs in professional sports are posted on www. teamworkonline.com and their companion Twitter account. Individual segments of the industry have professional trade association magazines, websites, Facebook pages, Twitter accounts, or newsletters that list job openings.

There are also several commercial electronic sport job services that require job seekers to pay a registration fee for access to sport job classified websites. Some sport organizations such as the PGA offer a résumé bank service (of PGA-trained professionals) that is designed to help sport organizations identify qualified candidates. Sport job seekers need to acquaint themselves with the variety of sport-related employment vehicles available and should make it a habit to subscribe to and read these publications and visit sport-related job websites.

For the most part, the sport industry may be described as a hidden industry because most sport organizations do not broadcast job openings in daily newspapers or through general employee recruitment vehicles such as general employment websites. Sport managers tend to be much more targeted in their staffing efforts and focus on those recruitment strategies that are efficient in that they are cost effective and most likely to provide them with a viable candidate pool.

Word-of-mouth, trade advertising, and internal promotion are utilized by sport managers because they are targeted strategies. In an attempt to only attract legitimately qualified candidates, sport organizations tend to focus on recruiting employees through sport-specific vehicles. Sport managers recognize that any general broad announcement of a sport position is likely to result in hundreds of résumés. In fact, many sport organizations receive hundreds of unsolicited résumés a year. For the human resource manager, processing these résumés is a laborious task that is neither an efficient use of time nor particularly productive. That is why sport managers have consciously devised recruitment strategies that are most likely to yield a pool of legitimate candidates.

Some organizations have adopted an on-line application process. The software used to accept and provide initial screening of applicants helps to create efficiencies in the candidate review process by immediately eliminating incomplete applications. The software can also be set to eliminate those candidates who do not demonstrate minimum position requirements or fall outside of established parameters.

As position requirements become greater and more specialized, the search strategy usually becomes more narrowed. Where staffing of entry-level positions is usually done through a more broad-based approach such as general or trade industry advertising, top-level executive management searches are much more focused on strategies related to industry networking. For example, a general manager of a professional sport team seeking to fill a senior-level marketing position is more likely to network with industry colleagues or sources than place a general advertisement in the local newspaper.

Although this approach to human resource recruitment in sport organizations has been productive, it is not without its problems. A targeted approach to recruitment may fail to identify strong candidates that exist outside of the scope of the search. For example, while Stephen, the young man introduced at the beginning of the chapter, has developed a good network within the golf industry and reads trade publications, as a college student he might not be aware of certain positions in the industry that are advertised through word-of-mouth among industry professionals. The reality is that the word-of-mouth strategy has its limitations. There is no guarantee that individuals will pass along the appropriate information to good candidates. This approach is clearly unsystematic and relies on a busy network of colleagues who may or may not subjectively help to identify quality candidates. Another problem with the targeted recruitment approach is that it tends to perpetuate existing hiring patterns. Most people find it easy and comfortable to build relationships and network with people who are similar to one's self. However, for the sport industry to grow and take advantage of the skills and talents of a diverse population, it is necessary to broaden recruitment strategies so that opportunities in sport will be available to all.

All sport managers must be aware of their organization's policies and practices that pertain to staffing. Public sport organizations and sport programs in educational institutions are required to follow the specific human resource policies of their directing or sponsoring agency. For example, the city's general human resource department could carry out the human resource function for a municipal golf course. If there were a city policy that all jobs are to be announced in the local paper and be published in a municipal employee newsletter or posted to both the internal employee and the city website, this would be done even though the golf club manager may believe that it would be unlikely to reach qualified candidates in this fashion. Similarly, a college athletic department may be required to internally post a job for a new soccer coach even though the athletic director believes that there is currently no qualified internal candidate for the job.

It is important, however, not to overlook existing employees. Internal promotion has historically been a successful recruitment strategy. Sport organizations, like other businesses, often emphasize job advancement. Career growth can be a powerful motivator for improving human performance and retaining talented employees.

More recently, as sport organizations have recognized the necessity of extending their recruitment horizons so that they may find the right people with the right skills, they have had to broaden and become much more innovative in their recruitment strategies. Box 9.4 lists some of the approaches now being used.

BOX 9.4 RECRUITMENT STRATEGIES IN SPORT ORGANIZATIONS

- Recruiting on the Internet using sport-related sites such as teamworkonline.com, workinsports.com, jobsinsports.com, womensportsjobs.com, gamefacesportsjobs.com, and others.
- Networking at industry trade shows or at professional association conferences or meetings.
- Using social media sites; electronic networking through professional and affinity sites (e.g. LinkedIn.com).
- Sending recruiters to beaches, ski areas, and other recreational locations to hand out t-shirts, water bottles, and other branded materials encouraging new applicants.
- Recruiting on college campuses – sending job announcements to the faculty of sport management programs.
- Seeking referrals from colleagues or industry peers.
- Creating a volunteer program where prospective candidates are invited to participate and become familiar with the sport organization.
- Hosting Careers in Sports job fairs or seminars.
- Using direct mail to target specific categories of people with the desired skills, such as professional association members (e.g. Association of Luxury Suite Directors).
- Using sport job head hunting, executive search firms, or industry résumé banks.
- Sponsoring internships to create a relationship with students who will soon be entering the workforce.

The key point here is that it is often no longer sufficient just to rely on word-of-mouth, trade advertising, or internal promotion to effectively identify viable candidates. Attracting the most skilled and talented job applicants now requires creativity and initiative in terms of the sport organization's recruiting efforts. This is not to say, however, that importance of networking within the industry has diminished. Sport organizations will continue to rely on candidate referrals. At a time when sport management programs are becoming more pervasive and competition for sport jobs is at an all-time high, sport organizations are likely to rely on this strategy to help them hone in quickly on serious candidates.

For example, many sport organizations will utilize the internship as a prospective employee-screening program. Through the internship, the sport organization is able to effectively assess the performance of the intern to determine whether or not he or she has the skills and/or personal traits that the organization deems necessary for success. This strategy has helped sport managers to identify highly skilled potential employees, while helping the organization from making the human resource mistake of hiring someone who looks qualified on paper, but who fails to live up to the organization's performance expectations. For this reason, it is critical that students treat the internship seriously and conduct themselves as if they are being auditioned for future work. While any organization is unlikely to hire an intern that performed poorly, the consequences of poor performance are magnified because of the reliance on industry peer referrals across the sport industry. Managers in sport organizations rely on friends, peers, and colleagues within the industry to identify qualified candidates. It is not unusual for an intern site supervisor to assist a highly regarded intern in identifying and securing employment with other sport organizations when no position is available within the host organization. Peer recommendations are usually given a great deal of weight by sport managers and, therefore, a glowing reference can open doors for the job seeker. Conversely, a negative performance appraisal by an internship site supervisor may become an insurmountable obstacle for someone seeking employment in the sport industry.

For a student to improve his or her chances of securing a positive reference upon completion of the internship, it is important that he or she make every effort to understand and abide by the organization's written and unwritten rules of conduct. Some sport organizations have formal intern handbooks or manuals that detail specific requirements and expectations for behavior. Written guidelines may detail policies for everything ranging from comp tickets, to dress code, to fraternization with players or clients. Other sport organizations have few written guidelines and, therefore, it becomes the intern's responsibility to initiate a discussion of organizational policy related to interns with the site supervisor and the faculty advisor.

In all situations, it is in the student's best interest to ask questions to clarify any concerns he or she might have about the organization's dress code, behavioral standards, and performance expectations rather than make an assumption that leads to a mistake that can have long-term negative consequences on his or her career in sport. As a general rule, the student should always treat the internship as a professional opportunity that serves as a critical building block for a successful career in sport.

The selection process

The process of evaluating applicants to determine if they are "fit" for the jobs that are available is called the selection process. In many ways, this phase of the staffing process has become even more challenging than the recruiting phase. Not only has it become more important than ever that the right person with the right skills is identified for each job, but there are also legal considerations that make important additional demands in terms of selection.

Selection and the law
There are several pieces of federal legislation that, in particular, shape and influence the selection process. The first, Title VII of the Civil Rights Act of 1964, guarantees all American citizens equal employment opportunity. This law forbids discrimination on the basis of sex, race, color, religion, or national origin. An organization cannot refuse to hire, train, promote, or transfer employees simply on the basis of any of these characteristics. This means that selection and all other employment-related decisions must be made on the basis of objective standards, such as the actual requirements of the job as indicated in the position description.

Similarly, the Age Discrimination in Employment Act and the Americans with Disabilities Act prohibit discrimination in employment decisions on the basis of age and disabilities respectively. Enforcement of these laws is the responsibility of the Equal Employment Opportunity Commission (EEOC), which has the ability to accept lawsuits and impose heavy fines against employers with discriminatory practices.

The key for managers, then, is to ensure a selection that focuses both on attaining the right "fit" in terms of the requirements of the job, but also provides equal employment opportunities to all applicants.

Testing
EEO guidelines define employment testing to include any procedure used as a basis for the employment decision. This means that employment testing, which may be considered as application forms, pencil and paper tests, performance tests, interviews, or education or experience requirements, must be administered and used in ways that avoid discrimination. Many sport organizations utilize testing as part of the selection process. In fact, it is important for the student to know that some sport organizations require intern candidates to undergo a battery of

319

Table 9.2 Types of employment tests

Type of test	Use
Psychological and personality tests	Measure personality characteristics felt to be essential for performance.
Pencil-and-paper honesty tests	Evaluate integrity/degree of comfort with risk for engaging in dishonest behavior.
Skills tests	Assess skills in areas such as math, English, written communication skills, computers, sport business, or general industry knowledge, etc.
Assessment centers, simulations	Evaluate more complex skill sets such as teamwork, organizational skills, leadership, etc. in a "hands-on" situation.
Drug tests	Check for the presence of controlled substances through chemical analysis of urine, blood, or hair samples.

tests as part of the selection process. These tests may include questions related to their knowledge of the particular business and the sport industry in general, or may require a specific skills demonstration such as the ability to write a press release or create a simple invoice. Table 9.2 summarizes some of the more common employment tests currently in use.

Pre-employment screening

In addition to the more formal testing techniques shown above in Table 9.2, reference and background checks are also important elements of most selection processes. In checking references, it is best to request multiple references, to speak with each of the individuals provided, and to focus the discussion on job performance rather than on areas that might be viewed as violating the applicant's rights to privacy. Pre-employment screening may also involve a search of public records or an electronic search of the individual's name using multiple Internet search engines.

Pre-employment screening for volunteers has become the subject of discussion in the sport industry particularly for those segments of the sport industry that deal with children or young adults, specifically youth sports, high school sports, college sports, youth development leagues, and recreation. There have been several well-publicized incidents of sport volunteers and coaches of youth sport teams physically or sexually abusing players. While many states require criminal and sexual criminal offender checks for employees working with children, laws do not always extend to volunteers. Sport managers must be extremely diligent in screening volunteers for programs that involve children. Many sport organizations require that Criminal Offender Record Investigation (CORI) and Sexual Offender Record Investigation (SORI) checks are completed

320

for all youth sport volunteers. Unfortunately, fees related to these checks may be prohibitive for some organizations and certainly not all potential offenders have criminal records.

As the members of our society become more mobile, many sport organizations are now conducting background checks as well as reference checks as a way to receive additional information about potential employees and volunteers. Through services available on the Internet, for example, it is now possible to receive credit reports, criminal conviction records, worker's compensation claims, court judgments, personal address histories, real estate records, and more. While extreme caution must be exercised, so as not to violate the applicant's privacy rights and existing privacy and discrimination laws, the responsible acquisition and use of this kind of information can help ensure that a sport organization does not hire someone who will become a problem for the organization and its employees, members, or clients.

The job interview

While the job interview is perhaps the most common of all employment tests, it is, in its most common forms, the least valid and least reliable predictor of eventual performance on the job. Most of the problems with the job interview are related to the fact that many managers are not trained in providing effective interviews. As a result, interviewer bias and inconsistencies in the way interviews are conducted tend to raise questions about conclusions drawn from the interviews.

To reduce the impact of interviewer bias and interview inconsistencies, two techniques are combined. The first is to require structured interviews in which specific interview questions are developed in advance, and each applicant is asked the same questions. This is combined with a multiple rater approach in which applicants are interviewed by a team of interviewers (in some cases, the search committee), or by a series of individuals, each of whom asks some of the pre-selected interview questions. This combination of multiple interviewers using a structured interview format tends to result in an employment test that is both fairer to the applicant and more useful to the sport organization. Many sport managers effectively utilize the search committee strategy.

TRAINING AND DEVELOPMENT

Because of the constantly changing demands of business, training has become an increasingly important human resource management process, not just for new employees but for virtually all employees. Training for new job-specific skills and/or professional development that contributes to the overall competencies and knowledge base of the employee are the responsibility of the sport organization.

Training of the worker does not stop with the initial employee orientation. While new employees and volunteers need a basic orientation to the organization, systematic continuous employee training programs are critical to the employee's or volunteer's long-term success with the organization.

In previous decades, most training focused on the basic skills needed to perform a specific job such as machine operator or concession worker, and much of that training occurred on the job. A volunteer, for example, might have been assigned the task of being a court monitor and was sent to the court with the instructions "just figure out what needs to be done and do it." Today's sport organizations have realized that in addition to specific job skill instruction, training efforts must increasingly focus on developing employees at every level including skills in teamwork, problem solving, communication, information systems, and creativity. Many sport organizations have instituted several on-going training activities that focus on helping employees to develop customer service, teamwork, and communication skills. Training initiatives include encouraging and supporting management staff's attendance at professional association conferences and industry shows; holding daily, weekly, and quarterly staff meetings that include an education and training session; and continually giving feedback to employees on their progress.

In providing continuous training for all of the organization's employees, there are two critical challenges: selecting the most appropriate approach for the particular type of skill being targeted, and ensuring an overall training design that is consistent with the fundamentals of how learning can best be facilitated.

Selecting the most appropriate instructional approaches

Part of the key to effective training is to select the training format most appropriate for the kind of learning being targeted. For example, learning about teamwork is likely to be more effective through approaches that include simulations (role plays) in which the trainees are actively involved in exercises designed to enhance teamwork, rather than through an approach involving simply viewing a video on teamwork. On the other hand, information intended to enhance the employee's understanding of a product or process can be very effectively communicated through video-based or computer-based instruction.

The most effective training designs match the area of training being targeted with the instructional approach most appropriate for that type of learning. In Chapter 3, the use of iPads and laptops for NFL player training was discussed. This computer-based training is supplemented with on-field demonstrations, classroom lectures, videos, and discussions. This is an example of how the most effective training and individual learning often combines two or more instructional approaches.

The fundamentals of effective learning

While there is obviously a wide range of options in terms of instructional approaches, there are a number of fundamentals for effective learning that should be present in every training program, regardless of which approach is chosen. These fundamentals for learning skills (behaviors) or information (understanding) are summarized in Box 9.5.

BOX 9.5 FUNDAMENTALS OF EFFECTIVE LEARNING

Learning goal(s): a clearly defined target in terms of what the trainee will be able to do or understand as a result of the learning.

Modeling: a demonstration of the targeted skill broken down to its key components with a meaningful detailed and engaging presentation of the key information.

Practice: multiple and varied opportunities to "try out" the targeted skills or understanding.

Feedback: reinforcement and information about performance during practice and beyond.

Whether the training is instructor led or computer based, or whether the training occurs in groups or individually, to be effective there must be clearly defined learning goals, effective presentation of the skill or information, and sufficient opportunity for practice and feedback.

Beyond these fundamentals, it is also important to realize that the most effective learning occurs when the individual has the opportunity to actually use the new skill or understanding on the job. This means that learning is most complete when the individual has the opportunity to continue to practice and receive reinforcing feedback as part of his or her day-to-day work. It is not enough that skills be practiced and refined in the training setting. For optimal learning, the reinforcement of new skills requires continued practice and feedback as part of the individual's regular work activities.

Whether a NASCAR pit crew member, volunteer customer service representative at a rodeo tour event, or professional volleyball tour marketing director, continued professional development is critical to success. All sport managers should ensure that their employees consider professional development and training to be part of their regular job responsibilities. Effective sport organizations continue to educate and support their employees long after the initial orientation is complete.

By doing so, they ensure that all members of the organization have the skills and understanding required for overall strategic effectiveness. Appropriate training programs then require instruction in the right skills, using the right mix of instructional approaches, delivered the right way in terms of the fundamentals of learning.

PERFORMANCE EVALUATION

Effective staffing and training are two of the core elements of an organization's human resource management system. A third is effective performance evaluation. Performance evaluation, sometimes called performance appraisal or performance planning and review, is the formal process of assessing how well each employee in the organization is performing his or her job. Perhaps no tendency in sport is stronger than the tendency to assess performance. In nearly every sport, performance is continuously monitored and statistical measures developed and constantly updated as a means of assessing individual, team, or organizational performance.

In professional golf, for example, key performance measures include average strokes per round, percentage of greens reached in regulation, percentage of tournaments in which the golfer "made the cut," and so on. For off-field employees, performance is measured in terms of numbers of tickets sold, percentage increase in sponsor renewal, or number of calls made. The point is that, in sports, measures of performance have emerged naturally to allow effective assessment of how well individuals or teams are doing their jobs. The challenge is to develop similarly effective means of assessing or measuring the work of everyone in the organization.

Performance evaluation formats

A wide variety of formats have emerged to evaluate work performance in organizations. Probably the most common general format involves the use of graphic rating scales. In this approach, employees are rated on a range of different traits (creativity, cooperativeness, initiative, etc.) or behaviors (see the example in Box 9.6 below) using a numerical scale indicating the level of performance in this area (1=low, 5=high), or the quality of performance (1=poor, 5=excellent), or the frequency of performance (1=never, 5=always). Box 9.6 shows an example of a particular type of graphic rating scale, a behaviorally anchored rating scale (BARS). Using the BARS technique, combinations of specific behaviors are used to determine the level of performance in the various areas of performance required in a specific position. In the example in Box 9.6, the scale shown is for communication skills. Other areas of performance required for the position, interpersonal skills, technical skills, and so on, would have separate BARS allowing evaluation of performance in each of those areas.

BOX 9.6 BARS EVALUATION OF COMMUNICATION PERFORMANCE

Presents ideas clearly and responds constructively to others' ideas.

10 = Communicates effectively in writing, one on one, in small groups, and with management.

 8 = Communicates effectively in writing, one on one, and in small groups; appears less comfortable communicating with management.

 6 = Communicates effectively in writing and one on one; appears less comfortable communicating in small groups and with management.

 4 = Communicates effectively in writing; appears less comfortable communicating one on one, in small groups, and with management.

 2 = Needs improvement in all phases of communication: written, one on one, in small groups, and with management.

Another common performance evaluation format is the Balanced Scorecard or management by objectives (MBO) approach described in Chapter 6. You will recall that, in the Balanced Scorecard approach, the manager works with individuals to define specific performance objectives for the individual consistent with the organization's goals. Some organizations combine BARS and Balanced Scorecard, using the rating scale component for those job requirements that are consistent year to year, and the goal-setting component for areas of performance that might be of particular importance in a given year. For example, an advertising sales position in a marketing department of a tour sport organization might be evaluated using BARS for the areas of performance relating to how well the individual deals with existing advertisers, but the organization uses a Balanced Scorecard approach for evaluating how well the individual performs in terms of attracting new advertisers or increasing sponsorship revenues for a tour event or series.

Performance evaluation and equal employment opportunities

Performance evaluation usually occurs on an annual basis for each employee, and the results of this evaluation are very often the basis for decisions on whether and how much to increase the employee's pay for the coming year, as well as for decisions relating to the future training opportunities, promotion, and potential reassignment of the employee. Because performance evaluation does provide the basis for so many important decisions relating to pay, future training, and promotion, the federal anti-discrimination legislation discussed earlier in the chapter requires that an organization's performance evaluation process be legally defensible. While the Equal Employment Opportunity Commission has not defined specific guidelines for a legally defensible performance evaluation process, research on a large number of court decisions on employment discrimination cases suggests four criteria (Kreitner, 2001).

A *job analysis* should be used to develop the performance evaluation instrument. Job analysis is the systematic assessment of what skills, personal characteristics, and other qualifications are actually required to perform the job successfully. Job analysis ensures that the evaluation process is focusing on the actual requirements of the job. It also minimizes the extent to which a manager's bias might result in different evaluation processes for different employees. Every employee with the same job description will be evaluated on the same items.

The evaluation should *focus on behavior*, rather than on traits or characteristics. This ensures that the actual performance of the individual is being evaluated, rather than the individual's personality or other traits. The problem with evaluating personality or traits – unless they are defined in terms of specific types of behavior – is that judgments on characteristics such as initiative or attitude tend to be very subjective and, for that reason, less consistent. The BARS approach represents the kind of behaviorally oriented format supported by these guidelines.

The performance evaluation process should be performed consistent with *specific written instructions.* Written instructions on exactly how to conduct the performance evaluation ensure that every employee is being evaluated using the same system. This reduces the likelihood that managers, for whatever reason, might treat different employees differently in terms of the evaluation process.

Managers should *review the results* of the evaluation with their employees. This guideline reflects what the courts have tended to view as one of the characteristics of a legally defensible performance evaluation process. But sharing the results of evaluation with the individual is also good management. If one of the key goals of the performance evaluation process is improved work performance, then feedback on work performance to the individual is essential. When conducted effectively, the performance evaluation process provides a valuable opportunity for the manager to recognize and reinforce positive performance, and to exchange views and information with the employee about how work performance might be improved.

In summary, each of these criteria for a legally defensible performance evaluation process represents an important guideline for an effective performance appraisal process. Organizations following these guidelines are creating a system of evaluation

326

that is not only more likely to be fair in terms of validity and reliability, but is more likely also to be more accurate in the judgments it produces for purposes of pay and promotion, and more productive in terms of enhancing future work performance.

COMPENSATION

The next core element of an effective human resource management system is compensation: the rewards individuals receive for performing the work of the organization. The challenge for sport organizations is to design a total compensation system that allows the organization to attract and retain individuals with the skills and qualifications it needs to be successful, supports a high level of work performance by its members, and allows the organization to remain profitable or financially viable into the future. There are a number of potential elements that can be included in an organization's compensation system.

Base pay

Base pay is the compensation provided for performing the basic duties required by a given job. Traditionally, salary ranges are established for each position in the organization. These salary ranges set the lowest level and highest level of base pay available for individuals in that position. Employees progress upward through the salary range for their position, most often on the basis of how long they have spent in the position, and how well they do their job as determined by their annual performance evaluation.

The salary ranges established by an organization usually reflect industry standards in terms of what the going rate is for similar positions at other companies in the same geographic area, or in the same or competing industries. Organizations research what other organizations are paying their employees in order to ensure that their own pay scales are high enough to allow them to attract and retain good employees while, at the same time, not paying more than the market requires.

Performance-based pay

In recent years, as organizations have focused on becoming more competitive by improving their performance, there has been an increased emphasis on compensation systems that reward employees for performance beyond the basic requirements of their jobs. Performance-based pay can include incentive pay, bonuses, or commissions, usually for attaining specific individual or team performance goals in terms of quality, efficiency, or productivity. For example, a salesperson might be compensated based on a percentage of ticket revenue developed, sponsorship fees collected, or gross premium sales. Similar to this is gain sharing or results sharing in which employees receive additional financial compensation in return for contributing to the organization's overall success as measured by increased profits, reduced expenses, or some other indicator of improved organizational effectiveness.

Another form of performance-based pay is pay-for-skills or pay-for-knowledge in which additional compensation is awarded to employees who learn and successfully apply new skills or knowledge considered valuable to the organization's success. For example, a sport program supervisor who completes a course in advanced life saving or emergency medicine or achieves certification in athletic training may be financially compensated for his or her new skills.

Actually, there has been some criticism of the increasing emphasis on performance-based pay. Critics argue that it can be difficult to measure performance in some jobs, such as customer service, or jobs where the focus is on the quality of what is done, rather than the number of units produced. Critics also charge that tying pay to performance focuses employees' attention on reaching short-term goals rather than on the kind of problem solving that can use up a lot of time over the short term, but significantly improve performance over the longer term. In an attempt to overcome such possible negative effects, some sport managers have financially awarded creativity or new ideas. Even if the ideas have produced poor results or have failed outright, some managers believe that risk-taking and creative problem solving should be encouraged and, to ensure that employees remain committed to trying new things, they will provide bonuses for unconventional thinking and creative problem solving.

Finally, unless managed carefully, pay for performance programs can result in employees competing with each other to be judged "above average" or "exceptional," rather than working together for the good of the organization. For example, some sport managers create friendly competitions among sales teams in an effort to motivate high performance. One negative outcome of these competitions is that employees assume a win-at-all-costs attitude and may focus on sabotaging other sales teams or employing high-pressure sales strategies that may be detrimental to the organization in the long run. These criticisms represent important warnings to sport organizations as they attempt to use pay to motivate work performance.

Another compensation issue of concern to sport managers and students entering the sport industry is salary scale. There is a general misconception that sport salaries are high. Media stories reporting the gargantuan salaries of professional athletes do not represent compensation on the off-field side. Generally, salaries in sport, particularly starting salaries, are low. Organization type, i.e. non-profit or for-profit, often affects salary scale as does industry segment and organization location.

While senior-level executives and staff may be well compensated in some sport organizations, entry-level salaries are generally very low. Because of the glut of potential employees who are willing to work for little or nothing just to be in sport, sport salaries are generally deflated. The reality for most sport managers is that they need to pay their dues. They must work long hours – often nights and weekends – at pay levels that are lower than other business enterprises. Success in the sport industry is often about perseverance and dedication. It is possible to move up the ladder within the sport industry and to be well compensated for skills and demonstrated performance.

Benefits and other non-financial compensation

In addition to direct pay, or financial compensation, there are also non-financial forms of compensation. The most common forms of non-financial compensation are called benefits. Typically, these include medical and life insurance, vacation, holiday, and other paid-time benefits, and some form of company-sponsored retirement or savings programs. Most often, the costs of these benefits are shared with the employee, i.e. the employee pays a percentage of his or her health plan and retirement plan contribution.

Finally, there are other forms of non-financial rewards that can vary from organization to organization. For sport organizations, these types of benefits are particularly useful for compensating poorly paid employees and/or thanking volunteers and cultivating volunteer support. These range from dinners and event tickets to access to special events, company-sponsored trips, golfing privileges, jewelry, facility use, merchandise discounts, and clothing. At many tour sport events, there are special functions held specifically for volunteers. They may include concerts, luncheons, and/or receptions with tour athletes.

For employees, other rewards might include additional vacation time and flex scheduling, or organizations paying for college courses and other forms of career development opportunities. The key to an effective compensation component of the overall human resource management process is to develop a combination of pay, performance incentives, benefits, and other non-financial rewards that will enable the organization to attract and motivate a high-performance workforce.

EMPLOYEE WELLNESS

Clearly, one of the major challenges of human resource management in sport organizations is maintaining employee health and wellness. For the sport organization, athlete health and wellness is directly linked to the individual's ability to perform.

329

Support personnel, such as athletic trainers, sport medicine professionals, therapists, and counselors, are seen as critical to assuring that the athlete is in optimal physical condition. Specialized equipment, staff personnel, and medical services are all provided. As with other non-sport organizations, general employee wellness is seen to be important to the organization in terms of lessening employee absence, containing health costs to the organization, and facilitating overall employee performance.

Safety and the U.S. government

In 1970, the U.S. Government created the Occupational Safety and Health Administration (OSHA) to set health and safety standards for the American workplace, and to monitor organizations to ensure work conditions are free from recognized hazards. OSHA requires that employers maintain conditions consistent with federal safety standards. Employers must also submit to periodic workplace inspection and record and report all workplace accidents and injuries. Where violations of safety standards are found, OSHA is able to levy penalties for each violation with increasing penalties if the violation is not corrected in a timely fashion.

Alcohol and substance abuse

The history of alcohol and substance abuse with prominent sport figures is a long and storied one. Clearly, one of the most serious threats to wellness in the sport workplace is the prevalence of a variety of dangerous substances including alcohol and drugs. This is a problem that is not unique to sport and it impacts all of society. Many organizations, both sport and non-sport, have required drug testing. There are legal restrictions that place limits on testing employees, and the tests themselves are not always reliable, leaving employers open to lawsuits.

In addition to testing, many organizations have taken the route of providing employees with substance abuse and other emotional or behavioral problems access to an employee assistance program (EAP). Employees who are identified as needing assistance are referred to the program. Through the program, an employee's problem is evaluated and options for treatment are confidentially discussed, and appropriate referrals or treatment are provided usually through an outside provider or agency.

The EAP approach has actually expanded in recent years to include programming for the full range of employee health and wellness issues that impact workplace productivity. In school-based sports particularly, there has been an emphasis on education of athletes and employees through programs such as the NCAA's Champs/Life Skills program. In professional sports organizations, agents, unions, and other governing bodies play a role in educating their employees (including athletes) about the potential dangers of illegal substance use.

A wellness approach to employee health

There is actually a much better reason than the existence of OSHA or substance abuse problems for organizations to focus on the health and safety of their employees. The fact is that a healthy workforce is simply more productive than a workforce where employees are unable to perform their jobs well as a result of accident, injury, illness, or unhealthful behaviors. It is for this reason that employers are increasingly taking a wellness approach to employee health.

A wellness approach focuses on preventing accidents, injuries, or illnesses before they happen. In this approach, employees are encouraged to engage in a range of behaviors and activities associated with better health. These include improved nutrition and regular exercise, stress management training and employee counseling for personal problems, programs for reducing or eliminating the use of alcohol, tobacco, and other unhealthful substances, and regular medical examinations. While there are definite expenses associated with supporting a wellness approach to employee health and safety, these expenses are generally found to be much lower than the potential productivity gains from a healthy workforce.

In the area of performance-enhancing drugs, however, the line between personal health and human performance often becomes blurred. Athletes often believe that in order to maximize their abilities, they must use supplements or other chemical interventions to achieve peak performance and be competitive with other athletes who might also be using artificial means to achieve results. Realizable gains through chemicals, however, may be dangerous and may have long-term negative consequences, but it is often difficult to convince an athlete of potential long-term negative health effects when they can see the immediate gains in size, strength, and speed. There is also the ethical question of whether sports organizations see it in their best interest to curb the use of these substances when the organization itself is benefitting directly from the newly developed skills of its athletes who are winning games, setting records, and attracting fans.

EMPLOYEE RELATIONS

The final challenge of human resource management that we will discuss is the challenge to maintain a productive and mutually satisfying relationship between employees and the organization. Fairness and competency in implementing each of the processes already described in this chapter are essential for positive employee relations. But there are other challenges as well. Some of the most prominent include unions and collective bargaining, sexual harassment, and government-mandated accommodations for employees.

Unions and collective bargaining

Employees usually form unions as a way to improve their ability to have an impact on their working conditions, on how they are paid, how work is scheduled, and so on. The federal government formed the National Labor Relations Board (NLRB) to ensure that there would be a fair and orderly process for workers seeking to form a union. Employees interested in forming a union must first obtain the signatures of 30 percent of the potential members of the union. Once this is done, the NLRB supervises an election in which employees vote by secret ballot as to whether they support the formation of a union. If a majority of those voting vote in favor of the union, the NLRB certifies the union as the employees' official representative in negotiating with management.

Collective bargaining is the process of negotiating a labor contract that is acceptable both to management and employees. Typically, the labor contract that is negotiated contains agreements about wages and hours; conditions of employment; promotion and layoff; discipline; benefits; overtime vacation; and rest periods; as well as grievance procedures (Griffin, 2000). Union members have the opportunity to accept or reject the terms suggested in the proposed contract by voting for or against it. Again, ratification of a new collective bargaining agreement requires a majority of those voting.

If relations between management and employees are not well managed, the collective bargaining process can become extremely difficult, with employees sometimes resorting to work slowdowns or labor strikes as a way to express their displeasure. As management and unions have learned to cooperate more effectively in the negotiation process, collective bargaining agreements have become an important tool for ensuring positive relations between employees and the organization, and for making workers and the workplace more productive.

Sexual harassment

A second area of challenge in terms of employee relations is the need to maintain a work environment free from sexual harassment. Sexual harassment is generally considered to include unwanted sexual attention or behavior, either directly toward a specific group or individuals, or contributing to an offensive or intimidating work environment.

Sexual harassment is never acceptable, but as a result of the Civil Rights Act of 1964, employers are considered legally responsible for maintaining a work environment free of the conditions that constitute sexual harassment. The consequences of failing to maintain such an environment can be considerable in terms of legal settlements, fees, and lost employees. What is much more difficult to calculate are

332

the costs to these organizations in terms of the increased difficulty of attracting and recruiting skilled and talented workers who will now question working for a company with the reputation resulting from the publicity from lawsuits.

For all of these reasons, most American businesses now have formal programs to ensure an environment in which sexual harassment is clearly unacceptable. Sexual harassment represents a serious threat to the goal of positive employee relations. Reducing this threat to the lowest possible level will pay off, not only in avoiding costly legal battles, but also in the value of achieving a more productive work environment.

Americans with Disabilities Act

There are two other areas where the government has intervened to ensure fair treatment of employees. The first is in the area of accommodating the needs of workers with disabilities. In 1990, Congress passed the Americans with Disabilities Act (ADA). This law requires employers to make "reasonable accommodations" for qualified individuals with known disabilities.

In the years since the passage of the ADA, court cases have provided clarification of what is meant by reasonable accommodation and known disabilities. As employers' legal responsibilities continue to become clearer in this area, the ability of employers to respond to the needs of workers with disabilities will continue to improve.

Family and Medical Leave Act

In 1993, Congress passed the Family and Medical Leave Act (FMLA). With some exceptions, the FMLA requires employers with 50 or more employees to provide up to 12 weeks of unpaid leave to eligible employees during any 12-month period. The unpaid leave can be for births, adoptions, the care of sick children, spouses, or parents, or for the employee to recover from their own illness (Hall and Walker, 1993).

SUMMARY

In this chapter, students were introduced to the tour sport industry. The tour sport segment consists of a single or series of sport competitions at various locales throughout a tour season. They may feature individuals (as in golf) or teams (as in volleyball) that compete in a tournament-type or championship event format either on the basis of one single event or as part of a series. The tour sport industry consists of three distinct segments. The first segment is known as traditional tour sport and encompasses traditional sport competitions such as golf, tennis, or auto racing

333

where individuals and teams may compete in one event and/or as part of a championship event series. The second segment is outdoor adventure/action sports that feature non-traditional sport activities such as freestyle stunt skiing, BMX, snowboarding, surfing, log rolling, or skateboarding. Examples of these types of tour sport series included in this segment are the X Games and the Dew Tour. The third segment is tour sport entertainment that is usually commercial in nature and features sport activity that is usually scripted to some degree and has predetermined outcomes. Examples of this segment are the WWE and Harlem Globetrotters.

This chapter also focuses on the people factor in sport organizations through the examination of the human resource function. Both employee and employer perspectives of the human resource function are presented. Human resource management is described as the responsibility of management to establish and maintain specific programs and systems needed to attract, develop, and support a high-performance workforce. The human resource function is directly tied to the organization's strategic initiatives and may be viewed in the context of two separate human resource tracks – on-field personnel management and off-field, front-office, or business-side personnel management.

The sport organization must employ a human resource management system that includes job analysis, human resource planning, recruiting and selection, training and development, performance evaluation, compensation and reward systems, and employee safety and wellness. The human resource manager's responsibility also includes complying with organizational policies, legislation, and guidelines established by the sport organization's governing bodies.

MANAGEMENT EXERCISE: YOU ARE STEPHEN PAUL

Imagine that it is you, not Stephen Paul, the sport management student introduced in the opening discussion case in this chapter, who is looking for a position in the tour sport industry.

1 How would you go about finding a job in this industry segment? Identify the first three steps in the process.
2 Identify the special skills, experience, or knowledge you can bring to the tour sport organization.
3 Develop or review your own résumé. Determine the institutional resources available to assist you in putting together a professional résumé; what skills, experience, or knowledge do you have that differentiate you in the sport marketplace, and how would you go about creating your own personal brand?
4 Investigate the types of entry-level positions available in international tour sport organizations, and determine whether these positions are of interest to you.
5 To learn more about your chosen field, interview a sport management professional to determine the following: how he/she obtained his/her present position; educational background; use of internship; types of skills needed to perform their job; any advice for someone just starting out in the sport business.

CHAPTER 10

MANAGING CHANGE AND THE PROFESSIONAL LEAGUE SPORT INDUSTRY

INTRODUCTION

Throughout this book, you have been presented with the notion that management is a complex organizational task made more challenging by the dynamic nature of the sport industry. Change is both the most daunting challenge confronting management and the most promising opportunity. Change threatens to overwhelm the organization on the one hand and yet, at the same time, it reveals unprecedented possibilities. New competition, new technology, and new performance standards are just some of the changes that managers must not only anticipate, but must bring about.

Change is inevitable. The question is not whether to accept the challenge of change but rather how to manage change to make it as productive as possible and a process for strengthening and renewing the organization. In this chapter, you will be introduced to the principles and process of managing change. The classic model of organizational change proposed by Lewin (1951) is introduced as a simple theoretical framework for managing change. Strategies for overcoming resistance to change and for effectively bringing about change in the organization will be identified. Lastly, the concept of the learning organization will be introduced.

There may be no better segment in all of the sport industry than professional league sport to examine the process of managing change. Professional league sport has evolved from its humble beginnings to multi-million dollar businesses today. Professional league sport organizations are high-profile organizations that must constantly change and evolve to fulfill their mission and cultivate stakeholder support.

336

Check the stats

Purpose
To provide highly competitive athletic events and competitions to spectators either at a sport venue or through media platforms. Professional team sport organizations are commercial in nature and are driven to generate a profit for ownership interests.

Stakeholders
Players, agents, player unions, coaches, franchise management personnel, franchise employees, franchise owners, league management personnel and employees, broadcast networks, franchise and league sponsors, sport media including broadcasters and reporters, professional sports analysts, stadium, arena, and ancillary service companies and personnel, fans.

Size and scope
Professional sport leagues and teams exist throughout the world. Major professional sport leagues revolve around sports such as soccer, baseball, hockey, football, rugby, cricket, and basketball. In many places around the world, professional sports are a multi-billion dollar enterprise.

Governance
Professional leagues are governed through a league system that has centralized management power. Franchise owners share collectively in decision making and establishment of league-wide policies and rules for league and franchise operation. The power of oversight and rule implementation falls to a commissioner and/or league presidents. Additional shared functions such as negotiation of broadcast rights, league sponsorships, merchandising, licensing, revenue sharing, all-star game or championship event management and personnel issues (player drafts, discipline, player contracts, trades, salary cap, or luxury tax oversight), units, or divisions are managed through the league or commissioner's office. Through the collective bargaining process, players' unions and representatives (and, in some cases, officials groups) participate in enterprise governance and policy setting.

Inside look: America's game

In the words of author Michael MacCambridge (2004), "In the second half of the twentieth century in the United States, professional football's popularity as a spectator sport grew to eclipse that of Major League Baseball," and has become "one of the few solid pieces of common ground left on the increasingly balkanized map of American popular culture." It was during the 1960s when the percentage of Americans who identified professional football as their favorite sport nearly doubled, and by the early 1970s, the NFL's Super Bowl gained national holiday status.

337

MacCambridge cites various reasons for this shift: that football was better on TV than baseball; and that football reflected more accurately American culture and its infatuation with power, passion, technology, and teamwork. MacCambridge also credits Commissioner Alvin "Pete" Rozelle for engineering the game's transformation from what a former NFL player described as a "localized sport based on gate receipts and played by oversized coal miners and West Texas psychopaths to a national sport based on television ratings." This occurred in large part because, according to MacCambridge, Rozelle was masterful at tailoring the NFL's image for a broad middle-class audience. He argues that Rozelle sold sports as they'd never been sold before – "a sophisticated passion, rather than a trivial juvenile pursuit," while articulating a vision of competitive balance in terms of revenues, competition, collaboration, and corporate outreach (2004, pp. xiv, xvi, xix).

Rozelle encouraged owners to think in terms of the well-being of the league rather than the success of individual franchises. He promoted the idea of competitive balance in which organizational structure, strategies, policies, and procedures were put into place to help to ensure that every team had an opportunity to rise to the top during any given season. He was able to unite owners, coaches, and players and to get them to buy into a shared vision of what is good for the league is essentially good for all.

Rozelle essentially laid the foundation for what many people believe is the world's preeminent professional sport league. In essence, the NFL is often viewed as the gold standard of professional team sport leagues, and has earned this reputation for several reasons. NFL franchises are considered to be some of the most valuable franchises in the world (Hambrecht, 2012). The league has the most lucrative television contracts in professional sport in the world. Of the league's $9 billion of revenue in 2011, $4 billion came from television rights (Gaines, 2011). It has developed valuable partnerships with a wide variety of industry-leading corporations. NFL-licensed products and apparel are consistently among the top selling in professional sport. Its broadcasts repeatedly bring in record audience numbers and it has enjoyed relative labor stability.

Yet, despite these positive metrics, the league still faces challenges. Head injuries such as concussions, policies related to player safety, medical coverage of retirees, and impending player lawsuits (that claim the league and helmet companies knew about potential dangers and failed to inform the players) are all subjects of concern (Schwarz, 2007; Nocera, 2012). Current Commissioner Roger Goodell must also deal with a four-year trend of diminishing league-wide attendance (Hayes, 2012).

THE CHALLENGE OF CHANGE IN PROFESSIONAL SPORTS

Professional league sport is probably the most high profile of all industry segments. It attracts the most media attention, and being a fan or supporter of a particular team has become an important part of many people's daily lives across the globe. Millions of fans around the world discuss their teams over coffee in the office and at the local pub. The business of professional league sport is a multi-billion dollar enterprise that is intensely scrutinized by a world community through television, radio, and Internet broadcasts, social media, and countless newspapers and websites. The professional league sport segment is very big business that incorporates sponsors, media partners, and thousands of support organizations and personnel.

Despite the fact that professional team sport leagues have been generally stable and have enjoyed a great deal of success in the last decade, significant changes at all levels of professional sport organizations have occurred. Changes in technology, sport medicine, drug testing, nutrition, equipment, and training have had a major impact on athletes and their games. Changes in the economy have affected consumer spending, sponsorship revenues, and merchandise sales. The emergence of new media technology has shaped not only how we consume professional sports, but how we interact with these organizations as well. New professional leagues and teams have come into the marketplace and others have relocated. Labor relations are an on-going challenge with words such as lock-out, strike, and collective bargaining agreement becoming part of the daily discussions of professional sports. In European leagues, a poorly performing franchise may be relegated to a lower division while another team is promoted (relegation system). Those who work in sport management in the professional team sport segment recognize that this industry sector is dynamic. For the professional sport manager, the challenge of change is the challenge to make change not a problem for the organization to overcome, but rather a key competency for the organization as it continues to pursue improvement and success.

Professional league sports: an overview

Professional league sports are characterized by their delivery of the highest level of sport competition and that athletes who play professionally are financially compensated for participation. The professional league sport industry in the U.S. (which includes Canadian franchises in all leagues except the NFL (until the Buffalo Bills move to Toronto)) includes over 1,500 organizations. The dominant professional sport leagues in the U.S. are the National Football League (NFL), Major League Baseball (MLB), the National Hockey League (NHL), and the National Basketball

Association (NBA). This group of leagues is often referred to as the "Big Four." Other professional leagues include the Women's National Basketball Association (WNBA), National Lacrosse League (NLL), Major League Lacrosse (MLL), and Major League Soccer (MLS). Professional league sport organizations also include minor league teams where, for sports such as hockey, baseball, and basketball, these leagues may be affiliated with professional franchises and serve as feeder programs. Minor league organizations may also operate independently for the purpose of spectator entertainment and/or player development.

Professional leagues and organizations can be found around the world and not only include baseball, basketball, football, and hockey, but also feature other popular sports such as cricket, soccer, and rugby. As outlined in Chapter 9, sports such as golf, tennis, and auto racing offer professional competitions, series, and leagues, but these sports are traditionally considered to be part of the tour sport industry segment because they tend to feature athletes competing individually rather than in teams and because series and events rotate from site to site.

Major league professional team sport organizations are primarily located in large metropolitan areas where teams can pull from a large population to sell their tickets and build their fan base. Large markets also offer the benefit of an established corporate community from which they can create sponsorship partnerships, sell advertising, and maximize other marketing opportunities. Minor league franchises are often located in secondary markets. All professional franchises require top-quality facilities, appropriate amenities, infrastructure, and other resources that support the franchise operation and league competition.

Professional team franchises are organized in a league structure and, for the most part, are privately held, although there are some publically held franchises. The league system requires that member franchises follow the policies, guidelines, procedures, and rules of the league. This system creates interdependence between the individual teams and, theoretically, the competitive balance between franchises that is necessary for organizational success and long-term sustainability. Historically, team owners have recognized that, without member competitors, the league and the team will fail. Some of the tools that have been employed to guarantee that teams stay viable include revenue sharing (gate receipts, national television and broadcast rights fees, licensing and merchandising, and expansion fees), the player draft system, and the granting of territorial rights. Other important league matters include labor relations, scheduling, league expansion or contraction, championship format, and the establishment of rules, policies, and procedures as they relate to operations and competition.

Understanding change in sport organizations

To understand change, it is necessary to examine why change occurs. Slack (1997) says that change emanates either from external sources or from within the sport organization itself.

External forces

Impetus for change in the external environment seems to originate from either one of two sources: external stakeholders or external conditions. External stakeholders may include the federal or local government, governing bodies, competitors, feeder organizations, media, fans, licensees, and sponsors.

Effects of pressure to change exerted by external stakeholders are easy to identify. For example, in the U.S., the federal government as an external stakeholder has investigated the use of performance-enhancing drugs in sports including professional baseball. Their work has forced several professional sport organizations to look more closely at their existing drug testing policies.

While external stakeholders include specific constituent groups, external conditions include general trends, interests, or factors that directly impact the operation of the sport organization. External conditions may include the economy, waning interest, or rising popularity of a particular sport, the political, religious, or social climate, and development of new technology. An example of a change brought about by an emerging environmental trend was the establishment of the Women's United Soccer Association in the U.S., which was seen to be a direct outcome of the U.S. women's World Cup victory in 1999 (Wagenheim, 2011). This league then folded in 2003. In 2007, the Women's Professional Soccer League was founded. The league was a restructuring of the old league spurred by continued interest in the sport in the years following the USA women's winning of the gold medal at the 2004 Olympic Games. Play began in 2009 on the heels of the U.S. women winning the 2008 Olympic gold medal and also the 2009 Women's World Cup. An increase in participation in girls' soccer programs is a direct result of the increased popularity of the sport in the U.S. and the high-profile success of the women's teams. The link between the U.S. women's success in the international arena to growth of women's soccer at all levels, including the attempt to establish professional leagues, is undeniable (Wagenheim, 2011).

The advent of new media technology is another example of change, and it has resulted in one of the most perplexing challenges faced by professional league sport managers. For example, many professional franchise managers agree that the development of broadcast technologies has significantly changed the operation of sport organizations. New national and international markets were opened up; new fans were reached; and new sources of revenue were made available. Evidence of the change brought about by the Internet, social media, and wireless can be seen in the operation of professional sport organizations around the world. Live game broadcasts are now streamed to electronic devices around the world. Sports scores, news, and updates are available to fans almost instantaneously through their smart phones and other devices. Fans are talking to one another around the globe and ordering merchandise and tickets on-line all hours of the day and night.

Internal forces

While external sources exert pressure on the organization to change, internal forces lead to change as well. Slack suggests that an emphasis on service quality, a move to self-managed teams, and the demand for flexible operating procedures have produced pressures for change from within the sport organization. Change may also be triggered by such simple operational activities as the hiring of a new employee, the development of a new policy, or the cutting of a budget item (Slack, 1997).

The construction of a new sport facility is a good example of how change can be driven from within. With the construction of a new sport facility, for example, the team may see opportunities to develop new revenues or offer new programs and services to ticket buyers. This change in venue may also require the hiring of new staff ranging from ushers to concession workers to promotional staff. A new security plan will need to be devised. New signage and new parking policies will need to be developed. New scoreboards may give rise to new sponsorships and promotional opportunities. In this example, it is easy to see how change in one area is likely to bring about change in other areas.

Categories of change in professional sport

Whether the impetus for change comes from internal or external sources, the manifestation of change occurs in one of four areas within the sport organization: technology, structures and systems, products and services, and people (Slack, 1997). Technological change refers to a change in production methods, service provision, or equipment based upon the development of new technology. Examples would include the adoption of new ticketing software, website development, or creation of a fan loyalty card program that rewards fans for swiping their fan loyalty card at kiosks in the arena so that they may accumulate loyalty points that may be used to purchase tickets or merchandise.

Structural and system changes encompass those changes to the organization's structural elements including division of labor, reporting structure, or organizational control. The creation of a social media coordinator position within the marketing department is a great example of how structural and system changes are manifested as the result of environmental change.

Product and service changes reflect changes to operational areas including the basic supply of goods and services, marketing, finance, and facility management. One example would be the adaptation of environmentally friendly stadium strategies such as recycling cans and bottles and replacing restroom paper hand towels with hand blow dryers. Other changes to products, services, and facilities might include the creation of gluten-free concession menu items or adding a kids fan club and playground area within the stadium. Changes to functional operational areas might include expanding promotional activities to incorporate social media platforms.

Lastly, changes in the people area involve human resource-related concerns. For example, these might include a change in player draft strategy or the hiring of a new coach. It may also include a change in internship programs or the shift to an on-line employee application process.

The domino effect of change

While it is useful to examine change on the basis of how it affects each of these areas – technology, structures and systems, products and services, and people – change does not occur in isolation. As in the example of a team moving into a new stadium, change in one area is frequently related to change in another area. There is, in fact, a domino effect for sport organizations whereby one change brings about subsequent changes throughout the organization.

This type of network of change is not unusual. In fact, there is little doubt that as long as professional sports exist, there will be both internal and external pressures to grow, improve, and innovate. For the professional league sport organization, change is not only inevitable, it is necessary.

IDENTIFYING THE CHANGE

Regardless of the specific change that an organization might pursue, effective management of the change process begins with comprehensive understanding in two areas. First, there should be a vision of the desired change or a comprehensive set of goals that define the change for the organization. Nowhere is vision more critical than in the process of achieving effective change. Management must develop a comprehensive set of goals that is so specific it will communicate an unmistakable vision of what the changed organization will look like. Second, there needs to be an understanding of the factors and forces that are likely to influence and shape the change process. The manager needs to carefully assess and consider all possible influences emanating both from the internal and external environment and should necessarily forecast how these factors will shape the change process.

343

Developing the vision

Consider the cases of former NFL Commissioner Peter Rozelle and current NFL Commissioner Roger Goodell. Both men led the league into unprecedented periods of growth and stability (Galica, 2012). Both men were able to stabilize and grow the league through their leadership and ability to unite a diverse group of constituencies. Both men talked to owners, players, media members, corporate sponsors, and fans and asked them to share their concerns and aspirations for the league. They then began to carefully articulate a vision for the NFL for all league stakeholder groups. Both men's visions involved enhancing all aspects of the game. For Rozelle, the vision was to establish the NFL as the premier professional sport league in the U.S. For Goodell, the vision was to continue to grow the game and to recommit to player safety so that the league will ensure its own sustainability while continuing to reach even greater heights as the premier professional team sports business. A look behind the scenes of Goodell's commissionership would show that he created a comprehensive set of goals that would include things like negotiating a new collective bargaining agreement, sponsoring a long-term study into the effects of head injury in NFL players, and ensuring that member franchises have optimal stadium and related facilities. Other goals might include negotiating of optimal media contracts and reaching new international markets through media or scheduling of games at non-U.S. sites. Goodell's vision for the future of the NFL is not only well conceived, but represents a thoughtful and strategic idea that positively positions the league for the future.

Goodell's actions demonstrate what management expert Noel Tichy calls envisioning, a process that involves not just management, but the entire organization:

> The visioning process is creative and often chaotic. A vision is a group effort. It is what the group believes to be important. It is also a work in progress, an architectural rendering that constantly gets modified. As many people as possible should be involved, thinking "out loud" and getting feedback from many different stakeholders.
>
> (Tichy, 1993, p. 118)

The first responsibility of the sport manager in directing change involves not just stating one's individual philosophy or ideas about what the organization should look like or what changes should occur, but instead, he or she must include all members of the organization in the thinking and planning process.

Leadership researchers Warren Bennis and Burt Nanus come to the same conclusion:

> The leader only rarely was the one who conceived of the vision in the first place. Therefore the leader must be a superb listener, particularly to those advocating new or different images of the emerging reality ... Successful leaders, we have found, are *great askers*, and they do pay attention.
>
> (Bennis and Nanus, 1985, p. 492, original emphasis)

Managing change and the professional league sport industry

In managing change, the sport manager's first responsibility is to "get" the vision, to listen, and to "think out loud" in conversations throughout the organization for the purpose of developing a specific set of goals that will define exactly what the change should look like in his or her organization. Through a vision that can be directly translated into clearly defined goals and with a strong and specific sense of exactly what the change should be, the manager can then turn to the next task in the change process. This task involves understanding all the forces and factors that will affect the organization as it pursues the change goals.

Force field analysis

Social scientist Kurt Lewin (1951) developed a process for identifying and analyzing the forces operating in a change situation that he called force field analysis. Lewin suggested that in any organizational change effort, two kinds of forces affect the change operating in any change situation: driving forces and restraining forces.

Lewin defined *driving forces* as forces or factors in the situation that initiate, assist, and support the change. Driving forces include such things as changes in the organization's environment that make change necessary or that represent an opportunity to the organization. They include key individuals and groups within the organization who are in favor of and support the change. They also include the availability of training, technology, and other resources necessary for the change to be effective. Driving forces might also include information or experiences that make clear what will happen if the organization doesn't change.

To understand the effect of driving forces in bringing about change, one needs only look at how the leagues might decide to move, add, or drop franchises from the league. MLS' decision to add franchises recently in Philadelphia, Portland (OR), Seattle, and Toronto may be the result of driving forces including the desire to reach smaller cities with a strong soccer interest, and national and international viewership for its media broadcast partners.

Restraining forces are forces or factors working against the change, forces generating resistance at the individual and corporate culture levels. In many ways, restraining forces are the opposite of driving forces. They include opposition from key individuals and groups within the organization, and lack of availability of training and other resources needed for the change to succeed. Restraining forces might also include negative information or experiences relative to the change. Restraining forces working against the MLS decision to add teams may be a lack of quality domestic players and increased travel costs. A force field analysis for NFL rules changes that might enhance player safety are shown below in Box 10.1.

For change to be effective, managers must begin with a careful and complete force field analysis. They must first identify the driving forces in the situation and make

345

full use of them to overcome the obstacles to change. Perhaps more importantly, managers must also correctly identify the restraining forces in the situation and develop strategies to eliminate or minimize them as the change moves forward. Only when this depth and scope of understanding has been achieved is the sport manager ready to begin actually implementing the change process.

BOX 10.1 FORCE FIELD ANALYSIS FOR NFL AND PLAYER SAFETY RULES

Driving forces Reasons for rules changes	Player injury results in loss of player asset Team health care costs rise with injuries Attendance/audience may drop when marquee players are injured Player injury results in poor team performance Loss of fans Loss of audience Drop in merchandise sales Loss of sponsorship Fans complain about brutality Ethical and moral concerns about long-term health issues for players Lawsuits NFL alumni suffer long-term health problems Negative public opinion – the NFL is inhumane
Restraining forces Reasons against rules changes	Possible perception that game is soft and uninteresting Loss of fans Costs to retrain officials Backlash from broadcast partners, sponsors Head injury research is incomplete Player resistance Owner resistance Negative impact on successful brand

---

IMPLEMENTING THE CHANGE PROCESS

Once the change goal has been clearly defined, and the analysis of the force field relative to that goal has been completed, the task for the sport manager is to begin to implement the change plan. Again it is Kurt Lewin who provides a simple theoretical model for understanding how change is brought about within organizations. While there are several theories that may be useful for the manager in understanding how to manage change, Lewin's theory provides a good starting point for students interested in examining how change takes place within an organization. According to Lewin, there are three stages in a successful change process:

1   The *unfreezing* stage, during which the organization addresses the problems of
    resistance and prepares its people for change;
2   The *actual change* stage, during which the new beliefs and new behaviors are
    communicated, modeled, and initiated;
3   The *refreezing* stage, during which the new beliefs and behaviors are supported
    and reinforced.

To achieve the change goal, the manager must manage each of these stages effectively.

Stage 1: unfreezing – reducing the resistance to change

Change does not come easily, for individuals or for organizations. For reasons we
will discuss below, both individuals and organizations tend to resist change vigor-
ously. The first stage in the change management process, then, focuses on reducing
the resistance to change. This resistance to change in organizations exists at the
individual and at the organizational levels. At the individual level, the source of
resistance to change appears to be our human nature. At the organizational level, it
is the "corporate culture" that tends to resist change.

Stress: the human response to change

The changes required for organizations to be competitive in today's dynamic environment are not minor. People are being asked to learn and use technology that may
not have even existed a few years earlier; to do more work, faster and with greater
quality than ever before; and, in the case of sport organizations, to successfully
adapt to new rules and regulations that are continuously being promulgated by governing bodies. Often, the natural response to change of this dimension or magnitude
is what is called the stress response (Seyle, 1976).

The *stress response* is the fight-or-flight response that prepares us for action when we
are in danger. Unfortunately, most people view major change as a potential source
of danger, and their natural reaction is one of stress. People become anxious about
whether they can do what the change requires in terms of using new technology, doing
different work than they are used to, and doing more of it, faster and with greater quality. People worry about whether there will still be a place for them in the organization.
From a needs perspective, change represents a threat to people's security, and often
their natural reaction is to resist and defend against this perceived threat.

For example, as the media has increasingly scrutinized the off-field behavior of professional athletes, additional pressure has been placed on players, agents, coaches,
public relations staff, and owners to set standards for acceptable behavior and then
attempt to bring about such behaviors. Athletes' access to social media has added
additional opportunities for athletes to behave badly and embarrass themselves or
their organization. For some coaches, this job requirement is outside their comfort
zone. They are used to breaking down game films, assessing athletes' skills, and

347

devising game strategies. Monitoring athletes' personal lives and being asked to comment on this by the media is a daunting task to them.

For the public relations specialist, the advent of social media creates additional work as well as new demands for expertise and skills in that area. Public relations staff may wonder if they can be effective with this new aspect of their job. To escape the stress associated with these additional responsibilities, the initial response of the employee is often one of resistance. Their view can often be that these new responsibilities should be given to someone else. In fact, many coaches and public relations/media relations/communications department members have successfully lobbied their managers for the creation of new positions to handle this work.

As in these examples, the human response to change in organizations tends to be negative. Not only will people question how the change affects them individually, but they also question how the change will affect the organization. Change may be resisted because stakeholders question the outcomes of the change, i.e. do we really need a Facebook page and isn't it becoming obsolete anyway? For the employee, the question is whether or not this change will be worth the necessary investment of time, effort, and money. Is this change good for everyone? Will some of us be left behind? Do the benefits of this change outweigh the total costs to the organization and all of the stakeholders? For this reason, effective change must begin with strategies to help people to get beyond this initial stress response to enable them to fully adapt to the requirements of the change.

According to management change theorist Robert Kriegel, people are the most critical element of successful change,

> people are the gatekeepers of change. They have the power to breathe life into a new program or kill it. If they're excited and positive; it's open sesame. If they're not – and that's most of the time – it's clang! The gate's slammed shut in your face.
>
> (Kriegel, 1996, p. 5)

Corporate culture

The other major source of resistance to change in organizations is corporate culture, the term used to describe the set of beliefs, norms, and values that are shared by the members of an organization. These beliefs, norms, and values have to do with the way the organization operates, and what is important in that organization. Researchers Terrence Deal and Allan Kennedy (1982) suggest that corporate culture tends to be created and communicated by the stories an organization tells about itself, by the language it uses, by whom the organization celebrates as its heroes, and by its rituals and ceremonies.

Professional league sport organizations are famous for the kinds of stories, language, and rituals that communicate the beliefs and values of sport teams and leagues throughout the world. For example, international football/futbol/calcio (soccer) fans around the world identify closely with local, regional, and national teams. They may dress in team colors, paint their faces, chant throughout the game, drink excessively, and engage in acts of violent hooliganism (see also Chapter 2). It is not unusual for professional hockey fans to throw their ball caps on the ice when a player scores three goals in a game, "the hat trick." In professional baseball in Japan, hitters commonly touch or brush the home plate after a home run to show respect for the next hitter. In India, some teenage Islamic girls are playing basketball in the hopes of securing a position on one of the semi-professional circuit club teams which offers full-time jobs to talented players, lodgings, and a lifetime job upon retirement (Westhead, 2011). Their actions fly in the face of centuries-old Islamic traditions. Some professional sport leagues have instituted diversity hiring programs for the purpose of expanding the pool of qualified minority applicants and employees.

In a very real sense, the beliefs, norms, and values communicated through these actions, stories, rituals, and heroes provide a mental road map to the members of a sport organization. They define and reinforce in people's minds what is important in the organization and "the way things are done around here." Because it requires a shift in current practice, change represents the most serious kind of threat to an organization's corporate culture. Change requires a new set of beliefs, new norms, and new values. It not only requires new heroes, new language, and new rituals; change renders the old heroes, language, and rituals obsolete.

As shown in Box 10.2, for the process of change to be successful in an organization, management must recognize both the potentially intense individual human resistance to change and the equally intense collective resistance rising from the organization's corporate culture and utilize the appropriate strategy to diminish their negative effects. The first step in managing change, therefore, is to deal with the reality of this resistance. Management's task in the "unfreezing stage" is to reduce this resistance to change at both the individual and the organizational level. The resistance must be "unfrozen" and thawed to enable the personal and organizational flexibility necessary to accept and embrace the change.

Strategies for reducing resistance to change

John Kotter and Leonard Schlesinger (1979) have identified a number of strategies (shown in Box 10.2) for reducing individual and organizational resistance to change in organizations. For our purposes, this collection of strategies for unfreezing can be divided into two categories: agreement-oriented approaches and the coercive approach.

Agreement-oriented approaches to unfreezing

Four of the options identified by Kotter and Schlesinger – education and communication, participation and involvement, facilitation and support, and negotiation and agreement – can be described as agreement-oriented approaches to preparing people for change. Each of these four options represents an effort to work with people to help them accept the need for the change before moving forward. As a result, these approaches each have the important advantage of being more likely to maintain the bond of trust between managers and the other members of the organization. The assumption is that resistance to the change will lessen as management takes the time to address people's concerns and to reach agreement about how best to achieve the change.

In some change situations, however, these agreement-oriented approaches to unfreezing may not be possible. For example, it is conceivable that no amount of lobbying, education, participation, facilitation, or negotiation could prepare a sport organization for the kinds of change required when there is an immediate threat to the athletic program, student-athlete, or athletic department staff member. This brings us to the second category of unfreezing that involves a more coercive approach.

Coercion as a strategy for unfreezing

Coercion is the process of imposing change on an organization. It is the process of requiring people to perform new tasks, or to perform their old tasks in new ways, or to perform in conditions that might be dramatically different from what they have been accustomed to, whether they agree or not. Coerced change is not voluntary, it does not involve education or facilitation or negotiation, and it is usually not

350

gradual. Coercion is used when the need for change is too urgent to permit the more time-consuming, agreement-oriented option.

Coercion would be a valuable strategy for a minor league team that faced problems arising from an incident involving one of its players. The player, who was driving home from the stadium after an away game team bus trip, was arrested for driving intoxicated after causing an automobile accident with injury to the other driver. With the looming possibility of the loss of the player and a lawsuit against the team from the other driver, the general manager and ownership might immediately institute a policy of no alcohol service on team buses.

In such a scenario, the sport managers involved determined that the severity of the incident and the likely irreparable harm to participants, the general public, and the franchise were so heinous that coercion to bring about changes to the team's policy on alcohol service was the only available option. This change was not voluntary; the change was required for all personnel on team buses. The general manager and owners were convinced that the change could not be optional nor brought about in participatory fashion. At the very least, in their minds, there was not enough time for further education, participation, and negotiation in dealing with the issue. For the general manager and the owner, the change was necessary for the organization's survival and the safety of players and the general public; so the change was coerced.

Some critics might argue that coercion is not a strategy for reducing resistance to change, but rather is a process of imposing change despite continuing broad-based resistance. While there is some validity to this position, there are grounds for viewing coercion as a legitimate means to reducing resistance. Based on his research on the relationship between feelings and behavior, Harvard psychologist Jerome Bruner concluded: "You more often act yourself into feeling than feel yourself into action" (1973, p. 24). According to Bruner, people tend to adjust how they feel about something to the reality of the situation. This suggests that even if people are forced into change, once they realize that they can survive new conditions and may even benefit by them, their resistance to the change may at least be reduced, if not eliminated entirely.

Some experts still question whether coercion might not actually increase resistance among resentful employees over the longer term. They point out that the problem with forcing people into change is that you then find yourself operating an organization with a crushed and battered workforce. Defenders of coercion as an approach for unfreezing, on the other hand, argue that coerced change can still be implemented in ways that respect the needs and dignity of people. Still others point out that, given the pressure on organizations to change rapidly in response to opportunities and threats, there may be no effective alternative.

Stage 2: the actual change

Once resistance to change has been reduced to the extent possible, the task for managers is to begin the actual change. The new behaviors, the new approach, and the new priorities required by the change must be preached, modeled, and initiated. In other words, you can't expect people to follow you from the old way to the new way until it is clear to them, in the most specific terms possible, just what the new way is, what it means, and that they are an important part of the process.

We have already pointed out that a clear definition of the change goal is essential even prior to beginning the change process. We have also discussed the importance of getting constituents to become invested in the change and take responsibility for the change by participating in the shaping of the vision and resultant change goals. But even the most inspiring vision will not move an organization unless it can effectively be shared. In the second stage of the change process, the challenge for managers is to *communicate* the change both within and beyond the organization through words and actions.

Words

Words are a powerful force in focusing our attention and mobilizing our energies. Anyone who has heard the motivational words of a coach before a big game understands the power of the spoken word. Change is a political process in which the forces for improvement attempt to overcome the forces of resistance and the status quo. Effective change can be viewed as the result of an effective campaign, and words are a potentially powerful weapon in deciding the outcome of that campaign.

We said at the outset that effective change begins with a clear and comprehensive vision of exactly what the change means and looks like for the organization. The challenge in this second stage of implementing the change is to find the words, the phrases, and the stories that will enable the stakeholders of the organization to share the change vision and to begin to act on it. The sport manager must truly be an organizational coach who encourages, motivates, and energizes members of the organization and other constituencies with his or her enthusiasm for the change.

Actions speak louder than words

As important as an effective change message is, however, all the words in the world will not be as effective as the example of a leader, especially in communicating new behaviors and values. There is often no more effective way to help people understand the change vision than to have "the new way" modeled for them by the manager.

Words can yield a variety of interpretations in terms of the kind of behaviors people *think* they mean. But a manager's actions provide a clear model of exactly the kind of behavior that is required. In the case of change, imitation is more effective than interpretation. A manager who wants people to take a more team-based approach with their people, for example, will almost certainly get better results by taking a more team-based approach him or herself rather than just by making a speech on teamwork. The same is true for a sport manager who wants to see his or her staff spending less time in their offices and more time talking and working with their people. If the manager wants his or her staff out of their offices and talking with people, the best way to achieve this is to lead by example. The actions of the leader, *if they are consistent with their words*, simply provide a much clearer message about the kind of new behavior required by the change.

Communication in actions and in words is the essential task of the manager in the second stage of the change process. Only through a strongly shared sense of exactly what the change is, expressed compellingly in words and shown dramatically in the leader's actions, will the organization be able to begin to move from where it has been, to where the change seeks to take it.

Stage 3: refreezing/re-architecting

Lewin (1951) termed the third and final phase of the change process "refreezing." *Refreezing* is the process of reinforcing the change, once it emerges, to ensure that it endures over the long term. If the new patterns and the new behaviors developed in the change phase are genuinely to take root and prosper, they must become embedded in the very fabric of the organization, and they must yield positive results. This is what Tichy means by "re-architecting": designing and building the structures and support needed to sustain the new behaviors and beliefs far into the future.

For change to endure and prosper, the new ways of doing things must become part of an overall positive experience for the people doing them. To achieve this, the refreezing phase requires the elements shown in Box 10.3 below. In other words, successful change requires the development of an entirely new corporate culture focused on the new behaviors and the new beliefs.

BOX 10.3 ELEMENTS OF REFREEZING/RE-ARCHITECTING

- Recognizing the heroes and champions of change;
- Celebrating the successes of the change;
- Rewarding commitment to change.

Recognizing heroes

Successful change requires heroes, individuals, and groups who adopt the new behaviors and run with them. The heroism can take many forms, from the sport information director who works extra hours to prepare a last-minute press release to the booster club member who solicits a major gift from his own company to support the athletic program. Clearly, the successful achievement of change requires the support and dedication of many people. Refreezing the change requires the recognition of those individuals and groups who actively participate in and lead the change.

Sport managers traditionally recognize their heroes through awards and publicity programs. Heroes are awarded trophies or plaques for their contributions as a matter of tradition. However, the celebration of heroes need not necessarily take the form of a certificate of appreciation, logo golf shirt, or golden cup. Heroes may be recognized through other positive feedback strategies such as writing a feature story about the hero in the team's newsletter; offering the hero an all-expenses paid trip to a desirable away game; or recognizing the hero during half-time ceremonies. Some sport organizations celebrate their heroes by providing them with premium sport event tickets, inviting them to participate in the championship parade, or inducting them into the team hall of fame.

Sport managers must take the time to identify and recognize heroes. In doing so, they not only clarify the direction of the change, but also reinforce the emerging value that views trying the new behaviors as nothing short of heroic.

Celebrations

Celebrations are a powerful way to emphasize and reinforce values and behaviors through a positive social experience. Celebrations are community events that dramatically enrich the experience of the group and the individual. In recent past years, organizations have begun to recognize the power of celebration. Initially during this period, celebrations were organized around employee anniversaries: five years with the firm, ten years, 25 years, and so on. Over time, the forms of celebration in sport have multiplied from the informal office pizza party to a more formal team dinner. Some sport managers recognize staff members who have championed change and brought about desirable results through celebratory lunches, trips, or golf outings.

One of the most well-known and traditional celebrations in sport has been the raising of championship banners to the roof of the arena or the retiring of a hero's uniform number (or, in the recent case when quarterback Peyton Manning joined the NFL's Denver Broncos, the number 18 – previously retired in 1963 in honor of former Bronco Frank Tripucka – was "unretired" and given to the new QB. To his credit, Tripucka said: "I would be honored to have him wear it. It's been retired for [almost] 50 years. That's enough" (Kils, 2012, p. 1)). While these types of celebrations are often reserved for those athletes or coaches whose performance on the court or on the ice is worthy of recognition, employees as organizational champions may be recognized through a variation on that theme. For example, a sales executive who created and implemented a new system for securing corporate sponsorships may be worthy of having his or her own team jersey created. The jersey might then be hung from the office ceiling for a week. One common staff celebration includes the employee of the month award. It is not unusual to see professional teams recognize their employees for excellent service or extraordinary ideas that bring about positive change.

The common thread in these celebrations is that they are community events marking community achievement, whether in terms of athletic performance, sales, service, or just completing another productive week. If a change is to become a genuine part of the life of the organization, it must be celebrated as it unfolds and advances. Recognition and appreciation of the achievement of the change goals must be raised to the level of community celebration. Only very reluctantly do we give up our celebrations; so celebrations, in a sense, serve as insurance that the changes will endure.

Reward

As important as recognition and celebrations are for refreezing or reinforcing the new behaviors required by change, pay and promotion remain among the most powerful means of reinforcing behavior in organizations. The ultimate indicators of an organization's priorities are still most clearly reflected in what you get paid for and who gets promoted. Basing pay and promotion decisions on progress made toward adopting the new behaviors sends a powerful signal that the organization is serious about the change.

For example, if a corporate sales manager has been asked to lead efforts to secure new corporate sponsorships for a new arena and a group sales representative is asked to increase group ticket sales, then some significant portion of their compensation should be based on how well they perform in these new areas. Additionally, their success may be rewarded with promotions to the assistant director level. Designing reward systems that directly reinforce the change priorities of an organization can be difficult. By paying and promoting change champions and change heroes, however, and by rewarding the early adopters of change, the organization is sending a clear message about what matters now through one of the most important channels it has.

Change in organizations is a marathon, not a sprint. Many managers will say that for significant change to be achieved and genuinely to take root will take closer to a decade than a year. The message from this section is that effective change should be viewed as a managerial triathlon of three events: unfreezing, the actual change, and refreezing. Only successful performance in all three will enable the sport manager to achieve the goal of effective change.

MANAGING CONTINUOUS CHANGE

In the past, any organizational change tended to be viewed as an infrequent event that would likely be followed by a period of stability for the organization. Once a change occurred, the organization would continue in the new direction. However, in today's dynamic environment, change is never ending. Once the three-part change process is complete, it is time to start all over again. It may be argued that change is an on-going process and management of change is an ever-present concern that must be viewed as a critical responsibility of management.

The "calm waters" versus "white-water rapids" metaphors

Many years ago, management professor Peter Vaill used the term "calm waters" to describe the conditions under which a manager navigates change. Vaill compares organizations to large ocean liners traveling calm waters with a crew that had made the trip together dozens of times. Under "calm water" conditions, change is usually required only when the occasional storm appears. The "ship" (the organization) makes a change in course to avoid the storm but, once the storm passes, the ship resumes course toward its destination.

As we have noted throughout this book, conditions in more recent times have changed how sport organizations do business. The effects on management and operations are dramatic. According to Vaill, the environment is no longer one of calm waters with only occasional storms, and organizations are no longer like large ocean liners with a veteran crew. The organization, says Vaill, is

> more akin to a forty-foot raft than to a large ship. Rather than sailing a calm sea, this raft must traverse a raging river made up of an uninterrupted flow of permanent white-water rapids. To make things worse, the raft is manned by ten people who have never worked together, none have traveled the river below, much of the trip is in the dark, the river is dotted by unexpected turns and obstacles, the exact destination of the raft is unclear, and at irregular frequencies the raft needs to pull to shore, where new crew members are added and others leave.
>
> (1991, p. 32)

In the permanent white-water rapids described by Vaill over 20 years ago, he described how organizations need to be not merely capable of implementing an occasional change, but *built* for change, with constant change as one of their fundamental goals. His insights are even more relevant today.

While this approach may result in a successful organization that is constantly innovating and creating change, a word of caution is necessary. Change, in and of itself, is not always inherently beneficial to the organization. Some managers, in an attempt to become bigger, better, faster, more competitive, or more innovative, can dramatically increase employee stress levels, dramatically drain resources, and diminish the quality and service of existing programs or initiatives.

Author Robert Kriegel (1996) identified how organizations fail in their attempts to innovate and manage change for their own benefit. Change can and does fail when an organization tries to do too much all at once, tries to move too quickly, initiates changes that are impractical, or impossible, or fails to fully consider existing resources or potential consequences of the change. Ill-advised organizational change initiatives can create a workplace that resembles a "panic zone" where employees are rushed, stressed out, reactive, nervous, and scared (Kriegel, 1996, p. 299). Kriegel warns that, in this environment, communication breakdowns occur, creativity suffers, good judgment is threatened, and people shift into crisis management mode. The lesson is that while innovation and change require a certain amount of risk taking, sport managers must not abandon logic, common sense, and sound business practices when positioning their organization as change leaders. Managers must never forget the people component of change.

Thriving on chaos: the innovative organization

Tom Peters, one of the world's leading management theorists, suggests that an organization successfully built to seek out and thrive upon change would have a clear competitive advantage. Peters' point is that, in a genuinely chaotic environment, an organization built to *thrive* on chaos will certainly do better than one built merely to *survive* the chaos. According to Peters, the goal of the innovative organization is to create an organization for which the continuous "white-water rapids" are a source of competitive advantage and not a source of continuous insecurity and dread. Peters has suggested a set of principles that typify what he calls the *innovative* organization, a blueprint for designing organizations to actually thrive on chaos. A number of Peters' principles for creating such an organization include setting goals for innovation, investing in applications-oriented small projects designed to facilitate innovation, encouraging pilot-testing of new ideas, and supporting innovation champions (Peters, 1987).

According to Peters, the goal of the innovative organization is to create an organization *designed* for "white-water rapids," an organization whose ability to "thrive on chaos" represents a competitive advantage over organizations for whom change somehow represents a continuing problem.

The learning organization

Back in Chapter 1, we learned of the concepts of learning organizations in the context of the NFL's legal battle with former licensee American Needle. As noted in Chapter 1, Peter Senge (1990) has suggested a different prescription for prospering as organizations such as the NFL face turbulence and change. According to Senge, the only organizations that will successfully adapt to the conditions of continuous change are those that are constantly engaged in learning from their own and others' experiences. Only organizations that are deeply committed to continuous learning will be capable of the continuous adjustments necessary for success in a fast-paced, constantly changing environment. While learning may be a management responsibility, according to Senge, it is not exclusively – or even primarily – the task of managers. Organizations in general at all levels must become more "learningful." A culture of change-readiness must pervade the entire organization.

Jon Spoelstra, President of Professional Sports Franchises Division, Mandalay Baseball Properties LLC of Mandalay Entertainment, widely considered to be one of the industry's most innovative and successful sports marketers, suggests that sport organizations must change and innovate to survive in today's sport industry (Spoelstra, 1997). For Spoelstra, who also served in executive positions with several professional team sport organizations, the key is creating an organization that not only rewards and values innovation and change, but encourages it. By creating think-tank sessions away from the office for employees, rewarding even innovative failures, and recognizing budding superstars of innovation, Spoelstra was able to create an organizational culture within the team sport organizations that thrived on "little experiments" which often gave birth to "breakthrough ideas" that greatly increased ticket revenues (Spoelstra, 1997). Sport organizations must be willing to embrace change, harness it, and realize its promise of improving and enhancing the organization. Successful organizations are those that create change, embrace change, and lead change rather than those that seek to be sensitive to change, react to change, or adapt to change (Kriegel, 1996). Sport organizations that integrate change readiness into their culture are those organizations that question existing beliefs, assumptions, and standards while seeking out opportunities to innovate, to lead, to take risks, and to challenge existing ways of doing things.

EPILOGUE: MLS INTERNATIONAL

What's the most popular sport in the world? Football, right? Not American football, but the sport most of us call soccer. So why isn't soccer as popular in the U.S. as it is in, say, Argentina, Ghana, Turkey, or Qatar (host of the 2022 FIFA World Cup)? Most of you probably played soccer at some point as a child, and many of you may have kept on through high school or beyond. So people play soccer in America (as the data in Chapter 4 indicate). So why isn't Major League Soccer – the continent's highest level of pro soccer – more popular? Why does the NFL get crowds of nearly 100,000 at their games, while MLS is happy to draw 20,000 to theirs? Yes, the NFL has been around longer. We learned above about how the NFL developed into the presence it is now over a period of decades. The same could be true for MLS. Give MLS 80 or 90 years and let's see where they go, you might think.

But the biggest impediment for MLS is its clear inferiority to other professional leagues, mostly those in Europe. Teams in England's Barclays Premier League are stocked with the best players from around the world. MLS? Not so much. In fact, several of the best U.S. players play for teams in the U.K. And most Americans know that our pro leagues are the best of their type in the world, as is the case with the NHL, NBA, and MLB. And with so many European league games available today through various media outlets, it is just as easy to watch Norwich City versus Wigan Athletic at the DW Stadium as it is Sporting KC versus the Houston Dynamo.

So how does MLS counter the reality that its product is inferior to pro leagues in the U.K., Germany, Italy, and Spain? One possibility is to take the route often suggested by U.S. leagues in their efforts to reach foreign markets: expand internationally. But rather than place an MLS franchise in London to play in the U.S. against Chivas USA and the San Jose Earthquakes, why not seek to have an MLS team located in the U.S. play in the Barclays Premier League? Maybe the previous year's league champion, or a team of U.S. all-stars? Wouldn't this draw more fans to the sport to see a U.S. team battling every week against the likes of Arsenal, Chelsea, and Tottenham Hotspur? Couldn't you draw more than 20,000 to see Manchester United play in the U.S. in something other than an exhibition match? Would there be barriers? Sure. But is it worth a try to grow the sport in the U.S.?

SUMMARY

Professional sport is a segment of the sport industry that has changed dramatically and continues to pose a challenge for the sport manager. The sources of change include the changing environment, advancing technologies, new structures and systems, products and services, and people concerns. Professional team sport organizations face continuous pressures from outside and inside the organization to grow, improve, and innovate.

Managing the change involves developing a vision and translating the vision into clearly defined goals. Through force field analysis, the manager undertakes the task of understanding the factors supporting the change and the sources of resistance.

Implementing the change process includes three stages. The first stage, unfreezing or awakening, must prepare people and awaken them to the need for change. The second stage is the change or envisioning stage. In this stage the goals of the change are defined, clarified, and communicated. The third stage, refreezing or re-architecting, requires that reward structures be created to reinforce the change as it begins to happen to ensure that it endures over time. Without the successful completion of all three stages, the process of change becomes more dubious.

But making even the most successful change is probably not enough. One of the most significant changes for management is that, in today's rapid-paced environment, change never ends. Continuous change is the new requirement. This means that management must develop organizations built for change. Tom Peters describes the innovative organization designed to thrive on chaos. Peter Senge outlines the terms of the learning organization, in which everyone learns from their experience and makes the adjustments required by whatever change lies ahead. Jon Spoelstra argues that successful sport organizations must be willing to challenge the status quo, question common conventions, and encourage risk taking. Clearly, good sport managers are those that can quickly shape their organizations and adapt to change in an ever-increasingly dynamic environment. Excellent sport managers are those that will initiate change and create organizations where change is the norm and innovation is the standard.

MANAGEMENT EXERCISE: GOODELL TO GREAT

In this chapter, we have introduced NFL Commissioner Roger Goodell, one of the most powerful professional team sport managers in the world. What few people know about Goodell is that he represents the model of what many aspiring professional team sport managers hope to become. On August 8, 2006, Goodell, who slept with a football at age six, became commissioner. Goodell had always wanted to play professionally but had a knee injury during his freshman year in college and told everyone he knew that his dream was to work in the NFL. When Goodell was named to succeed Commissioner Paul Tagliabue, he became, in essence, the patron saint of professional team sport interns everywhere.

Goodell's story is a familiar one to everyone who has toiled at the lower rungs of the ladder for professional team sport organizations. While working part-time as a bartender as he finished his undergraduate studies, Goodell received a stream of rejection letters from NFL teams to whom he had sent his résumé. When he finally got a chance through an NFL internship program in 1981, he jumped at the opportunity. In 1983, he worked for the New York Jets as a public relations intern cutting out newspaper articles. Mike Kensil, the former vice president of operations with the Jets, said of Goodell:

The thing that impressed you was no job was too small. He is such a dog-gedly hard worker. And he has the ability to talk to people and hear what they're saying, yet at the same time, get his point across. When he left to go back to the league office at the end of the year, we were all saying this guy was going to go somewhere. Little did we know ...

(Battista, 2006, p. 8)

In his near decade as commissioner, Goodell has overseen many significant changes to the game including the negotiation of a new collective bargaining agreement, the integration of technology into the NFL operational landscape, and the signing of one of the most lucrative broadcast partnerships in history. He has taken a firm stance on improving player safety through research and disciplinary action against players and coaches who were involved in creating a bounty system under which players were financially rewarded for aggressive hits that injured other players. He has widely been lauded as one of the best commissioners and most powerful men in all of professional team sports (Gloeckler and Lowry, 2007; Rosenberg, 2012). Not bad ... for an intern.

QUESTIONS FOR YOU TO CONSIDER

1   Explain how the evolution of the role of commissioner came about in governing professional league sport organizations. What internal and external environmental changes served as the impetus for the creation of the commissioner's role?

2   Identify and explain the significant driving forces and restraining forces that are likely to bring about organizational change in the NFL within the next five years.

3   Research your own favorite professional sport team franchise to determine ownership and franchise value. Explain how valuation for professional league sport franchises is calculated.

4   Compare and contrast the structure and operations of professional leagues in three different countries.

5   Explain how professional team sport organizations are utilizing social media to enhance their brands.

361

REFERENCES

1 The sport management challenge and the branded and licensed sport product industry

Ain, M., Clemmons, A.K., Cook, L., Dooley, J., Feldman, B., and Haney, T. (2010, August 23). College football confidential. *ESPN Magazine*, pp. 80–94.

Belson, K. (2010, January 7). American Needle: From green celluloid visors to caps of all kinds. *New York Times*, p. B15.

Belson, K. (2012, May 22). A hobby to many, card collecting was life's work for one man. *New York Times*. Accessed July 2, 2012, from: http://www.nytimes.com/2012/05/22/sports/baseball/baseball-card-collecting-was-lifes-work-for-jefferson-burdick.html?pagewanted=all.

Belson, K. and Schwarz, A. (2010, January 7). Antitrust case has implications far beyond N.F.L. *New York Times*, pp. B13, B15.

Berry, R.C. and Wong, G.M. (1993). *Law and business of the sport industries: Common issues in amateur and professional sports, Volume II* (rev. ed.). Westport, CT: Praeger Publishers.

Bhanoo, S.N. (2010, June 12). Those earth-friendly products? Turns out they're profit-friendly as well. *New York Times*, p. B3.

Birnbach, L. (ed.) (1980). *The official preppy handbook*. New York: Workman Publishing.

Branch, J. (2009a, March 22). Want to tread on Jeter's turf? Yankees grass is now a brand. *New York Times*, pp. A1, A21.

Branch, J. (2009b, April 21). The authenticator. *New York Times*, pp. B12, B15.

Brennan, C. (2012, February 16). All-star Lin? Put him in, Commish. *USA Today*, p. 3C.

Broughton, D. (2010, January 4–10). Sports and this court: How the nine sitting justices have ruled on industry-related cases. *Street & Smith's SportsBusiness Journal*, p. 10.

Burke, J. (2011, August 22). The 18 best-dressed ladies on the tour. Bleacher Report. Accessed July 9, 2012, from: http://bleacherreport.com/articles/814894-lpga-the-18-best-dressed-ladies-on-the-tour#/articles/814894-lpga-the-18-best-dressed-ladies-on-the-tour/page/19.

Byrne, J.A. (1992, October 23). Paradigms for postmodern managers. *Business Week/Renewing America*, p. 63.

Caldwell, D. (2010, August 22). With merchandise sales down, Nascar has high hopes for tiny cars. *New York Times*, p. Y5.

Chamberlain, G. (2012, March 3). Olympic brands caught up in abuse scandal. *The Guardian.* Accessed July 7, 2012, from: http://www.guardian.co.uk/business/2012/mar/03/olympic-brands-abuse-scandal?INTCMP=SRCH.

Chang, J. with Halliday, J. (2006). *Mao: The unknown story.* New York: Anchor Books.

Chozick, A. (2012, April 9). Apps take positions in the Topps baseball lineup. *New York Times,* pp. B1, B4.

Clarkson, M.B.E. (1995). A stakeholder framework for analyzing and evaluating corporate social performance. *Academy of Management Review, 20,* pp. 92–117.

Connor, T. (2012, January). Totally prepped. *Connecticut Magazine.* Accessed July 7, 2012, from: http://www.connecticutmag.com/Connecticut-Magazine/January-2012/Success-Stories-Totally-Prepped/index.php?previewmode=on.

Davis, F. (1992). *Fashion, culture and identity.* Chicago: University of Chicago Press.

Donaldson, T. and Preston, L. (1995). The stakeholder theory of the corporation: Concepts, evidence, implications. *Academy of Management Review, 20,* pp. 65–91.

Duerson, A. (2007, March 19). Back on Topps. *Sports Illustrated,* p. 30.

Fayol, H. (1949). *General and industrial administration.* New York: Pittman.

Football and antitrust (2010, January 13). *New York Times,* p. A26.

Freeman, R.E. (1984). *Strategic management: A stakeholder approach.* Englewood Cliffs, NJ: Prentice-Hall.

Garfield, C. (1992). *Second to none.* Homewood, IL: Business One Irwin.

Gladden, J.M. (2007). Managing sport brands. In B.J. Mullin, S. Hardy, and W.A. Sutton (eds) *Sport Marketing* (3rd ed.) (pp. 171–187). Champaign, IL: Human Kinetics.

Goldstein, W. (1989). *Playing for keeps: A history of early baseball.* Ithaca, NY: Cornell University Press.

Gorn, E.J. and Goldstein, W. (2004). *A brief history of American sports.* New York: Hill and Wang.

Graham, S. (2004, January 19–25). Kevin Plank's drive makes Under Armour an industry overachiever. *Street & Smith's SportsBusiness Journal,* pp. 8–9.

Helyar, J. (1994). *Lords of the realm.* New York: Random House.

Hiestand, M. (2002, August 19). Sports gear so out of style it's in style. *USA Today,* p. 3C.

Horovitz, B. (2009, December 7). Nike CEO knows how to just do it. *USA Today,* pp. 1B–2B.

Jones, T.M. (1995). Instrumental stakeholder theory: A synthesis of ethics and economics. *Academy of Management Review, 20* (4), pp. 404–437.

Kaplan, D. (2010, January 4–10). All four unions, credit-card issuers among the "friends of the court" filing briefs in the case. *Street & Smith's SportsBusiness Journal,* p. 9.

Katz, D. (1993, August 16). Triumph of the swoosh. *Sports Illustrated,* pp. 54–73.

Kennedy, P. (2012, July 15). Who made that? *New York Times Magazine,* p. 21.

King, B. (2010, January 4–10). Supreme Court weighs a game changer. *Street & Smith's SportsBusiness Journal,* pp. 1, 8–11.

King, B. and Kaplan, D. (2010, January 18–24). NFL, Needle, get their high court moment. *Street & Smith's SportsBusiness Journal,* pp. 1, 28.

Levere, J.L. (2012, April 5). New Balance celebrates its homemade footprint. *New York Times,* p. B2.

Levine, P. (1985). *A.G. Spalding and the rise of baseball: The promise of American sport.* New York: Oxford University Press.

Li, T. (2011, January 18). Li Ning drops on poor Q4 sales. *China Daily.* Accessed June 27, 2012, from: http://www.chinadaily.com/hkedition/2011/01/18.html.

Lipsey, R. (ed.) (1996). *Sports marketplace.* Princeton, NJ: Sportsguide.

Liptak, A. and Belson, K. (2010, May 24). N.F.L. fails in its request for antitrust immunity. *New York Times.* Accessed July 26, 2010, from: http://www.nytimes.com/2010/05/25/sports/football/25needle.html.

Liu, J. (2012, June 27). Sports firms bet their shirts on London. *China Daily*. Accessed July 2, 2012, from: http://www.chinadaily.com.cn/bizchina/2012-06/27/content_15525356.htm.

Macur, J. (2011, June 19). The fairway as runway. *New York Times*, p. Y6.

Mandell, R. (1984). *Sport: A cultural history*. New York: Columbia University Press.

McCarthy, M. (2012, March 6). Lin is real deal; some products are not. *USA Today*, p. 3C.

McGeehan, P. (2012, February 10). A point guard's sudden emergence catches retailers off guard. *New York Times*, p. A19.

McGrath, B. (2012, April 16). On the runway: Inquisition. *The New Yorker*, pp. 40, 42.

Metcalf, H.C. and Urwick, L. (eds) (1941). *Dynamic administration: The collected papers of Mary Parker Follett*. New York: Pittman.

Mintzberg, H.A. (1980). *The nature of managerial work*. Englewood Cliffs, NJ: Prentice-Hall.

Murphy, K. (2012, July 20). Rockets gain Lin's skills and international fans. *New York Times*, p. B14.

New uniforms kick off debate (2011, September 7). *USA Today*, p. 7C.

Nichols, M.A. (1995, April). A look at some of the issues affecting collegiate licensing. *Team Licensing Business*, 7 (4), p. 18.

Nocera, J. (2008, April 12). China tries to solve its Brand X blues. *New York Times*, pp. B1, B8.

Olson, E. (2010, September 1). Under Armour wants to dress athletic young women. *New York Times*, p. B3.

Our story (2012). Vineyard Vines. Accessed July 5, 2012, from: http://www.vineyardvines.com/ourstory.

Owen, R. (1825). *A new view of society*. New York: E. Bliss & F. White.

Oznian, M. (2011, October 3). The Forbes Fab 40: The world's most valuable sports brands. *Forbes*. Accessed July 2, 2012, from: http://www.forbes.com/sites/mikeozanian/2011/10/03/the-forbes-fab-40-the-worlds-most-valuable-sports-brands-3.

Pak, J. (2012, May 24). The layers of Linsanity. *The Harvard Crimson*. Accessed July 2, 2012, from: http://www.thecrimson.com/article/2012/5/24/harvard-jeremy-lin-linsanity-commencement-2012.

Pennington, B. (2012a, July 9). Daring from tee to green: The clothes, not the shots. *New York Times*, p. D7.

Pennington, B. (2012b, July 22). On par: For McElroy, slumps in the game and shoulders. *New York Times*, p. Y7.

Plata, C. (1996, September/October). Ducks & dollars. *Team Licensing Business*, 8 (6), p. 38.

Protecting your trademark: Federal registration rights and responsibilities (2012). United States Patent and Trademark Office. Accessed July 2, 2012, from: http://www.uspto.gov/trademarks/basics/BasicFacts_with_correct_links.pdf.

Roberts, D. (2011, October 26). Under Armour gets serious. *CNN Money*. Accessed July 8, 2012, from: http://management.fortune.cnn.com/2011/10/26/under-armour-kevin-plank.

Sandomir, R. (2011, June 22). After 3,000, even dirt will sell. *New York Times*, pp. A1, B13.

Sandomir, R. (2012a, May 22). Yet another outsized Ruthian moment. *New York Times*, p. B13.

Sandomir, R. (2012b, June 24). Lin, with a trademark application, is guarding a word that defined a craze. *New York Times*, p. Y7.

Say, J.B. (1803/1964). *A treatise on political economy*. New York: Sentry Press.

Schmidle, N. (2010, August 22). Inside the knockoff factory. *New York Times Magazine*, pp. 38–45.

Scorecard: Of a certain age (2003, June 9). *Sports Illustrated*, p. 23.

Senge, P.M. (1990). *The fifth discipline: The art and practice of the learning organization*. New York: Doubleday.

SGMA's wholesale study tallies $77 billion in sales (2012, May 24). Sporting Goods Manufacturers Association. Accessed June 26, 2012, from: http://0-www.sbrnet.com. wildpac.wne.edu.

Simmons, B. (2004, December 20). The sports guy. *ESPN Magazine*, p. 12.

Simon, H.A. (1965). *The shape of automation for men and management.* New York: Harper & Row.

Smit, B. (2008). *Sneaker wars: The enemy brothers who founded Adidas and Puma and the family feud that forever changed the business of sport.* New York: Ecco.

Sports merchandising industry loses its creator, David Warsaw (1996, July/August). *Team Licensing Business*, 8 (5), p. 18.

Tanier, M. (2011, September 15). There's an exciting clash on the field. Oh, that's the uniform. *New York Times*, pp. A1, B16.

Tanier, M. (2012, April 4). In Nike's rollout, flash everywhere but in the uniforms. *New York Times*, p. B16.

Thomas, K. (2010, December 10). Sports stars' catchphrase: "If I say it, I own it." *New York Times*, pp. A1, A3.

Tung, A. (2012, June 16). "Made in China" gains acceptance. *China Daily.* Accessed July 2, 2012, from: http://www.chinadaily.com.cn/bizchina/2012-06/16/content_15506619.htm.

Vamplew, W. (1989). *Pay up and play the game: Professional sport in Britain, 1875–1914.* Cambridge: Cambridge University Press.

von Bertalanffy, L. (1951, December). General systems theory: A new approach to the unity of science. *Human Biology*, pp. 302–361.

Weinreich, M. (2012, March 30). Tale of trading card reflects Knicks' season. *New York Times*, p. B13.

Wilker, J. (2010). *Cardboard gods: An all-American tale told through baseball cards.* New York: Seven Footer Press.

Winn, L. (2009, August 24). The last iconic baseball card. *Sports Illustrated*, pp. 49–53.

Wood, L. (2000). Brands and brand equity: Definition and management. *Management decisions*, 38 (9), pp. 662–669.

2 Globalization and ethics and international and Olympic sport industry segments

About FARE (2012). Football Against Racism in Europe. Accessed July 13, 2012, from: http://www.farenet.org.

About the USOC (2012). United States Olympic Committee. Accessed July 21, 2012, from: http://www.teamusa.org/About-the-USOC.aspx.

About us (2012). London Organizing Committee for the Olympic Games. Accessed January 3, 2013, from: http://www.london.2012.com/aboutus.

Ashe, A. (1992, August). What does the future hold for blacks in sport? *Ebony*, pp. 132–133.

Blum, D.E. (1993, April 21). Forum examines discrimination against black women in sport. *Chronicle of Higher Education*, pp. A39–A40.

China-made U.S. uniforms raise ire (2012, July 12). *Associated Press.* Accessed July 14, 2012, from: http://www.espn.go.com/new-york/story.

Conway, R. (2012, June 12). Euro 2012: Uefa investigates allegations of racism by fans. *British Broadcasting Service.* Accessed July 13, 2012, from: http://www.bbc.co.uk/sport/0/football.

Davis, K. (1975, June). Five propositions for social responsibility. *Business Horizons*, pp. 19–24.

Dawes, M. (2012, November 2). WADA back USADA sanctions against shamed Armstrong. *Daily Mail*. Accessed January 4, 2013, from: www.dailymail.co.uk/sport/othersport.

Faster, higher, stronger (2012, June 29). *Warsaw Voice*. Accessed July 21, 2012, from: http://www.warsawvoice.pl/WVpage/pages/article.php/25038/article.

FIFA has built up cash reserves of $1.3B after $631M profit for '10 World Cup (2011, March 4). *Street & Smith's SportsBusiness Daily*. Accessed July 19, 2012, from: http://www.sportsbusinessdaily.com/Daily/Issues/2011/03/Mar-4/Events-and-Attractions/FIFA.aspx.

Financial Report 2011 (2012, May). 62nd FIFA Congress. Accessed July 21, 2012, from: http://www.fifa.com/mm/document/affederation/administration/01/60/80/10/fifafinanzberichteinternet.pdf.

Friedman, M. (1970, September 13). The social responsibility of business is to increase profits. *New York Times Magazine*, pp. 13–14.

Gifford, C. (2006). *The Kingfisher soccer encyclopedia*. Boston: Houghton Mifflin.

Hums, M.A. (1996). Increasing employment opportunities for people with disabilities through sports and adapted physical activity. *Proceedings from the Second European Conference on Adapted Physical Activity and Sports: Health, well being and employment*. Leuven, Belgium: ACCO.

International Sport Federations (2012). International Olympic Committee. Accessed July 19, 2012, from: http://www.olympic.org/content/the-ioc/governance/international-federations.

IOC Code of Ethics (2009). International Olympic Committee. Accessed July 19, 2012, from: http://www.olympic.org/Documents/Reports/EN/Code-Ethique-2009-WebEN.pdf.

IOC Fact Sheet: Women in the Olympic Movement (2012). International Olympic Committee. Accessed July 19, 2012, from: http://www.olympic.org/Documents/Reference_documents_Factsheets/Women_in_Olympic_Movement.pdf.

IOC Olympic Charter (2011). International Olympic Committee. Accessed July 19, 2012, from: http://www.olympic.org/Documents/olympic_charter_en.pdf.

IOC Olympic Marketing Fact File (2012). International Olympic Committee. Accessed July 19, 2012, from: http://www.olympic.org/Documents/IOC_Marketing/OLYMPIC-MARKETING-FACT-FILE-2012.pdf.

IOC publishes final reform recommendations (1999, November 24). *The Independent*. Accessed July 19, 2012, from: http://www.independent.co.uk/sport/general/ioc-publishes-final-reform-recommendations-741696.html.

Jacoby, N.H. (1973). *Corporate power and social responsibility*. New York: Macmillan.

Karasz, P. (2012, April 2). Hungarian president resigns amid plagiarism scandal. *New York Times*. Accessed July 19, 2012, from: http://www.nytimes.com/2012/04/03/world/europe/hungarian-president-pal-schmitt-resigns-amid-plagiarism-scandal.html.

Lapchick, R. (1996). *Racial report card*. Boston: Northeastern University Center for the Study of Sport in Society.

Litsky, F. (2002, May 25). U.S. Olympic chief quits over her lies on college degrees. *New York Times*. Accessed July 19, 2012, from: http://www.nytimes.com/2002/05/25/sports/olympics-us-olympic-chief-quits-over-her-lies-on-college-degrees.html?pagewanted=all&src=pm.

Macur, J. (2012, June 22). Armstrong could lose more than titles if guilty of doping. *New York Times*. Accessed July 19, 2012, from: http://www.nytimes.com/2012/06/23/sports/cycling/lance-armstrong-could-lose-5-million-if-guilty-of-doping.html?_r=1.

Mallon, B. (2000, May). The Olympic bribery scandal. *Journal of Olympic History*, pp. 11–13.

Mamudi, S. (2012, June 12). Coca-Cola, Visa, P&G pin big hopes on Olympics sponsorships. *Dow Jones Newswires*. Accessed January 27, 2013, from: http://english.capital.gr/dj/news.asp?details=1527531.

Marchand, D.A. (2010, February). An inside look at the International Olympic Committee. *IMD*. Accessed July 21, 2012, from: http://www.imd.org/research/challenges/upload/TC014_10_An_inside_look_at_the_International_Olympic_Committee.pdf.

Mario Balotelli faces racism at Euro 2012; UEFA charges Croatia with racial abuse, chants (2012, June 16). *The Huffington Post*. Accessed July 13, 2012, from: http://www.huffingtonpost.com.

Pound, R. (2006). *Inside the Olympics: A behind-the-scenes look at the politics, the scandals and the glory of the Games*. Hoboken, NJ: John Wiley & Sons.

Rice, F. (1994, August 8). How to make diversity pay. *Fortune*, pp. 79–86.

Senn, A. (1999). *Power, politics, and the Olympic Games*. Champaign, IL: Human Kinetics.

Shropshire, K.L. (1996). *In black and white: Race and sports in America*. New York: New York University Press.

Sturdivant, F.D. and Vernon-Wortzel, H. (1990). *Business and society: A managerial approach* (4th ed.). Homewood, IL: Irwin.

The organisation (2012). International Olympic Committee. Accessed July 21, 2012, from: http://www.olympic.org/about-ioc-institution.

The role of the CGF (2012). Commonwealth Games Federation. Accessed July 19, 2012, from: http://www.thecgf.com/games.

VANOC Reports (2010). Vancouver Organizing Committee for the 2010 Olympic and Paralympic Winter Games. Accessed July 21, 2012, from: http://www.2010legaciesnow.com/vanoc.

Wallechinsky, D. and Loucky, J. (2012). *The complete book of the Olympics*. London: Aurum Press.

Whitley, D. (2012, August 13). Olympics 2012: Women rule London – no cynicism necessary. *The Sporting News*. Accessed December 17, 2012, from: www.aol.sportingnews.com.

Wilber, D. and Marimow, A. (2012, June 18). Roger Clemens acquitted of all charges. *The Washington Post*. Accessed July 19, 2012, from: http://www.washingtonpost.com/local/crime/roger-clemens-trial-verdict-reached/2012/06/18/gJQAQxvzlV_story.html.

3 Information technology (IT) management and the sport media

McManus, J. (2012, March 23). Female athletes connect with Twitter. *ESPNW*. Accessed July 15, 2012, from: http://www.espn.go.com/espnw/mobile.

Muret, D. (2012, February 27). When will mobile concessions catch on? *Street & Smith's SportsBusiness Journal*. Accessed July 15, 2012, from: http://www.sporsbusinessdaily.com.

Nethery, R. (2005, November 28–December 4). ESPN faces rapidly changing market. *Street & Smith's Sportsbusiness Journal*, p. 23.

Newcomb, T. (2012, February 3). How the iPad is revolutionizing the NFL. *Popular Mechanics*. Accessed July 15, 2012, from: http://www.popularmechanics.com.

Ostrowski, J. (1998, December 21–28). In any currency, ESPN a cash machine. *Street & Smith's Sportsbusiness Journal*, p. 25.

Pistons giving high-tech swag to season ticket holders (2012). Accessed April 7, 2012, from: http://www.thehoopdoctors.com.

Super Bowl ads cost average of $3.5M (2012, February 6). *ESPN New York*. Accessed July 15, 2012, from: http://www.espn.go.com/newyork.

4 Developing goals and school and youth sports

2010–11 high school athletics participation survey (2011). National Federation of State High School Associations. Accessed June 21, 2012, from: http://www.nfhs.org/content.aspx?id=3282&linkidentifier=id&itemid=3282.

About HSLDA (2011). Home School Legal Defense Association. Accessed June 18, 2012, from: http://www.hslda.org/about.

About Pop Warner Little Scholars, Inc. (2012). Pop Warner Little Scholars, Inc. Accessed June 17, 2012, from: http://www.popwarner.com/aboutus/pop.asp.

Bob Gardner named NHSH executive director (2010, February 9). National Federation of State High School Associations. Accessed July 17, 2010, from: http://www.nfhs.org/content.aspx?id=3831.

Borden, S. (2012, March 4). Soccer's new model forces high school players to choose. *New York Times*, pp. Y1–Y2.

Branch, J. (2009, November 28). Seeing other side in land of "Hoosiers." *New York Times*, pp. B9–B10.

Bunbury: College soccer's top honors (2010, Winter). *Through the arch*, p. 14.

Bundgaard, A. (2005). *Muscle and manliness: The rise of sport in American boarding schools.* Syracuse, NY: Syracuse University Press.

Collins, J.C. and Porras, J.I. (1998). Building your company's vision. *Harvard Business Review on change* (pp. 21–54). Boston: Harvard Business School Press.

Conaboy, C. (2011, August 1). Heading off problems. *Boston Globe*, pp. G11–G12.

Daniel, A. (2011, September 9). NHL: 20 best Shattuck-St. Mary's hockey alumni. Bleacher Report. Accessed May 22, 2012, from: http://m.bleacherreport.com/articles/84230.

Drucker, P. (1973). *Management: Tasks, responsibilities, practices.* New York: Harper & Row.

Frequently asked questions (2010). National Alliance for Youth Sports. Accessed June 22, 2012, from: http://www.nays.org/Who_We_Are/frequently_asked_questions.cfm#1.

Hardy, S. (1997, April). Memory, performance and history: The making of American ice hockey at St. Paul's School, 1860–1915. *The International Journal of the History of Sport*, 14 (1), pp. 97–115.

Hersey, P. and Blanchard, K. (1981). *Management of Organizational Behavior.* Englewood Cliffs, NJ: Prentice-Hall, pp. 108, 382.

History of AYSO (2011). American Youth Soccer Organization. Accessed June 21, 2012, from: http://ayso.org/AboutAYSO/history.aspx.

Hruby, P. (2011, November 22). Natalie Randolph more than just a coach. *ESPNW*. Accessed June 14, 2012, from: http://espn.go.com/espnw/more-sports/7269929/natalie-randolph-more-just-coach.

Hunter, K. (2010, July 15). Shattuck-St. Mary's School – Center of hockey excellence. *The Hockey Writers*. Accessed May 24, 2012, from: http://www.thehockeywriters.com.

Hyman, M. (2010, January 31). A survey of youth sports finds winning isn't the only thing. *New York Times*, p. Y-9.

Ivy League presidents approve concussion-curbing measures for football (2011, July 20). The Ivy League. Accessed June 20, 2012, from: http://www.ivyleaguesports.com/sports/fball/2011-12/releases/Ivy_League_Presidents_Approve_Concussion-Curbing_Measures_for_Football.

James, C.L.R. (1993). *Beyond a boundary.* Durham, NC: Duke University Press.

Jennings, R. (2012, March 4). Beren Academy loses in state finals. *ESPN Dallas/Fort Worth.* Accessed June 15, 2012, from: http://www.espn.go.com/statefinals/beren-academy-run-ends.

Joyce, G. (2008, May 5). There's something about St. Mary's. *ESPN Magazine*, pp. 80–85.

Kumar, A. (2012a, February 5). Bill aims to give home-schooled students access to public high school sports. *The Washington Post.* Accessed June 18, 2012, from: http://www.

washingtonpost.com/local/dc-politics/bill-aims-to-give-home-schooled-students-access-to-public-high-school-sports/2012/02/03/gIQAedHLsQ_story.html.

Kumar, A. (2012b, March 1). Va. senators sack "Tebow Bill": home-schoolers kept off public school rosters. *The Washington Post*. Accessed June 18, 2012, from: http://www.washingtonpost.com/local/dc-politics/tebow-bill-defeated-in-va-general-assembly/2012/03/01/gIQAjCIjlR_story.html.

Little League chronology (2010). Little League Baseball, Inc. Accessed May 28, 2012, from: http://www.littleleague.org/learn/about/historyandmission/chronology.htm.

Longman, J. (2011a, May 27). Where soccer players grow. *The New York Times*, pp. B9, B13.

Longman, J. (2011b, August 11). Tackling by moonlight. *The New York Times*, pp. B13, B17.

Longman, J. (2012, February 9). Home schoolers are hoping to don varsity jackets in Virginia. *New York Times*, pp. A1, B12.

Macur, J. (2010, May 10). A coach used to tests insists players pass theirs. *New York Times*, pp. D5–D6.

McLachlan, J. (1970). *American boarding schools*. New York: Scribner.

Mission statement (2012). Virginia High School League. Accessed June 18, 2012, from: http://www.vhsl.org/about.mission-statement.

Mulvaney, E. (2012, March 7). TAPPS draws renewed criticism for rejection of an Islamic academy. *The Houston Chronicle*. Accessed June 15, 2012, from: http://www.chron.com/news/houston-texas/article/TAPPS-draws-renewed-criticism-for-rejection-of-an-3387164.php.

O'Connor, A. (2012, June 13). Trying to reduce head injuries, youth football limits practices. *New York Times*. Accessed June 17, 2012, from: http://www.nytimes.com/2012/06/14/sports/pop-warner-football-limits-contact-in-practices.html.

Ogilvie, V. (1957). *The English public school*. London: B.T. Batsford.

O'Hanlon, T.P. (1982, Spring). School sports as social training: The case of athletics and the crisis of World War I. *Journal of Sport History*, 9 (1), pp. 15–25.

Pilon, M. (2012, March 2). In reversal, a Jewish school gets to play. *New York Times*, pp. B9–B10.

Pop Warner announces new national rule changes regarding practice and concussion prevention (2012, June 13). Pop Warner Little Scholars, Inc. Accessed June 17, 2012, from: http://www.popwarner.com/football/2012rulechanges.asp.

Quarstad, B. (2012, February 5). Shattuck-St. Mary's announces 13 students sign National Letters of Intent for 2012. *IMSoccer News*. Accessed May 23, 2012, from: http://www.insidemnsoccer.com/2012.

Quinn, R.E. and Rohrbaugh, J. (1983). A spatial model of effectiveness criteria: Towards a competing values approach to organizational analysis. *Management Science*, 29 (3), pp. 363–377.

Rohan, T. (2012, June 14). Pop Warner weighing research and risk in concussion prevention efforts. *New York Times*. Accessed June 17, 2012, from: http://www.nytimes.com/2012/06/15/sports/pop-warner-football-rules-limiting-contact-raise-new-questions.html.

Schwarz, A. (2011, April 3). Madden puts concussions in new light in his game. *New York Times*, pp. Y1, Y9.

Section 130: Purpose of high school athletics (2011). *Texas Association of Private and Parochial Schools Manual: Athletic and fine arts rules*. Accessed June 16, 2012, from: http://www.tapps.net/ConstitutionByLawsManual.html.

Shattuck-St. Mary's hockey (2012). Shattuck-St. Mary's School. Accessed May 24, 2012, from: http://www.hockey.s-som.org.

Shealer, S. (2010, February 4). Shattuck-St. Mary's – its system works. *ESPN Rise*. Accessed May 23, 2012, from: http://www.espn.go/high-school/boys-soccer.

Smith, M. (2010, June 14–20). Female football coach gets deal with Crons. *Street & Smith's SportsBusiness Journal*, p. 9.

SSM alumni find gold and silver at 2010 Olympics! (2010, Winter). *Through the arch*, pp. 10–12.

SSM history (2013). Shattuck-St. Mary's School. Accessed January 26, 2013, from: http://www.s-sm.org/about/ssm-history.

State laws concerning participation of homeschool students in public school activities (2011, May). *Home School Legal Defense Association legal research supplement*. Accessed June 18, 2012, from: http://www.hslda.org/docs/nche/Issues/E/Equal_Access.pdf.

Stedry, A.C. and Kay, E. (1964). *The effects of goal difficulty on performance*. New York: General Electric/Behavioral Research Service.

Structure of Little League Baseball and Softball (2010). Little League Baseball, Inc. Accessed May 28, 2010, from: http://www.littleleague.org/learn/about/structure.htm.

Swanson, R.A. and Spears, B. (1995). *Sport and physical education in the United States* (4th ed.). Dubuque, IA: Brown & Benchmark.

URJ encourages Texas Association of Private and Parochial Schools to reconsider decision about playoff games on Shabbat (2012, February 29). Union of Reform Judaism. Accessed June 17, 2012, from: http://urj.org/about/union/pr/2012/?syspage=article&item_id=84846.

5 Decision making and the health and fitness industry

Agor, W. (1986, January–February). How top executives use their intuition to make decisions. *Business Horizons*, pp. 49–53.

Etzioni, A. (1989, July/August). Humble decision making. *Harvard Business Review*, pp. 122–126.

Hoffman, M. (1998, July). Buyer profile: In Gold's we trust. *Health & Fitness Business News*, p. 16.

International Health and Racquet Sportsclub Association Trends Report and Resource Center (2011). International Health and Racquet Sportsclub Association. Accessed July 20, 2012, from: http://www.ihrsa.com.

International Health and Racquet Sportsclub Association Trends Report and Resource Center (2012). International Health and Racquet Sportsclub Association. Accessed July 20, 2012, from: http://www.ihrsa.com.

Janis, I. (1982). *Groupthink*. Boston: Houghton Mifflin.

Peters, T. and Austin, N. (1985). *A passion for excellence*. New York: Random House.

Shakeshaft, J. (2012, February 13). The 21 most innovative gyms in the U.S. *The Greatist*. Accessed July 20, 2012, from: http://www.greatist.com/fitness.

Simon, H.A. (1957). *Administrative behavior*. New York: Free Press.

Straff, N.D. (2012, January). The best gyms in America for every work out. *Fitness Magazine*. Accessed July 20, 2012, from: http://www.fitnessmagazine.com.

Vroom, V. and Yetton, P. (1973). *Leadership and decision making*. Pittsburgh, PA: University of Pittsburgh Press.

YMCAs take another hit in tax wars with private clubs (2000, February). *Health & Fitness Business News*, p. 23.

6 Strategic management and the sport facilities industry

Abell, D.F. (1980). *Defining the business: The starting point of strategic planning.* Englewood Cliffs, NJ: Prentice-Hall.

Andrews, K.R. (1971). *The concept of corporate strategy.* Homewood, IL: Dow Jones Irwin.

Blanchard, K. (1993). *Raving fans: A revolutionary approach to customer service.* New York: William Morrow & Co.

Carlson-Thomas, C. (1992, February). Strategic vision or strategic con: Rhetoric or reality? *Long-range planning,* pp. 81–89.

Cohen, A. (2006, August). Just subtract water? *Athletic Business,* 30 (8), pp. 36–48.

Collins, J. (1997). It's not what you make, it's what you stand for. *Inc.,* 19 (14), pp. 42–45.

Collins, J.C. and Porras, J.L. (1996). Building your company's vision. *Harvard Business Review,* 74 (5), pp. 65–77.

Drucker, P.F. (1954). *The practice of management.* New York: Harper & Bros.

Ellerbrook, R. (2011). New England Parks and Recreation Association. Personal communication.

Farmer, P., Mulrooney, A., and Amon, R. (2001). *Sport facility planning and management.* Morgantown, WV: Fitness Information Technology, Inc.

Fisher, M.L., Hammond, J.H., Obermeyer, W.R., and Raman, A. (1994, May/June). Making supply meet demand in an uncertain world. *Harvard Business Review,* pp. 83–89.

Fried, G. (2010). *Managing sport facilities* (2nd ed.). Champaign, IL: Human Kinetics.

Hammer, M. and Champy, J. (1993). *Re-engineering the corporation: A manifesto for business revolution.* New York: HarperBusiness.

Horrow, R. (2001, January). Sharing the cost. *Stadia,* pp. 56–60.

Kaplan, R.S. and Norton, D.P. (1993, September/October). Putting the balanced scorecard approach to work. *Harvard Business Review,* 71 (5), pp. 134–147.

Kaplan, R.S. and Norton, D.P. (1996, January/February). Using the balanced scorecard as a strategic management system. *Harvard Business Review,* 74 (1), pp. 75–86.

Maynard, M. (2010, November 19). Wrigley set for football, with odd ground rules. *New York Times.* Accessed July 20, 2012, from: http://www.nytimes.com.

Patterson, I. (2006, April). Sport for all. *Stadia,* pp. 74–77.

Porter, M. (1985). *Competitive advantage.* New York: Free Press.

Sashkin, M. and Kiser, K.J. (1993). *Putting total quality management to work.* San Francisco: Berrett-Koehler.

Schendel, D.E. and Hofer, C.W. (1979). *Strategic management: A new view of business policy and planning.* Boston: Little, Brown.

7 Designing the organization and sport agency

2011 MLB first-round draft pick signing bonuses (2011, August 16). *The Associated Press.* Accessed May 31, 2012, from: http://www.huffingtonpost.com/2011/08/16/2011-baseball-draft-signing-bonuses-mlb_n_928180.html.

Agent regulations (2012). National Football League Players Association. Accessed June 12, 2012, from: https://www.nflplayers.com/About-us/Rules--Regulations/Agent-Regulations.

Alli Sports and Mountain Dew announce long-term extension and new Dew Tour (2012, April 16). Alli Sports. Accessed June 20, 2012, from: http://www.allisports.com/dew-tour/tour-info.

Andrews, M. (2012, June 4). SoxProspects.com: Previewing 2012 draft. *ESPNBoston.com*. Accessed June 12, 2012, from: http://espn.go.com/blog/boston/red-sox/index/_/count/46.

Atkinson, C. (2012, March 30). Wasserman Media Group making growth pay with $25 million investment. *New York Post*. Accessed June 18, 2012, from: http://www.nypost.com/p/news/business/naming_his_price_zUB6c3mRRnyXwhtgNmHoFK.

Bane, C. (2012, April 17). Changing Dew Tour. *ESPN.com*. Accessed June 20, 2012, from: http://espn.go.com/action/story/_/id/7823954/dew-tour-scale-three-yearly-events.

Berry, R.C. (1990). Representation of the professional athlete. In American Bar Association Forum on the Entertainment and Sports Industries (ed.) *The law of sports: Doing business in the sports industries* (pp. 1–6). Chicago: ABA Publishing.

Berry, R.C. and Wong, G.M. (1993). *Law and business of the sport industries: Common issues in amateur and professional sports, Volume II* (rev. ed.). Westport, CT: Praeger Publishers.

Blum, R. (2001, April 5). Welcome to the age of $2 million men. *Boston Globe*, p. C3.

Bodley, H. (2000, December 22). Free agency: One of the best things in baseball players' lives. *USA Today*, p. 10C.

Brady, E., Upton, J., and Berkowitz, S. (2011, November 17). Salaries for college football coaches back on the rise. *USA Today*. Accessed May 31, 2012, from: http://www.usatoday.com/sports/college/football/story/2011-11-17/cover -college-football-coaches-salaries-rise/51242232/1.

Briny Baird (2012). ESPN Golf. Accessed June 24, 2012, from: http://www.espn.go.com/golf/player/_/id/18/briny.baird.html.

Burke, M. (2008, September 1). The most powerful coach in sports. *Forbes*. Accessed December 3, 2008, from: http://www.forbes.com.

Carney, M. (1998, July). The competitiveness of networked production: The role of trust and asset specificity. *Journal of Management Studies*, 35 (4), pp. 460–478.

Carroll, J.M. (1999). *Red Grange and the rise of modern football*. Champaign, IL: University of Illinois Press.

Chandler, A.D. (1962). *Strategy and structure*. Cambridge, MA: MIT Press.

Conklin, D. and Tapp, L. (2000). The creative web. In S. Chowdhury (ed.) *Management 21C* (pp. 220–234). London: Pearson Education.

Conway, R. (1995). *Game misconduct: Alan Eagleson and the corruption of hockey*. Toronto: MacFarlane, Walter & Ross.

Covell, D. (1999). B3: The bikes, blades, and boards tour. In M.A. McDonald and G.A. Milne (eds) *Cases in sport marketing* (pp. 195–208). Sudbury, MA: Jones and Bartlett.

Crasnick, J. (2005). *License to deal: A season on the run with a maverick baseball agent*. Emmaus, PA: Rodale.

Crouse, K. (2011, August 6). As Lochte raises profile, image makers dive in. *New York Times*. Accessed June 20, 2012, from: http://www.nytimes.com/2011/08/07/sports/as-lochte-raises-profile-image-makers-dive-in.html?pagewanted=all.

Dobrow, M. (2011). *Knocking on heaven's door: Six minor leaguers in search of the baseball dream*. Amherst and Boston, MA: University of Massachusetts Press.

Dorish, J. (2011, November 12). Average salaries in the NBA, NFL, MLB and NHL. *Yahoo!Sports*. Accessed May 31, 2012, from: http://sports.yahoo.com/nba/news?slug=ycn-10423863.

Dudley Hart (2012). ESPN Golf. Accessed June 24, 2012, from: http://www.espn.go.com/golf/player/_/id/18/dudley.hart.html.

Forbes, G. (2001, June 8). '82 strike changed salary dealings forever. *USA Today*, p. 14C.

Foster, G., Greyser, S.A., and Walsh, B. (2006). *The business of sports: Text and cases on strategy and management*. Mason, OH: Thomson South-Western.

Freedman, J. (2012a). The 50 highest-earning American athletes. *SI.com*. Accessed May 31, 2012, from: http://sportsillustrated.cnn.com/specials/fortunate50-2011/index.html.

Freedman, J. (2012b). The 20 highest-earning international athletes. *SI.com*. Accessed May 31, 2012, from: http://sportsillustrated.cnn.com/specials/fortunate50-2011/index.20.html.

Frequently asked questions (2012). Major League Baseball Players Association. Accessed May 31, 2012, from: http://mlb.mlb.com/pa/info/faq.jsp.

Gimino, A. (2011, November 22). Rich Rodriguez' compensation: Nearly $2 million per year, five years. *Tucson (AZ) Citizen*. Accessed June 13, 2012, from: http://tucsoncitizen.com/wildcatreport/2011/11/22/rich-rodriguezs-compensation-nearly-2-million-per-year-five-years.

Greenberg, M.J. (1993). *Sports law practice*. Charlottesville, VA: The Michie Company.

Hawkins, S. (2000, December 13). Texas on the money with Rodriguez. *Boston Globe*, p. F6.

Helyar, J. (1994). *Lords of the realm*. New York: Ballantine Books.

Hoffer, R. (2006, July 31). It's great to be average. *Sports Illustrated*, pp. 56–66.

Kanter, R.M. and Buck, J.D. (1985). Reorganizing part of Honeywell: From strategy to structure. *Organizational dynamics*, 13, pp. 6–20.

Katzenbach, J.R. and Smith, D.K. (2003). *The wisdom of teams: Creating the high-performance organization*. New York: Collins Business Essentials.

Lester, P. (1990). Marketing the athlete: Endorsement contracts. In G. Uberstine (ed.) *The law of professional and amateur sports* (pp. 23-1–23-36). Deerfield, IL: Clark, Boardman, and Callaghan.

Lowenfish, L. (1980). *The imperfect diamond: A history of baseball's labor wars*. New York: Da Capo Press.

McAleenan, G. (1990). Agent–player representation agreements. In G. Uberstine (ed.) *The law of professional and amateur sports* (pp. 2-1–2-85). Deerfield, IL: Clark, Boardman, and Callaghan.

McCarthy, M. and Wieberg, S. (2006, November 17). Reviled or loved, agents get results. *USA Today*, p. 15C.

Mickle, T. (2012, May 14). Wasserman Media Group creating new actions sports and Olympic division. *Street & Smith's SportsBusiness Journal*. Accessed June 19, 2012, from: http://www.sportsbusinessdaily.com/Daily/Issues/2012/05/14/Labor-and-Agents/WMG.aspx.

NFL combine training (2012). IMG Performance Institute. Accessed June 19, 2012, from: http://www.imgacademies.com/img-performance-institute/pro-athlete-training/nfl-combine-training.

Nightengale, B. (2012, April 4). 2012 MLB salaries: $20 million players multiply. *USA Today*. Accessed May 31, 2012, from: http://www.usatoday.com/sports/baseball/story/2012-04-04/MLB-player-salaries/54015334/1.

Pay structure of minor league baseball players (2010, March 17). National Sports and Entertainment Law Society. Accessed May 31, 2012, from: http://nationalsportsandentertainment.wordpress.com/2010/03/17/pay-structure-of-minor-league-baseball-players.

Peters, T.J. and Waterman, R.H., Jr. (1982). *In search of excellence*. New York: Harper & Row.

Rodriguez finalizes $275 million deal with Yankees (2007, December 13). *Associated Press*. Accessed June 12, 2012, from: http://sports.espn.go.com/mlb/news/story?id=3153171.

Rosenthal, G. (2012, February 29). Peyton Hillis can't stop changing agents. *NBC Sports: ProFootballTalk*. Accessed June 13, 2012, from: http://profootballtalk.nbcsports.com/2012/02/29/peyton-hillis-cant-stop-changing-agents.

Ryzik, M. (2012, June 9). The making of an Olympic sex symbol. *New York Times*. Accessed June 19, 2012, from: http://www.nytimes.com/2012/06/10/fashion/ryan-lochte-olmypic-swimmer-and-sex-symbol.html?pagewanted=all.

Sander, L. and Fain, P. (2009, June 12). Coaches' contracts are fertile ground for conflict. *The Chronicle of Higher Education*, pp. A1, A23, A24.

Schein, E.H. (1985). *Organizational psychology* (3rd ed.). Englewood Cliffs, NJ: Prentice-Hall.

Snow, C.C., Miles, R.E., and Coleman, H.J., Jr. (1992, Winter). Managing 21st century network organizations. *Organizational Dynamics*, pp. 5–20.

Sperber, M. (1993). *Shake down the thunder: The creation of Notre Dame football*. New York: Henry Holt.

Stanger, S. (2012, June 7). Alli Sports and Dogfunk join forces. *Graffy, Inc.* Accessed June 20, 2012, from: http://www.graffyinc.com/alli-sports-and-dogfunk-join-forces.

Torre, P.S. (2009, March 23). How (and why) athletes go broke. *Sports Illustrated*. Accessed June 13, 2009, from: http://sportsillustrated.cnn.com/vault/article/magazine/MAG1153364.

USA quickfacts (2012). U.S. Census Bureau. Accessed May 31, 2012, from: http://quickfacts.census.gov/qfd/states/00000.html.

Weber, M. (1947). *The theory of social and economic organization* (eds and trans. A.M. Henderson and T. Parsons). New York: Free Press.

Wertheim, L.J., Yaeger, D., and Schecter, B.J. (2000, May 29). Web of deceit. *Sports Illustrated*, pp. 67–80.

White, G.E. (1996). *Creating the national pastime*. Princeton, NJ: Princeton University Press.

Wieberg, S. (2006, November 17). To Oklahoma, Stoops worth more than his weight in gold. *USA Today*, p. 16C.

Wieberg, S. and Upton, J. (2007, December 5). The money game. *USA Today*, pp. 1A–2A.

Yasser, R., McCurdy, J.R., Goplerud, C.P., and Weston, M.A. (2011). *Sports law: Cases and materials* (7th ed.). Cincinnati, OH: Anderson/LexisNexis.

8 Motivation and leadership and intercollegiate athletics

2011–2012 NCAA Division I Manual (2011). Indianapolis, IN: National Collegiate Athletic Association.

About us (2012). Horizon League. Accessed January 8, 2013, from: www.horizonleague.org/aboutus.

Ashburn, E. (2011, July 1). The U. of Arizona's president finds an unexpected new field of employment. *The Chronicle of Higher Education*, p. A11.

Bamberger, M. (2008, February 11). The court supreme. *Sports Illustrated*, pp. 63–64.

Beech, M. (2004, March 1). A global racquet. *Sports Illustrated*, p. 30.

Bennis, W.G. and Nanus, B. (2003). *Leaders*. New York: HarperCollins.

Blake, R.R. and Mouton, J.S. (1982, February). How to choose a leadership style. *Training and Development Journal*, pp. 38–45.

Blake, R.R. and Mouton, J.S. (1985). *The managerial grid III*. Houston, TX: Gulf Publishing.

Bowen, W.G. and Levin, S.A. (2003). *Reclaiming the game: College sports and educational values*. Princeton, NJ: Princeton University Press.

Brady, E., Upton, J., and Berkowitz, S. (2011, November 17). Salaries for college football coaches back on the rise. *USA Today*. Accessed January 8, 2012, from: http://www.usatoday.com/sports/college/football/story/2011-11-17/cover- college-football-coaches-salaries-rise/51242232/1.

Brennan, E. (2012, March 29). Q & A: NCAA president Mark Emmert. *ESPN.com*. Accessed April 9, 2012, from: http://espn.go.com/blog/collegebasketballnation/post/_/id/56723/qa-ncaa-president-mark-emmert.

Burns, J.M. (1978). *Leadership*. New York: Harper & Row.

Byers, W. with Hammer, C. (1995). *Unsportsmanlike conduct: Exploiting college athletes*. Ann Arbor, MI: University of Michigan Press.

Carey, J. (2011, May 6). NCAA yet to receive letter from Justice Department on BCS. *USA Today.* Accessed May 6, 2011, from: http://www.usatoday.com/sports/college/football/2011-05-05-ncaa-justice-department_N.htm.

Commissioner LeCrone (2012). Horizon League. Accessed January 29, 2012, from: http://www.horizonleague.org/aboutus/staff-directory/jonathan-b-lecrone.html.

Conger, J.A. and Kanungo, R.N. (1988, July). The empowerment process: Integrating theory into practice. *Academy of Management Review,* pp. 473–474.

Covell, D. and Barr, C.A. (2010). *Managing intercollegiate athletics.* Scottsdale, AZ: Holcomb Hathaway.

Davis, S. (2009). *When March went mad: The game that transformed basketball.* New York: Henry Holt.

Fleishman, E.A., Harris, E.F., and Burtt, H.E. (1955). *Leadership and supervision in industry.* Columbus, OH: Ohio State University Bureau of Business Research.

Gardner, H. with Laskin, E. (1996). *Leading minds.* New York: Basic Books.

Gems, G.R. (2000). *For pride, profit, and patriarchy: Football and the incorporation of American cultural values.* Latham, MD: The Scarecrow Press.

Gonzales, A. (2011, July 1). Larry Scott's vision realized in new Pac-12 Conference. *The Arizona Republic.* Accessed July 9, 2011, from: http://www.azcentral.com/sports/articles/2011/03/30/20110330pac-12-conf.html.

Handlin, O. and Handlin, M.F. (1970). *The American college and American culture: Socialization as a function of higher education.* New York: McGraw-Hill.

Harris, C. (2012, February 20). Fiesta Bowl case: Junker pleads guilty to felony charge. *Arizona Republic.* Accessed February 23, 2012, from: http://www.azcentral.com/arizonarepublic/news/articles/2012/02/21/20120221fiesta-bowl-case-junker-pleads-guilty-felony-charge.html.

Harris, C. and Rough, G. (2011, May 5). Maricopa county officials to investigate Fiesta Bowl gifts. *The Arizona Republic.* Accessed May 6, 2011, from: http://www.azcentral.com/news/articles/2011/05/05/20110505fiesta-bowl-investigation-gifts.html.

Harris, C. and Wagner, D. (2011a, March 29). Fiesta Bowl probe offers look at John Junker's excesses. *The Arizona Republic.* Accessed May 5, 2011, from: http://www.azcentral.com/news/articles/2011/03/29/20110329fiesta-bowl-probe-junker-expenses.html.

Harris, C. and Wagner, D. (2011b, March 29). Fiesta Bowl report puts BCS role in jeopardy. *The Arizona Republic.* Accessed May 5, 2011, from: http://www.azcentral.com/news/articles/2011/03/29/20110329fiesta-bowl-report-lavish-spending-activities.html.

Harris, G. (2011a, March 30). BCS also looking at Fiesta's future role in championship. *The Arizona Republic.* Accessed May 5, 2011, from: http://www.azcentral.com/news/articles/2011/03/30/20110330fiesta-bowl-ncaa-license.html.

Harris, G. (2011b, April 29). Ruling on Fiesta Bowl's fate expected in May. *The Arizona Republic.* Accessed May 6, 2011, from: http://www.azcentral.com/news/articles/2011/04/29/20110429fiesta-bowl-ruling-in-may.html.

Hersey, P. and Blanchard, K.H. (1982). *Management of organizational behavior: Utilizing human resources* (4th ed.). Englewood Cliffs, NJ: Prentice-Hall.

Higgs, R.J. (1995). *God in the stadium: Sports and religion in America.* Lexington, KY: University of Kentucky Press.

Holmes, B. (2010, January 5). Somber Trojans try to carry on after sanctions. *Los Angeles Times.* Accessed January 5, 2010, from: http://www.latimes.com/sports/college/basketball/la-sp-usc-basketball5-2010jan05,0,4415152.story.

Interview: Mark Emmert (2011, February 14). Frontline: Money and March Madness. *Public Broadcasting Service.* Accessed April 8, 2012, from: http://www.pbs.org/wgbh/pages/frontline/money-and-march-madness/interviews/mark-emmert.html#2.

Johnson, D. (2011, July 14). Mark Emmert: Is this man qualified to be NCAA president? *The Bleacher Report.* Accessed April 8, 2012, from: http://bleacherreport.com/articles/767226-mark-emmert-is-this-man-qualified-to-be-ncaa-president.

Justice Department questions legality of B.C.S. (2011, May 4). *The New York Times.* Accessed May 5, 2011, from: http://www.nytimes.com/2011/05/05/sports/ncaafootball/05sportsbriefs-JUSTICEDEPAR_BRF.html?_r=1&scp=1&sq=BCS%20justice%20department&st=cse.

Katz, D., Maccoby, N.M., and Morse, N. (1950). *Productivity, supervision, and morale in an office situation.* Ann Arbor, MI: University of Michigan Institute of Social Research.

Kelderman, E. (2008, May 23). New data show many colleges footing large share of athletic expenses. *The Chronicle of Higher Education,* p. A15.

Kirkpatrick, S.A. and Locke, E.A. (1991). Leadership: Do traits matter? *Academy of Management Executive,* 2 (5), p. 49.

Klein, G. (2010, July 1). USC parts ways with running backs coach Todd McNair. *Los Angeles Times.* Accessed July 31, 2010, from: http://www.latimes.com/sports/la-sp-0702-usc-todd-mcnair-20100702-16,0,5492341,print.story.

Klein, G. and Dwyre, B. (2010, July 20). Pat Haden is USC's new athletic director. *Los Angeles Times.* Accessed August 1, 2010, from: http://www.latimes.com/sports/la-spw-usc-haden-garrett-20100721,0,623315,print.story.

Kotter, J.P. (1998). What leaders really do. *Harvard Business Review on leadership* (pp. 37–60). Boston: Harvard Business School Press.

Kouzes, J.M. and Posner, B.Z. (1987). *The leadership challenge: How to get extraordinary things done in organizations.* San Francisco: Jossey-Bass.

Kouzes, J.M. and Posner, B.Z. (1990, July–August). The credibility factor: What followers expect from their leaders. *Business Credit,* 92, pp. 24–28.

Lapointe, J. (2003, February 9). New chief brings college presidential seal to the N.C.A.A. *New York Times,* 8-7.

Layden, T. (2002, November 18). The loneliest losers. *Sports Illustrated,* pp. 69–71.

Lawson, H.A. and Ingham, A.G. (1980, Winter). Conflicting ideologies concerning the university and intercollegiate athletics: Harper and Hutchins at Chicago, 1892–1940. *Journal of Sport History,* 7 (3), pp. 37–67.

Lester, R. (1995). *Stagg's University: The rise, decline, and fall of big-time football at Chicago.* Urbana, IL: University of Illinois Press.

Lewis, Jr., S.R. (2001, Spring). The game of life. *Carleton College Voice,* pp. 9, 56.

Lincoln, C. (2004). *Playing the game: Inside athletic recruiting in the Ivy League.* White River Junction, VT: Nomad Press.

Manz, C.C. (1992, July–August). Self-leadership ... the heart of empowerment. *Journal for Quality and Participation,* pp. 80–85.

Maslow, A. (1970). *Motivation and personality* (2nd ed.). New York: Harper & Row.

Moss, I. (2010, June 30). CU must iron out details, including exit cost, for move to Pac-10. *Denver Post.* Accessed July 6, 2010, from: http://www.denverpost.com/colleges/ci_15405676.

Murphy, A. and McKnight, M. (2011, March 30). Fiesta Bowl probe results in Junker dismissal, casts pall over BCS. *Sports Illustrated.* Accessed July 11, 2011, from: sportsillustrated.cnn.com./fiesta-bowl-junker/index.html.

NCAA Presidential Task Force on the Future of Division I Athletics (2006). *The second-century imperatives: Presidential leadership – institutional accountability.* Indianapolis, IN: The National Collegiate Athletic Association.

NCAA sanctions against SC. (2010, June 10). *Los Angeles Times.* Accessed July 21, 2010, from: http://www.latimes.com/sports/la-sp-0611-usc-sanctions-list-20100611,0,2933056.story.

NCAA statement on Department of Justice BCS letter (2011, May 5). The National Collegiate Athletic Association. Accessed May 5, 2011, from: http://www.ncaa.org/wps/wcm/connect/public/ncaa/resources/latest+news/2011/may/ncaa+statement+on+department+of+justice+bcs+letter.

Nethery, R. (2004, December 6–12). Cutting a deal in college sports. *Street & Smith's SportsBusiness Journal*, pp. 28–31.

Oriard, M. (2001). *King football: Sport and spectacle in the golden age of radio and newsreels, movies and magazines, the weekly and the daily press.* Chapel Hill, NC: University of North Carolina Press.

Pennington, B. (2008, March 12). It's not just an adventure, it's a job. *New York Times*, pp. C15, C18.

Pugmire, L. (2010, January 7). Mayo's agent denies player accepted cash of gifts for play at USC. *Los Angeles Times*. Accessed January 8, 2010, from: http://www.latimes.com/sports/college/basketball/la-sp-oj-mayo-usc7-2010jan07,0,3855281.story.

Quarterman, J. (1994). Managerial role profiles of intercollegiate athletic conference commissioners. *Journal of Sport Management*, 8, pp. 129–139.

Randazzo, R. (2011, March 30). Tostitos' sponsorship up in the air. *The Arizona Republic*. Accessed May 5, 2011, from: http://www.azcentral.com/business/news/articles/2011/03/30/20110330tostitos-sponsorship-up-air.html.

Rushin, S. (1997, March 3). Inside the moat. *Sports Illustrated*. Accessed August 7, 2008, from: http://find.galegroup.com/itx.

Sack, A.L. and Staurowsky, E.J. (1998). *College athletes for hire: The evolution and legacy of the NCAA's amateur myth.* Westport, CT: Praeger.

Schoenfeld, B. (2006, June 19–25). Tough times in Tucson. *Street & Smith's SportsBusiness Journal*, pp. 1, 29–33.

Selcraig, B., McCallum, J., and Keteyian, A. (1986, October 6). In the kingdom of the solitary man. *Sports Illustrated*. Accessed August 7, 2008, from: http://find.galegroup.com/itx.

Shapiro, B.J. (1983, Winter). John Hannah and the growth of big-time intercollegiate athletics at Michigan State University. *Journal of Sport History*, 10 (3), pp. 26–40.

Sheldon, H.D. (1969). *Student life and customs* (rev. ed.). New York: Arno Press.

Simon, R.L. (1991). Intercollegiate athletics: Do they belong on campus? In J. Andre and D.N. James (eds) *Rethinking college athletics*. Philadelphia: Temple University Press, pp. 43–68.

Single, J.L. (1980, November). The power of expectations: Productivity and the self-fulfilling prophecy. *Management World*, 19, pp. 37–38.

Skinner, B.F. (1953). *Science and human behavior.* New York: Macmillan.

Skinner, B.F. (1972). *Beyond freedom and dignity.* New York: Alfred A. Knopf.

Smith, M. (2009, December 7–13). Five issues for the next NCAA president. *Street & Smith's SportsBusiness Journal*, pp. 1, 25–27, 29–30.

Smith, R.A. (1971, December). Origins of faculty attitudes toward intercollegiate athletics: The University of Wisconsin. *Canadian Journal of History of Sport and Physical Education*, 2 (2), pp. 61–72.

Smith, R.A. (1988). *Sports and freedom: The rise of big-time college athletics.* New York: Oxford University Press.

Smith, R.A. (2011). *Pay for play: A history of big-time college athletic reform.* Chicago: University of Illinois Press.

Sperber, M. (1998). *Onward to victory: The crises that shaped college sports.* New York: Henry Holt.

Sweitzer, K.V. (2009, Winter). Institutional ambitions and athletic conference affiliation. *New Directions for Higher Education*, 148, pp. 55–63.

Thamel, P. (2010a, June 5). Conferences consider expansion, not tradition. *New York Times*, pp. B9, B11.

Thamel, P. (2010b, June 7). Pacific-10 and Big Ten step toward expansion. *New York Times*, pp. D1–D2.

Thamel, P. (2010c, June 10). Officials scrambling to save Big 12, which may lose 2 teams. *New York Times*, p. B14.

Thamel, P. (2010d, June 11). Analysis: Uncertainty marks start of expansion. *New York Times*, pp. B9, B12.

Thamel, P. (2010e, June 12). Nebraska moves to Big Ten and pushes Big 12 to brink. *New York Times*, pp. B9, B12.

Thamel, P. (2010f, July 29). Sanctions will take heavy toll on U.S.C. *New York Times*, pp. B11–B12.

Thelin, J.R. (1996). *Games colleges play: Scandal and reform in intercollegiate athletics.* Baltimore, MD: The Johns Hopkins University Press.

Trinity men's squash tops Yale in dramatic fashion for 13th straight national title (2011, February 27). Accessed March 5, 2011, from: http://athletics.trincoll.edu/sports/msquash/2010-11/releases/Men-s_Squash_G_201011.

Trinity squash player withdraws from national singles championship (2010, February 26). Trinity College. Accessed April 11, 2010, from: http://athletics.trincoll.edu/sports/msquash/2009-10/news/Men-s_Squash_50910.

Turner, P.V. (1984). *Campus: An American planning tradition.* New York: The Architectural History Foundation.

U.S.C. announces penalties for men's basketball team. (2010, January 4). New York Times, p. D6.

Vroom, V.H. (1964). *Work and motivation.* New York: John Wiley & Sons.

Wachter, P. (2011, February 20). Squashing the Ivies. *New York Times Magazine*, pp.36–39.

Wachter, P. (2012, January 20). After 14-year run, squash juggernaut loses a match. *New York Times*, pp. B10, B12.

Watterson, J.S. (2000). *College football: History, spectacle, controversy.* Baltimore, MD: The Johns Hopkins University Press.

Wharton, T. (2011, May 5). Utah A.G. pleased feds look into BCS. *The Salt Lake Tribune*. Accessed May 5, 2011, from: http://www.sltrib.com/sltrib/sports/51751393-77/bcs-utah-ncaa-letter.html.csp.

What they're saying about USC sanctions. (2010, June 10). *Los Angeles Times*. Accessed July 21, 2010, from: http://www.latimes.com/sports/la-sp-0611-usc-ncaa-quotes-20100611,0,5281908.story.

Whitford, D. (1989). *A payroll to meet: A story of greed, corruption, and football at SMU.* New York: Macmillan.

Wieberg, S. (2003a, January 10). Brand takes control, such as it is, of NCAA. *USA Today*, p. 11C.

Wieberg, S. (2003b, August 5). Brand: Athletics pricey, worthy. *USA Today*, p. 11C.

Wieberg, S. (2003c, August 15). NCAA's Brand: Fiscal fitness up to schools. *USA Today*, p. 1C.

Wieberg, S. (2005, January 8). Brand focused on containing costs in NCAA. *USA Today*. Accessed January 13, 2005, from: http://www.usatoday.com/sports/college/other/2005-01-08-ncaa-convention_x.htm.

Wieberg, S. (2010, April 28). Washington's Mark Emmert named new NCAA president. *USA Today*. Accessed April 8, 2012, from: http://www.usatoday.com/sports/college/2010-04-27-ncaa-president-emmert_N.htm.

Wieberg, S. (2011, June 30). BCS director Bill Hancock "confident" after Department of Justice meeting. *USA Today.* Accessed July 11, 2011, from: content/usatoday.com/communities-justice-department-antitrust.

Wodraska, L. (2010, July 3). Utah officially accepts Pac-10 invitation. *Salt Lake Tribune.* Accessed July 6, 2010, from: http://www.sltrib.com/sltrib/sports/49781044-77/utah-utes-pac-scott.html.csp.

Wolverton, B. (2006, November 24). NCAA defends tax-exempt status as Congressional scrutiny of colleges increase. *The Chronicle of Higher Education,* p. A42.

Wolverton, B. (2008a, January 25). Athletes' hours renew debate over college sports. *The Chronicle of Higher Education,* pp. A1, A23.

Wolverton, B. (2008b, March 14). The joy of benchwarming. *The Chronicle of Higher Education,* pp. A1, A7.

Woods, D. (2012, March 13). Report: Butler eyes move to Atlantic 10. *Indianapolis Star.* Accessed April 7, 2012, from: http://www.indystar.com/article/20122013.

Yaeger, D. (1991). *Undue process: The NCAA's injustice for all.* Champaign, IL: Sagamore Publishing.

Yaeger, D. with Henry, J. (2008). *Tarnished Heisman: Did Reggie Bush turn his final college season into a six-figure job?* New York: Pocket Books.

Zidich, J. (2011a, May 15). Fiesta trauma is far from over. *The Arizona Republic.* Accessed July 11, 2011, from: http://www.azcentral.com/arizona.May-2011-15-fiesta-trauma.html.

Zidich, J. (2011b, July 1). Fiesta has to be on the same page as IRS, BCS. *The Arizona Republic.* Accessed July 11, 2011, from: http://www.azcentral.com/arizona.July-2011-1-fri.html.

9 Human resource management and the tour sport industry

Bernstein, V. (2012, February 26). Nascar remains low on its main fuel. *New York Times,* p. SP10.

Griffin, R. (2000). *Fundamentals of management* (2nd ed.). Boston: Houghton Mifflin.

Hagstrom, R.H. (1998). *The NASCAR way: The business that drives the sport.* New York: John Wiley and Sons.

Hall, M. and Walker, B.S. (1993, August 5). Federal family leave act: Provisions at a glance. *USA Today,* p. 2B.

Kreitner, S. (2001). *Understanding management.* Boston: Houghton Mifflin.

Murphy, K. (2010, October 28). DuPont extends sponsorship of Jeff Gordon's 24 Team. *The Final Lap – Nascar News, Radio, Podcast.* Concord, N.C. Accessed July 18, 2012, from: http://www.finallap/2010.com.

Volunteers in sport (2011). Australian Bureau of Statistics. Accessed July 18, 2012, from: http://www.abs.gov.au/austats.

Welcome to Lumberjack World Championships (2012). Lumberjack World Championships. Accessed July 18, 2012, from: http://www.lumberjackworldworldchampionships.com.

Why should I network? (2012). Work in Sports. Accessed July 18, 2012, from: http://www.workinsports.com/wiscareeradvice.

10 Managing change and the professional league sport industry

Battista, J. (2006, July 30). A lifetime spent preparing for the top job in the N.F.L. *New York Times*, 8-1, 8-6.

Bennis, W. and Nanus, B. (1985). *Leaders*. New York: Harper & Row.

Bruner, J.S. (1973). *On knowing: Essays for the left hand*. New York: Atheneum.

Deal, T.E. and Kennedy, A.A. (1982). *Corporate cultures: The rites and rituals of corporate life*. Reading, MA: Addison-Wesley.

Gaines, C. (2011, November 15). The N.F.L. is heading towards an attendance crisis and here's why. *Business Insider Sports Page*. Accessed July 18, 2012, from: http://www.businessinsider.com.

Galica, T. (2012, June 27). How Roger Goodell solidified his sport as the best American sports commissioner. The Bleacher Report. Accessed July 18, 2012, from: http://www.bleacherreport.com.

Gloeckler, G. and Lowry, T. (2007, September 26). Roger Goodell: The most powerful man in sports. *Business Week*. Accessed July 18, 2012, from: http://www.businessweek.com.

Hambrecht, W. (2012). Sports market report. WR Hambrecht+Co Sports Finance Group. Accessed July 18, 2012, from: http://www.wrhambrecht.com.

Hayes, J. (2012, July 8). N.F.L. attendance numbers dropping, football losing popularity? Yahoo Sports. Accessed July 18, 2012, from: http://www.sports.yahoo.com.

Kils, M. (2012, March 20). Frank Tripucka "honored" to unretire No. 18 for Peyton Manning. *The Denver Post*. Accessed July 18, 2012, from: http://www.blogs.denverpost.com.

Kotter, J.P. and Schlesinger, L.A. (1979, March–April). Choosing strategies for change. *Harvard Business Review*, pp. 109–112.

Kriegel, R. (1996) *Sacred cows make the best burgers*. New York: Warner Books.

Lewin, K. (1951). *Field theory and social science: Selected theoretical papers*. New York: Harper & Row.

MacCambridge, M. (2004). *America's game: The epic story of how pro football captured a nation*. New York: Random House.

Nocera, J. (2012, February 3). The cost of football glory. *New York Times*, p. A21.

Peters, T. (1987). *Thriving on chaos*. New York: Harper & Row.

Rosenberg, M. (2012, June 6). Vilma faces tough task against the most powerful man in sports. SI.com. Accessed July 18, 2012, from: http://www.sportsillustrated.cnn.com.

Schwarz, A. (2007, January 18). Expert ties ex-player's suicide to brain damage. *New York Times*, p. A1.

Senge, P.M. (1990). *The fifth discipline: The art and practice of learning organizations*. New York: Doubleday/Currency.

Seyle, H. (1976). *The stress of life*. New York: McGraw-Hill.

Slack, T. (1997). *Understanding sport organizations*. Champaign, IL: Human Kinetics.

Spoelstra, J. (1997). *Ice to the Eskimos*. New York: HarperCollins.

Tichy, N. (1993). Revolutionize your company. *Fortune*, pp. 114–118.

Vaill, P. B. (1991). *Managing as a performing art: New ideas for a world of chaotic change*. Hoboken, NJ: Jossey-Bass.

Wagenheim, M. (2011, July 29). Growth of women's soccer gets a kick from national team success. SportsNola. Accessed July 18, 2012, from: http://www.sportsnola.com.

Westhead, R. (2011, May 1). In India, teenage girls face down Islamic traditions with basketball. *The Star World News*. Accessed July 18, 2012, from: http://www.thestar.com.

INDEX

137–8; management exercise 163–4; miscellaneous other for-profit clubs 138, 139; not-for-profit clubs 138, 139; and Planet Fitness (PF) 161–2; programs and services offered by clubs 139–40; size and scope 136–7; spin-offs/ancillary health and fitness services/products 141–2; supplements 142
health and safety: of employees 329–31
health/sport supplements 142
heroes, recognizing of 354
Heskey, Emile 64
hockey: and SSM 103–8
Hodler, Marc 59
Holden, J.R. 67
Home School Legal Defense Association (HSLDA) 127, 128, 129
home-schooled participants 126–30
Hooper, Ibrahim 118
Horizon League 274, 275, 276, 277
Horrow, Rick 168
Hughes, Joe 269–70
human resource management 305–35; athlete/performer/talent track 305–7; compensation 327–9; devising a strategy 213–14; employee relations 331–3; employee health and wellness 329–31; function of 308; human resource planning 310–14; importance of 308–9; job analysis 310, 326; job/position descriptions 310–11; management exercise 334–5; off-field/front-office/business side 307; on-field 306–7; performance evaluation 324–7; player development systems 306; staffing 314–21; training and development 321–4; understanding strategic requirements 313; working with volunteers 309
human-resource related change 343
Hunter, Paul 98
Hunter, Torii 217
Hyndman, Sarah 5

Iman Academy (Houston) 117, 120, 121
IMG (International Management Group) 219, 227
in-house management 171
incentives: and performance motivation 275–6
information: gathering of and decision-making process 145–7
information overload 91
information systems 80–2, 97
information technology 70–99; and auto racing 80; benefits 98; and career

development 87; challenges 87–96; and change 341–2; communication with stakeholders 84–5; conversion of data into information 87–8; cost considerations 94; decision support system (DSS) 81, 82; definition 80; deleterious effects 98; enhanced communication through IT 83–6; ensuring information is on TRAC' 88–90; and ESPN 71–4; experiments with mobile technology for sports concessions 85–6; facilitating of commercial exchanges 85–6; feedback on performance 82–3; information overload and poor systems mismanagement 91; information systems available 80–2, 97; and leaks 92–3; management information system (MIS) 81; negative consequences of 94–6; product and service innovations through 86–7; and sabotage 93–4; and security 92–3; social media platforms and benefits 75–7; and training 91–2; transaction-processing system (TPS) 80–1
innovation 17–18
innovative organization 357
integrity 21–2
Inter Collegiate Athletic Association of the United States (ICAAUS) 256
intercollegiate athletics 246–98; and conference management 272–3; establishment and evolution of industry 253–8; and Fiesta Bowl 248–53; governance 247–8; and leadership 279–94; management exercise 295–8; and performance motivation see performance motivation; player development 306; size and scope 247; spending on Division I athletics 288–91; and squash 259–61; and women 258
Intercollegiate Football Association (IFA) 255
internal forces: and change 342
International Association of Venue Managers (IAVM) 166
International Federations (IF) 50, 51–2
International Management Group see IMG
International Olympic Committee see IOC
International Skating Union (ISU) 50
international sport: overview 44–5
International Sports Federations (IFS) 43
Internet 86
internship 318
interviews, job 321

Manchester United 2
Mandalay Baseball Properties LLC 358
Manning, Peyton 354
Marinatto, John 287
marketing of athletes: and sport agencies 216
Maslow, Abraham 268
matrix structure: and organizational design 231–3
May, Michael 28
Mayo, O.J. 265, 266
Medora (Indiana) High School 111–12, 113, 114, 115
Meister, Barry 242
memorabilia and collectibles 15–16, 21
mercenary athletes 67–8
merger and acquisition 182–3
Messersmith, Andy 212, 220
Mike Boyle Strength & Conditioning 138
Mile High Performance Fitness Clubs (MHPFC) 163–4
Miles, Les 215–16
Miller, Marvin 10, 212, 220
minor league ballparks 166–8
minor league baseball player salaries 209–10
Mintzberg, Henry 13
mission statement 174, 175–6
MLB (Major League Baseball) 9, 20, 21, 79, 339; average salaries 208; negotiating signing bonuses 210
MLB Players' Association 10, 220
MLS (Major League Soccer) 134, 345, 359
Moorad, Jeff 241
Moore, Harold 256
Morgan, Alex 96
Mueller, Mark 124
Muslims 117–18

Naismith, Dr. James 247
Nanus, Burt 344
NASCAR (National Association for Stock Car Auto Racing) 19, 20, 302; and sponsorship 304–5
National Alliance for Youth Sports (NAYS) 101
National Collegiate Athletic Association see NCAA
National Federation of State High School Associations (NFHS) 101, 102
National Football League see NFL
National Football League Players' Association (NFLPA) 213
National Governing Bodies (NGBs) 43
National Hockey League see NHL

National Association of Intercollegiate Athletics (NAIA) 247
National Interscholastic Athletic Administrators Association (NIAAA) 102
National Junior College Athletic Association (NJCAA) 247
National Labor Relations Board (NLRB) 332
National Olympic Committees 50, 52–3
National Organizing Committees (NOCS) 43
national youth league organizations 102–3
NBA (National Basketball Association) 339–40
NBC Sports 234, 235
NCAA (National Collegiate Athletic Associatiin) 9, 77, 179, 246, 256, 257–8, 264, 267; Champs/Life Skills program 330; Constitution 247–8; leaders/leadership 280–94; Task Force report 288
needs theory 268–70, 276
network structure: and organizational design 233–5
New Balance (NB) 26–7
New Era Sports & Entertainment 266
New York Yankees 2, 15, 79
NFL (National Football League) 9, 77, 337–8, 344; challenges faced by 338; force field analysis 346; legal dispute between American Needle and 32–5, 358; and Nike 35, 35–6; vision for 344
NFL Network 79
NHL Enterprises 0–10
NHL (National Hockey League) 77, 339
Nielsen rating 87–8
Nike 1, 4, 7, 8, 10, 29, 65; and NFL 35, 35–6; sustainability activities 20; treatment of factory workers 20, 25; and World Cup (2010) 20
non-profit organizations 171
Norris, Ty 19
North American Soccer League 221
North Beach Tennis Club 311–12, 313, 314
not-for-profit health and fitness clubs 138, 139
Nowinski, Chris 122

Obama, Barack 250–1
Occupational Safety and Health Administration (OSHA) 33
O'Connor, Anahad 123
Octagon 232–4, 241
Olson, Elizabeth 36
Olympic Charter 48, 58, 61; Rule (41) 68

388